Pskov

RIGA

R Dvina

SOVIET UNION

Polotsk

Smolensk

R Memel

Wilno

Kaliningrad

MINSK

Białystok

OLAND

R Bug

R Pripat

R Dnieper

R Vistula

WARSAW

BREST

ÓDŹ

Lublin

KIEV

Kielce

Chelm

Sandomierz

LVOV

KRAKÓW

ADY

Kamieniec Podolski

CARPATHIAN MOUNTAINS

HUNGARY

ROMANIA

BUDAPEST

POLAND

POLAND

Tim Sharman

COLUMBUS BOOKS
LONDON

First published in Great Britain in 1988 by
Columbus Books Limited
19-23 Ludgate Hill
London EC4M 7PD

Chapter decorations are reproduced from decorative paper
cut-outs from the village of Kadzidlo

British Library Cataloguing in Publication Data

Sharman, Tim
    Poland——(Travelscapes).
    1. Poland——Description and travel——1981-
    ——Visitors' guides
    I. Title
    914.38'0456   DK4081

    ISBN 0–86287–327–4

Designed by Vera Brice
Maps by Vera Brice and Leslie Robinson
Set in Linotron Erhardt by Falcon Graphic Art Ltd
Wallington, Surrey
Printed and bound by Richard Clay Ltd, Bungay, Suffolk

For Ewa, Aleksander and Mikołaj here,
Romek and Danuśia there.

CONTENTS

ILLUSTRATIONS

MAPS

The following symbols are used
in the maps:
- ✝ Church or monastery
- ♜ Castle
- ∴ Ancient monument
- △ Mountain peak
- ♨ Viewpoint

Preface

The first thing to be said about Poland, a country which has had more than its share of bad press, is that it is a fascinating and exciting place which is easy enough to visit. Well organized tours of the main cultural centres – Gdańsk, Warsaw and Kraków – are available, but when it comes to experiencing what is unique about Poland the independent traveller will have a more richly rewarding time. Landscape and cultural heritage are, after all, only a part of any nation, however much they may be the part which attracts from afar – and Poland's mountains and lakes, castles, cathedrals and art collections do attract many. But often what travellers remember most clearly and describe most enthusiastically are the social encounters. Poland is, quite definitely, a special society.

Devout, patriotic and stubborn in their defence of a land that has so often been a battlefield and has even been removed completely from the European map, the Poles are a breed apart, as they are only too willing to tell the world. But there has to be more to life than mere survival, even against the odds which have confronted this nation during the past few centuries. Intensely aware of their history, the Polish are a highly literate and cultured people who treasure what has survived and in their turn produce books, films, plays and music in prodigious quantities. And churches. Thousands have been built since the Second World War and many hundreds are still under construction, often to the most adventurous designs. Would that the same care were put into Polish residential accommodation.

What is surprising is that such a turbulent past has spared so much. The landscape, more varied and beautiful than maps suggest, is studded with dramatic reminders not only of the days of medieval fortifications and missionary monks, but also of the golden age of the Polish nobility: on the huge estates, great palaces were planted, built by Italians and crammed with tapestries from Flanders, paintings from Holland, and furniture, porcelain and gold from just about everywhere.

In many rural areas of Europe today the landscape is empty, but

11

rural Poland is full of people. Polish farmers have never wholeheartedly embraced large-scale state agriculture but have stuck with their hard-won family plots and straggling wooden villages. Theirs is a hard and unremitting life but, by definition, it is agriculture on a human scale. At harvest times whole families gather to help get in the potatoes or neatly stack the little bundles of hay; on my wanderings I have often felt as if I were in a time warp, carried back to a pre-motor age where man cuts and horse hauls. And there are still so very many horses, pulling their long wooden carts to good old-fashioned markets.

When such a lifestyle is combined with the steep green hills which culminate in the high Tatra Mountains, then the effect can be quite magical to behold. For me, these southern hills contain some of the most beautiful, most visually comfortable places in all of Europe, and the great log houses, set on ridges of thin turf, are among the most handsome structures ever devised. A by-product of the barely modernized rural lifestyle is that many of the traditions of folk weaving, painting, embroidery and carving still flourish, and gorgeous regional costumes are regularly worn to church, for weddings and for other such celebrations just as naturally as working clothes are worn to the fields. Traditional music, too, continues in many regions as a private rather than a public entertainment. I often recall a summer evening in the mountains when I came across two teenaged boys practising their violins on the porch of their farmhouse, framed by the rock peaks of the Tatras and a nearby pine-clad ridge.

From the long ridge of mountains marking Poland's southern frontier, great rivers wend northwards across the rolling and forested plain, passing ancient hilltop towns and cathedral cities such as Kraków, former capital of Poland. Kraków is a wonderful city, with its ancient streets, its impressive cloth hall in the vast market square where trumpets sound the hours, and its great riverside rock topped by a royal castle and a cathedral where the bones of many Polish kings lie in exquisitely carved tombs, Kraków came through the last world war relatively unscathed, but Warsaw, Gdańsk and Wrocław, all rich and ancient cities, were reduced, along with many smaller places, to rubble. By an astonishing act of faith, they have been rebuilt, and often perfectly enough to make it seem that not a stone has been touched for centuries: a truly remarkable and heroic feat.

In this book I have set out to explore a country which both deserves and needs to be better known and understood, setting the ancient towns, cities and palaces in their historical as well as their geographical contexts. I consider myself lucky to have visited Poland for the first time on foot, making an unforgettable journey which introduced me to the legendary hospitality of the country people as well as to many delightful out-of-the-way places. For young people, this is quite a sensible way to travel in summer, using a network of hostels known as *schronisko* – usually village and town schools turned into dormitories providing basic accommodation at a minimal price. Holders of international student cards are also granted special discounts in regular student hostels which can be found in towns throughout the country. At the other end of the scale are the five-star international hotels, indistinguishable from those in any other country. In between these extremes there is a host of alternatives from smaller, older and less luxurious hotels, to motels often set in lovely landscapes, private rooms (look for the *noclegi* sign), rented cottages, and modern camp sites complete with cabins, restaurants, tent sites and sites for caravans.

A caravan, in fact, is probably the best way to see Poland and certainly the cheapest, for as well as using the official sites it is possible to spend the night in absolute safety in any village, town or even city, where many carparks are guarded day and night. For the really adventurous, it would be quite possible to travel around using nothing but public transport, which ranges from domestic airlines and city trams to long-distance trains and buses, local buses, and even tiny narrow-gauge steam railways which wander around the countryside calling on the most remote villages.

If you are bringing a car, you will need to carry your car registration documents, insurance green card and, if you intend to stay longer than two months, an international driving licence. Vehicles can also be rented in Poland but all foreign drivers must in any case pay for petrol with vouchers available from hotels or travel offices and paid for in convertible currency. Remember that petrol stations are thinner on the ground here than in western Europe and that there is sometimes a queue because pumps are not self-service. So carry a can and top up whenever you see a quiet petrol station, rather than wait until you are low.

On the matter of driving in Poland, a few words are necessary. On the open road the maximum speed allowed is 90 kph (54 mph) and in built-up areas 60 kph (37 mph) unless, of course, there are signs indicating otherwise. These limits are monitored by mobile radar units, often set up in the most surprising places, and on-the-spot fines can be anything from 1,000 to 5,000 *złotys*, so be careful. Being a foreigner is no defence with the police *(milicja)*, who sometimes also make spot checks on travellers, asking to see passports and car documents, so keep them handy. Do not drink any alcohol at all when driving – not even one beer on a hot day: it is strictly forbidden. Given Polish hospitality, this can be a problem, but the fact that you will be driving is always a valid excuse for not taking the proffered glass. There are as yet few parking meters in Poland, and in many cities, notoriously in Warsaw, cars park quite legally across pavements. But parking outside a legal zone is again punishable by on-the-spot fines.

Pedestrians too must be aware of the few rules which apply to them, notably the orderly crossing of roads in cities only at pedestrian crossings and even then not until the crossing lights are green. It is very annoying to be waiting beside an empty street with a red light against you, but that is the rule. Tickets for trams and buses must be purchased before your journey from a kiosk *(ruch)*, and can be bought cheaply in any number.

There are many specialist holidays available in Poland, usually organized by *Polorbis*, the Polish state tourist organization (known as *Orbis* within Poland). Many Germans and Americans take fishing or hunting trips there, shooting beautiful deer and elk, duck and boar, an activity of which I heartily disapprove. Better by far to take a horseback holiday, available for anyone from the beginner to the experienced cross-country rider, in one of a dozen centres in the northern forests, or to laze in one of the many long-established spas which will treat a great variety of ailments under strict medical control. In winter, skiing holidays can be taken on gentle nursery slopes or out on the big mountainsides. Polorbis has offices in several countries and will happily provide many detailed brochures and other information. Its London address is: 82 Mortimer Street, London W1. Tel: 636 2217/4701/9030.

To enter Poland you must first obtain a valid visa from the visa section of your local embassy or consulate. Alternatively, if you are booking an organized tour, this will be done by the travel office. Once you are in the country, a fixed amount of convertible currency – that is, Western money – must be exchanged for each day of your stay. This can be done either in advance, in one lump sum at the border, or week by week, in which case the larger hotels or any local *Orbis* office will change the money. But beware. You need to exchange the correct amount, keep all the receipts for changing and have the right stamp put on your visa each time; otherwise you will be asked to settle up on the spot when you come to leave the country.

One other technical point concerns registration upon arrival in Poland. All foreign visitors must register with the police within 24 hours of entering the country. If you are staying at an hotel or even a campsite this is done automatically and yet another stamp is put on your visa card. If you are caravanning or staying with friends, make sure that at some stage during your stay, the sooner the better, you collect some of these stamps. The basic message is that the more of any kind of rubber stamp you can collect, the better the Polish bureaucrats will like it.

With photography, common sense applies, as in most activities. Certain buildings or places will display a sign showing a camera with a diagonal red line drawn through it, which means that photography is forbidden. Signs, however, can be old, hidden or lost, so the basic rule is that no pictures can be taken of railways or railway stations, airports, bridges or anything of a military nature, which includes personnel as well as vehicles, planes and camps, etc. All this has to be stated but does not of course represent a problem for most visitors. Be sure, though, to take an ample supply of your favourite photographic film because, with the exception of certain colour-print films which are sometimes stocked by branches of the *Pewex* hard currency shops, Western film stock is not available.

Leaflets explaining all the above mentioned rules are available in English from any *Polorbis* travel office when a visa or flight is booked.

The name *Cepelia* crops up quite often in this book and refers to the chain of state shops selling the products of Poland's many skilled craft-workers. *Cepelia* shops contain a wealth of truly beautiful regional folk items, each one hand-made and marked with the name and address of its creator, which means that from an indexed map or atlas the village of origin can be found. There is no export duty payable on *Cepelia* goods up to the value of 5,000 *złotys* per item, which covers most things apart from large items of furniture and the biggest and most gorgeous of the *gobelin* wall hangings. But even the smaller *gobelins* can be exquisite works of art, made from hand-spun and naturally dyed wools to either traditional or modern patterns. *Cepelia* shops are found in even the smallest places and stock a huge range of objects including ceramics, woodcarvings, folk pictures painted on glass, leather bags, belts and slippers, painted chests and boxes, wooden toys and kitchen tools and wonderful textiles which can be bought off the roll.

Poland is renowned for its fine woollen textiles and these can be found made up into garments of high quality, if not of the latest fashion. Men's suits are a good buy, for example, as are certain types of overcoat. Shoes are another Polish speciality, although it is true to say that the best are exported. Do not spurn a department store in a small town or even a village, for desirable items can often be found there which have long since been snatched up in the city. Toys are worth considering if space allows and if you can find the good old-fashioned wooden ones. What may come as a surprise to visitors is the wide range available of Polish, Russian and other eastern European music recordings and books. Recordings on disc or cassette by many very fine ensembles and soloists can be bought at relatively cheap prices, and books available in English include works of reference, classical fiction and Polish history, photographic albums and local guide-books. For those who will be exploring the network of byways, seeking out particular villages, the indexed Polish road atlas is essential, but it may be easier to buy at a specialist bookshop before leaving home. It is called *Samochodowy Atlas Polski*.

I have no wish to encourage alcoholism but there is more to vodka than an English pub would know. There are vodkas flavoured with rowan-berry, with lemon and even with pepper or cherry, as well as golden vodka and, perhaps most famous of all, *zubrówka*, flavoured with the grass that bison feed on, a blade of which will be found floating in every bottle. The best place to buy these is in the ubiquitous *Pewex* shops (most hotels have at least one branch). Otherwise they stock mostly imported goods which can be bought only with convertible currency.

Many Poles who have worked abroad or have relations there who send money home to them have official foreign currency bank accounts and use this money to keep themselves supplied with difficult-to-get luxuries available only at *Pewex* shops. Favourites are whisky, American cigarettes, chocolate and jeans, all of which can be bought by visitors at prices usually lower than at home. I always make a point of buying my blue jeans at *Pewex* plus a little brandy for the Christmas pudding, and travelling lately with young children I find it a sure place to get vitamins, fruit juice and even powdered baby milk.

Just a word about sales staff in shops. Where demand always outstrips supply, as inevitably it does in Poland, and most shops are state-owned and not, therefore, subject to the usual laws of competition, there is little incentive for the sales staff to care overmuch for the customer's wants. Do not be shocked when shop staff treat you as a second-class citizen, which they will do in the big cities. There are many private shops where the service is good; generally I have found that people are more polite in the smaller places and in the south of the country. This applies also to restaurants and cafés. Customer-attention is one area which Poland must improve if it is to make the most of its tourist potential.

There is a great contrast between the food which will be found in ordinary restaurants and that which is eaten by the Poles at home. Visitors who have or who make Polish friends will be the recipients of much good old-fashioned hospitality and a fine spread will be laid before them which will include a variety of cold meats, any local speciality, beautiful soups such as *barszcz*, the famous beetroot soup, and gorgeous home-made cakes. The problem is that you never know what sacrifices have been made to ensure that a memorable meal is laid on for you.

Restaurants (restauracja) in the top hotels will have no problems in providing a full menu of both traditional Polish dishes and international fare. Everyday restaurants, however, vary widely in both menu and décor and are often large refectory-like places, full of tobacco smoke and with a very basic menu offering perhaps meatballs, potatoes and *sauerkraut* as a main dish. Herrings of one sort or another are a favourite starter, often served in sour cream (*śledź w śmietanie*). Another is steak tartare (*befsztyk tatarski*), a mixture of raw meat, sardine, egg, onion, oil, pepper and salt. Pancakes with cabbage and mushrooms (*naleśniki z kapustą i grzybami*) are very tasty and make use of the golden-brown boletus mushrooms rather than the white ones, which the Poles call by the French name of *champignons* and rate less highly. Mushrooms in a cream sauce are also possible to find (*pieczarki w śmietanie*). Soups, of course, are always available and in great variety, but the most common is *barszcz*. Fish soup (*rybna*) will be met with in the north and potato soup (*kartoflanka*) everywhere. In my experience the tomato soup (*pomidorowa*) is often rather thin, which cannot be said of the vegetable soup (*jarzynowa*). Cucumber soup (*ogórkowa*) is delicious in the summer.

The choice of main dishes available will vary from a selection of two or

17

three in a simple restaurant to a more enticing array in a hotel or big city establishment. The most widespread and basic menu will include minced beef rissole (*kotlet mielony*), usually served with potatoes (*ziemniaki*) and vegetables. More often than not there will be *bigos*, surely the national dish. This is made from *sauerkraut*, fresh cabbage, onions and a variety of meats—usually pork—and was traditionally served after the hunt. Many Polish families make *bigos* in large amounts as it tastes better with each reheating. Particularly Polish and worth seeking out are mushroom-stuffed beef rolls in sour cream (*zrazy zawijane*), served with buckwheat (*kasza*) instead of rice. Cabbage leaves stuffed with minced beef and rice (*gołąbki*) can be delicious, but I have never had the courage to try Polish tripe (*flaki*), even though it bears little resemblance to the British version, being seasoned with ginger, nutmeg and marjoram and garnished with Parmesan cheese.

The most common pudding is a glass of stewed fruit (*kompot*), from which one drinks before spooning out the fruit. The most common fruits used are plums (*śliwka*) and cherries (*wiśnia*). (Plums are also found in those delicious dumplings (*knedle*) which are served in milk bars as well.) *Kompot* can be served with a different fruit, in which case it is known as *pierozki*. Pancakes with fruit or cheese (*naleśniki*) and sour-milk pancakes (*racuszki*) are also very popular. If you want ice-cream, just ask for *lody*, which is also widely available from street kiosks.

Despite these hints, the visitor will inevitably be faced with an incomprehensible menu at some stage and must turn to a more detailed phrase-book or advice from the waiter: *Co pan poleca?* (What do you recommend?) Only in the smartest places need one be ashamed to point at something already served at another table.

To ask for the bill simply wave your hand until someone sees it, which may take some time, or use the official words from the phrase book: *Proszę o rachunek.*

Milk bars (*Bar Mleczny*) are very useful places for a quick meal, usually self-service. A variety of hot dishes is available, mostly without meat. Typical examples are beans in tomato sauce (*fasolka po bretonsku*), dumplings with plums (*knedle*), potato dumplings (*kopytka*), macaroni (*makaron*), fried mushrooms (*pieczarki z patelni*), potato pancakes (*placki*) and salad (*salata*). Many bars are privately run and offer hot snacks such as hot dogs.

Cafés (*Kawiarnia*) are found everywhere, serving mostly tea (*herbata*) and cakes (*ciastka*), the best of which is often the cheesecake (*sernik*). In the early morning, however, the café will serve breakfast (*śniadanie*), usually egg dishes such as an omelette (*omlet*), ham and eggs (*jajka na szynce*) or scrambled eggs (*jajecznica*). Most big towns have a branch of *Hortex*, famous for cakes and ice-creams.

1

Warsaw:
The Old Town and environs

Approached from the west, on the Berlin to Moscow road, Warsaw proclaims itself with a tall spire that is visible for many a mile. Unlike those of other cities of the north European plain, however, Warsaw's spire is neither Gothic nor does it sit upon a great nave. The 234 metres of the Palace of Culture — Uncle Joe's Cathedral, as it is irreverently dubbed by some — are decidedly secular in origin. Built between 1952 and 1955, it was the gift of the Soviet Union. Such a building is easily despised, either on political or on aesthetic grounds, but I have grown fond of it, a slender concrete tower with just enough decoration to persuade the eye that it heralds more than a mere functional complex.

But whatever your opinion, the place is unavoidable, placed as it is next to the city's main shopping centre; and it does have the great merit of providing from its 30th-floor balcony a full panorama of the low, spreading city, the Vistula and the surrounding Mazovian countryside. From such a vantage point the eye is drawn inevitably towards the horizon, but for the visitor to Warsaw it is better to summon a little courage, some knowledge and especially some imagination, and look downwards to contemplate the capital city itself.

Plac Defilad, the huge open space of grass, statues and car parks surrounding the foot of the tower was once a warren of busy, narrow streets. To the north, today's tidy grey apartment blocks are in the district of Muranow, once Warsaw's Jewish quarter, later the horrific closed ghetto of the Nazi occupation. Beyond them are two great cemeteries. One, deserted and overgrown, belonged to one of the largest Jewish communities in Europe. The other, tidy, fresh-flowered and much visited, is Catholic, like most of Poland's population. To the north-east is the seemingly timeless red-tiled roofscape of Warsaw's medieval walled town, standing on a bluff above the river. Seemingly, because for the years between 1939 and the 1950s that roofscape simply was not there, thanks to the brutal efficiency of the Nazi war machine.

The recreation of Warsaw has become legendary but it is still worth dwelling upon the reality from which it arose when surveying the wide avenues and busy shops, the palaces and parks and, of course, the narrow cobbled streets of the Old Town, the Stare Miasto. Of the 987 pre-war buildings listed as of historic value, 782 were reduced to ruins: 87 per cent of Warsaw's housing, 91 per cent of industrial plants, 80 per cent of state and municipal buildings, 75 per cent of schools, and an estimated 850,000 Polish people were destroyed there. Eisenhower visited Warsaw in 1945 and pronounced it more tragic than anything he had ever seen. In 1947, the American writer John Gunther was still appalled and stunned by the scene, although by then the clearing up and rebuilding were well under way: 'In Warsaw it is impossible over large areas to identify any buildings at all, or even to see where street intersections were, because the ruin is total, the devastation is complete. Almost every vista looks like a jumble of enormous broken teeth.'

The decision to reconstruct Warsaw had been made even before the new Polish government reached the city in 1945, but when the two men appointed to direct the operation, architect Roman Piotrowski and his deputy, Józef Sigalin, first set eyes on the hundreds of hectares of deserted rubble, they had serious doubts about the task. For along with the buildings, most of the archives and city plans had gone. Even the sewers and tram lines had been systematically wrecked as the Germans withdrew, a straightforward act of revenge for the nuisance caused by the recent uprising. With so many landmarks obliterated, with nearly all records destroyed, natives of Warsaw were lost in their own home town. Some suggested moving the capital to the less damaged industrial city of Lodz, but walking around Warsaw today, or visiting dour Lodz, convinces one that the right decision was made. The miracle of Warsaw's rebirth is now part of the heritage of all Poles: the car park at the Palace of Culture is filled at any season with buses from far-away villages and factories, as new generations visit the sights and witness the history they know so well.

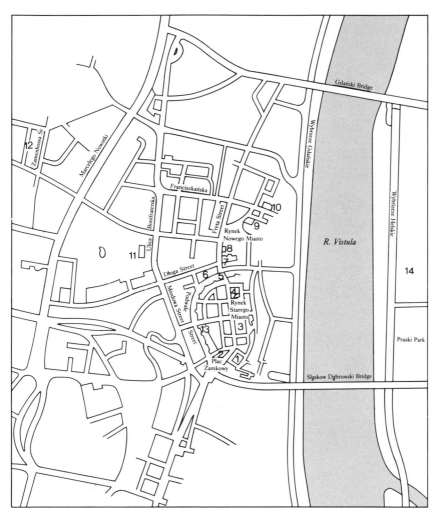

1 Royal Castle
2 Statue of Zygmunt III Wasa
3 St John's Cathedral
4 Warsaw Historial Museum
5 Barbican

6 St Paul's Church
7 St Jacek's Church
8 Marie Curie's House
9 Church of the Holy Sacrament
10 Church of the Virgin Mary

11 Krasiński Palace
12 Jewish Monument
13 Kilminski Statue
14 Zoo

Most of historic Warsaw can be enclosed by a long narrow strip on the left, that is the west, bank of the Vistula with the Old Town at the northern end and the summer palace of Wilanów eleven kilometres away to the south. The downstream end of this strip, where the walled medieval town sits on its steep bluff, is the highest point in the vicinity, an obvious defensive site to protect a much-used river crossing. Important as this crossing point had been for centuries, and prospering as it did with its settlement of timber and grain merchants and its increasing function as a trading post, it was not until 1413 that Warsaw became the capital of the independent principality of Mazovia, and only in 1596 was it proclaimed the seat of the Kingdom of Poland. For several centuries before that, the southern city of Kraków had been home for the court, but following the formation of the dual state of Poland-Lithuania the establishment moved north to be closer to the centre of the vast territory now to be administered, territory that stretched almost to Moscow in the east and to the Black Sea in the south. And if twentieth-century politics seem complex and difficult to follow, they are as nothing to the tangled web of dynastic marriages and territorial wheeling and dealing of medieval Europe. For their part, Polish kings of the period were related to the ruling families of Sweden, Bohemia, Hungary, Brandenburg, Brunswick, Saxony and Transylvania.

The early prosperity of Warsaw is apparent from an inventory of 1546 listing 700 brick houses, nine churches and three hospitals, the whole protected by a double row of ramparts enclosing an area of about twelve hectares (30 acres). The city's undoubted hey-day was the eighteenth century. At that time, before the partitions by Austria, Prussia and Russia which removed Poland from the map of Europe for more than a century, Warsaw was one of the finest and most cultured cities of Europe, famed for its palaces and parks, its educated and liberal nobility.

I was about to say that some of those medieval buildings remain, and in a way they do. So meticulous was the rebuilding of the Old Town after the Second World War that, for the innocent eye, it is impossible to detect that all the houses, shops and churches in the narrow streets leading to the market square have been assembled since 1945. Old photographs, plans and books were traced and examined, memories were raked over; even the noble townscapes of Bernardo Bellotto, known, like his more famous uncle, as Canaletto and court painter here from 1767, provided valuable clues to the layout and details of the city. It is perhaps small recompense for the destruction and loss suffered, but Warsaw has been able to reconstitute itself much as it pleases, choosing to recreate the most splendid period of its history, picking which original features of buildings to retain, which later additions to ignore. From a foreign perspective this may seem to be a fine game, almost playing with time itself, selecting where in the past to live, but in 1945 it was a deadly serious business to the surviving Poles, nothing less than reconstructing the very heart of the nation. For once, against all the odds, Humpty Dumpty was put together again.

To explore the old town is the first aim of most visitors to Warsaw; it gives the best understanding of the city's life and development. The classic view of any riverine town is from the opposite bank, in this case from Praski Park in the Praga suburb. This can be reached by tram from most parts of the city or by foot from the Old Town itself.

From **Praski Park**, with its zoo and pleasant wooded paths, it is possible to walk to the very edge of the wide, shallow Vistula, to sit on one of the large and smooth glacial stones that litter the bank, and contemplate the medieval outline of the old city. There are not many cities with such an unspoiled river bank. Little river traffic will be seen these days, even though boats of shallow draught can navigate the Vistula, but in previous centuries it was a busy trade route with great rafts floating grain, salt and many products of the upstream forests from Kraków, Kazimierz and other towns of the south. The raftsmen, known as *flisak*, were a hardy and, in common mythology, honourable band who guided their cargoes for hundreds of kilometres to reach Warsaw or, much farther, the rich sea port of Gdańsk. Journey over, they walked back along the river bank to their home towns and villages, tough men armed with sticks and axes, famed for purveying rough justice to wrongdoers met along the way. But you will see no *flisak* today, not even in Canaletto's richly detailed 'A General View of Warsaw as seen from Praga' in the National Museum. Considering all the events of the past 200 years it is amazing how similar is the silhouette today to that portrayed by the artist, but then maybe this picture was used to check the accuracy of the rebuilding. The most prominent buildings are the Royal Castle, the Zamek Krolewski, marking the southern edge of the walled town, the rearing gable of St John's Cathedral and, to the north, the brick-built Gothic belfry of the Church of the Virgin Mary.

Cross the Śląsko-Dąbrowski bridge on foot or by train to the obvious starting place for an exploration of the Old Town, **Castle**

Square (Plac Zambowy), an impressive space dominated by the pink castle walls and a column supporting a bronze statue of Zygmunt III Waza, the monarch who first made Warsaw a royal seat in the sixteenth century and who combined the duties of king of Sweden with those of his Polish crown. His monument was first erected in 1644 by his son Władysław and stood hereabouts in what was then a small square outside the walled city's Kraków Gate, looking south down the elegant avenue of palaces then, and now, known as Krakowskie Przedmiescie, meaning simply Kraków suburb, being the route that eventually leads to that distant city. The gate is long gone but Zygmunt himself is in fine shape, having survived Nazi dynamite with little damage and been remounted on a new column in 1949.

Fine as Zygmunt's view is, he stands with his back to a better. Plac Zamkowy is wedged between the colourful stucco of the houses facing out from the tight grid street plan of the medieval town and the rosy façade of the Royal Castle (Zamek Krolewski). This side of the castle, originally protected by the town walls, had no need of fortification and what is seen today is simply one wing of a large palace which evolved from the wooden fort that first marked out this spot as a power base in the thirteenth century. The present stucco walls rise directly from the stones of the square, three storeys of large windows, a high red-tiled roof and a central clock tower with bulbous cupola, a Renaissance palace in all its old glory. Or rather, in all its new glory, because the Zamek Królewski is brand shining new, coated with real gleaming gold — yet hung with genuine Renaissance tapestries and paintings.

It is not unusual to visit a grand palace, even Versailles or Blenheim, but there is something a little eerie about a new-minted Renaissance palace. After my first visit in 1981 I was left with the impression of having been to a celestial Ideal Home Exhibition, a show palace for heaven-sent monarchs; but in truth the castle is a remarkable microcosm of nearly four centuries of Polish history. Considering the problems that have beset Poland and its economy for so many years, it was a remarkable and illuminating achievement to rebuild such a place from an empty site in so short a time. The decision to reconstruct the castle was not taken until 1971, and yet on a July morning in 1974 a huge crowd watched as in solemn ceremony the clock in the main Zygmunt Tower was restarted, with the hands at 11.15, the hour at which they had been so violently stopped on Black Sunday in September 1939, the day when Nazi artillery first shelled the castle.

The money for the rebuilding came from private donations large and small as well as from the many Poles living abroad; local people also contributed thousands of hours of labour to the project. The years prior to the Second World War had been devoted to assembling a magnificent collection of furniture and paintings and turning the castle into a public museum. The fact that many of the present furnishings and pictures are the originals is thanks to heroic efforts in 1939 by museum staff: during the bombardment, and with some loss of life, they mounted an emergency evacuation of everything that was not nailed down, plus some things that were. Some paintings and furniture were initially taken to the relative sanctuary of the National Museum, later, of course, to be looted by the Germans, but a remarkable amount of original material has been brought together to furnish the new castle. It was obvious even then, survivors have said, that one day the castle would be restored, so even sections of decorative plaster were carefully removed to be used as patterns for future craftsmen. Following the 1944 uprising, what was still left of the castle was systematically blown up by German sappers, but sections of carved stonework were rescued from the rubble and carefully stored. Many of the windows, doorways and even fireplaces therefore contain pieces of the original stone, and these are quite obvious to the eye. There are even a few items bearing original gilt, which lacks the shine of the new.

Guided tours of the castle, for which it may be necessary to book several hours in advance, start at an entrance in the north-east corner of Plac Zamkowy and take in the Gothic cellars and the galleries and apartments on the ground and first floors. Once inside, there is a very good guide book available in English, French and German, packed with colour photographs of the interiors and a lot of history — useful, as most tours are conducted only in Polish, unless you are travelling with a well organized group. The castle has been refurbished in a variety of styles, but generally the aim has been to recreate the atmosphere and décor of the eighteenth century and in particular the reign of the last king, Stanisław-August Poniatowski, from 1764 until 1795, when the monarchy was abolished and the king exiled to St Petersburg.

A unique feature of this grand building is that it was conceived as both a parliament and a royal residence, with the accent heavily on the parliamentary function. Warsaw had been a convenient location for meetings following the 1569 Union of Lublin, and the first joint Polish-Lithuanian Sejm or parliament was in session from April to July

1570 at the then much smaller Castle. The background to this union was that Zygmunt August, the last Jagiellonian king of Poland, had no heir and was concerned about the stability of the state after his death. Until 1569 the long relationship between Poland and its neighbour and ancient rival, the Grand Duchy of Lithuania, had been based on a political marriage back in 1386 but, faced with the growing power of Muscovy in the east and the prospect of a divisive squabble for the succession, Zygmunt called a meeting of the nobles of both countries in the old city of Lublin, with the idea of creating a Commonwealth. This great political experiment called for a joint parliament and an elected king, and following Zygmunt's death in 1572 several thousand gentry of the new dual state met on the fields of Wola, just outside Warsaw, and elected a Frenchman, Henri Valois, as king. This Commonwealth survived for 223 years, ruled by eleven elected kings, seven of whom were foreigners. Amongst a very mixed bag, one of them, it is claimed, fathered 300 children. The era of elected kings started inauspiciously with the weak Henri Valois fleeing from Kraków in the middle of the night upon hearing that his brother, King Charles IX of France had died. Eager to claim the French throne and out of place amongst the down-to-earth Poles, he left Poland in secret, failing to consult either parliament or his court advisers. The ideal of democratic institutions, therefore, has long been and has remained important to the Poles, although it has to be said that the common people were not at all involved in the royal election process, remaining bound as serfs to their local lords and masters. But a surprising ten per cent of the population did qualify as gentry, at a time when in France and England the figure was about one per cent.

The new expanded régime was given metaphoric expression in the three wings added to the existing castle between 1598 and 1619, creating the layout seen today, which is a five-sided structure enclosing a large courtyard. Kraków was still the official capital but with parliament sitting every year or two for several weeks, the king came to spend more time in Warsaw, and so royal apartments were added, though like the parliament they were the property of the state and not the king. At a time when most of Europe was ruled by absolute monarchs, Poland was run by a respected parliament where the king acted much as a chairman in what became known as the 'Democracy of the Gentry'. Coming at the end of Poland's golden century of enlightenment and intellectual achievement, when its scholars, scientists and writers were the equal of any, this neo-classical form of government and the era it represents made an indelible mark on the character of Polish society. The rebuilt castle, therefore, is more than a mere tourist attraction: it is a glorious symbol of Poland's image of her own past.

The tour begins in the north-east wing in what are known as the **Jagiellonian Rooms,** overlooking the Vistula. They were laid out in their present arrangement around the year 1600, incorporating the former residence of Zygmunt August. All the Jagiellonian rooms are decorated with original furniture, ceramics and paintings from the sixteenth century. The Flemish tapestries are particularly fine examples from the Brussels workshops, including 'The building of the tower of Babel' and 'The tragedy of the Jewish people', made in 1572 and an ironic survival in the city that saw the destruction of so many thousands of Jews. Beneath these rooms is a large subterranean hall with cross-vaulting supported on a single central pillar, the only structure from the period that survived the 1939–45 war intact.

Also overlooking the river on the ground floor are the three great chambers that were used by the **Sejm,** the parliament of the Commonwealth. In these pillared halls hang portraits of the dukes of Mazovia and more Flemish tapestries, and here the deputies would debate, the king and the public listen. The Sejm was designed with an area especially for spectators who followed debates closely as well as attending the opening ceremonies of each session, every bit as grand as those still held in London. The Sejm was designed around 1570 by Giovanni Battista Quadro, just one of the many Italians who migrated to northern Europe, putting into practice the new ideas from beyond the Alps which show up at this period in buildings throughout Poland, following a proposition by a Lithuanian deputy.

It was in these splendid rooms during the interregnum of 1573 that the future structure of the state was decided, and the decisions made on how to elect future kings. These same rooms witnessed the beginning of the end of the kingdom in 1652, when a Lithuanian deputy proposed the principle of a unanimous vote for any decree was allowed by the Sejm, the notorious *liberum veto.* A single deputy could now throw out not only the measure on which he was voting but all measures passed by parliament in that session: the affairs of state were in the hands of any individual dissenter. This system was the subject of much ridicule by visitors to Poland, one of whom observed that 'wise debates in the Diet were closured [*sic*] by the drawing of swords, and no patriot was ashamed to raise a faction or to call in a foreign power'.

The Oxford historian J. M. Thompson, writing earlier this century, thought Poland's political systems then 'might have been suited to a wandering tribe of savages. In the fixed and civilized society of Europe they meant sheer anarchy and dissolution'. The wonder, then, is that the state continued until 1795.

The state could, and often did, survive without a monarch. It was the fabric of the state itself which was at risk. To summarize crudely a complex situation, in the absence of a dynastic monarchy towards which loyalties could evolve over generations, nobles were looking solely to their own interests, which included those of their foreign allies. The state, in other words, was fragmenting into a confederation of principalities.

Above the parliamentary chambers are the **Royal Apartments,** the most important chamber being the **Canaletto Room**, the walls of which are almost completely covered with a series of 24 views of Warsaw painted by Bellotto in the 1770s. It can easily be understood how the clarity and precision of these large pictures would have aided those responsible for Warsaw's reconstruction. Opening off this room and built into the ancient Grodzka Tower of the Mazovian dukes is a delightful **Royal Chapel,** a tiny circular sanctuary, richly decorated, with all the columns and capitals gilded. The altar has long since disappeared but a 'Madonna and Child' from the studio of Rubens hangs here, and on a pedestal, as meaningful as any sacred relic, is an urn containing the heart of Tadeusz Kościuszko (leader of the popular insurrection of 1794 and a hero of the American War of Independence) which had been carefully carried to safety on the very first day of the Second World War.

First of the royal apartments in the wing facing the river is an audience chamber with a throne and one of the many beautiful inlaid wood floors in the castle, all reconstructed from surviving details and photographs; this one features a large central rosette in different coloured woods. The four overdoor paintings representing 'Wisdom', 'Pity', 'Justice' and 'Courage', however, are originals by another talented Italian, Marcello Bacciarelli, court painter to the last king Stanisław-August Poniatowski. Bacciarelli was head of the Royal Academy of Painting, an institution commissioned by the king to teach native Polish artists.

The **King's Bedroom,** dressing-room and study are again richly decorated with panels and pictures that were removed before destruction. In the bedroom, however, the glass chandelier was a gift in the

1970s from the President of Austria and a suite of eighteenth-century tapestry-covered furniture was presented by Princess Alexandra on behalf of the British people. Some of the Castle's contents were in fact originally taken away as marriage dowries or looted centuries before by Swedes or Prussians. Most extraordinary of these, perhaps, was the sixteen-metre-long paper frieze showing the wedding procession of Zygmunt III in 1605, which was taken from the castle by King Charles Gustavus during the Swedish wars of 1655 and returned in 1974 by Olof Palme. But the most dramatic stories tell of objects that left the city during the Nazi occupation, a Matejko painting, for example, being rolled up and carried in a rucksack during the 1944 uprising. Clocks, pictures, books, armour, furniture and porcelain have all found their way back to Warsaw thanks to a widespread understanding of the terrible cultural losses suffered by Poland in the Second World War. Maybe the most surprising restorations among many from the Soviet Union were the standards and banners confiscated by Russian troops during the uprisings of 1830 and 1863, one inscribed in Polish and Russian: 'In the name of God, for our freedom and yours'.

Farther along the **East Wing,** through the lavish **Throne Room,** the Knights' Hall and the exquisite Green, Yellow and Marble Rooms is the **Ballroom,** largest salon in the Castle and scene of the greatest war-time loss. It was in this room, lined with gilded columns and large mirrors, that Napoleon, being introduced in 1806 to local dignitaries, is reputed to have commented on the great number of beautiful women Warsaw possessed. His remark turned out to be more than a passing interest; the young Countess Marie Walewska soon became his mistress and, according to legend, hers was the one voice which finally persuaded the Emperor to form the short-lived Duchy of Warsaw. Despite these distractions, though, even Napoleon must have noticed that the entire ceiling was covered by a wonderfully executed painting of allegorical figures and landscapes, the work, like so much else in the Castle, of Bacciarelli. On 17 September 1939 this enormous ceiling, titled 'The Dissolution of Chaos', was destroyed in the Nazi bombardment.

In the upper **North Wing** is a series of rooms that once belonged to the royal children but now contain displays of historical paintings by Jan Matejko, a nineteenth-century master whose romanticized images of Poland's past have become part of the national heritage. The **Library**, built by Domenico Merlini between 1780 and 1784, in the north wing of the adjoining Pod Blacha Palace, was the only castle building not destroyed in 1944. Its long, marble-columned gallery is decorated with bas-relief medallions representing both arts and sciences, and with many marble busts. During the nineteenth century the royal book collection was dispersed but the gallery remains as an example of the forms of decoration favoured at the court of King Stanisław-August. This king, who for 30 years from 1764 ruled over this great palace, is, if little else, an interesting character who has not always been well served by history. He was placed on the throne by his one-time mistress, Catherine the Great of Russia, who expected him to be a pliant puppet in her plans to control Poland. His many enemies within Poland considered him weak and concerned only with paintings and palaces, but in truth he was an intelligent and learned man in an impossible situation: the head of a country fast approaching breaking point. Stanisław proved to be less a tool than either Catherine or his uncles would have wished. Seeming in the first years of his reign to perceive Poland's predicament, he sought to introduce fundamental reforms in fields as diverse as monetary control, education and the military establishment. in 1765 he established the first truly secular school in Poland, the Collegium Nobilium, and a great educational campaign was begun in which both literature and the theatre were fully involved. He was also behind the publication of a new periodical, the *Monitor*, modelled on the London *Spectator* and highly critical of the ignorance, conservatism and religious intolerance that bedevilled the country. The king also supported moves to develop basic industries, such as mining, and to improve agriculture: in short, to do those things successfully practised already in many other European countries.

The rebuilding of the castle was a part of his plan for the monarchy to be seen to be both present and powerful, but Stanisław's popular fame continues to rest with his achievements in promoting and organizing artistic and intellectual life in the capital. Quite understanding the power of a picture, one of the projects he took most seriously was the establishment of a school where Poles would be trained in the craft of historical painting, for in this way he hoped that a more accurate view of Poland's own past could be presented to the country. Amongst many other reponsibilities in the king's artistic programme, the stewardship of this new academy was given to Marcello Bacciarelli, who became one of Stanisław's closest friends and advisers; he was one of the regulars at the famous Thursday dinners hosted by the king and attended by a great variety of intellectuals, scholars and artists. An important absentee from these intimate affairs was the Russian ambassador, a man who saw himself as the real power behind the throne; thus Stanisław could relax and discuss openly with his free-thinking friends all the problems of state as well as the latest scientific and artistic news and gossip from both home and abroad.

Invariably foreigners meeting the king were impressed by him. The English historian Willian Coxe, visiting in 1778, wrote: 'The King of Poland is handsome in his person, with an expressive countenance, a dark complexion, Roman nose, and penetrating eye; he is uncommonly pleasing in his address and manner, and possesses great sweetness of condescension, tempered with dignity.' This dignity was tested in 1771 when during a spate of conspiracies to overthrow the king, Stanisław was abducted at night from his carriage as it approached the castle and dragged across-country for many hours before being able to send to the city for help. The final indignity, however, was reserved for 1795 when, after the third partition of Poland by Austria, Prussia and Russia, he was forced to abdicate. As he left the castle he had so lovingly rebuilt and decorated, a silent crowd filled the streets and when the tearful Stanisław tried to address them his Russian guards forbade him. Three years later he died in his Russian exile, aged 65. He deserved better than to have been the king of Poland in the eighteenth century.

Returning once more to Plac Zamkowy, it is time now to explore the rest of recreated Warsaw. The only public transport allowed inside the walls is the *dorożka*, the horse-drawn cab, which can be hired from the Old Town market square to potter round the nearby streets. Although they are a picturesque and pleasant indulgence, there is really no substitute for that best of all ways of travelling and seeing — walking.

Before ever I set foot in Warsaw I knew, of course, the story of the old city's rebirth but was still not sure what to expect. At worst it could have been a medieval theme park with a turnstile at the gate, and perhaps it would have been in some countries. The real miracle of Warsaw, though, is not that the buildings and back alleys, the churches and cafés, the palaces and parks have been brought back from the grave, but that the result should have so much atmosphere, so much life. Despite the tourists and the gift shops, the line of horse-drawn cabs, the ice-cream parlour and the pizzeria, it is the peeling paint of the burghers' houses, the dark, disappearing lanes and the old ladies with their string bags of bread, which make this a real town and not a movie mock-up. Obsessed as Poland is with its past, now that in the new heart of old Warsaw something of that past has been so perfectly resurrected, the concerns of everyday life are quite properly modern and ordinary. In many ways this is due to properties being managed by cooperatives, ensuring that a great variety of people live in the few streets squeezed between the Market Square and the red brick wall that still encloses much of the area. The fact that such an attractive centre has not become the exclusive territory of a social élite is perhaps one advantage of socialist institutions.

Before diving into the cathedral or a museum, a slow stroll through the streets of the Old Town to soak up this special atmosphere should be rewarding. In Plac Zamkowy there is a shop that sells guides, maps and postcards, the latter being very useful for the determined hunter of specific buildings who has no native language: just wave the appropriate picture in the face of a local and invariably directions are forthcoming, even comprehensible. And there are plenty of Kawiarnias where tea and cake can be taken at leisure; coffee, the *kawa* suggested by the title, is, when available, far more costly. Undoubtedly, in such cafés, a delightful old custom will be witnessed: the kissing of the female hand by an arriving or departing male is still widespread amongst young people, and universal with their elders.

The present (restored) layout of Plac Zamkowy has been thus only since the early nineteenth century when the Kraków Gate and adjoining sections of wall were removed, the plan being to open up a much larger area to form a vast new square after the fashion of the time, but fortunately, in my view, this came to nought. From the north exit of the square, walk down the deep and narrow Swiętojańska Street past St John's Cathedral on your right and into the **Old Town Market Square (Rynek Starego Miasto)**. Without doubt the first place to visit is the **Warsaw Historical Museum**, housed in a maze of small rooms, corridors and stairways in the old burghers' houses on the north side. Considering that the city archives were destroyed during the war, an astonishing amount of material has been gathered, the period of war-time occupation being particularly well covered. The one-way route through the labyrinth starts with a series of models that speculate upon the very earliest settlements in the area, each room containing contemporaneous objects. The region was inhabited, of course, long before the Slavic tribes came on the scene; there is a Mesolithic site just a few kilometres upstream from Warsaw. The proto-Slavs were on the move in eastern Europe throughout the Bronze Age and early Iron Age, together with many other ethnic groups, and it is not until ploughing became established as a means of cultivation that a stable society developed. The early cultural centres, though, were not on the middle Vistula but on the Baltic coast, in the Poznan-Gniezno area, and in the south and south-west around present-day Kraków and Wrocław. Warsaw was a late arrival on the scene, though the indications are that several fortified settlements existed in the area by the ninth and tenth centuries. The models in this large and well arranged collection show the development from a simple wooden fort protected by earth ramparts and a fence to the first Gothic houses in the vicinity of the Market Place, dating from early in the fourteenth century.

The year 1339 was a significant one for the growing town. The Polish king, Kazimierz the Great, brought a legal action there against the Teutonic Knights, a powerful warrior order founded during the Third Crusade by Germanic nobles, following their annexation of traditional Polish territories in the northern provinces of Pomerania and Kujawy. Two eminent representatives of Pope Benedict XII were summoned from Rome to conduct and witness the hearing, which ended with all the disputed lands, including the city of Gdańsk, being returned to Polish control. Not surprisingly, the Knights rejected the proposal, but it was a laudable attempt to settle claims in a civilized manner and it put Warsaw on the European map. Then, in 1413, the town became the residence of the dukes of Mazovia; they abandoned Czersk, 35 kilometres upstream, when the Vistula, moving freely on the flat plain, gradually edged away from their old capital. The rapid growth of Warsaw in the fifteenth century, when the New Town, the Nowe Miasto, sprouted beyond the northern wall, paralleled a general rise in prosperity throughout Europe; in 1526, the principality was incorporated into the Polish kingdom following the death of the last of the Mazovian dukes.

Six centuries after the dispute between the Teutonic Knights and Kazimierz the Great the first German air raids on Warsaw took place. Not surprisingly, the most moving displays in the museum are those that tell the story of the city between 1 September 1939 and 17 January 1945, when the Soviet armies finally drove out the occupiers. The city had been taken once before, in 1655, when the Swedish armies had looted and burned, but the German action was the most complete attempt to obliterate a cultural capital and its million-plus inhabitants.

Photographs, posters, proclamations, identity cards and personal letters all tell the horrible story of Nazi occupation, of the ghetto resistance and the awful scenes following the 1944 uprising, when commando teams dynamited street after street until nothing but the occasional jagged remnant of a church or palace appeared above a welter of broken brick. A film show depicts this savage destruction and contains never-to-be-forgotten images of the effects of war. It is a harrowing but perhaps obligatory experience, bringing home an essential difference between the inheritance of an island nation such as Britain and a country of the European mainland. Even the most sympathetic knowledge and imagination can scarcely comprehend the effect of such a terror as the Nazis unleashed upon Poland.

The last displays in the museum depict the amazingly rapid reconstruction of Warsaw's basic buildings and services following the War. As early as 23 January 1945, it is reported, 6,000 people arrived from somewhere in answer to a call for volunteers to clear the main streets of rubble, and in June that year a special commission was set up to plan the city's future shape.

For many centuries the **Market Square** had been the focus of Warsaw's everyday life and until 1817 a town hall, built in the fifteenth century, had sat right in the middle surrounded by market stalls. Had that survived until the war, no doubt it too would have been rebuilt. Better, I think, the present open space amidst the narrow streets, especially after the experience of the museum just left. The freedom to wander across the square allows a good view of the surrounding houses with their lofty decorations and odd attic lanterns looking for all the world like stranded dolls' houses. The first stone houses, built by wealthy burghers and merchants, were modernized in the seventeenth century by the addition of baroque façades, often with very fine doorways. In the nineteenth century, it seems that these houses almost fell down without assistance from bombs or dynamite. As a modern, commercial city developed beyond the walls, the merchants left the Old Town to live and trade in the wide new avenues; poorer folk moved in and the usual pattern of structural degradation followed. Warsaw's first inner city problem was spotted early this century and a society formed to preserve such cultural relics as the Stare Miasto represented. Again following a familiar pattern, writers and artists took up residence and finally, in the 1920s and 1930s, the façades were restored and painted.

Undoubtedly one reason for the comfortable atmosphere in the square is that no attempt has been made to keep the place picture-book perfect: on many houses the paint is peeling and there is nothing of that sanitized, almost plastic-coated appearance of many historic West German town centres, such as Hamelin or Helmstedt. In a perverse way Warsaw seems more genuine and not just because fragments like carved portals and ornamental grilles were recovered from the rubble and correctly located in the new structures.

The four sides of the square are named after activists from the eighteenth-century Polish Enlightenment. The north, Strona Dekerta, has the only house to have survived the war with its walls standing; it is through this house that the **Historical Museum** is entered: known as **Pod Murzynkiem**, meaning 'under the little negro', it bears on its façade a sculpted negro head, indicating that the original owner, Jacob Dziannotti, traded in spices. Many houses have internal courtyards, the easiest to see being that behind the 400-year-old wine bar, Winiarnia Fukiera, entered from the rear, at 44 Piwna Street. The joyful noises emanating from it at most times will no doubt lure all but the sternest abstainer. On the first floor there is a museum of wine-making.

On the eastern side, Strona Barssa, is a museum named after one of Poland's legendary sons, the Lithuanian Adam Mickiewicz, frequently referred to as the Polish Byron, whose life (1789–1855) embraced the European Romantic period, of which his was the best known native voice. Without doubt his beautiful and powerful verse is better known and more meaningful to the modern Pole than is Byron's to his British counterpart. His initial fame was achieved with verses published whilst teaching at the University of Wilmo, the Lithuanian capital, but his membership of a students' secret society led in 1823 to his enforced exile from Russia, from where, in 1829, he travelled to Paris, never to return to his native soil. The epic verse he produced in exile initially reinforced his reputation as the greatest contemporary voice of the Slavonic world after Pushkin. But he seems to have been temperamentally unable to hold down any of the many teaching and editorial posts his fame brought him, becoming a sad and increasingly mystical man, his muse flown, and with a wife and six children to support. His unquenchable belief that the Bonaparte family were destined to lead his country to freedom brought him much scorn and indirectly led to his death in 1855. Sent to Istanbul by the French Government on a peculiar mission, the aim of which was to raise an army of Polish exiles to fight against Russia, he contracted cholera. His body was returned to Paris but in 1890 was disinterred and, among great rejoicing, buried in Kraków's Wawel cathedral, alongside the greatest figures of Polish history. Not easily translated, his best known works are historical dramas and verse narratives, such as 'Dziady' (Forefather's Eve) and 'Pan Tadeusz', an epic discribing Lithiania and its gentry in the period prior to Napoleon's 1812 campaign. The museum has a permanent exhibition detailing the poet's life and a variety of temporary displays on various aspects of Polish literature.

The burghers' houses of the southern, Zakrzewskiego, side of the square are the usual handsome and well decorated affairs but better known to me as the home of the *Hortex* restaurant where, just a few years ago, the first-floor window tables were the scene of a very sedate wedding party at which the guests drank champagne and my new wife and I imbibed tea. Why we chose tea on such an occasion is beyond recall, if not reason.

Two streets lead from each of the far corners of the square, seeming to present many options, but the land behind the east side falls quickly away towards the river, with steps leading down close to the potently named Dung Hill, where for centuries domestic rubbish was thrown, a habit still rife throughout Europe. Perhaps one day Warsaw's Gnojna Góra will know the scratching of the archaeologist's trowel; much social history may be buried there.

From the north-western corner, Nowomiejska Street leads to the **Barbican** gateway beyond which is the New Town. A Venetian gentleman, one Giovanni Battista, was responsible for the design and construction of the stump-towered Barbican, built to protect the town's northern gate, but once the city spread beyond the walls such fortification had little purpose and the gate was removed at the end of the seventeenth century, the towers being partly demolished a hundred years later. Shortly before the Second World War a section of the wall was reconstructed but complete restoration of the Barbican towers and much of the remaining wall took place only in the years 1952 to 1954. The narrow cobbled road through the red-brick fortification always has its complement of 'sixties-style people displaying but, it seems, rarely selling pictures, beads and other artless souvenirs. It is possible to climb up on to the wall and walk along its narrow top to the circular Marshal Tower, from where there is a broad view down to the river; the tower vaults were once a prison. Beside the tower is an 1855 figure of Syrena, the mermaid who is the symbol of Warsaw, albeit a freshwater variety, I suppose. She is reputed to have popped up out of the river and ordered two children, Wars and Sawa, to found a city, whence the Polish name for the capital, Warszawa. Syrena has unintentionally given her own name to many shops and cafés and also to a rather quaint Polish car, usually grey in colour with matching clouds of exhaust.

Just beyond the Barbican are two impressive churches facing on to Freta Street. On the left is the baroque St Paul's, founded in 1699, and across the road stands the earlier and more handsome **Dominican Church of St Jacek,** completed in 1638; behind it is the largest monastery in Warsaw, dating from the 1690s. The church's façade and the decoration of the nave and aisles are early baroque, but there are some elements of Gothic in the chancel vaults and windows. On the north side is the ornate chapel of the Kotowski family, built in the 1690s by a renowned Dutchman of many talents, Tylman of Gameren. While serving as a makeshift hospital for insurgents during the 1944 uprising, both the church and the monastery were bombed and hundreds of wounded were killed. Just a few doors from the church at **No. 16 Freta Street** was born in 1867 a Maria Skłodowska, better known by her married name, Marie Curie. The house was destroyed in 1944 and since rebuilding has been the patriotically named Polonium Museum, devoted to the life and scientific work of the double Nobel Prize-winning discoverer of radium. Opened in 1967, the centenary of her birth, the collection illustrates her life, most of which was spent in France where she had gone as a young girl to study physics; she married her professor, Pierre Curie. On display are some of her scientific instruments and various mementoes, such as diplomas and prizes awarded for her discoveries.

Farther along Freta, past little shops and the house, No.5, where the German writer E. T. A. Hoffman lived, is the **New Town Market Place (Rynek Nowego Miasta),** well furnished with trees and sloping away to the right. Once the busy heart of the 'new' suburb, it is now a sober and dignified place, a quiet retreat after the bustle of the Old Town. The intention of the post-war reconstruction of the New Town was to recreate the architecture of the late eighteenth century and again one must be in awe of the immense amount of detailed research that was necessary to achieve the present scene. Dominating the bottom of the square are the white stucco façade and dome of the **Church of the Holy Sacrament,** another fine baroque piece by Tylman of Gameren. The floor plan is in the form of a stump-armed cross, creating a circular church with two side chapels, altar and entrance lobby. Tylman's commission came in 1683 from Maria Sobieska, the French-born wife of the mighty King Jan Sobieski, famed throughout Europe for his decisive intervention at Vienna in 1683 which finally turned the tide against the westward expansion of the Turkish empire. The church was the queen's votive offering for her husband's victory in that great battle. Inside is the funeral chapel of the Sobieski family, one of the last of the line, the great king's grand-daughter, Caroline de Bouillon, being remembered with a baroque memorial installed in 1746.

There is one more church in the New Town that is worth a visit and it can be located by its distinctive bell tower peering over the rooftops to the left of Tylman's dome of the Holy Sacrament. To get there, leave the Market Square by its northern exit, where the church will be seen to the right. Founded in 1411 by the duke of Mazovia as the parish church of New Warsaw, the **Church of the Virgin Mary** is the oldest in the suburb. It suffered at the hands of nineteenth-century builders who disguised its Gothic simplicity, but since the war it has been splendidly restored to its original character. During this work some fine examples of fifteenth-century polychrome decoration were discovered. The adjacent bell tower with its steeply pitched roof and scallop-edged and decorated gable, all in soft red brick, dates from the sixteenth century and is one of the landmarks when the town is viewed from across the river.

The church is in Kościelna Street which continues westwards to Franciszkańska where, on the corner of Zakroczymska Street there is a late baroque Franciscan church (1680), a three-aisled building with a shallow dome and twin steeples on its façade; then turn left on to Ulica Bonifraterska, by which a large open square is reached, dominated by a building truly deserving of the title of palace. The front elevation, nineteen windows long, of the **Krasiński Palace** is in classical north-Italian baroque and yet again is the work of Tylman. He built it between 1677 and 1682 for Jan Krasiński, governor of the province of Płock, and it was said at the time to be more magnificent than the royal residence. Krasiński sought the best architects, desginers and sculptors he could find. The neo-classical carving on the front and rear pediments are the work of the renowned Gdańsk sculptor Andreas Szlüter, as are the figures perched above. That a provincial governor could afford such a place is a good indication of the immense wealth and power accumulated by the nobility in Poland's golden age. The interior is richer even than the façade, although the present decoration dates from 1782 when fire damaged much of the palace. For many years it served as the State Treasury, but since post-war rebuilding the Krasiński Palace has been an appropriate home for the National Library's collection of manuscripts and old documents. Sadly most of the original collection of 40,000 documents was destroyed during the war, but great efforts have since been made to build it up and there is much of value here to students of Polish literature and music. Behind the palace the old formal gardens are now a public park, and beyond that is Muranów. Here in Zamenhofa Street, a monument commemorates the 1943 ghetto rising when some 17,000 Jews were killed and the remaining 50,000 deported to the death camps.

Just down the road from the Krasiński Palace at the crossing with Długa Street is another poignant reminder of the occupation. In the roadway is a manhole cover that should bring a cold shiver to anyone who has seen Andrzej Wajda's film *Kanał*, a story about the 1944 uprising and its pathetic dénouement when the insurgents, many of them teenagers, sought to escape from the besieged Old Town area by lifting such covers and retreating through the slimy sewers towards safer parts of the city. Needless to say many did not make it. Exhausted after weeks of fighting on near-starvation rations, some collapsed and were drowned. Others were victims of interception by German troops who threw grenades into the sewers. The Wajda film was part of a famous trilogy — *Our Generation, Kanał, Ashes and Diamonds* — which should be obligatory viewing at all schools to illustrate the brutalizing nature of war. Here, at the corner of Dluga Street and Miodowa (Honey) Street, there is a plaque in memory of the several thousand who escaped through the tunnels, and of those who did not.

As you follow Miodowa, which runs parallel to the Old Town walls and just one block away, the density of both palaces and history increases. During another conflict which resonates still in the Polish consciousness, the Kościuszko Insurrection of 1794, Miodowa saw intense fighting when the people of Warsaw attacked the residence of the Tsarist ambassador in nearby Podwale Street. This popular uprising was a crucial action in Poland's history, its origins — to simplify greatly a characteristically complex period in north-eastern Europe — lying in the anger and frustration felt by Poles at the interference in their affairs by the neighbouring states of Russia, Prussia and Austria. In 1772 and again in 1793, chunks of Polish territory had been partitioned by these powers and put under their rule. Kościuszko, a professional soldier by then famous for his role in the American War of Independence, secretly made his way into Kraków from his exile in France and led a briefly glorious campaign against the Russian garrisons. In Warsaw, awaiting Kościuszko's largely peasant army, local shoemaker Jan Kiliński led the attack on the hated Russian ambassador. As is the way with so many popular risings, however, anarchy spread before the gains could be consolidated, and both Russian and Prussian armies were quickly on the scene brutally to clear up the mess. The net result was that in 1795 the king was forced to abdicate, the partitions were completed and Poland's period of enlightenment was ended. There was to be no independence for Poland until 1918. Kościuszko himself survived the upheavals, dying in France in 1817, to be further immortalized in a poem published that year by John Keats:

> Good Kościuszko, thy great name alone
> Is a full harvest whence to reap high feeling;
> It comes upon us like the glorious pealing
> Of the wide spheres — an everlasting tone.

In Podwale Street, which means 'under the wall', there is a romantic statue of Kiliński, sabre aloft and obviously spoiling for a fight.

2

Warsaw:
The Royal Way

To detail all of Warsaw's noble mansions is a task beyond this volume. A Polish book covering just the biggest and best describes 52 palaces all within the modern city centre, any handful of which will give an impression of the city as it was 200 years ago.

In Miodowa alone, not a long street, there are by my count five palaces and two churches. **St Basil's** has three paintings by the highly competent eighteenth-century historical artist Franciszek Smuglewicz who had learned his craft in Rome. Across the road is the **Church of the Capuchins**, with its monastery, founded in 1683 by King Jan III Sobieski, and amongst its more gruesome relics this modest baroque house of worship contains the heart of Sobieski and the viscera of King August II, in addition to the tomb of the Polish Canaletto. On the same side is the **Palace of the Archbishops of Warsaw** and the formidable semi-circular entrance gate to the **Pac Palace,** now the Ministry of Health. This huge building was erected in 1681 by the inevitable Tylman of Gameren for the Radziwiłłs, one of the small group of noble families who had gathered unto themselves most of the hereditary and influential offices of state, together with vast estates, and were a lot wealthier than the Crown itself. The Czartoryski, Potocki, Branicki, Zamoyski and Radziwiłł dynasties more or less ran the joint republic of Poland-Lithuania, nominating contenders for the royal elections and generally wheeling and dealing with affairs of state, and it is impossible to travel around the country without coming across their palaces and parks and even whole towns built by them.

Unfortunately the Pac Palace is not open to the public so its beautiful chapel and amazing Moorish décor can be seen only in books, but just around the corner in Senatorska Street, once home of the capital's most fashionable shops, is a palace that is most definitely open to all comers. In fact I can boast that a splendid marble hall in the **Prymasowski Palace** was the scene of my marriage, not that this would impress locals, who know that the former Primate's residence contains the register office. It was certainly more grand than the corporation affairs common in Britain. The unhurried and dignified ceremony was presided over by a robed judge and an organist played melodies of our choice.

Senatorska, leading away from the Old Town, contains four more noble piles, all restored after war-time destruction. Here, as in many places throughout the country, little wall plaques are to be found, often with fresh flowers beneath, in memory of citizens who died on that spot at the hands of the Nazis. A 23-year-old poet, Krzysztof Baczyński, has his name engraved on the wall of the **Blanka Palace,** which itself stands next to the large **Monument to the Heroes of Warsaw,** a high stone slab surmounted by a formidable sword-waving female. Ulica Senatorska here enters **Plac Teatralny,** home of the Grand Opera and Ballet Theatre. The latter is a giant pseudo-classical block built in the nineteenth century and one of seventeen theatres in the capital. The first public theatre in Warsaw was opened in 1765 at the suggestion of Stanisław-August Poniatowski, a great connoisseur and patron of the arts who would probably have been happier alone with his books than running that complex nation. In the event, partition relieved him of his duties and Polish theatre began its long experience of operating in a cultural climate dominated by harsh foreign rule and censorship. The habits of the nineteenth century have persisted in Polish theatre, as in literature, the cinema and much else. Poles will say that you must always read between the lines; view a play or film knowing Polish history and problems, seeing the allusions, the hidden references to despised foreigners et cetera. In the next breath, they will say that no outsider could possibly understand anyway. Personally I think that all this is just a bit overstated. Worthwhile creative work, surely, has many levels of interpretation and meaning, the best of it dealing with universal themes. But Poles, generally speaking, take a great pride both in their nationalistic artists and in regarding themselves as the most victimized nation in Europe. There is a strong argument for this latter notion but it seems an unhealthy doctrine to carry into the twenty-first century. The inevitable interaction of history

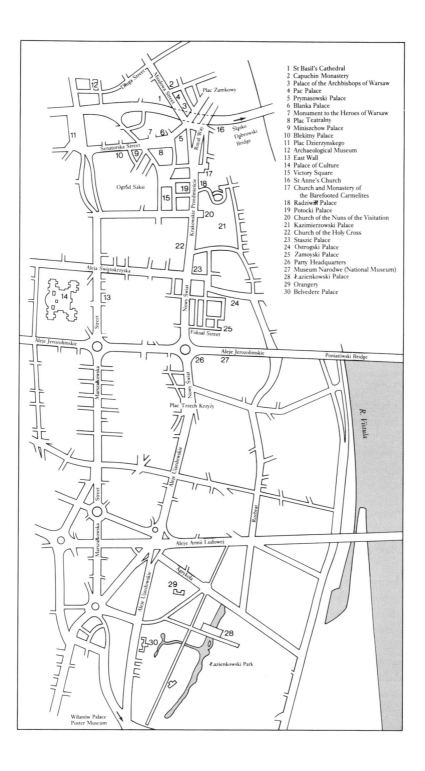

1 St Basil's Cathedral
2 Capuchin Monastery
3 Palace of the Archbishops of Warsaw
4 Pac Palace
5 Prymasowski Palace
6 Blanka Palace
7 Monument to the Heroes of Warsaw
8 Plac Teatralny
9 Miniszchow Palace
10 Blekitny Palace
11 Plac Dzierzynskego
12 Archaeological Museum
13 East Wall
14 Palace of Culture
15 Victory Square
16 St Anne's Church
17 Church and Monastery of
    the Barefooted Carmelites
18 Radziwiłł Palace
19 Potocki Palace
20 Church of the Nuns of the Visitation
21 Kazimierzowski Palace
22 Church of the Holy Cross
23 Staszic Palace
24 Ostrogski Palace
25 Zamoyski Palace
26 Party Headquarters
27 Museum Narodwe (National Museum)
28 Łazienkowski Palace
29 Orangery
30 Belvedere Palace

and theatre is apparent in the museum on the first floor of the Grand Theatre building.

Beyond the theatre, inevitably, are more palaces, the most notable being the **Mniszchów** and **Błękitny**; one of the latter's many claims to fame being that in 1816 a six-year-old Chopin gave a concert there. 1944 saw the destruction not only of the palace but also most of the priceless collection of a quarter of a million books and manuscripts held there since 1804, when it became home for the important Zamoyski library. Senatorska Street leads to **Plac Dzierżyńskiego,** named after an activist in the workers' movement who took part in the Russian Revolution of 1917 and has a monument here.

Just a couple of minutes' walk north, at the far end of Długa Street, is the **Archaeological Museum,** which lost only half its collection during the war. This is a good museum of its type, with treasure trove, relics and reconstructions illustrating the long history of settlement in the Polish lands up to the medieval period. Originally this was the city arsenal, put up in 1638 by a gentleman described as a 'general of artillery, traveller and poet'. At the outbreak of the 1830 November Insurrection it was stormed and looted by the people of Warsaw only to become a prison for the insurgents when the rising failed.

The wide tram-lined street south from Plac Dzierżyńskiego leads to **Marszałkowska Street** and the modern shopping centre. Like the towering Palace of Culture directly opposite, the glass and concrete blocks of the big department stores known as the **East Wall** were built on ground cleared of the rubble of former city streets. Started in 1961, this is the new commercial centre of the capital, with offices and apartments as well as four large stores, a cinema, theatre and numerous small shops, cafés and snack bars.

The department stores give a good indication of Polish styles and cost of living, given that the average income is known. At the time of writing it is about 23,000 *złotys* a month but inflation is still rife and is likely to remain so for some years yet. Some of the best purchases for visitors are of clothing, such as very fine — if traditional — suits, jackets and coats of pure wool. There are also plenty of shoes, these days, but the better styles are more easily found in the British high street, the name of the Polish game being 'export or die'. On a recent visit I snapped up some very solid wooden toys from a specialist department on the upper floors of the East Wall; such safe and well crafted toys and children's furniture can be found throughout the country. For a huge range of genuine folk-crafted items, there is a chain of shops under the *Cepelia* banner with at least one branch in even the smallest town and many more in the cities. Just over the road from the East Wall shops and next to the old Metropol Hotel is a large *Cepelia* with many items in carved soft wood; from spoons and spice racks to tables, cupboards and large painted chests traditionally used to store a country girl's trousseau. Perhaps the most exciting, and certainly the most expensive, are the *gobelins;* not garden gnomes but wall hangings hand-woven from naturally dyed wools of various textures. They vary greatly in size and price, some being true works of art. Many are based on traditional designs representing houses, trees and flowers in beautiful rich colours. Others are spectacular and haunting abstracts.

While in the vicinity of Marszałkowska Street, which continues its shop-lined way southward, some exploration must be made of the **Palace of Culture.** This giant, prestigious structure with its monumental entrance steps and portico contains all sorts of offices, several university departments, four theatres, three cinemas, a congress hall, the Technology and Zoological Museums, the Palace of Youth with its own sports hall, swimming pool and ballroom, plus various exhibition galleries and the 30th-floor viewing balcony. Guided tours are available and necessary. If you turn right in the entrance lobby and up some steps, there is an international bookshop crammed with scholarly volumes, mostly in Polish and Russian but with quite a few English-language volumes lurking amongst them. Most of these are on scientific subjects, but the sections at the back of the long high room are devoted to publications from other Eastern European countries. Here, beautifully illustrated Hungarian, Czech and German books can be found, outlining architectural and artistic history. So if Budapest, Prague or Dresden are on your itinerary it may well be easiest to buy a guide here. But if you do really long for the English language, it is a short step from the south side of the Palace across the busy Aleje Jerozolimskie to the British Institute building, in whose library all are welcome to peruse last week's *Daily Telegraph* or wallow in Waugh.

Behind the main stores of the East Wall is a pedestrian precinct, always crowded with shoppers, which is a regular meeting place and a good spot to observe local life. Nearby, narrow alleyways disappear through buildings towards internal courtyards where sometimes craftsmen's workshops or little boutiques can be found. Hot dogs and lottery tickets are sold in profusion here from tiny wheelless caravans.

47

A Polish partiality for eating in the street is satisfied by numerous other kiosks and hatches from which ice-cream is served, made in Italian machines that were imported during the phoney prosperity of the 'seventies, and such awful delicacies as *gofry*, sweet sugar-coated waffles. Much better are the various *bulka*, long thin pieces of French-style bread toasted and then garnished with a variety of dressings, the most popular being mushrooms — not our white variety, but the large brown ones which are feared by the British but adored by all other Europeans.

Turning north into any of the streets here will lead you eventually across the wide boulevard of Świętokrzyska to **Victory Square (Plac Zwycięstwa)**, which you will enter beside the new Victoria Hotel. This huge square, which has a busy and complex one-way system for drivers, opens out on its west side to the large **Saxon Gardens (Ogród Saski)**, that were the private grounds of a royal palace that did not get rebuilt after the war. Now the fragment of an old colonnade protects the tomb of the Unknown Soldier where guards stand on silent duty day and night.

Victory Square is yet another part of Warsaw that has seen violence as well as ceremony. In 1794 there was fierce fighting here, and in 1807 Napoleon reviewed his troops in the square, as later did the Tsarist Grand Duke. At the end of the nineteenth century a large Orthodox church was built in the square as a symbol of Russian domination, but after independence in 1918 it was torn down, an equally symbolic act. The north side of the square is closed by the back of the Grand Theatre, the road to the right of the theatre leading back into Senatorska Street and thence to Plac Zamkowy.

Our next destination, setting out from the Plac Zamkowy, is the National Museum, the Museum Narodowe, and the way there leads south from the Royal Castle along the Krakowskie Przedmieście. The first broad stretch of this avenue, the most impressive in the city and also known as the Royal Way, was developed as a market place in the fifteenth century and later was where the city council ceremoniously welcomed kings and nobles returning from military triumphs. The first notable building is **St Ann's Church**, perched on the edge of the Vistula escarpment and overlooking the modern east-west highway that burrows beneath. The church has evolved from one built on the site in 1454, and although the neo-classical façade dates only from 1788, much of the rich baroque interior is from the early seventeenth century. It was in front of St Ann's that princes from the Polish fiefdoms swore homage to the king in a ceremony that was later idealized by Matejko.

Because of the traffic and busy shops it is easy to disregard the architecture and innumerable monuments, but the shops themselves are not without interest. At No. 83 an establishment selling souvenirs and craftwork is named Lalka, meaning doll, and is a copy of a shop in a famous nineteenth-century novel of that name by Bolesław Prus, which describes in great detail everyday life in the city.

At the point where the street narrows and the palaces begin again is a monument to the poet Mickiewicz, close to the imposing baroque **Church and Monastery of the Bare-Foot Carmelites**, the façade of which, added in 1783, is regarded as the earliest example of classicism in Poland. Dominated by two storeys of columns, the façade is bedecked with sculpted figures representing saints of the Order and crowned with a copper sphere which represents earth, entwined by a snake biting into an apple. The interior is equally impressive and just as subtle. Next door is the large **Radziwiłł Palace,** a splendidly proportioned neo-classical affair set back from the road. Two wings form a courtyard, at the top of which is an equestrian statue of Prince Józef Poniatowski, nephew of the last king. Since 1918 the palace has been the seat of government, and is now home to the Presidium of the Council of Ministers.

Directly opposite, again set back in a fine courtyard fronted by huge decorative gates, is the **Potocki Palace.** Built in the usual mixture of styles, this is a residence quite characteristic of the mightly ruling families of the seventeenth and eighteenth centuries. Somehow I doubt that the Potockis would have approved of their neighbours, for Warsaw's first modern hotel, the Europejski, was built right next door on the site of yet another palace. Rebuilt since the war, like everything else around here, it is still luxurious, but has been replaced as the watering hole for business and journalist visitors by the glossy Victoria Hotel nearby. The corner entrance to the old hotel, though, leads to a cake shop with a most impressive interior. Great pillars rise to the ceiling, archways and alcoves frame a modest counter serving very good cakes and very expensive coffee.

Across from the Europejski is the still empty shell of what was the pre-war five-star hotel, the Bristol, a turn-of-the-century creation whose sumptuous *art nouveau* décor (known locally as the Secession style) was so famed that it is still possible to buy a little guide-book in English describing the place. It was at the bar of the Bristol that the world's press awaited war in 1939. The hotel, which is about to be restored to something of its former glory, was once owned by the great pianist-turned-politician Ignacy Paderewski.

A few steps on from the Bristol, past a little tree-filled square, is one of the best baroque buildings in town, the **Church of the Nuns of the Visitation**, its façade all columns and sculptures. It was designed, for a change, by Polish architects. Brought from France by Queen Ludwika in 1654, this order saw their first chapel here destroyed a year later during the Swedish wars, and the present structure was completed in 1734. I hesitate to use the word miracle with reference to a church but somehow this one came through the war virtually unscathed. A happier claim to fame is that Chopin used to play the organ here, perhaps to entertain the daughters of the nobility who made up the membership of the adjoining nunnery.

The next stretch of the Royal Way is dominated on the river side by the complex of converted palaces and especially constructed buildings of the University of Warsaw. The first buildings, directly on the pavement, could pass as fairly ordinary offices or apartments were it not for the slightly ridiculous carved muscle-men who have been stuck on the front of one section to support a balcony. Just above head height these four truncated Atlases, caught for ever, it seems, in mid-grunt, stare fixedly at the pavement. Their efforts support a building containing a precious collection of prints, drawings and architectural plans belonging to the university, the remnants of a pre-war collection of which 60 per cent was taken by the Germans, including original Dürer drawings. The prints library does hold occasional public exhibitions and it is well worth enquiring about these.

The main entrance to the large university campus is through a splendid neo-baroque gateway on the east side of the street, opening on to a tree-lined avenue at the bottom of which stands the old **Kazimierzowski Palace**. Now containing lecture halls and offices, this was originally built, just these few hundred metres from the city wall, as an out-of-town residence for King Jan II Kazimierz Waza in the seventeenth century, and then rebuilt in its present form a hundred years later. Blocking the view of the palace from the road is a large neo-classical library, home for a million books, and other university departments stand around this pleasant campus which has the great advantage for students of being in the centre of town. The west side of the street has many specialized and general bookshops and plenty of cafés where students sit for hours drinking black tea, examining their brown-paper parcels of new books or even writing essays. My wife claims to have written most of her thesis in the smoke-filled cafés of Krakowskie Przedmieście. Always worth a visit down this way is the **Russian Bookshop,** where well produced tomes on art and architecture in English, as well as posters, calendars and Soviet guide-books, can be found.

Poles are avid, well educated readers with a profound if chauvinistic knowledge of history, and their lust for learning was evident during the war when, closed by the Germans, the university went underground. Threatened by the death penalty for clandestine teaching, about 300 lecturers managed to continue their work. By 1944 about 9,000 students had received an education, several hundred gaining a master's degree, but the price was high. 162 professors and scientists lost their lives. By the war's end, about 80 per cent of all the university's buildings, libraries and equipment had also been destroyed.

Back on the Royal Way, on the west side, are the twin towers of yet another baroque church, the **Holy Cross,** badly damaged in the 1944 uprising when it was the scene of vicious fighting. Once again, though, the restorers have excelled themselves, and today it is a spacious and richly decorated place of regular worship, the focal point being an enormous carved and completely gilded altar dating from 1700. Sealed safely inside two of the pillars are urns containing the hearts of Chopin and the Nobel Prize-winning author Władysław Reymont. The church lends its name to the next turning on the right, Świętokrzyska Street, which is lined with modern shops and leads back westward to the East Wall and Palace of Culture.

As you proceed southward again, the road seems blocked by a large neo-classical building rather more impressive than elegant. Generally speaking, the farther from the Old Town one goes, the more modern the buildings become. This one, The **Staszic Palace,** dates from only 1820 and today it is the headquarters of the Polish Academy of Sciences. Appropriately enough, a statue and monument to Mikołaj Kopernik stands outside. Latinized, he becomes Copernicus, Poland's representative in the pantheon of science. To the statue's right the road narrows and changes its name to Nowy Świat, New World Street, and here in the sixteenth century there was little but open countryside and a dirt road leading out of town. Only in the seventeenth century did the rising bourgeoisie begin to build their homes here and today it is one of the busiest and best loved streets of the city. The first corner building on the right houses the faded grandeur of the Nowy Świat café, a famous student den. Ask for *sernik,* the cheesecake that is one of the country's specialities.

More local goodies of great renown can be found in an unpretentious little shop on the same side of the street, not far from a pet shop which spills its living wares on to the pavement. **Bliklego Ciastkarnia,** Mr Blikle's cake shop, is famed for its doughnuts, which have been produced here for more than a hundred years; the last Thursday before Lent is the traditional day to queue for this fattening confection. The shop has gained mention in several works of literature, but the only visible clues to its reputation are the signed photographs and sketches lining the walls. As for the other cakes on sale, they are good if undramatic, but any upmarket atmosphere the establishment might have had is destroyed by the presence of the ubiquitous ice-cream machine.

Some of the more interesting buildings of this district lie just behind the main road on the river side, in narrow streets jammed with cars parked right up on the pavement, a technique which is another local speciality. At the bottom of Ordynacka Street is the **Ostrogski Palace** where the Chopin Society and Museum are now housed and where, legend has it, a golden duck swims around in the vaults guarding a hidden treasure. I just hope that this dampness does not adversely affect the fine pianos upstairs.

Tucked away, if that is the expression for such a large place, in Foksal Street, further down on the left, is another palace with keyboard connections, the **Zamoyski,** from which a bomb was thrown at the Tsar's local governor, Count Berg, in 1863. The count survived this incident better than the palace, for in reprisal a horde of Cossacks was let loose inside it, and the invaluable contents were thrown into the street. Heaved from an upstairs window was a piano on which Chopin had played in his youth, an action lamented by Cyprian Norwid in his poem 'Chopin's grand piano'.

The next major crossing sees the wide Aleje Jerozolimskie cutting east to cross the river by the Poniatowski Bridge, which is presently and slowly being rebuilt with considerable disruption to the neighbourhood. There are two buildings of interest on this approach to the bridge, only one of which I suggest you enter without an appointment. The first grey, featureless block is the **Party Headquarters,** seat of the ruling Polish United Workers' Party whose initials PZPR will be seen in many places, such as posters and buildings. The second, and even uglier, grey, graceless block is an absolute must, for this is the home of the **National Museum,** built between the two world wars and looking like a monument to both. The museum has many branches throughout the country but this is the main collection of paintings, with some religious objects and Egyptian relics thrown in. Guidebooks big and small are available in several languages, but don't forget that Polish museums never open on Mondays. There are seven galleries open to the public: Ancient Art, Collection from Faras (Sudan), Medieval Art, Polish Modern Art, Polish Contemporary Art and two sections on Foreign Art. It would take a chapter to describe even the finest works on display so let me mention just some of the best known and some of my personal favourites.

For a good wallow in Polish history the Matejkos cannot be bettered: huge canvases, crowded with figures yet finely detailed in costume and context, each one a frozen frame from a past elevated to myth. 'The Battle of Grunwald' shows the fearful struggle of 1410 when a Polish army finally overcame the mighty Teutonic Knights; 'Rejtan' illustrates the moment when a noble threw himself across a doorway in the Royal Castle to prevent the 1795 documents of partition being given to the senate for final signature; 'Skarga's Sermon' shows an angry priest berating King Zymunt III Waza and a roomful of nobles during the 1606 rebellion of the gentry against the monarchy. All powerful, melodramatic stuff. Jan Matejko (1838–93) lived entirely during the period of partition, which obviously affected his attitude towards his art. He was possessed of great craftsmanship and artistry, but these monumental works, so beloved by Poles, are just too crowded, too Cecil B. de Mille, for my taste. As artistic images and not mere iconography, the details work better for me than the whole. Individual characters are impressive, a point emphasized by the studies and single portraits this painter produced, including a self-portrait showing the artist old beyond his years.

Probably the most famous of native painters, Matejko by no means stands alone. Less dramatic but no doubt more valuable as a historical record is a fine view by the younger Canaletto, looking south from the castle along the Vistula escarpment, which runs parallel to the Royal Way. The steep green bank with its trees and gardens looks much the same today — a pleasant retreat in the hot summer afternoons with its many little paths and parks.

One of the most startling pictures I have ever seen is Józef Chelmonski's giant canvas 'Czworka', which has a galloping four-in-hand wagon racing straight out of a muddy plain on to the viewer, or that is the impression. This effect is created by a low viewpoint and a highly distorted horizontal perspective, giving an image very like that obtained with a wide angle photographic lens. Small copies of this work and others of the artist's landscapes can be found on many an apartment wall in Poland.

The great discovery in Polish painting has been the work of Jacek Malczewski (1854–1929), a pupil of Matejko. His bright, haunting pictures reveal an obsession with Death, who appears not as a monster but as a welcoming angel with decidedly Polish features. A weird imagination is apparent in most of his canvases and especially in his many self-portraits, where he depicts himself as a Don Quixote look-alike and often handcuffed; a symbol, it would seem, of Poland's position at the time. These are unsettling but beautiful pictures that stand alone. Other impressive Polish artists include Olga Boznanska (1865–1940), one of the first female professional artists, who has nine splendid portraits on show, all of women. Stanisław Wyspianski is another adored artist, whose pastel portraits of sleeping children and likenesses of himself are widely reproduced, although he may be better known internationally as a dramatist; his symbolic play *Wesele (The Wedding)* was filmed by Andrzej Wajda. Tadeusz Makowski's simple, almost primitive, golden-brown pictures of gnomish cobblers and the like are very appealing, Andrzej Wroblewski's 'Execution' (1949) is disturbing, and Tadeusz Brzozowski's 'The Prophet' (1950) is decoratively melancholy. And there are many more. The newcomer to modern Polish painting has many pleasant surprises awaiting both here and in other galleries.

The **Medieval Rooms** are full of wonderful paintings, sculptures in wood and stone and beautiful madonnas, polychromy being dominant in ecclestiastical art of the time. In fact an anonymous carver of the early fifteenth century is charmingly known as 'Master of Beautiful Madonnas', which neatly describes his work. The recorded chant of plainsong gently pervades the rooms housing the ecclesiastical works, one of the most remarkable of which is a wooden triptych carved in Antwerp for use in a Gdańsk church. Dozens of amazingly detailed figures, all painted or gilded, can be studied at very close range and are quite worthy of the attention.

The **Foreign Art Galleries** are based upon the collection of Stanisław-August Poniatowski and are divided into North European, Italian and Russian schools from the fifteenth to the eighteenth century. This broad sweep takes in Flemish landscapes, Brueghel and

Cranach, Tiepolo and David; the latter's equestrian portrait of Stanisław Potocki being not at all unlike his mounted Napoleon in the Louvre. Later works include pictures by Courbet, sculptures by Rodin, drawings by Klee and Modigliani and lithographs and ceramics by Picasso, works which he donated to the museum shortly after the war. Elsewhere in the building are a library of art history and photographs, a department of coins and medals and one of prints and drawings dating from the fifteenth century. Examples of the goldsmith's art are displayed in the large **Collection of Decorative Art**, together with Gothic chalices, Limoges enamels, early jewellery, tapestries, locks and ceramics. It is altogether a fine museum and deserves an unhurried visit.

Back in Nowy Swiat, as you proceed south, the street enters Plac Trzech Krzyży, Three Crosses Square, in the centre of which stands the Church of St Alexander, in the form of a rotunda. Beyond the church and the left turn which goes down to the undistinguished building where since the 1920s the Sejm has sat in its purpose-built parliament, the road changes its name once more, becoming Aleje Ujazdowskie. This is a wider, more open avenue, originally called Calvary Way and lined with 28 shrines marking the Stations of the Cross but now flanked by late nineteenth-century mansions reduced to the rôle of foreign embassies, including the British and the Amercian. The British occupy a rather tatty Kensingtonian pile; the Americans a modern, insensitive slab of a place inside which I once spotted a sign reading 'Behind this door live some of the finest fighting men in the world'. Marines or diplomats, I wondered?

This smart end of town was formalized in the late nineteenth century with wide avenues radiating from green roundabouts, their designers influenced, no doubt, by Haussmann's Paris. A short walk ahead, across a complex junction under which a modern ring road hums, lies the first objective of this Royal Way.

Łazienkowski Park, known to everyone as Łazienki, was laid out in the second half of the eighteenth century around the summer palace of Stanisław-August, then some distance from town, and now is a public park, a splendid expanse of mature oaks and besquirrelled chestnuts, wide promenades and narrow twisting paths, pavilions and monuments, its crowning glory being the very graceful little **Palace on the Water**, the **Łazienkowski Palace** itself. When the king purchased the land in 1766, it had for many years been used for hunting, and at the northern end there was already a splendid quadrangular palace with a formal Italian garden,

Ujazdowski Castle, which had been built in 1600 and is presently being restored. Being a man of his time and a patron of the arts, the king no doubt took great pleasure in commissioning a new palace for himself together with other functional and decorative additions to the existing parkland, and so successful was his creation that Łazienki can be regarded as his greatest contribution to the nation; an artistic monument to a man who otherwise ruled over the dissolution of the state.

At all times of the year there are people in the park, but because of its size the only congregations are around the island palace, where all wanderings inevitably lead, and on summer Sundays around the Chopin monument where a crowd will be listening to an open-air piano recital. Several times throughout the day, at a grand piano sited beneath the big swirling bronze statue of the composer, eminent pianists perform his works. This is a modern innovation but based on a long tradition. Within sight of his summer palace the king had built an open-air amphitheatre modelled on the ruins of the one at Herculaneum, its stage set on a tiny islet in the lake. Up to 1,500 spectators can be seated on the steep steps, beneath statues representing classical and contemporary dramatists. On long summer evenings dramas are still performed in this idyllic setting but whether the actors can be heard above the quacking of the ducks and the wind in the willows, I cannot say. The king hedged his bets by creating another theatre in the old **Orangery,** designed like many royal buildings in Warsaw at that time by Domenico Merlini, Stanisław-August's official architect, and there can be few such elaborate edifices purpose-built both for the performance of drama and the growing of oranges. Nell Gwynn would have been in her element.

The Orangery theatre auditorium, constructed entirely of wood, has remarkable acoustics but, sadly, few performances are given here these days and the room, with its beautifully painted ceiling and its frieze featuring fashionable folk of the day, is now a gallery displaying casts of classical statues from the king's collection. In 1870 a new Orangery was built at the southern end of the park, a glasshouse splendid in its simplicity and set among a forest of roses.

The name Łazienki means nothing more than 'baths' and the present 'white wedding cake palace on the water', as one guide puts it, was built on the site of an earlier royal bath-house. Determined to have a home away from the eyes of parliament and the noise and smell of the Old Town, Stanisław-August followed previous nobles down the

Royal Way and developed the existing domed rotunda built in the 1680s by Tylman to shelter a bath moulded in the form of a grotto. Starting in 1775, a series of building programmes produced the gem of a palace that is today one of Poland's proudest possessions. Every bit as delicate and charming as Le Petit Trianon at Versailles, it has the advantage of standing on its own island in the long, narrow, tree-lined lake, so that numerous views of it appear through the willows as one follows the paths that surround the water. The classical façade with its colonnaded portico crowned with statues is by Merlini; the expensive interior by his Polish associate Jan Kamsetzer. Burned by the Nazis but not blown up, although holes were drilled in the walls ready for demolition charges, the whole has been restored in a typically thorough and tasteful fashion. Today it is a branch of the National Museum, displaying itself in all its eighteenth-century glory with original paintings, furniture, sculptures, clocks and even chandeliers, which were all carefully stored during the occupation. Where the royal tub once stood there is now a sculpture of Aphrodite emerging from her bath. The high and glamorous **Ballroom** is lined with busts and has allegorically carved fireplaces at each end. Little imagination is necessary to fill it with the bewigged hubbub of a summer ball, hooped frocks and shiny leather stepping out a perfect pavane on the polished marble.

Other rooms are equally elaborate and stunning. Next to the ballroom is a small gallery containing pictures from the royal collection, which include a Bacciarelli, and then an elegant dining-room. Upstairs are the royal apartments, exquisitely furnished with period pieces, and an exhibition telling the story of the palace and park. The whole atmosphere of the building is of lightness, impeccable taste and a prosperity that belies the true condition of Poland today, sadly, as much as it did in those days before partition. Within the park there are, by my reckoning and not including the café, at least fourteen buildings of interest, from the palace to a water-tower in the style of a Roman tomb and the White Cottage, a little pavilion where King Louis XVIII of France took refuge in 1803.

Back on the main road and itself backing on to the park is the **Belvedere Palace,** a large pile built in its present form in the late eighteenth century and today the residence of the President of the Council of State, who is nominally head of state; since 1972 this has been the widely respected Henryk Jabłoński. Like many another place in this town, the Belvedere has seen action in its day. During the partition it was the home of Grand Duke Konstanty, the Tsarist governor, and in November 1830 this dignified gentleman was forced to hide in the room of a lady-in-waiting while the insurrectionists searched for him. As well as being unwanted, Konstanty's reign was seen by locals as being somewhat weird. All his footmen had to be either two metres tall or midgets, and citizens guilty of misdemeanours, whatever their social position, were chained to wheelbarrows and forced to work in the gardens. From the Belvedere the ultimate destination of the Royal Way lies several kilometres farther on; down the hill, past the Soviet Embassy and Universus, the biggest bookshop in Warsaw, then through old suburbs and new tower blocks to the flat land beside the Vistula river.

King Jan III Sobieski, he who conquered the Turks at Vienna, must have felt a greater need than other monarchs to distance himself from parliament when he chose this site for his summer palace. Begun in 1677, the baroque fabric of **Wilanów** — from Villa Nova — progressed by affordable stages and was not completed until 1729, more than 30 years after the king's death. Once the extensive car park, the expensive restaurant and the souvenir shops have been passed, mature trees are all that separate the visitor from the large and very regal complex of buildings. The first structures to be sighted will probably be the high domed room of St Anne's Church and, close to the ornate entrance gates, the equally florid Potocki mausoleum. As only guided tours of the palaces are allowed, there may be a delay before gaining entrance, time that can be well spent looking around the gardens and studying the highly decorated building from the outside. To the south of the palace, beyond the Poster Museum, is an informal and wooded area full of glades and a variety of mature, not to say elderly, trees, sloping down to a large pond. At the farther side of the water a broad stream flows northwards to the Vistula, leading to the lower-level formal Italian gardens directly in front of the palace. Replete with fountains and statues, these are separated from the palace terrace by stairs decorated with sculptures representing the four states of love, designated somewhat cynically as Fear, Kiss, Indifference and Quarrel. An insight, perhaps, into court life at the time.

The garden façade of the palace is richly decorated with moulded plasterwork featuring busts of historical figures, and the ornate parapets are strewn with Sobieski family crests and more statues. On a south-facing wall is an elaborate sundial where gilded cherubs support a winged god, Chronos, whose pointer tells both the time and the sign of the zodiac — a clever device which was the work of Adam Kochański, scientist and royal librarian, and the famous Gdańsk astronomer Jan Hevelius. North, beyond the inevitable orangery, now a gallery of baroque statuary, is an area designated as an English Park and containing, confusingly, a Chinese pavilion.

Once one is inside the palace, with the mandatory felt slippers fixed to one's feet to give some protection to the floors, the tour proceeds through long galleries which are exquisitely furnished and retain the original wall and ceiling decoration. As in the Zamek Krolewski the goldsmith's art is much in evidence, providing a splendid setting for the fine collection of pictures assembled here from the household not only of Sobieski but of the subsequent owners of Wilanów, who have included the Czartoryski, Lubomirski, Potocki and, until 1945, Branicki families. In the gallery of Polish portraits there are more than 250 canvases from the sixteenth to the nineteenth centuries, as well as sculptures, medals, portraits on porcelain and those strange creations, coffin-lid likenesses. These were painted on hexagonal pieces of tin plate which could then be fixed to the coffin, but the custom seems to have been to remove them before interment. The furnishings have been arranged according to ancient inventories and the written reports of visitors during 200 years, each room being decorated according to its original function. Star exhibits include a writing table which belonged to Jan Sobieski and his wife's dressing table, a set of eighteenth-century English mirrors and a suite of rococo walnut furniture with Aubusson coverings. There are also among many other suites of furniture, chests and clocks, such exquisite things as a collection of sixteenth-century Limoges enamels and various *objets d'art* in wood, enamel and silver.

One of the first-floor rooms where careful restoration has revealed late seventeenth-century frescos is the **Quiet Room (Pokój Cichy)**. It is a strange, low place, its ceiling painted with naked goddesses, a chandelier suspended over an altar-like table. The only other furniture is a set of chairs with their backs against walls decorated to give the impression of a colonnade with gardens beyond. Perhaps this was a rainy-day retreat for the king, for the times when the real garden would have muddied his silk hose. To those who have visited the Royal Castle and National Museum, the full, walrus-moustached figure of Jan Sobieski will by now be familiar, usually portrayed astride his charger with a burning Vienna beyond and a few dead Turks underfoot. This image, like that of Stanisław-August

Poland

Poniatowski in his coronation robes, will be imprinted on the memory after any extensive tour of Poland; in each case so many copies have been made that it is difficult to recall which is the original. There are about 60 rooms at Wilanów, all so richly decorated that the brain becomes blurred with images of golden alabaster cherubs and coats of arms set against the glowing Pompeiian pink of the so-called Grand Crimson Room or the Genoese velvet of the Queen's Antechamber. It is all out of this modern world and almost too much for our more humble age. There is one room, however, in the earliest section of the palace, that is an oasis of simplicity compared to the rest of the building. This is the **Middle Room,** with its plain walls and lightly decorated beamed ceiling. And rather than keep up with the hectic pace of the guided tours in such establishments, I have found it possible to slip away from the back of my designated party and concentrate on a particular room or picture until the next group happens along.

Reference was made earlier to the **Poster Museum** and, having come thus far, take the opportunity to see a form of graphic art that is highly respected in Poland. There is a permanent display of Polish and foreign posters from a collection of about 25,000 items, and if you catch the right year there is the International Poster Biennale. Alternatively, there is a pleasant café close to the palace ticket-office. This serves hot meals or just more tea and cheesecake, and has a friendly tabby cat. I have so far scarcely mentioned food during this tour around Warsaw. In Poland it must be admitted that, fine as many traditional dishes can be, they are rarely so in ordinary restaurants and the cry that the best food is served at home is even more than usually true. So get invited to dinner by a Polish family to experience both hospitality and food at its best — you wil be served lots of cooked meats and maybe apple cakes, washed down, if you are not very careful, with too much vodka. Good meals are available in some restaurants, of course; the supply problems of the early 'eighties were thankfully overcome long ago — but the problem is service. It is an area where Poland must make an effort if it is to please visitors, many of whom collect food memories as others do snapshots.

That said, let me mention some names. There is no doubt that good food and service can be had at the Canaletto Restaurant in the Victoria Hotel and also at the Forum and Europejski hotels. The Europejski offers a more sedate atmosphere than the other two and also has a pleasant café. In the Old Town market place, the Bazyliszek Res-

60

taurant serves boar, venison and duck in season, and a summer speciality is a delicious *zupa owocowa,* cold fruit soup. In the north-east corner of the square is a place close to my heart: the Kamienne Schodki Café, which was the first place my wife and I went to after meeting. It is a nice old-fashioned place and, besides serving tea and cakes, it has a special candle-lit area where duck, the house speciality, is served. A short walk from the Old Town down towards the river is the large Retman Gdański Restaurant in Ulica Bednarska, a local favourite with a good selection of Polish dishes. But personally I am a café dweller rather than a restaurant man. Street cafés in summer from which to watch the world as it passes, a snug corner in winter with a book, black tea and a cake — there is no shortage of such places in Poland. One sign found throughout the country is *Hortex,* the state-run catering organization. Its fame is based upon a range of ice-cream sundaes but the small *Hortex* corner café in the Old Town square also serves one of the most famous and basic of Polish dishes, *barszcz.* Better known perhaps by its Russian name of bortsch, this spiced beetroot soup is served with a small, hot sausage-roll and makes a cheap and warming snack.

3

Mazovia

The region of Mazovia, or Mazowse, at the heart of which lies Warsaw, was never the richest area of Poland, being composed mainly of sand and clay. This great flat low-lying region is the meeting-place for all the rivers of eastern Poland; the Wieprz and Pilica joining the Vistula to the south of Warsaw, the Bug and Narew a little to the north. This combination of soil and water has not encouraged an abundance of market towns with cathedrals, or even many picturesque villages, but there is nevertheless plenty of interest which can conveniently be visited on a day trip from the capital. And if you stretch the area a little, there is an experience to be had here that is quite unique in the whole of Europe.

But it is not necessary to go far from Warsaw to find a landscape that is alien to most of us. Just to the north-west of the city, enclosed by the westward-curving Vistula, is a huge tract of dune and bog land, stretching for 40 kilometres and in places 20 kilometres wide. This is the **Kampinoski National Park (Puszcza Kampinoska)**, a fascinating remnant of the forest which once covered most of Poland and, for that matter, northern Europe. It is difficult terrain to get about on, being a mixture of pine forest on interminable sandy ridges interspersed with areas of soft marshland. But that which is difficult for man has proved to be ideal for many species of plant and animal. In previous centuries the only people who entered the forest, apart from the nobility who hunted bison and aurochs, were bee-keepers and pitch-burners whose abandoned cottages can still be found, but today it is a protected area and special permits are necessary in order to visit certain enclosed reserves. The serious naturalist or mushroom hunter is advised to go the the main office at Izabelin, where a guide can be hired and advice given, but for the general visitor who just wants the experience of being in such an atmospheric landscape, and the chance to glimpse wild boar or one of the hundred or so elk with their sad and ridiculous faces, it is best to head for the village of Palmiry. This is close to the main road from Warsaw and well served by buses from the centre. From here a small road takes you deep into the forest where there is a carpark and adjoining it a cemetery that was laid out on the spot where the Nazis carried out mass executions of Warsaw citizens. A glance at the memorial stones reveals that it was the community leaders and those of social renown, such as actors and sportsmen, who first stood beside the open ditches to be shot. Set in a clearing in the silent forest, it is a moving and thought-provoking place to visit.

Countless side trails head off into the trees and it is not necessary to travel far in order to feel alone in all the world, nor very much farther to be totally lost in a confusing wilderness. So it pays to be careful and keep to the marked tracks. The intrepid naturalist, however, will find many delights hidden away in the gloomy bogs or perched atop the alder, pine and birch groves. As well as the boar and elk there are roe deer, foxes, badgers, even the occasional wolf, and the birds include cranes and black storks, grey herons, falcons and marsh owls, the latter being difficult to spot thanks to the unsociable hours they keep.

During Poland's all too frequent times of trouble people have sought sanctuary in the forest which is so conveniently close to the city. In 1863 it saw fierce fighting as the mounted Tsarist troops flushed out the Warsaw insurgents, and in 1939 the Polish army fought bravely here against the confident and better armed Germans in an attempt to relieve the capital. During the Second World War it was an obvious base for the Resistance, though there were many casualties, as the partisan cemetery at the little forest village of Wiersz testifies.

If you have a car there is an interesting circuit to be made westward from Warsaw that takes in first the Kampinoski forest and then, just beyond its farthest edge, **Fryderyk Chopin's birthplace** in the little village of **Żelazowa Wola.** This lies a few miles north of Sochaczew on the main Poznań road, but by way of the forest it can be approached on country roads, which seems, somehow, much more fitting. The house itself is pleasant enough but rather modest and undistinguished

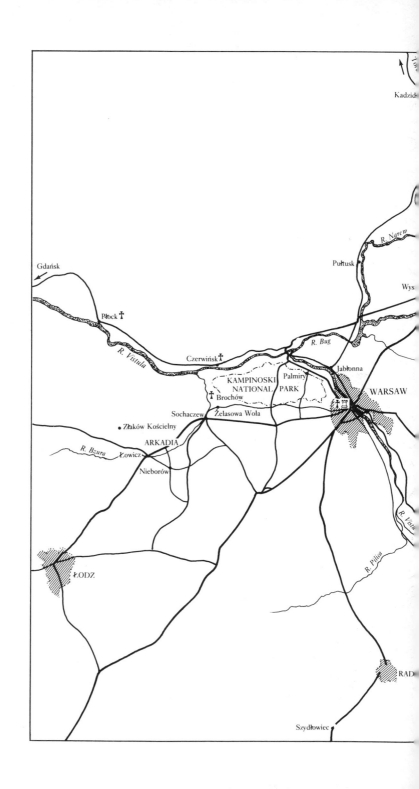

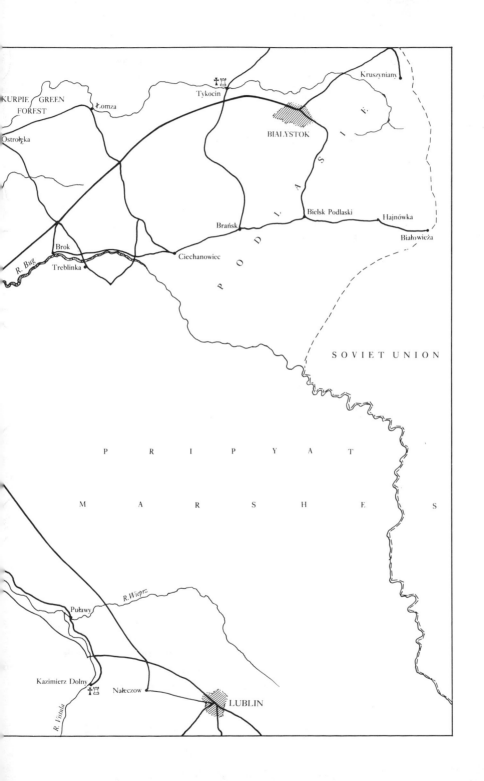

from the outside. It sits very well in the large garden, part formal and part natural, which slopes southwards to a small stream where a little island is reached by way of a footbridge. The small scale and peaceful atmosphere ideally befit a romantic image of the composer, but I dare say much has changed since this was Chopin's home, for although he was born here, in 1810, the family was living in Warsaw within a year. It is known, however, that he visited the place very often, right up to the summer of 1830 when he left Poland for ever. Today, the six-roomed house has the atmosphere of a shrine, so well is it restored; so clean and light and impeccably furnished to the period.

The room you will enter first was formerly the kitchen, and contains decorated beams typical of the period, as well as a copy of the well known portrait of the composer by Delacroix. The next room is the most important, containing the Steinway grand piano used by eminent interpreters of the master's music for Sunday recitals here from June until September. On these occasions the large windows are opened and the music drifts into the scented garden where the audience sits on the terrace or under the trees. Which is not a bad way to spend a warm summer Sunday. Elsewhere in the house are family pictures and other memorabilia associated with Chopin's life, including a cast of his left hand and copies of his earliest compositions. There is also a copy of his certificate of baptism in the house, but just eight kilometres to the north, in the old **Church of Brochów** beside the Bzura river, the original can be seen, which makes a good excuse to visit this rare example of an ecclesiastical fortress.

To continue the suggested circuit, head south from Żelazowa Wola and join the main road at Sochaczew, once a ducal seat but reduced to anonymity by the passage of too many wars, and then travel west for some 25 kilometres to **Łowicz**. At first glance the little town appears somewhat drab but it is an ideal place in which to find out about the surrounding countryside. The village people of this poor farming region are famous for the richness of their folk traditions, and in particular for their brightly coloured costumes. True enough, the streets are not thronged with gaily clad maidens, nor ever were they, but come the June festival of Corpus Christi there will be a long procession to the church in which many traditional and beautifully embroidered costumes can be seen. On other days of the year — excepting Mondays, of course — the best chance of seeing such attire is in the **Regional Museum**, which is housed in a sixteenth-century palace facing on to the cobbled market square.

This is one of the best museums in the country, and has a large collection of costumes. Many of these include a heavy wool skirt with brightly coloured stripes, worn with a black waistcoat and white full-sleeved blouse and topped off with an embroidered headscarf. There are also displays showing the history of the region, the evolution of local agricultural implements, cottage furniture, pottery, painted Easter eggs, and those uniquely Polish decorations, coloured paper cut-outs in the shape of cockerels, horses, people and a huge variety of complex natural and geometric patterns. These are still stuck around a cottage on walls and beams, adding a touch of colour to the generally dim rooms. In fact they can be seen in the back garden of the museum, into which two complete cottages have been squeezed, each furnished in a style that was common in the local villages until quite recently.

Before you leave the town, the big **Collegiate Church** directly facing the museum is worth a visit. In its earliest form, in the middle of the fifteenth century, it was a Gothic brick structure but it was remodelled several times, the final working over being done in the 1660s. A large building abounding in baroque decoration, it has a series of ornate tombstones and also several chapels, each with a beautiful vaulted ceiling. A marked contrast to the surviving houses in the smaller Old Market Place (Stary Rynek), with their simple but strong vaulted gateways large enough for a horse and cart. The Łowicz branch of the *Cepelia* folk-craft shops, just across the road from the museum, has a good selection of local items including some lovely *gobelins*, woven wall hangings featuring traditional patterns that bear a close resemblance to the paper cut-outs.

South-west of Łowicz, some 50 kilometres away, is **Łodź**. With a population of more than a million people this is the second largest city in Poland. But unless you have business or relations there it can be recommended only to fans of nineteenth-century industrial architecture. Such is the fame of the English Industrial Revolution that every country claims to have its own Manchester, and Łodź is Poland's. Large and grubby, it has a local museum, a very good film school and little else; so from Łowicz travel just a few kilometres south-east on the Skierniewice road to find two places more appropriate to a day which has included Chopin.

The first is a romantic park called **Arkadia,** laid out at the end of the eighteenth century by Princess Helen Radziwiłł and today preserved in its original form with pavilions and temples, a grotto to Sybil and a neo-Gothic ruin. In autumn it is especially good to walk by the lake kicking up great waves of golden leaves.

This experience can be repeated just down the road at the second stop, the village of **Nieborów**, which has the added attraction of a baroque palace by the indefatigable Tylman of Gameren. Now the palace is a branch of the National Museum, containing a large collection of *objets d'art*, paintings and furniture, but half of it is reserved as a place of retreat and work for Polish writers and artists. Would that such a scheme operated in Britain. The rooms that are open to the public are well worth a visit. Crammed with odd bits of furniture, Greek marbles, a huge and inviting double bed and a large and well stocked library, this has the feeling of a family house, albeit one belonging to a very special family. A glance at the bookshelves full of volumes in many languages brings home the cosmopolitan character of the old upper classes. Never able to resist a glance at other people's books, I noticed the *Letters of Walpole* and the *Letters of Byron* alongside the *Mémoires de General Pepe* and the *Fables* of La Fontaine, while next to a collection of verse by the Polish favourite Wyspiański stood *Thoroughbred Racing Stock* by Lady Wentworth and the beguilingly titled *Jennings' Landscape Annual.*

The main staircase is extraordinary, its walls and ceiling lined with blue and white Delft tiles. In the lobby is an equally unusual chair, carved to represent the woodman's craft. The arms are shaped like axes sunk into the seat and a pair of gloves is moulded over the back. The carving is impressive, but the chair looks horrendously uncomfortable. The gardens are planted with a variety of statues, Roman tombs and Gothic sarcophagi, and even a column covered in hieroglyphs, which was probably snaffled during some grand tour.

From Nieborów there are several ways of getting back to Warsaw, the simplest being to take the small road due north to join the main Poznań road by which one can then head east towards the capital.

There is one more town within easy reach of Warsaw which is worthy of mention but it is best visited when travelling alongside the Vistula on the road to Toruń and Gdańsk. This is Plock, yet another riverside settlement perched on a cliff. One of the oldest of Mazovian towns, it is also potentially one of the most interesting, but restoration work has only recently begun and it may be several years before the long, narrow, medieval section of the town recaptures some of the splendour of its past as a wealthy trading centre and the seat of bishops and kings. Each June the town is taken over by a national folklore festival, with poets, dancers and musicians of all regions taking part in what is bound to be a noisy and colourful event.

The promenade along the cliff top provides a panorama over the wide river and far below there is a little shipyard which makes riverboats. At the east end of this path are the old Bishop's Palace and the Gothic Noblemen's Tower, plus the **Cathedral** which, although it has lost all its twelfth-century Romanesque characteristics, contains a fascinating royal chapel with the tombs of King Władysław Herman, who reigned from 1079 until 1102, and his son Bolesław, who continued the family business until his own death in 1138. The story of these two gentlemen is not untypical of the time. Each succeeded to the throne by usurping his elder brother, in a period when Poland was attempting to gain full independence from the tentacles of the Holy Roman Empire. Since those days Bolesław has always been known by the sobriquet Krzywousty (Wrymouth), and recent delving into his tomb has revealed that his jaw was indeed deformed. Such nicknames were common in the Middle Ages, but were not, I am sure, mentioned in the presence of the monarch concerned. There was Bolesław the Chaste, Bolesław the Curly, Mieszko the Stumbling and — my own favourite — Władysław Spindleshanks. But convenient and amusing as such labels are, they surely obscure rather than enlighten those far-off days: as in the case of Shakespeare's Richard III, with his hunch, a nickname can prejudice for centuries any objective analysis.

On the road from Płock to Warsaw, just across the river from the western end of the Kampinoski forest in fact, is the little village of Czerwińsk, where the twin towers of one of the finest buildings to be found close to the capital rise above the river bank. This is the **Abbey Church of St John Lateran,** established way back in 1148. The basic structure is a stone Romanesque basilica, later rebuilt in Gothic, Renaissance and baroque, but the real treasures, discovered only in 1951, are the frescos, which date from the early twelfth century through all the stylistic periods up to the baroque. It is certainly worth turning off the main road to see them.

To the north-east of Warsaw, the Vistula is greatly enlarged by the combined waters of the Narew and Bug rivers which flow in from the east, draining a vast area of eastern Poland as well as the soggy wilderness of the Pripyat marshes across the border in the Soviet Union. Being mainly forest, this is not a region with too many man-made attractions, but it is a landscape that is quintessentially Polish, with quiet villages and resigned horses pulling creaky carts.

Searching out people to interview for a school geography book, I once drove out in this direction and found a circular route that extends a little beyond Mazovia but takes in several places worthy of a visit and also gives the traveller plenty of opportunity to soak up an atmosphere that is to be found nowhere else.

Leaving Warsaw in a north-easterly direction, keep to the E12 road for the 50 kilometres or so to Wyszków on the Bug river and then carry on a further 24 kilometres until, in the middle of a forest, a narrow road as straight as an arrow turns off to the right, signposted to Brok and Treblinka. Yes, the same Treblinka where 10,000 Poles and 800,000 Jews were murdered. In an effort to cover up their crime, much of the camp was destroyed by the retreating Nazis, but a monument has been erected on the site and some 17,000 symbolic tombstones installed. What remains of the camp can be found beyond Brok, just south of the Bug river.

Still following the river, the route leads to the small town of **Ciechanowiec,** where there is an open-air museum of the Skansen type first developed in Sweden, set in the grounds of an old palace. Here a typical oval-shaped forest village has been built using genuine buildings reassembled on the site. Half an hour spent here will give a good flavour of the life that has been lived in these parts for many centuries, regardless of changing frontiers and political systems. Every lifestyle is represented, from the simplest one-room cottage of a day labourer right through to the Neo-classicist palace, which itself houses many smaller exhibits. The peasant farmstead surrounded by its wooden picket fence is similar to many thousands which are still inhabited throughout the Polish lowlands, and the yeoman's manor house with its five rooms would probably be condemned in Britain, so basic is its hewn-log architecture and so primitive its sanitation. But these little homes of solid wood survive in many places and are easy to keep warm in the bitter Polish winters. Also on display are a village smithy, an arcaded granary, a windmill and a beam well — this last more often associated with the Hungarian plain, but still to be seen some cottage yards in Poland. Detailed research by the museum specialists has enabled them to plant up a cottager's field in the ancient chequered pattern, with buckwheat millet, hemp, flax, turnip and poppy; all the crops being used in one way or another on the site. In one little cottage there is a hens' nest built below the stove, a habit that survives in many country districts to ensure a supply of eggs through the winter.

From Ciechanowiec the road continues eastwards through Brańsk, Bielsk Podlaski and Hajnówka until at **Białowieża** you can go no further. The rest is forest — and just two or three kilometres away is the Soviet Union. This small village lies in the heart of the last primeval forest in Europe; a vast 125,000 hectares (312,000 acres), half in Poland, half in the Soviet republic of Bielorussia.

The first call upon arrival should be the **Museum**, which is one of the best of its type that I know. Close to the park entrance, it is housed in a purpose-built structure in the grounds of an old mansion and the English language guide-book will explain all you need to know about the forest, from the basic structure of the terrain and the critical level of the water table right through the history of the forest since the last Ice Age and details of its myriad forms of life. There are even stuffed and sad-faced elk and bison dating from the nineteenth century and a room full of similarly preserved birds. One room is devoted to historical methods of bee-keeping and wood distillation, others to plant protection, local archaeology, scientific research, edible fruits and fungi and many other topics.

The forest itself can be entered only with a guide, groups travelling on special horse-drawn carts. Here man is regarded officially as the predator and it is he who is controlled while the forest moves to its own profound and complex rhythms around the four beats in the bar of the seasons. So high are the trees and so dense the canopy that a few paces from the track take you into a strange, gloomy, green-shadowed world of soft earth and fallen, moss-eaten trunks. Most of it is a trackless wilderness where even the forest wardens get lost; they tell stories of spending the night sitting under a tree only to find the next day that they were just 50 metres from the edge of the trees.

Białowieża owes its survival to the kings and dukes of Poland and Lithuania, for whom this was a hunting forest. The first guards worked here in the fifteenth century, seeing off poachers and preserving the game for a royal death. Even so, it is a miracle that so much woodland has survived the many wars that have passed this way, although it was a different matter for the larger animals. King of this jungle is the European bison, an enormous yet passive beast who lived through all those royal hunts — such as that of King August III in 1752 which killed 42 bison and 38 elk — only to be eaten to extinction in the First World War by starving soldiers. In the 'twenties, three Białowieża bison were brought back from zoos and today their progeny amount to some 250 animals. Many others have been supplied back to zoos and to other European forests where they had become extinct. The unsurprising secret of this success, it seems, is simply to leave the bison alone in a core area of the forest which is strictly closed to all except the director of the park — at the time of writing a friendly bearded man by the name of Stanisław Kujawiak — and a handful of his specialists. There is, however, a viewing enclosure where several of the great brown beasts can be seen at close quarters.

Another creature who roams the woods but can be approached at certain places is the strong and stumpy tarpan horse, whose bloodline goes back to the original steppe horse and which is now being bred back to something like its original form after much interbreeding. The work done here on both of these species is highly regarded throughout the world and without a doubt the European bison owes its continuing existence to the people at Białowieża.

But though the bison and tarpan are the visible stars, the forest is its own firmament. It is not only tropical forests which teem with life; here, besides the 26 species of tree, the fauna comes in an unbelievable 11,000 different forms, 8,500 of which are insects. Which still leaves a lot to account for. Such as 206 species of spiders, 24 of fish, 228 of birds, 13 of bats, then hedgehogs, moles, voles, shrews — 19 different rodents, in fact — plus foxes, badgers, otters, raccoon dogs, polecats and, rarest of all these days, beavers, which were extinct in the Polish part of the forest by the early years of this century but have now crossed over from the Soviet side to colonize the many wet areas. The larger creatures tend to keep to the protected zones, knowing that they will remain undisturbed, but walking along the marked trails or riding in the horse-drawn wagons provided for tourists is still a unique experience and there is always the chance that a family of boar will be spotted rummaging around on the forest floor or that an elk will gaze cautiously upon you from a respectful distance. And this is a forest unlike any other. For one thing the trees here are huge; spruces soaring 50 metres to reach the light, oaks and hornbeams 30 or 40 metres. Some of the oaks are so ancient that they are designated 'Monuments of Nature' and named after kings. This is definitely not your typical English woodland.

Białowieża is a long way from almost anywhere and local accommodation is limited but a journey there and back is part of the experience, passing through a fascinating region of the European plain. Strictly speaking this is not Mazovia but the old province of Podlasie, which means 'under [or close to] the trees', and because it is so remote from towns and industrial centres, the old rural ways and beliefs continue. The only town left in the area since the Soviet frontier moved westward after the last war is Białystok, an old textile centre which lost much of its character during the fighting but makes a useful centre for these eastern marches. It is equipped, by Polish standards, with all mod cons. The road there leads from Hajnówka, 20 kilometres west of Białowieża, northwards across-country for 60 kilometres, crossing the young Narew river and passing numerous tiny and quite primitive villages.

Many people of this flat and green land are not Catholics, like the majority of Poles, but followers of the Orthodox Church, which was introduced during the years of Russian influence and domination. The first sighting of the little onion-domed churches will confirm your feeling that you have wandered off the map into a story by Tolstoy or Turgenev. And it is not only Orthodox Christians who live hereabouts but, amazingly, Muslims as well. In several villages to the north and east of Białystok there are tiny communities of Tartars, the last survivors of a population which was allowed to settle in the area in the second half of the seventeenth century by King Jan III Sobieski in return for military services rendered during the king's many campaigns. If you wanted to disappear, this would certainly be a good place to do so, and I know many Poles who have no idea that Muslims live in their country.

East of Białystok, at Kruszyniany, a tiny village tight against the Soviet frontier at the end of an long stretch of cobbled road, there is a little wooden mosque hidden away amongst some trees. On one memorable occasion we were escorted there by an old man with a war-won limp who served as its keeper. Inside all was polished pine with two benches for the men and a little gallery above for the women, who must, of course, remain out of sight. In such a damp, green and northerly place, it is strange to see Arabic script on tombstones alongside Polish and the crescent moon on a weathervane, but there they are, just surviving.

From Białystok my route heads off west down the main Warsaw road but after 30 kilometres **Tykocin** is an interesting diversion, just a few minutes north of the road. This was once a Mazovian frontier town, where the ruins of a royal castle are still to be seen, as well as a fine baroque church, a Cistercian monastery and, most unusually, a fortified synagogue complete with sabbatines — enclosures for the women — who were denied entrance to the temple. Next stop on the main road is Łomża with its cathedral standing above the Narew river and then, half an hour later, Ostrołęka, which announces itself with a giant paper-making plant.

Ostrołęka has very little of interest these days except for a very friendly local museum where costumes, tools, textiles and other artefacts of the neighbouring Kurpie Green Forest region are display-ed. Lying to the north of the town, this area again has a distinct local culture with its own styles of dress, music and dance. One of the most delightful afternoons that I have ever spent in Poland was with a village bee-keeper met in Ostrołęka Museum, who took us back to his home village of Kadzidło some 20 kilometres to the north, a thin-soiled and sandy place where few of the roads were surfaced. Life has never been easy in such a settlement, carved out of the pine forests, but since 1950 a craft cooperative has employed locals to make traditional things such as rugs, bedspreads and wooden kitchen tools. Our friend had an interest in local history, and a short time before had opened an exquisite little museum in the wooden cottage of his recently deceased grandmother, which he has filled with anything he could gather from around the district. It is a real delight. The walls are decorated with the local variety of the paper cut-outs and it is quite extraordinary to watch these being made. A square of paper is folded over and over until it can just be held in the fingers and then, after many quick snips with a giant pair of carpet scissors, the thing is unfolded to reveal a strutting cockerel or a complex floral pattern. Such things can be bought in the shops, but I treasure most the cut-out made here in front of my eyes by a nine-year-old who was hardly bigger than the scissors she wielded so deftly, while behind me an old man played even older tunes on a peculiar accordion operated by a foot pump. These are the moments that Poland can offer to anyone prepared get off the beaten track and trust to non-verbal communication and a phrase-book.

The main road continues south-west all the time, following the Narew river, and the last place of interest before Warsaw is **Pułtusk,** a medieval town actually built on an island in the river. Napoleon had one of his toughest tussles here while on the road to Moscow. In December 1806 his infantry sank to their knees and the horses to their hocks on the soft Polish roads; such is the nature of Mazovian clay. Entire artillery pieces were lost beneath the surface, and the greatest army in the world was stuck like a host of flies in wet paint. In despair Napoleon wrote that in Poland he had discovered a new element, namely mud.

After Pułtusk the Narew broadens, flooded by a new dam north of Warsaw, and a long bridge carries the road over the new stretch of water. This has become one of the capital's playgrounds, with weekend cottages around the shores and a host of sailing dinghies and windsurfers dotting the water. Just 20 kilometres north of the centre of Warsaw the road meets the Vistula at **Jabłonna,** where there is an eighteenth-century palace by Merlini which once belonged to Prince Józef Poniatowski. The palace now belongs to the Academy of Sciences and is closed to the public, but the park is a splendid place, with fine old trees, a mock Chinese pagoda, a neo-classical orangery and, in the main avenue, a triumphal arch erected in honour of Poniatowski, a national hero of the partition period who led Polish troops against both Russian and Austrian forces and was made a Marshal of France by Napoleon after his role in the advance on Moscow and the retreat. His sole object in supporting Napoleon was to gain independence for Poland. While covering the emperor's rearguard at the Battle of the Nations outside Leipsiz in 1813, his Polish lancers were trapped and, mortally wounded, Poniatowski rode his horse into the river rather than surrender.

My final Mazovian excursion is one of the most popular outings from Warsaw, and none the worse for that. It can be visited on a day-trip from the capital, but if you are touring by car it would make sense to use the route to head into south-eastern Poland towards Kraków and the mountains. There are three parallel roads from the capital towards Kazimierz Dolny, the objective of this expedition, and which one you choose depends entirely on the time you have available. By the main Lublin road it is about 130 kilometres and the journey will be direct but uninteresting. Of the other two, the road down the west bank of the Vistula is rather narrow but calls on many attractive little riverside villages, while the wider east-bank route provides a good history lesson as the innumerable war memorials flash by. In 1944, swept out of the Soviet Union, the German army dug in behind the Vistula and successfully delayed the Red Army's progress. Numerous battles and skirmishes took place across the river as the Soviets, with Polish units, established bridgeheads on the west bank.

Both of these roads converge on Puławy; take the narrow road south into the low hills which form the western edge of the Lublin uplands. Very soon this road emerges from the trees to follow the river bank once again before becoming totally confused in the tiny one-way streets of **Kazimierz Dolny.** Parking is difficult in the little town so it is best to stop in the big car park by the river and walk for five minutes into the square.

Small as Kazimierz has always been, it was a key trading town in the sixteenth and seventeenth centuries, sitting at the point where the Vistula river and its accompanying road crossed an important east-west trade route. Here grain from large estates in the region was stored and transferred to river boats and rafts for shipment down to Gdańsk and subsequent export; the nobles meanwhile growing fat on the profits and importing all those luxury furnishings which in many cases still adorn their palaces. Unfortunately this immense and well documented trade did little to benefit the men and women who worked in the fields. At a time when in western Europe feudalism was drawing to an end, the clock was being put back in Poland, Prussia, Hungary and other eastern European countries, and a man who in 1500, for example, was bound to contribute one day's unpaid labour each week to his local lord was forced by 1600 to give six days. An almost colonial economy developed around such places as Kazimierz; all the benefits of cheap food went to the rapidly changing societies of western Europe, including Britain, while the resulting wealth was squandered on the beautiful objects so admired by today's visitors. With the serfs having to eat inferior grains and nothing being put back to improve the land or the lot of the farmers, it was a classic situation — still to be seen, of course, in various parts of the world.

What cannot be denied is that today Kazimierz is both thriving and charming, favoured by artists as much as by tourists. The old **Market square**, the glory of Kazimierz on which its fame rests, is another cobbled affair with a wooden wellhead in the middle. It is lined on three sides with houses, those on the south side being among the most famous in the country. The tall arcaded pair in the bottom corner of the square, built by the Przybyła brothers in 1615, are the stars of many a tourist poster. Richly adorned with sculptures in the Polish Renaissance style, their carvings have been softened by age, but they still make an extraordinary impression and must have caused a stir when first built. Still the centre of activity even without its market, the square is open at the top end, where a steep hill rises to the **Church** which dominates everything below. It has an all too familiar history: built as a Gothic structure in 1350, it was remodelled in a Renaissance style at the end of the sixteenth century. Inside there are many precious objects of ecclesiastical art, such as the 1620 organ and pulpit and the stucco decorations of the vaulted nave and presbytery.

Behind the church, small lanes continue up the dry limestone hill past cottages shrouded with flowers towards the ruins of a castle built by Kazimierz the Great. The ruins are no more than that, but from their site there is a splendid view back over the town and across the Vistula to the plain beyond. For those with the time and the legs for it, there is a fourteenth-century watch-tower farther up the hill again and an even broader vista to be seen.

The town can be seen from another angle if you leave the square at the lower end and head for a smaller hill which is topped by a Franciscan church and monastery built in around 1590, later enlarged and crammed with the usual baroque ornamentation. This is still a fully functioning house of religion, though there is also a museum which describes the history of the establishment. But the real attraction is to get a view back over the cottage-clad hillside and the old roofscape of the town. Below the monastery, in Senatorska Street, which has a clear stream flowing alongside it, there are three more Renaissance houses, not quite so splendid as those in the square but still very ornate, one with its attic topped with carved saints and various fantastic creatures. This is now the local museum which, as usual, will provide many insights into the history of the district, including that of the Jewish community, which survived from the time of Kazimierz the Great only to be destroyed by the Nazis. The old synagogue is now the local cinema. Close to the museum is a baker's shop which makes bread in the shapes of cockerels and crayfish, sold as much for souvenirs as for nourishment.

Kazimierz Dolny, then, is a delightful place in a beautiful setting, a place in which to wander around on a summer's day. Take a stroll down to the river to find the few remaining granaries still standing from the sixteenth century, or even cross by ferry to the opposite bank where the haunted ruins of Janowiec Palace stand. But be warned that each July the town is crammed with spectators and colourful contestants for the Festival of Folk Bands and Singers, which attracts performers young and old from all regions of the country. For a week the market square jumps to the clatter of wooden shoes and the whine of the country fiddle, and the few hotel rooms are booked solid.

For those driving on to Lublin (40 kilometres to the east and described in the next chapter), the road from Kazimierz through the low hills is interrupted half-way by the eccentric nineteenth-century villas of Nałęczów, a spa set amongst the trees renowned for both its temperate climate and an ability to treat heart diseases and nervous depression — common complaints everywhere, it seems.

In this review of Mazovia I have so far made no mention of the region directly south of Warsaw, and for good reason. This is a land of prosperous fruit farmers, all, it would seem, with new and incredibly ugly flat-roofed houses stuck in the middle of their orchards, following the well established *nouveau riche* tradition of flaunting wealth. In Poland this means building the biggest box affordable, even if one or two of its floors are windowless and reserved for hanging the washing. Very often these houses are put together over several years by the members of the family themselves, who gather the scarce materials as and when they can. One fashion is to cover the outside of your red-brick container with slivers of broken mirror in several colours, to quite astonishing effect.

There is, however, one place worth a visit if you are travelling down the Warsaw-Kielce-Kraków road, and that is **Szydłowiec**, which lies some 30 kilometres past the industrial town of Radom and within sight of the Holy Cross Mountains which mark the southern boundary of Mazovia. This is an ancient site where there is evidence of an organized flint industry which thrived some 8,000 years ago, and a sandstone quarry which has been worked since medieval times. Most of the town, which has one of the largest Jewish cemeteries in Poland, is made of this stone. The late Gothic church has beautifully carved altars from the beginning of the seventeenth century and the town hall is a classic example of Polish Renaissance architecture. The real attraction, however, is in the perfectly moated castle, which houses a museum of folk-music instruments including primitive drums and tambourines, strange wooden rattles that both look and sound like bird scarers, solid wooden fiddles, ceramic whistles shaped like birds and horses, accordions and century-old goatskin bagpipes of exotic appearance. It is altogether a good town to stop in for a couple of hours.

4

The Lublin Uplands

Called in Polish Wyżyna Lubelska, this region is a compact geographical area. It was touched on briefly in the last chapter: the Vistula cuts its western extremity at Kazimierz Dolny. This was the land of corn that supplied the riverside granaries, its fertility being due to a thick layer of wind-blown soil known as loess that was deposited after the last Ice Age on top of a bed of chalk, thus ensuring both good drainage and easy working. There are few towns on the uplands and even villages are sparse, but Lublin itself makes up for that. Without doubt it is one of the half-dozen most interesting towns in Poland, a tight hilltop cluster of narrow alleys and squares, tall churches and cramped merchants' houses.

Unlike the old town centres of Warsaw and Gdańsk, Lublin escaped wartime destruction and is only now in the middle of a restoration programme which will turn it into even more of a showplace. As it is, the place reeks of age and of glories long past. An evening stroll through the echoing cobbled streets imparts the atmosphere of an old Italian town, or even of somewhere farther east. And that is not altogether inappropriate, because Lublin developed, like so many towns in eastern Europe, on a trade route which linked the Baltic and central Europe to the early Russian capital of Kiev and on to the Black Sea and the Middle East.

It is all too easy for those of us from the western islands of this continent, obsessed with the ancient history of the Mediterranean, to ignore the influence of overland links between prosperous Middle Eastern countries and northern and central Europe. From the tenth century chronicles have accounts by Arab and Persian merchants who travelled up the great Russian rivers and around the steppe lands that butt against the Carpathian Mountains and there is no reason to believe that this route had not operated for generations. By these routes they travelled regularly, and sometimes by camel train, to the important markets at Kraków, Wroclaw and even Prague. Lublin lies on the higher ground that made passage through the marshy lands of the Ukraine possible, a route followed to this day by major roads, which go east to Kiev and south-east across the modern frontier to Lwów (now Lvov), an important Polish city until it became part of the Soviet Union in the territorial changes that followed the Second World War.

Today Lublin is somewhat stranded in eastern Poland, but walking around the old town it is quite obvious that there was once immense wealth here. The peak of its fortunes came during the period from the fifteenth to the seventeenth century, when the Polish Lithuanian Commonwealth reached 'od morza do morza', 'from sea to sea', as they proudly say, referring, of course, to the Baltic and the Black Seas. In fact this was the largest political unit in Europe at the time, as a glance at any historical atlas will show. In the Kraków archives there is the 1645 ledger of an Italian merchant who traded in Lublin. This lists the great number of fabrics sold in the town that year; they included taffeta from London and velvet from Florence, which indicates the prosperity of the city at the time. And where there was money there was culture. Amongst many other artists, a gentleman known only as Jan of Lublin in the first half of the sixteenth century composed for the organ a famous *Tabulature* which is one of the monuments of early Polish music.

In recent years Lublin has expanded again, spreading beyond its two hills — one each for the town and the castle — and is developing as an industrial and educational centre. Its Catholic University, the only one in Eastern Europe, was founded in 1918 and now has about 2,500 students reading Theology, Christian Philosophy, Canon Law and the Humanities, including the History of Art. But it is the Old Town which is going to take the attention of the visitor. The motorist would do best to head for the **Castle** where there is a large car park; everything is then within easy walking distance.

From here, the castle looms above and you must climb a flight of steep broad steps to reach it. The initial appearance of this edifice is a surprise to the uninitiated, because the main building is an enormous whitewashed and supposedly neo-Gothic block erected in the 1820s, which smacks more of Hollywood-Arabic than of any earlier European style. Built on the ruins of earlier castles it is now the **Lublin Museum** and well worth a visit. There are sections devoted to archaeology, local ethnography, European painting, decorative art, numismatics and iconography, but heaven knows under which category one very strange exhibit should come. Heaven, come to think of it, is hardly an appropriate term to use. It is a large table, dated around 1637, on which there is a hand-shaped print which appears to be burned into the surface. Legend has it that this is the mark of the devil himself, summoned by an old lady to sort out a dispute over some land. If it is true, then the devil has mighty small hands.

In the ethnographic galleries there are some splendid old pots and pans, plus the usual colourful displays of local costumes, some with a distinctly oriental flavour and all beautifully stitched. Delicately embroidered blouses and scarves are arranged around the walls in flat

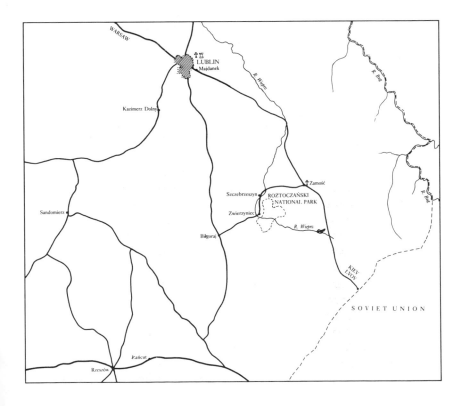

glass cases like so many pinned butterflies and just as colourful. Wood carving, a Polish speciality, is well represented; there are models of folk orchestras, complete with all their instruments, and several Nativity scenes, representing many hours of patient winter whittling. One peculiar wooden item, which looks rather like a metre-long bicycle pump, turns out to be a device used by young men to squirt water over girls on Easter Monday morning, a custom still widely practised, though today a drop of water suffices rather than a dowsing.

The fine arts section covers Polish painting from the fifteenth to the twentieth century, and includes some foreign pictures as well. The earliest work is a triptych from the 1640s featuring the Assumption, but the obvious star is Matejko's enormous 'Unia Lubelska' which depicts a roomful of assorted nobles from Poland and Lithuania contemplating the formal union of their two countries, still referred to as the Union of Lublin in acknowledgement of the city where the treaty was sealed on 1 July 1569. The picture is a typical and masterly example of Matejko's romantic historicism. Nearby is another of his giants, 'The Admission of the Jews to Poland' which no doubt touches a few raw nerves among visiting Poles. Jews first arrived in Poland in the early Middle Ages; a charter confirming their liberties was issued in 1265 and later expanded by Kazimierz the Great at the time of the Black Death. It is extraordinary to think that during the eighteenth century — so it is claimed — one third of the world's Jews lived in Poland.

Much of the castle hill is a large empty courtyard surrounded by the nineteenth-century walls, although there are two fourteenth-century towers surviving and also the little **Church of the Holy Trinity** which, according to castle records, was built in the 1320s. In the early decades of the fifteenth century a group of painters from nearby Ruthenia, nowadays part of the Ukraine, covered the inside of the church with frescos which show a marked Byzantine influence. The walls and the single supporting column are covered in biblical imagery, scenes from the Old Testament stories and the life of Christ, and alone are worth a visit to Lublin. Like so much else in this country it seems a miracle that they have survived at all, particularly as these stunning paintings, regarded as some of the finest frescos in Europe, were plastered over in the nineteenth century and only rediscovered years later. If evidence were needed of this part of Poland's connections with Byzantium and the Middle East, the bold, simple zig-zag pattern over the arched door to the presbytery should suffice. During the Nazi occupation the castle was used as a prison and some 400,000 people, mostly Jews, passed through on their way to the camps. On the eve of liberation there were still 450 prisoners in the place, all of whom were shot. Simple memorial tablets in the church record these terrible acts.

The castle is connected by a walled path along a short, low ridge to the Grodzka Gate on the east side of the Old Town and from there Grodzka Street runs straight ahead to a market square which is dominated by a town hall simply too large for the space available. Needless to say, it was not always like this. The earliest building on the site was started in 1389 and 200 years later became the seat of a royal tribunal, but the real damage was done in 1781 by Merlini — he who designed the beautifully proportioned palace in Warsaw's Łazienki Park — who this time got it all wrong. Or, more likely, the commissioning body asked the impossible. This neo-classical monstrosity completely ruins what could be a beautiful square and it is a pity that it has not been removed, both to make some open space in the centre of the town and to allow the burghers' houses to be properly seen.

Back in the square, the Lubomelski house at No. 8 boasts a wine cellar decorated with fourteenth-century frescos as if to prove their pedigree, while the Sobieski mansion at No. 12 is adorned on the outside with Renaissance sculptures. This house seems to have been a haven for royalty on the run; Charles XII of Sweden sheltered here in 1703 and Peter the Great did the same in 1707.

Uilca Zlota, Gold Street, runs from the square to a Dominican church and monastery, built in the mid-fourteenth century but reconstructed in the early seventeenth in a style that can only be called Lublin Renaissance, only to be well and truly overlaid with the baroque later on. Unspoilt though, are the magnificent **Chapel of the Firlej Family (Kaplica Firlejowska)** built between 1615 and 1630, and the extraordinary eighteenth-century painting in the south aisle which shows some of the miracles claimed from a fragment, now lost, of what was believed to be the true Cross. This relic was paraded through the streets when danger threatened and is reputed to have been responsible for quelling fires and halting plagues.

The entrance to **Lublin Cathedral** is just outside the old walls and reached by the Brama Trynitarska, Trinity Gate, in the south wall. Built in the Renaissance at the end of the sixteenth century, it was rebuilt 200 years later following a fire and this baroque interior remains intact, although the exterior did not escape the neo-classicists of the early nineteenth century. It is not an especially memorable building although the two rooms of the sacristy are interesting for the strange acoustics of the one and the *trompe-l'œil* ceiling of the other. This latter is by the Moravian painter József Majer, who was also responsible for most of the baroque decoration.

There are not many commercial attractions in the Old Town at present — few shops or cafés, for example — but maybe all that will change when the restoration is completed. It is well worth wandering through the large doorways of the houses and apartment blocks, however, in order to get some idea of their labyrinthine construction around a central courtyard; another influence, perhaps, from the east. The modern city with its noisy trams and crowded streets is reached by way of the Kraków Gate at the top of the sloping Old Town, but do not miss the local history museum within the gate tower itself. The main street lies straight ahead and goes by the ever popular name of Krakówskie Przedmieście, although it altogether lacks the grandeur of its Warsaw namesake. The few interesting buildings outside the Old Town lie around **Plac Wolnosci,** just to the south of this shopping thoroughfare, where there are the Sobieski palace, two Cistercian churches and, best of all these, the **Church of the Assumption (Kościoł Wniebowzięcia).** This was built between 1412 and 1426 by King Władysław Jagiełło in thanks for his great victory over the Teutonic Knights at Grunwald in 1410. Inevitably it has been modified several times but has retained very fine plaster decorations to the presbytery vault in the local Renaissance style.

Up until 1939 Lublin had one of the largest Jewish communities in Poland and in the still rather tatty Old Town it is not difficult to imagine their presence in the narrow streets and alleys, their black felt hats and corkscrew curls bobbing in and out of the dark doorways as they went about their business. But if a single Jew remains in Lublin today I would be most surprised, because just three kilometres down the road are the chilling remains of Majdanek, third largest of the concentration camps after Auschwitz and Treblinka. In fact, during the early stages of the War the Lublin Uplands were designated by the Nazis as a 'reservation' for Jews until such time as the war was over or a 'final solution' was decided upon to the perceived problem of Jewish influence in the Reich. Thousands of Jewish families were dumped in the region and left to get on with life as best they could, and surviving letters tell a sad story of their deprivations in the freezing winters. As it turned out, Majdanek was a part of the 'final solution', and it is estimated that 360,000 prisoners were murdered there. In October 1944, soon after Lublin had been taken by the Soviet armies, Majdanek was designated as a museum. Several of the camp buildings house displays which tell the gruesome story.

For a brief period in 1944, just as in 1918, Lublin served as the seat of a new and controversial Polish government. A group of Polish socialists who had sought refuge in the Soviet Union, subsequently to be known to history as the Lublin Committee, immediately set up camp in this, the first large town to be liberated, and coordinated the establishment of the new Socialist government, much to the displeasure of other political groups which existed both abroad and within the Resistance movements. From 1569 to 1944, the name of Lublin has marked turning points in the history of Poland.

Considering its history and fame, Lublin today is a bit of a disappointment and will be so until such time as the restoration programme is completed, but there is compensation just 80 kilometres down the road to the south-east, where a real delight is in store for those who press on that far. The town of **Zamość** has been restored; wonderfully so and with good reason, for this is one of the most perfect surviving towns planned in the Renaissance in Europe, classified by UNESCO as a monument of the greatest historical and artistic value. It is a monument that is also a symbol of the shining years of Polish culture. The ideas of the Renaissance took root in Poland as they did everywhere in Europe and they found fertile soil, inspiring a great flowering of intellectual and artistic achievement. The trinity which dominated the period consisted of Mikołaj Kopernik (1473–1543), better known as Nicholas Copernicus, the man whose pronouncements that the earth moved around the sun sent shockwaves far and deep; Jan Kochanowski (1530–84), a poet both brilliant and sublime who confirmed vernacular Polish as a literary language and produced a body of work which set a marker for centuries to come; and Jan Zamoyski (1542–1605), Chancellor of the Kingdom, Hetman to the Crown, architect of the 'democracy of the nobles' (whereby the king was elected by the nobility), kingmaker and general diplomatic fixer throughout central Europe, as well as an accomplished scholar. All three were examples of *'l'uomo universale';* all educated in Padua as well as Kraków; true Renaissance men.

Zamość was the creation of Zamoyski. It was his concept of the perfect city: an entirely new town set amongst green fields and designed for only 6,000 people; a town that would reflect not only his new-found status and power but become a centre of learning to rival Kraków and, not unimportantly, a wealthy merchant town on the old trade route and a power base for his progeny. Zamoyski started life as a minor noble in possession of just a handful of villages on the Lublin Uplands, but during his remarkable career he accumulated vast estates covering many thousands of hectares and including about 200 villages, plus the tenancy of huge royal estates in the Ukraine. The heyday of his power was during the ten-year reign of Stefan Batory, the Hungarian prince who was elected to the Polish throne in 1576. He chose as a site for his great experiment the fields of his native village of Skówka, and as architect, Bernardo Morando from Padua, the influential Italian town where Zamoyski had studied. Starting the project in 1580, Morando followed Italian planning theory of the day, laying out the town on a grid plan with public buildings at each corner, a large central market square and a palace for the boss, all enclosed by a formidable defensive system of walls and ditches. The details of the defences were modified over the years to keep pace with improved methods of attack — an all too familiar story — but in all its essentials the town stands today as created by Morando. And very splendid it is too.

The focal point of the whole ensemble is the main square, nowadays called **Plac Mickiewicza** after the poet, which is a light and open space surrounded by arcaded burghers' houses and dominated on the north side by the magnificent town hall. The houses of the square, and indeed of the whole town, are restricted to two storeys plus attics, and it is this human scale of construction that contributes so much to the relaxed atmosphere of the place. The **Town Hall** is something of an anomaly, however, the monumental double steps and first-floor verandah having been added in the eighteenth century and the tower heightened at about the same time. Some purists I have come across profess to be offended by this addition, but the square is quite able to carry the visual weight and, after all, what is wrong with a touch of kitsch? It is added to here by the occasional performance of slightly sanitized folk-dancing on the verandah itself. In fact, the building serves to emphasize the overwhelming unity of the town. A famous revolutionary figure from the early years of this century who was born in Zamość was Rosa Luxembourg, and a room in the town hall is devoted to her life, which was spent struggling to establish an international social-democratic party.

The other three sides of the square each have eight houses broken in the centre by the main thoroughfares of the town, the western exit aiming directly at the front door of the palace. All the houses here are worthy of a close examination, although, sadly, most of the high decorative attic fronts collapsed in the nineteenth century and have not been replaced. Many of the wall decorations were also lost at that time but enough survive to serve the imagination. The best of these decorations, complete with attics, can be seen on the five houses that stand to the right of the town hall, each boldly painted above the white arcade in its own strong colour. The blue house in the corner has intricate vine-like patterns across its front, while the maroon house next door has splendid window surrounds plus angels in alcoves, griffins and recumbent lions. In the gloom beneath the arcades there are many richly carved stone door architraves with ancient heavy doors leading to vaulted passageways from which the many little shops are entered.

The local **Museum** is at No. 26 Ormiańska Street, where not only the usual fascinating exhibits are worth attention but also the house itself, which has original wooden ceilings and beams decorated with rosettes.

Within eleven years of the founding of the town there were already 217 houses within the walls, homes for craftsmen and merchants from many countries. There were a number of Armenians and also Greeks, Hungarians, Italians, Jews, even Scots. In fact there were many Scots amongst the merchants of Eastern Europe, and their journals are valuable sources by which one can learn about the life and trading practices of the time. It must have been an exhilarating place in those early days, with wagons loaded with merchandise and the more comfortable carriages of the merchants themselves rolling into the brand-new town from all corners of the continent, the women looking at the new houses, the men weighing up the competition and the opportunities. And it was not only merchants Zamoyski attracted to his toy state. Intent upon creating a cultural as well as a commercial town, he built in 1594 an impressive Academy, still existing in a modified form, which he filled with illustrious scholars, poets and scientists, and a printing house was established to propagate their work. Furthermore, and as if to emphasize his religious tolerance (an intellectual and no doubt sincere fashion of the day), the founder commissioned a fine synagogue, now the library, Armenian and Greek Orthodox churches and Morando's finest piece, the **Collegiate Church.**

The church can be found just beyond the south-west corner of the square, its west door facing across the road to the much changed palace, which now serves as the local court-house. Begun in 1587, it is a three-aisled basilica surrounded by chapels, slender pillars supporting a high vaulted roof. The separate bell tower is a baroque structure erected in the 1760s and contains one of the largest bells in the country. The stucco and stone decorations of the presbytery are Morando's work, as is the lavishly decorated organ loft, but thankfully signs of the heavy, gilded hand of the baroque are almost absent from the dignified interior. Among the family chapels is the Zamoyski family's, and next to it the Rosary Chapel which houses a typically sumptuous Russian icon. In the nave there is a cycle of pictures that have been attributed to Tintoretto's son, depicting the life of St Thomas. My overriding memory of this church, though, is of the occasion when, intent upon a solitary exploration, I threw open the west door early in the morning to find the place packed and teh organ moaning low over the silent, kneeling congregation.

The old **Greek Orthodox Church** on the southern edge of the town was built so close to the wall that it too had to be fortified. It is now a Catholic church with many interesting Renaissance details and some original stucco decorations which conservators have recently restored to their original polychromy.

On the eastern side of the town there is a collection of old buildings, the most fascinating being a large and much decorated slab known by the strange name of **Podkarpie**, which can only mean 'under the carp'. Perhaps at one time it had such a fish amongst its embellishments. Originally there had been a wooden monastery on this site; this was rebuilt in the seventeenth century into brick baroque with its own hospital, but the whole institution was dissolved under the Austrian occupation that followed the 1795 partitions. When restoration is complete it should be one of the great attractions of the town and already there is a restaurant, the Hetmanska, in the basement. The neighbouring Franciscan Church has also seen some changes of mood within its baroque walls, becoming an ammunition dump and barracks under the Austrians and a cinema after 1918, but now it has settled down to life as a College of Fine Arts, which numbers among its pupils apprentice stone carvers who are working on the restoration of the Podkarpie as well as other Zamość buildings.

Just across the road are two of the town gates, the original Lwów Gate by Morando and an enlarged gate in a rather monumental classical style, which was constructed in 1820; the old gatehouse was then turned into a prison. From here the New Town of Zamość can be seen just down the road, deliberately built at a distance so that the Old Town could remain unspoiled by the proximity of the inevitable new blocks. Next to the old gate is a massive brick structure almost 100 metres long which is an early nineteenth-century gun emplacement, and to the north, around the line of the old walls, a similar pile threatens the north-eastern approaches to the town. Looking at these massive defence works, one is left in no doubt that the citizens and lords of little Zamość have always invested well in protection, and their track record over the centuries bears this out. Rarely were the formidable walls, moats and bastions breached, and the defence in 1656 against the 'Swedish Flood' was particularly gallant. The siege by the troops of King Charles Gustavus, who earned the title of 'Hurricane of the North', is wonderfully described in the Nobel Prize-winner Henryk Sienkiewicz's novel *The Deluge*.

The original northern Lublin gate would not have been a target for the Swedish troops, however, because Zamoyski had it bricked up in 1588, almost as soon as it was built, to commemorate the fact that the Austrian Archduke Maximilian, whom the Chancellor had defeated and taken prisoner at the battle of Byczyna, had passed through it. If Zamoyski had a weakness, it was a hatred for everything Habsburg, and Maximilian had been encouraged by his own family and by Austria's allies within Poland to enter the country and claim the throne following the death of King Stefan Batory. From this gate the street back to the main square passes the little Church of St Catherine, behind which is the large slab of the Academy, unrecognizably changed from its original arcaded form and now a branch of the Marie Skłodowska-Curie University of Lublin. The few streets north of the square, behind the town hall, must not be missed for they include an open market square where fruit, vegetables, local mushrooms and soft cheese can be bought, while in Zamenhof Street there is a very decorative Renaissance synagogue that is now a library. There is also a little square that was once the salt market (Solny Rynek), an important trading place. South of the square there used to be a water market where fresh supplies could be purchased in the days before piped mains.

As so often in Poland, there is also a museum detailing the sufferings of Zamość in the last war, but this is some way south of the town in a nineteenth-century fortification known as the Rotunda.

The road south from Zamość leads eventually to the mountains of the far south-east of the country, but for now head west through small villages to meet up with the Vistula at Sandomierz.

5

Małopolska

Palaeozoic beds may sound like something for back-pain sufferers, but they are the hills emerging through the Polish plain which separate Mazovia from Małopolska, or Little Poland, and Sandomierz is where these hills meet the Vistula river. Broadly speaking, the region of Malopolska runs from here down to the Jura Krakowska, the limestone hills which run north-west from Kraków, but the outline is vague as this was never a formal administrative area. Together with Wielkopolska (Greater Poland) this region was the basis of the original Polish state a thousand years ago. Gniezno and Poznań were the royal seats in the north before the capital moved down to Kraków and the fertile area around the upper Vistula and its tributaries. Outside the main towns of Kraków, Kielce and Częstochowa, the area is not densely populated. The rolling landscape of birch woods, open fields and soft green valleys is a place of small villages, often with large churches or ruined castles indicating a past more glorious than the present. Generally it is an area through which Poles as well as foreigners tend to drive, anxious to reach Kraków or the mountains, but a little courageous detour down back roads will reveal many a delight.

Sandomierz itself, however, dramatically sited on a cliff overlooking the Vistula, is well known and much visited. The way into the Old Town is from the north side of the hill, where the Opatowska Gate still stands in what remains of a town wall erected in the middle of the fourteenth century by Kazimierz the Great. I have never attempted to drive through this gate and over the cobbles and suggest that drivers park outside the walls and, as they say, proceed on foot. The strong

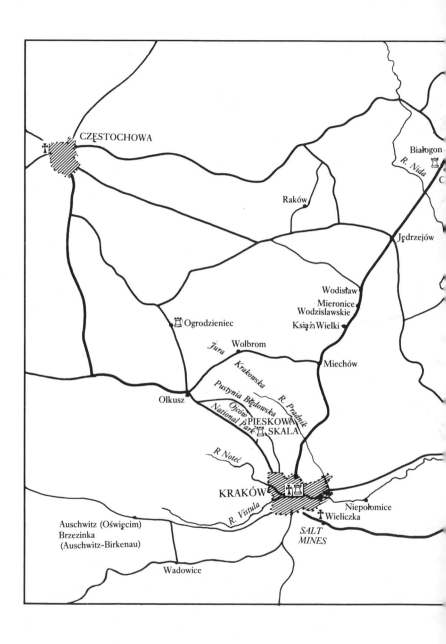

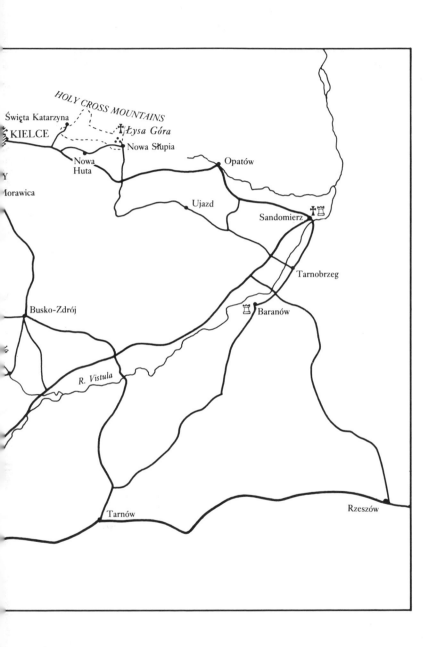

defences which are still visible are a sign of the town's strategic importance on the same trade routes that have been mentioned in connection with Lublin and Zamość; the old roads, that is, from southern Russia through to central Europe. In 1259, in fact, just a few years after Sandomierz was granted its charter, the Tartars came along this road on their probing westward raids, destroying both Lublin and Sandomierz, and within a hundred years the Lithuanians had followed, leaving the mainly wooden town a smoking ruin. It was only after this raid that the town was laid out on the plan preserved to this day. A large stone castle and strong defensive walls were an obvious measure of insurance.

The narrow road through the town gate, Ulica Skopenki, leads directly into the **Market Square,** a large and sloping space dominated by the mixed Gothic and Renaissance town hall and edged with fine old houses. Today the market is held elsewhere and the bustle of the old days, when spice merchants from beyond the Black Sea traded with cloth-makers from Kraków and farmers from just beyond the walls, can only be imagined. The town hall is typical of many surviving in Poland, a tall and narrow red-brick box of a building with a decorated attic and a hexagonal tower which was added in the 1620s to the original fourteenth-century structure. The little belfry is an eighteenth-century addition. Both of the streets going south from the square end up at the castle, Zamkowa running beside the old west wall and 1 May Street leading from the bottom corner of the market past the **Cathedral.** This is a typical edifice for such a town; it was built in 1360 on the site of a Romanesque church dating from the end of the twelfth century and had a baroque façade and towers added in 1670. The interior retains its cool, elegant Gothic structure with a cross-barrel vaulted roof, richly sculpted decorations on some of the pillars and keystones and a splendid choir and organ dating from 1682. In the presbytery there are murals in a Byzantine-Ruthenian style similar to those seen at Lublin, whilst in the aisle early eighteenth-century paintings depict the massacre of the local people by the Tartars in 1259 and the blowing up of the castle by the Swedes in 1656.

Behind the cathedral is the fifteenth-century house which was the home of a giant of Polish history, himself a historian. By any standards Jan Długosz (1415–80) was an outstanding scholar, working from 1455 until his death on primary sources to produce a monument as breathtaking as any cathedral. His chronicle, consisting of twelve great books, described Polish history from its very beginning right up to his own generation and the last years of his life. Written in the style of Livy, his critical yet sympathetic analysis of the evidence marks him out as a Renaissance man of the first order and the founder of the serious study of history in his country. Before the Second World War, the **house of Jan Długosz** was handed over to the local diocese to be used as a museum, and today it has substantial archaeological and ethnographic collections, including a collection of sacred art, which makes up the main body of the exhibition, an interesting series of folk paintings on glass, a large selection of ceramics including tiles, and furniture from the seventeenth to the nineteenth century. Amongst the sacred art there are many precious paintings from the fifteenth century, the most spectacular and interesting being the early 'Three Saints' from the Kraków workshops and 'The Mystic Marriage of St Catherine', a work attributed to the circle of the German Lucas Cranach and very reminiscent of the great man's style. There is also a rare twelfth-century sculpture of the madonna and child, a constant theme, of course, in Catholic Poland, and one deserving a book of its own. There is a lot more in the Długosz house, so be sure not to miss it.

Just beyond the cathedral is the castle, built in 1520; rebuilt, of course, in 1656 and recently restored, but more interesting is the Romanesque **Church of St James** just along the road. Shaded by large lime trees, it is believed to be the very first brick basilica in Poland, dating from 1250. The typically Romanesque portal on the north side is a good example of the arched doorways of the time, and the wooden ceiling above the nave is a tribute to the skill of the old carpenters. The oldest tomb inside is from the thirteenth century, but inevitably it is the baroque accretions which proclaim themselves most loudly, particularly the Chapel of the Sandomierz Martyrs with its profusion of alabaster and polychromy enclosing a wooden tomb in the shape of a sarcophagus. In the free-standing bell tower are two of the oldest bells in Poland, one cast in 1314, the other in 1389. The land around this church is the site of the town destroyed in 1259 by the Tartars, and excavations have uncovered a large early settlement. In one of the little houses they found a real prize in the form of a set of twelfth-century chessmen carved from horn, reckoned to be the oldest set in Europe and the second oldest in the world. It was left, perhaps, by one of those spice merchants from Persia.

This southern end of the hilltop town is perched not on rock but on a high cliff of soft loess soil, and during excavations it was discovered that the hillside was riddled with tunnels, but the intitial excitement at the idea of opening these up as a tourist attraction quickly faded when it was discovered that, the more they were tampered with, the more signs of subsidence were reported in the streets above. Fearful that the whole edifice of Sandomierz would tumble down into the river, the town's officials called in experts from all directions, and a complex and innovative system of fixing the town's foundations was finally installed, at great cost but to the inhabitants' great relief. For Sandomierz to have self-destructed would have been particularly painful. It only survived the Second World War by the initiative of a certain Colonel Skopenko of the Red Army who, knowing the beauty of the town, turned the 1944 battle for the river crossing away, thus saving it from almost certain destruction. A few artillery shells into that soft and crumbling hillside may have been all that was needed to precipitate an avalanche of medieval masonry. The thoughtful colonel died further west during the battle for the Odra crossing, but his last wishes were fulfilled and he is buried in Sandomierz.

Needless to say, as the town was built to protect a river crossing, there is today a bridge across the river, just beneath the town, but there is not too much on the other bank to capture the attention; with one notable exception, that is. Some 25 kilometres south, beyond Tarnobrzeg, dubbed the sulphur capital of Poland because of the huge deposits of the yellow element found there since the war, there is in the village of **Baranów** a splendid castle that is much featured on travel posters. It is rather out of the way unless you are heading south on the Tarnów or Rzeszów roads, but Baranów is one of the best preserved of Renaissance country houses, thanks, in fact, to the wealth brought by the sulphur for it is that state organization which has restored the place, using it for company receptions and for housing special guests and as a holiday retreat for the workers, as well as a museum for the industry.

On three sides of a courtyard run two storeys of beautiful arcades which are reached by steps rising each side of the entrance. To the innocent eye it is pure Italian, the slender columns supporting light and perfect arches, the whole surmounted by a steep red roof. One of the doors leading from the courtyard has a magnificent carved portal and inside there are equally fine stucco decorations by Giovanni Battista Falconi, another transalpine traveller who was active in Poland between 1625 and 1660. The owners were the Leszczyński family, and the Italian architect was Santi Gucci, who started work in 1579. Incredibly, our old friend Tylman of Gameren also managed to make

The Palace on the Water in Warsaw's Łazienki Park was built in the
eighteenth century as a summer residence for Poland's last king, and is now a
museum and art gallery.

Above: Castle Square, Warsaw, with King Zygmunt III's column, the Royal Castle and, on the left, the cathedral roof emerging from the medieval Old Town. Everything seen here has been totally rebuilt since 1945.

Below: Castle Square is the start of the Royal Way, the historic route which passes many of the capital's most interesting buildings, including the Church of the Barefoot Carmelites and the statue of the great nineteenth-century poet, Adam Mickiewicz.

Świętojańska Street leads from Castle Square to the heart of the Old Town. The national flags are flying to mark the May anniversary of the ending of the Second World War.

The Old Town Market Place. The row of rebuilt burghers' houses seen here contains a museum describing the history of Warsaw, including pictures of the war-time destruction.

Totally demolished by the Nazis, the Royal Castle was rebuilt only in the 1970s and is now a luxurious museum full of pictures, furniture and *objets d'art* associated with the monarchy.

Above: A part of Warsaw's medieval Old Town from across the Vistula. The high gable and bell tower belong to the Cathedral of St John.

Below: Łowicz. Wood carving is a continuing and widespread tradition in Poland; wherever possible buildings are richly decorated.

Lublin. The Trinitarska Gate towers above the medieval Old Town, where the narrow streets contain examples of most styles of European architecture.

Zamość. The Town Hall (1591) is the focal point of this Renaissance-inspired town, built by the remarkable and Italian-educated Polish Chancellor, Jan Zamoyski.

his mark here a hundred years later by enlarging the west wing. The Lubomirski family was another well known owner of the house before it went into a long decline that ended only when the sulphur riches arrived.

The main road turns away from the Vistula at Baranów and heads south, but the bold driver can follow the east bank of the river all the way to Kraków, using very tiny roads that are nothing more than spidery threads on even the best map. But bravery will be rewarded. 'Rustic Ruritania' goes some way towards describing the little villages of Małopolska, lost in a time warp with their tiny wooden churches, strong brown horses and human bodies disfigured by work. It was on these back roads some years ago, testing the endurance of an ageing car, that I came across an old man and his horse ploughing a strip of land close to the river. He told me that his wife was dead and his children all gone to the city to find work in factories, that his land amounted to no more than a small English paddock and yet was divided into thirteen of these strips scattered all over the district, so that for every hour he worked the land he spent another travelling to the next strip. He had his land and he had his independence — but at what price. Such small farms are slowly being amalgamated, usually after a death, but there are still tens of thousands of such holdings in Poland. Close to Kraków are the rich farmers with their tractors and orchards but the area down here by this stretch of the river belongs to another age.

Now from the river to the hills, and to reach them you have to cross the great brown god of the Vistula, which means back-pedalling to the bridge near Baranów or to Sandomierz itself. From the castle on the cliff at Sandomierz, the Holy Cross Mountains (Góry Świętokrzyskie) run westward for more than 100 kilometres in a series of parallel ridges which, although in no way Alpine, are in places very steep for long stretches and reach the quite respectable height of 600 metres. They are not, of course, as dramatic as the great rock wall of the Tatras in the far south but they are far more accessible and greatly favoured by lovers of forests and the hardy walkers who trek their length on carefully marked trails.

Kielce is the capital of this attractive hill country and although it is by no means the most exciting of cities most routes converge on it, the direct route from Sandomierz following the line of the ancient road taken by the spice merchants and passing between two ridges of the hills.

To the west of the small town of Opatów the valley between the mountain ridges narrows and the road passes beneath the highest peaks of the **Holy Cross Mountains** where villages cut out of the woodland run up the slopes. These always lead to good footpaths, many of which cross over the ridges. The highest ridge lies to the north of the road and its central section, which includes the Bald Mountain (Łysa Góra), is a national park. The vast areas of broken quartzite rock, bare on the summits, are an unusual and dramatic feature of the upper slopes — and one destined to destroy your footwear when you wander off the tracks. To reach the park headquarters and the natural history museum, aim for the conspicuous TV mast, reached via the little village of Nowa Huta. A stiff climb leads to the top of Łysa Góra where there is a complex of buildings, including the museum, around a Benedictine abbey which was established by monks from the Italian monastery of Monte Cassino. It may seem a ludicrously remote place for any kind of establishment, but bare mountaintops seem always to have had a magnetic attraction for worshippers, and this abbey turns out to have been built on the site of an even earlier pagan place. But all the prayers through the centuries brought little luck to this bald mountain; from 1825 until 1945 the monastery served as a prison. Today's pilgrims come for the view over the forested hills and distant villages, and to visit the museum.

Directly beneath the east flank of the hill, in the village of Nowa Słupia, which is about fifteen minutes' walk from the summit or about 20 kilometres by a roundabout road, is a museum which tells an altogether different story of these hills. For the first thousand years AD, the small but accessible beds of iron ore hereabouts were the basis of one of the most extensive iron-working centres in Europe, and the **Museum of Ancient Metallurgy** has been erected over an unearthed complex of old smelting furnaces. In fact the whole region is dotted with old ironworks and many villages betray their origins by their names. The previously mentioned Nowa Huta, for example, means 'new foundry'.

From the summit of Łysa Góra there is a trail running along the mountain ridge, descending some 12 kilometres to the west from the 612-metre-high point of the Łysica (where legend has it that witches congregate) to the village of Święta Katarzyna, which is one of the most popular centres for trekking in the country. As well as the little churches and picturesque villages that are scattered around the Holy Cross Mountains there are the usual poignant memorials to victims of the Nazi occupation. In a country of plains, this wooded outcrop provided cover for partisans, who were hunted down in turn by the occupiers. But despite the war and the mining, the tourists and the improved roads, there are still many who live an isolated life amongst the trees here.

Kielce is few people's favourite town despite its fine location among the hills. Much of the atmosphere of the place is dominated by nineteenth-century buildings in the centre and the usual post-war estates of tower blocks in the suburbs, the town being an expanding industrial centre. But there are several buildings worthy of a visit as well as the folk section of the Świętokrzyskie Museum which is in the main square. This building also contains a local history section. Just down the road, in the old palace built by the bishops of Kraków, one-time owners of Kielce, is a large gallery of Polish painting. The prize exhibits here, though, are the seventeenth-century interiors. There are three elaborate plafond ceilings, designed by an Italian and executed by Dutch and Flemish artists, although a local influence is apparent in the splendidly painted larchwood ceiling of the grand dining-room.

There are two main roads running south from Kielce, one to Kraków and the other to Tarnów, both of which have their attractions, but there is also a network of small roads visiting ancient places which should not be missed, so it is difficult to plan a simple tour to catch the main features of this lower, green and rolling region of Małopolska. On the basis that most southbound travellers will be heading for Kraków, I will suggest a couple of interesting ways of getting there. First the pretty route.

Due south from Kielce, road No. 128 heads for Busko-Zdrój and Tarnów but after about fifteen kilometres, at the village of Morawica, it swings to the left, leaving a narrower road to go straight on. This is the one to take for **Pińczów**, 20 kilometres or so further on through a land of gently sloping fields cultivated in the traditional strips with just the occasional patch of woodland.

Pińczów, a charming and sleepy little place beside the Nida river, with a ruined castle perched above it, once stood at the very heart of a fundamental and controversial period of change in the land. The Reformation which so confused Europe in the sixteenth century reached deep into pious Poland, coinciding with the expansion of printing and a local movement for the use of the Polish language in literature and education. This trend was fiercely opposed by the

University of Kraków, the leading institute of learning in the country then as now. Into this climate came a group of Aryans, a sect which rejected the dogma of the Trinity, to found the Academy of Pińczów in 1551 which soon attracted pupils from Bohemia, Germany and France as well as from within Poland. All beliefs, it seems, were welcomed, and a printing house was set up so that the ideas debated here could be disseminated far and wide. Needless to say, many powerful people were angered by all this, but the fashion spread and several nobles who had been educated abroad and breathed the fresh air of the Renaissance also set up printing presses and employed tolerant and humanistic teachers for their families. The role of little Pińczów in this complex story is outlined in the local museum, which is housed in a Gothic cloister in the town centre.

There are two Renaissance churches, with their high red roofs and white walls, a synagogue and, hidden amongst the trees of a park, a rococo palace from 1780. The building of the original printing house also survives, as does a handsome Paulite church and monastery. The dominant family in Pińczów were the Firlejs, one of whom had been Grand Marshal of the Crown. But more interestingly, perhaps, this was for many years the base and workshop for the artist and architect Santi Gucci, a Florentine who worked in Poland between 1550 and 1590 and rounded off his long career by becoming court architect to King Stefan Batory and his wife Anne of the old Jagiełłon family, whose tomb he designed for the Zygmunt chapel in Kraków. Alongside the castle on the hill is the beautiful **Chapel of St Anne,** built by Santi Gucci in 1600.

So from the soft green depths of the countryside the ripples of Pińczów's influence spread at many levels. Today the town is a delight, one of those places which are rarely mentioned in guide-books but have an atmosphere and character that linger long after more famous monuments have merged in the memory to a smear of gold leaf and marble. For those who are so inclined and equipped there is a campsite by the river and the chance of horse-riding at a nearby rest centre.

Just 20 more kilometres down the Nida valley there is yet another historic little town, Wiślica, which has gently subsided over the centuries so that now it is marked only on the better maps, one of which will be needed to find it. **Wiślica** was an important centre in the Middle Ages and a seat of the early Piast dynasty, but many mysteries remain as to its origins and only since the Second World War have excavations revealed the full extent of what was obviously a glorious past and thus widened the narrow beam of light which is all that illumines the earliest days of the Polish state. An early chronicle mentions that in the ninth century the then mighty Moravian state, based in the region which is now central Czechoslovakia, subdued the capital of the Wiślanie, or Vistulan, tribe of Slavs and baptized their chieftain, and it now seems that Wiślica was that very place. Fragments of a tenth-century church have been discovered which include a Romanesque font carved from local gypsum and dated some time around the year AD 880. Beneath the crypt of the collegiate church, itself completed in 1380, remnants of another church have been uncovered, including a gypsum floor adorned with carved figures and a border decorated with motifs of plants and animals which is one of the earliest and most beautiful Romanesque remains in the country.

The splendid church that still stands there has a high, plain and calming interior. In the presbytery there are frescos from the four-teenth and fifteenth centuries in the same Byzantine-Ruthenian style seen at Lublin and Sandomierz, and also an unusual tiled floor with an engraved stone tablet featuring Kazimierz the Great. The separate Gothic bell tower, not as high as the great roof, was built by the Sandomierz chronicler Jan Długosz, who built himself a house in the town centre in the 1460s. Another fragment of Wiślica's days of influence is known to history as the 'Wiślica Statutes'. These are thought to date from around 1350, and represent the first codification of common law in Poland.

As in the case of many places, especially those close to the Vistula, all was very nearly lost in September 1939 when the Polish army grouped here to battle vainly against the German *blitzkrieg*. But somehow the town survived, quiet and agricultural in the soft, reedy valley.

Once across the Nida river at Wiślica the country road continues south-westward, aiming directly for Kraków which is some 70 kilometres distant. It is a fascinating run through a dozen little wooden villages and tracked for some of the way by a narrow-gauge railway which, for reasons best known to its forgotten makers, twists crazily through the landscape calling on the remotest hamlets and farms. Such railways are one of the great joys of Poland, recommended to all with the time and patience to get to their destination and, given the vagaries of the timetable, back again. Usually the toy-like carriages are pulled by little fat and greasy steam locomotives, though sometimes the

101

lines are served by miniature diesel railcars. Once I was on such a train when it was energetically flagged down in the middle of a forest by a young couple, which was a bit ostentatious considering our speed of progress.

If time or inclination favours a quicker journey to Kraków than the back roads, it is easy enough to turn down to the main riverside road which enters the famous city past the smoking furnaces of Nowa Huta; not the village of the mountains near Kielce but a post-war steelworks and suburb built to 'proletarianize' balance to the great academic city just down the road. To travel this long road on a wet night with the shadowy bulk of the furnaces spewing flame is an eerie experience.

But from Kielce there is another and more direct route to Kraków. This entails following the main E7 trunk road south from the centre of Kielce, past the pump factory at Białogon and beneath the imposing ruins of Checiny castle. Having passed a delightful wooden baroque church, some 40 kilometres from Kielce, you will come to the town of Jędrzejów which boasts a most unusual exhibition in its **Gnomonical Museum,** where there are some 800 astronomical instruments and sundials on display. The museum is to be found at No. 8 in the market place, where the Przypkowski family made a lifetime's collection of these items. In 1962 they presented the whole assemblage to the state, and the museum was opened in the house, extending for obvious reasons into the back garden, which is dominated by one particularly enormous sundial. Perhaps the most fun is King Stanisław Leszczyński's eighteenth-century device; attached to a small cannon this fires a shot automatically at noon. One of the older exhibits is a stardial dated 1524, and the scholar will find an extensive library and archives of relevant literature.

The town seems to have a long and honourable connection with time-keeping, because at No. 7 in the market place there once worked a Mr Patek, who went on to found a most famous firm of Swiss watchmakers. Maybe it was he who inspired the Przypkowski family next door to start collecting more basic methods of marking the hours.

Like Pińczów and Wiślica, Jędrzejów was a place of considerable influence in the early days of the state, thanks to a large Cistercian abbey just outside the town which was founded in 1140 by French monks sent to spread the word in these remote parts. The late Romanesque basilica of the abbey church was built at the end of the thirteenth century and has been modernized several times since. Now it has a rich late baroque interior from the 1730s, with illusionist frescos, many ornate epitaphs to long-dead abbots and a typically ornate chapel in memory of the first Polish chronicler, Wincenty Kadłubek, who died here in 1223. In the nineteenth century the town had a successful textile industry but today its economy depends in the main on local agriculture which is dominated by fruit and tobacco. A great deal of the latter is grown in Poland, which is just as well considering that most Poles smoke like the proverbial flue.

Amongst the tobacco fields just a few kilometres to the east is Raków, a little village that reinforces Małopolska's reputation as the birthplace of a rational Polish culture, for it was in this village, once known, astonishingly, as the 'Polish Athens', that a tolerant and humanistic group of scholars known as the Polish Brethren established the **Academy of Raków,** which was the first to teach the revolutionary scientific theories of Copernicus, Kepler and Galileo at a time when Rome had marked the works of these great men on their infamous Index of proscribed books. But even the tolerant King Władysław IV could not resist the pressure of the Jesuit-led conservatives in the established Church, and in 1632 the Academy and its famous printing house were closed. The Counter-Reformation, here as elsewhere, brought the beast of intolerance into the open and so the opportunity to create a more sensible society was lost.

Back on the main road there is an interesting sidelight thrown on those times by Wodzisław, another small and ancient town, where the Calvinist church served as a synagogue from 1621 until the fateful year of 1939. At the next village, Mieronice Wodzislawskie, there is an early Gothic church which will appeal to collectors of ecclesiastica, the painted decorations being from the first half of the fifteenth century.

The landscape hereabouts becomes considerably more lumpy and the next little town, **Miechów,** sits above several small river valleys, an early junction on the old trade routes. Two great fires have destroyed much of the old centre, but in the market place the parish church survives with both Gothic and Romanesque fragments visible, its tall free-standing tower unusually crowned with a globe. The neighbouring monastery has a small ornamental garden encircled by beautiful Gothic-Renaissance arcades making a perfect place for quiet contemplation, which may be welcome at this stage of the journey. The not so distant presence of Kraków makes itself known about here by an increasing number of new houses in the villages as well as the appearance of little holiday chalets, favourite refuges for town-dwellers forced to live in cramped tower blocks. In complete contrast to the architectural styles from the past, the new houses are mostly home-made efforts erected with little regard to appearance; they vary from unplastered brick blocks to castellated wooden sheds, and there is plenty of scope for personal ingenuity inspired by a most unreliable supply of materials.

Cheating again, I propose yet another delaying tactic before entering Kraków by this route. At Miechów a road cuts due west towards the little town of Wolbrom, which I walked through on a trek to Istanbul in 1980. It is situated in the heart of the Jura Krakowska, which is a ridge of limestone extending 100 kilometres north-west from the great city as far as Częstochowa. This is typical limestone country, with ravines, thin soils and few trees, and the whole ridge is inclined with a sharp and broken scarp on the western edge. In one extraordinary place just below this scarp there is a large area of sand and gravel called the Pustynia Błędowska which is so desert-like that Rommel trained his Afrika Korps there during the occupation.

For the sake of convenience and a certain structural tidiness I will at this point mention Częstochowa in more detail, although strictly speaking it lies just within the old province of Silesia. Although the old town is a famous place and one that is crucial to Poland's Catholic majority, a large industrial centre has been imposed on it and there is little of interest remaining except for the one supreme attraction. On a hill at the western edge of the town stands the Paulite **Monastery of Jasna Góra,** a large collection of mainly brick buildings supported by stout defensive walls which proved their worth in 1655 by withstanding repeated assaults from the Swedish armies which had swept down from the Baltic. Four gates have to be negotiated to gain entrance to the monastery, where in a Gothic chapel the object of the greatest veneration in the country is to be found. It is a painting, obscure in origin but thought to be a southern Italian creation, although it is certainly Byzantine in character. Known as the **Black Madonna** or **Our Lady of Częstochowa,** it is a portrait of the Virgin reputed to have been painted by the hand of St Luke himself, and is believed by some to have miraculous properties. The faithful put the successful defence against the Swedes down to the presence of the picture, and one legend tells the tale of the Tartar soldier who, trying to steal the picture during a 1430 raid, found it becoming ever more heavy. In a rage of frustration he slashed at the image with his sword, whereupon blood gushed from the figure of the Virgin. To this day the face does actually have a small cut in the canvas but a more credible explanation is that, after the sacking of the monastery and the desecration of its icons by the Tartars, medieval artists restored the picture, leaving a cut as a memento or even as evidence upon which to create the myth and thus increase the power of the image.

Twice daily in a solemn and crowded ceremony golden screens are drawn back and the congregation can glimpse the face which they may have trekked for weeks to see. Jasna Góra is a great site, and every year thousands of walkers converge on the shrine on Assumption Day, 15 August. The biggest crowd seen on the hill was probably that which flocked in 1979 to see Pope John Paul II on his first return to his native land since his elevation from the job of Archbishop of Kraków. But where there are crowds there is business, and the steps outside the main entrance are thronged with stalls selling cheap plastic souvenirs. Even the nuns have got into the act, their own stall crowded with slightly up-market souvenirs, and very angry one of them became when I attempted to photograph her in action. Business must be brisk because on any day of the year there are coaches parked below the hill waiting for village or factory groups to kneel and pay their pennies in what may be an annual or a once in a lifetime visit.

Of course such a potent force is wide open to exploitation and in the seventeenth and eighteenth centuries, when both the Church and the nation were going through a bout of insecurity, various cults were formed which climaxed in 1717 with the coronation of the Black Madonna as Queen of Poland, an ill-concealed attempt by the clergy to maintain a direct hold over the populace. But there are attractions other than the purely religious at Jasna Góra which, a touch ironically perhaps, means bright or shining hill. The **Church Treasury** is packed with precious objects of incalculable value including gold, jewellery, embroidered fabrics and arms, making it one of the richest collections in the country. Over the centuries pilgrims from the humble to the mighty have deposited gifts here and the whole ecclesiastical complex is an Aladdin's cave of treasures, including a famous library with a huge collection of old books and manuscripts. It is little wonder that the name of Częstochowa crops up on all the tourist itineraries of Poland.

And so back to the Jura Krakowska, which in the late Middle Ages formed the frontier between Małopolska and the Bohemian-controlled territory of Silesia. At that time a line of fourteen castles was built along the dry ridge by Kazimierz the Great which gave the hills their nickname of 'Trail of the Eagles' Nests', but all are ruined now, some picturesquely so. I visited one of the largest ruins, Ogrodzieniec, late one summer evening and, armed with a branch full of ripe cherries which had been presented to me by two village girls, settled down amongst the fallen stones to enjoy my sunset repast and watch the usual procession of cows being led home either by old women or small children.

South of Ogrodzieniec, unless you are walking or dodging around on back roads, the major E22 road is met at Olkusz, an old mining town which extracted lead and silver back in the thirteenth century. The church here retains sections of a beautiful fifteenth-century altar, one of the finest specimens of Polish Gothic painting. Just outside the town, leave the main Kraków road and take a small turning on the left, which leads to the lovely gorge of the Prądnik river and the Ojców National Park, a typical and attractive limestone landscape crowned, quite literally, by the legendary castle of **Pieskowa Skała**. Perched on a rock high above the road, this is one of the most beautiful buildings in the country, dating from the fourteenth-century reign of Kazimierz the Great. The real splendour of the place, however, lies in the Renaissance rebuilding done around 1580, the courtyard with its slender columns and arcades being the finest and most photographed part. There are two permanent exhibitions in the castle; one detailing the history of the place and the other showing a magnificent selection of paintings entitled 'The evolution of European Art from the Middle Ages to the middle of the nineteenth century'. There are also temporary exhibitions on various historical subjects and a large library. Carefully restored in recent years, the castle provides an interesting cross-section of building styles, from the Gothic tower through the Renaissance arcades and grotesque carvings to the mid-seventeenth-century chapel with its 'whispering acoustic' in the crypt. More prosaically, there is a terrace café which provides splendid views along the narrow wooded valley, a nearby feature being a 20-metre limestone pillar left stranded on the valley side, which because of its shape is known as Hercules' Club.

It was more than the natural beauty of the area that brought the designation of National Park to the valley in 1956. The calcareous microclimate harbours a remarkable population of wildlife as well as splendid beech, fir and hornbeam woods and the endemic Ojców birch. Among rare birds there are eagle owls, dippers and mountain thrushes, and I have seen glorious swallowtail butterflies beside the stream. As you would expect of limestone, the valley is riddled with caves, and the earliest known remains of human habitation in Poland have been found in those around the village of Ojców. Now they are home to large colonies of bats, although guided tours can be made into a couple of these gloomy places. Legend has it that some time around the year 1300, Władysław the Short sought refuge in the caves during the struggles with Wenceslas of Bohemia for the Kraków throne, but it is more likely that he went to Ojców castle itself, which is known to have existed since at least 1109 and today is a ruin on yet another outcrop. The gate-tower of the castle is still intact, hiding behind huge limestone boulders on a steep and twisting path with the remains of an unusual fourteenth-century octagonal tower beyond. I can vouch for the fact that at dusk this is a very spooky place with all the atmosphere of a horror film, including the beating of bat wings close overhead.

Finally the little road leaves the green bed of the valley and, through a narrow gorge, climbs the short distance to the main road. This leads very quickly to the smoky blur on the horizon that is the city of Kraków.

6

Kraków: the Old Town

There are so many legends surrounding the origins of Kraków that this chapter could fairly begin with the words 'Once upon a time'. For example: once upon a time, long, long ago, a greedy dragon lived in a cave beside the Vistula river, at the foot of the rocky Wawel Hill. Such was his hunger that he ate everything and everyone who passed his way — cow, sheep or man. Not surprisingly, his existence caused anguish to mothers and shepherds alike for miles around, for nothing was safe so long as he lived. Enter our hero, by the name of Krak. He determined to achieve fame by killing the monster, but he planned to use cunning rather than physical force. Filling a dead sheep with sulphur he quietly placed it on the river bank as close to the cave as he dared. The dragon fell upon the carcass and devoured it in one gulp, but the sulphur burning in his stomach gave him such a great thirst that he drank and drank from the river until he burst into a thousand pieces and once more the river bank was safe.

Today, beside an unpretentious opening at the foot of Wawel, there is a modern sculpture of the dragon every bit as horrible as he could possibly have been himself, and almost as dangerous, with its jagged torch-cut edges. Krak, of course, was supposed to have founded a town on top of the dragon's rocky home but, quaint as the story is and long as man has lived on Wawel, the historians tell a far more interesting tale as to the founding of Poland's most famous and glamorous city. And let there be no doubt of the importance of this stony outcrop in the nation's history. Referring only to the great cathedral on the hill's summit, a certain Bishop Józef Olechowski

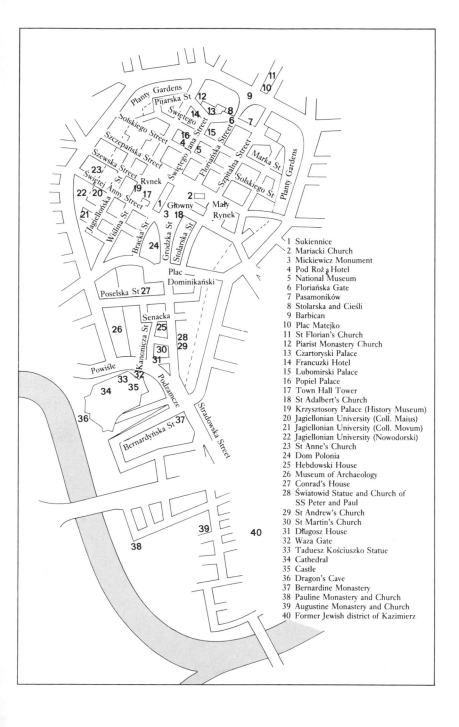

1 Sukiennice
2 Mariacki Church
3 Mickiewicz Monument
4 Pod Różą Hotel
5 National Museum
6 Floriańska Gate
7 Pasamoników
8 Stolarska and Cieśli
9 Barbican
10 Plac Matejko
11 St Florian's Church
12 Piarist Monastery Church
13 Czartoryski Palace
14 Francuzki Hotel
15 Lubomirski Palace
16 Popiel Palace
17 Town Hall Tower
18 St Adalbert's Church
19 Krzysztosory Palace (History Museum)
20 Jagiellonian University (Coll. Maius)
21 Jagiellonian University (Coll. Movum)
22 Jagiellonian University (Nowodorski)
23 St Anne's Church
24 Dom Polonia
25 Hebdowski House
26 Museum of Archaeology
27 Conrad's House
28 Światowid Statue and Church of
   SS Peter and Paul
29 St Andrew's Church
30 St Martin's Church
31 Długosz House
32 Waza Gate
33 Taduesz Kościuszko Statue
34 Cathedral
35 Castle
36 Dragon's Cave
37 Bernardine Monastery
38 Pauline Monastery and Church
39 Augustine Monastery and Church
40 Former Jewish district of Kazimierz

wrote in 1787 that 'Even had no history of Polish lands ever been written, it could largely be read in its walls and stones.'

Accepting that the steep-sided limestone plateau overlooking the curving river must have been every palaeolithic boy scout's perfect campsite, a glance at the map explains why this particular site developed at an early date into a major trading centre. The Vistula flows here through a narrow gap between the Jura Krakowska and the foothills of the Carpathian Mountains which rise immediately to the south of the city. In the earliest days it was natural and convenient for travellers to pass through this geographic gateway, and that oft-mentioned trade route from the Black Sea and Kiev passed through on its way to Prague and western Europe. Altogether seven known trade routes converged on Kraków, including three that wound through the Carpathians to the plains of Hungary.

Excavations on and around Wawel have revealed traces of habitation going back maybe 50,000 years, including sites that appear to have been flint workshops and the settlements of people who hunted large and long-extinct mammals, if not dragons. But for the past 1,500 years the area has been continuously occupied by Slavic people who sought protection here and at other such sites behind ramparts of earth and timber. The Vistulans or Wiślanie, previously met up-country in the heart of Małopolska, were the earliest group known by name, but the first mention of Kraków in the chronicles is dated AD 965 and comes, significantly, from the quill of a Jewish merchant based in Spain, one Ibrahim ibn-Yaqub. He makes it clear that by then the town had an important market which was visited by traders from many countries.

Where there was trade there was power, and where there was power the Church was never far away. In fact the year after Ibrahim wrote his chronicle, the first recognizably great Polish leader, the northern-based Prince Mieszko I, was baptized as part of a deal with the neighbouring Holy Roman Empire which involved his marriage to a Bohemian princess from Prague. Clerics, it seems, were amongst her dowry — missionaries sent to convert the Slavs to the Catholic faith. But it was another 34 years before an archdiocese was created in AD 1000 at Gniezno comprising the dioceses of Wrocław, Kołobrzeg and Kraków, and the Christian mission on Wawel Hill was recognized by the Church of Rome. Within 40 years the Piast monarchy under Kazimierz the Restorer moved its capital from Gniezno to Kraków following a damaging war with Bohemia which left the Gniezno region less than secure, and it was not until 1609 that the court left Kraków and settled in Warsaw.

There was more to Kraków, though, than the Wawel Hill. In AD 1000, the Vistula was less disciplined than today and divided into several branches so that Wawel was an island, but settlements of wooden houses and little churches quickly developed on dry land both to the north and the south. The river now runs tidily between solid banks, but it is still possible to identify those early sites within the modern city.

Most obvious of these and the focus for most visitors to Kraków is the **Rynek**. This outsize and unique market place with its huge central Cloth Hall, ancient towers and elderly flower-sellers is ample evidence of the town's medieval wealth, and at all times of the year it is the bustling heart of the Old Town, busy with locals and tourists alike. Once described as 'Kraków's drawing-room', it is a vast rectangle surrounded by blocks of ancient streets which are packed tight with churches and museums, hat shops and bookshops, tailors and grocers; the whole ensemble bound around with a green thread of shady parkland where the city wall once stood. The first moment of arrival in the market place is astonishing and memorable as the high walls of the side streets fall away to be replaced by the sky, silhouetting the tall twin towers of the revered **Mariacki Church**, or **Basilica of the Blessed Virgin Mary**, which dominates the north-east corner of the square. If that first moment coincides with the passing of an hour, then the experience is intensified by the sound of a melancholy trumpet call known as the *hejnał*. The trumpet cries out four times from the highest of the church towers, the quality of the sound changing as the horn is directed to the four corners of the compass in turn. Each slow, almost sobbing, sometimes wavering call is always cut short in mid-phrase, a custom which will already be familiar to travellers who have been near a radio at noon on any day in Poland, because at that hour an ancient microphone collects the sound and transmits it live across the nation; it is both a vivid reminder of past dangers and the celebration of a living legend.

The story goes that during the Tartar raids of the fourteenth century the watchman on duty in the church tower sounded the alarm at the approach of the invaders but was struck in the throat by a Tartar arrow before the call was completed. The call breaks off at exactly the same point to this day. I cannot help thinking that if he had played his alarm to a faster beat he could have been away before the arrow flew. But to hear the call is a strangely moving experience, causing many to stop and gaze up at the tiny figure just visible through the tower window. We were once privileged to climb the tower, and after an endless trudge up ancient wooden stairs and open catwalks suddenly emerged through the floor of a little room to be greeted by a chubby, friendly-faced young man in the blue uniform of a fireman. The fire department traditionally undertakes this work, having inherited the role from the early watchmen. Krzysztof Daniel was only 23, but he had already been doing the job for four years. The trumpeters normally work in pairs on 24-hour shifts with a 48-hour break between, but he claimed to be bored by his task. Normally the duty pair play cards and listen to the radio for their cue. Then one of them will take the trumpet from its case and perform a few practice runs before sounding the bell by pulling at an old rope and then going from window to window to play the age-old call. Although there are heaters of a kind, it must be bitterly cold up there in the winter and the biggest danger, we gathered, was from that warming glass of vodka, but our man swore that he had never once been late with the alarm. Heaven help him if he ever is. I feel that the city would grind to a halt if the trumpet did not sound, even in the wee small hours. Now that I have been to the top and witnessed the ceremony, I listen every time I hear the noon broadcast on Polish radio for the creaking of the boots as they pass across the wooden floor and the scrape of the little window opening and closing, knowing just what is happening in that little tower-top room.

The view from up there is, of course, spectacular, with the whole Stare Miasto (Old Town) laid out patchwork-fashion below, the little coloured ants of people criss-crossing the square, and school parties and lovers gathered around the statue of the poet Mickiewicz, a traditional meeting-place. To the south, Wawel Castle broods on its rock and far to the west rises the mound of earth piled 30 metres high in the 1820s in memory of Tadeusz Kościuszko, supposedly from soil collected from all the battlefields where the great patriot fought for his country's independence. In the middle distance are the multifarious roofs of the Old Town, the panorama pierced by church towers and split by narrow streets. The view due north leads the eye straight down Floriańska Street to the solid stone gate that leads to the Planty Gardens.

The trumpeter's tower at 80 metres is quite a bit taller than its twin, a difference that can, of course, be explained by a legend involving the two brothers who built the church, a fit of jealousy and a large knife, supposedly the one which hangs to this day in the Sukiennice, the old cloth hall. All of these tall tales can be found in the local guide-books, of which Kraków is never short. The taller tower begins as a square structure but then becomes octagonal, with a Gothic spire which was added in 1478. An unusual gilt crown was placed over the spire in 1666 and sits half-way down, as if wedged. From ground level the church is a not very impressive mass of old red brick without much decoration — except, that is, for a splendid old sundial. There are three doors, and the one to the south still has chains beside it where wrongdoers were exposed to public humiliation.

Once inside, past the thirteenth-century stoups where the devout still dip their fingers, the first impression of the church is quite stunning: a high vaulted ceiling in dark blue with golden stars. The second impression one has is of solitary worshippers at prayer amidst the slowly bobbing troops of tourists while the monotonous voice of a guide explains some detail or other to a silent group. **Mariacki** was founded in 1221 as a parish church and remodelled in its present form during the following century as a two-aisled basilica with no transept and an elongated presbytery. The nave and chapels were added in the fifteenth century. The only surviving fragments of the original Romanesque church are some of the foundations and the bases of the columns which separate the aisles from the nave.

As this was a parish church, every wealthy burgher, merchant and tradesman aspired to leave his mark, and that many succeeded can be seen by the number of inscriptions on the superb altars, memorials and chapels here. But the ultimate superlatives must be saved for the **high altar,** commissioned in 1477. An amazing thirteen metres by eleven of intricately carved linden wood in the form of a triptych, this is indisputably one of the greatest pieces of Gothic art in the whole of Europe. When folded it exhibits twelve reliefs illustrating scenes from the life of the Holy Family, all of gilded wood and additional polychromy. When opened, it reveals six scenes: Annunciation, Nativity, Adoration of the Magi, Resurrection, Ascension and Pentecost. The main scene, the Annunciation, shows a group of apostles supporting Mary, framed by an arc. Within the arc is a pageant of Kraków citizens, from knights to vagabonds, merchants to students. The realistic poses and details of expression, gesture and dress are quite breathtaking to anyone who has ever tried his hand at whittling a stick. So individual are the faces, so obviously portraits, that I can image the scene during the service of consecration. Many an eye must

113

have remained open during the prayers, eager to identify acquaintances and see who had been immortalized as a vagabond.

It is hardly surprising that this stunning work took the sculptor Wit Stwosz some twelve years to complete after receiving the commission. He was not a Pole, but came from Nuremberg where he was born Veit Stoss, and ironically it was from that city of war-crime tribunals that the altar was recovered in 1946, having been looted by the Nazis. It took 64,000 man-hours of work to restore it to its present condition, and during this process the polychrome was discovered beneath several layers of later paint. The altar is available for viewing when services are not being held, sometimes in an open position, sometimes closed. The times are shown outside the church.

In the right-hand aisle there is a baroque altar with a huge stone crucifix believed also to be the work of Stwosz because of the delicacy of its carving, and there is yet another cross ascribed to the master over the arch dividing the nave from the chancel. Stwosz's work did not go unrecognized at the time: the city council exempted him from payment of all dues and taxes in appreciation of his contribution to the church.

The altar aside, Mariacki is full of interesting features. It contains many finely carved statues, tombs and tablets, baroque altars with paintings by renowned artists from Venice, Holland and Germany, and six opulent chapels built in the fifteenth century. In the chancel is a wall painting by Jan Matejko, executed around 1890 and featuring angels playing musical instruments beneath a frieze designed around the coats of arms of kings and bishops and the emblems of the Kraków guilds. The windows at either end of the great church could not be more different. The high windows in the chancel are so ancient that little light filters through the mosaic of blue and red glass to reach the exuberantly carved stalls and the two extraordinary monuments on either side of the nave arch, the Montelupi family's on the right, the Cellari's on the left. At the west end, facing the square, the window between the towers was last glazed at the end of the nineteenth century, in an *art nouveau* style by one of Kraków's most beloved sons, Stalisław Wyspiański, with help from his friend Józef Mehoffer, a painter for whom stained-glass windows were to become something of an obsession.

At the eastern end of the church, behind the sacristy, there is a Renaissance extension which houses the rich **Treasury**, where liturgical vessels from the fourteenth to the eighteenth century can be seen, as well as a valuable set of historic vestments worn by bishops and other church officials. There was a more prosaic exhibition in a side chapel during one of my recent visits: a vividly illustrated attack upon abortion, which of course is all part of the service for the Church in Poland. By some diocesan equation rooted in the distant past, Mariacki is also the parish church for a nearby village, so if you are very lucky you may find a real country wedding taking place right here in the city centre. And Polish villagers in their best outfits are worth seeing, even if they are not decked out in traditional costume.

Back in the Rynek itself, the unavoidable focus is the huge **Cloth Hall (Sukiennice)**, which for centuries was used as a covered market. At the time that Kraków received its town charter in 1257, there was a line of open market stalls here which were later roofed and then replaced by a stone building. In the middle of the fourteenth century, Kazimierz the Great permitted a Gothic brick structure to be built in its place, a fraction over a hundred metres long. Then in 1555 a fire seriously damaged the place and, as was the fashion, an Italian architect, Giovanni il Mosca, known locally as Padovano, was entrusted with the rebuilding. The most beautiful feature of his design was the attic storey, still surviving and reached by ornate staircases at each end of the building. The crests of the roof parapets were decorated with carvings showing human faces of immense ugliness, twisted in pain or given animal features; binoculars come in handy for taking a close look at the survivors.

The interior of the Sukiennice is still the haunt of traders. The gloomy central aisle is lined with stalls selling items of folk craft, from cheap and cheerful wooden toys to expensive and beautiful woollen wall hangings. You will also find amber jewellery, pine boxes painted and plain, wooden decorative plates, dolls, candlesticks, wood carvings and much else, some kitsch but some of genuine worth. In summer, needless to say, this cool avenue is the busiest place in town. To shop for similar things in a more leisurely manner, head for the several *Cepelia* and other craft shops in or near the square.

In later years the upstairs storage rooms of the Sukiennice were converted into stately chambers for municipal functions, and today they house a gallery of Polish painting which includes three Matejkos, including 'The Prussian Homage', which took place in 1525 in the square below, and 'Kościuszko at the Battle of Racławice' at which a largely peasant army scored a famous victory over Tsarist troops during the 1794 insurrection. Matejko himself cut quite a heroic figure and during his years as Professor of Art in Kraków so intimidated his students with his obsession with historical images that the story is told of one student who, having produced a gentle landscape, justified his work by explaining that it showed the road down which Władysław the Short once rode to seek sanctuary at Ojców. Other well known artists featured are Chełmoński and Brandt, Olga Boznańska and Aleksander Gierymski, but my favourite picture here is Schindler's nineteenth-century girl preparing for a bath. It is a good gallery — light and spacious and yet not so large that the appetite is dulled by a surfeit of exhibits.

I have no doubts, however, that many more hours will be passed downstairs in the two cafés which sit under the arcades of the east and west sides, both nineteenth-century additions to the Sukiennice. Long and narrow, spilling out on to the square during the summer, these are among the best and most popular cafés in the whole of Poland. Plush red upholstered seats are set out in alcoves where regulars seem able to maintain their debating centres whilst visitors search for a seat. One of the regulars from the early years of this century who went on, quite literally, to make a name for himself was a Mr Ulyanov. He changed his name to Lenin and things have never been quite the same since. Tea, coffee, cheesecake and ice-cream are the normal fare, but early risers can enjoy breakfast. And downstairs on the east side (the side where the Mickiewicz statue stands) is one of the more acceptable public conveniences to be found in Poland, worth every *grosz* of the five *złotys* demanded by our lady of the saucer, who might well have been a descendant of the gargoyles on the roof.

There is still plenty of detail and atmosphere to absorb in the spacious square. As always, the pigeons seem to outnumber humans and there is even a legend to explain the presence of so many of them. They are, apparently, awaiting the return of their king from exile, when they will become courtiers once again. No one has told them that the monarch in question spent his royal fortune in another land and never had any intention of returning. So the pigeons wait and the building conservators get angry because nothing seems to deter them.

The most obvious object not yet described is the **Town Hall Tower**, stranded just beyond the south-west corner of the Sukiennice. It no longer has a town hall to lean against, which perhaps accounts for the fact that this 70-metre tower of medieval stone and brickwork stands not quite vertically. The town hall was completed in 1383, but frequent fires finally deprived it of its original Gothic spire, the present baroque crown being added in 1680. In 1820, during the short-lived Kraków Republic which was formed during the partitions, a campaign was launched to clean up the square, which had accumulated many shanty-like buildings, particularly around and leaning on the Sukiennice. Being in a bad state of repair, the body of the town hall was also dismantled. Recent restoration has cleared the old cellars, however, and created there a catacomb-like café, splendid in every respect except that it is difficult to catch the eye of one of the decorative waitresses who seem always to be hidden behind a column or round a corner.

Over in the south-east corner of the square, its green copper roof clashing with a cluster of overhanging trees, is the oldest building in the Rynek, **St Adalbert's Church.** Legend has it that St Adalbert (955–997), bishop pf Prague and friend of the Polish Prince Bolesław, preached on this spot before setting out on a mission of conversion to Northern Prussia from which, to no one's surprise, he did not return alive (his body *was* returned). The fascination of this little building lies in the fact that it is possible to distinguish pre-Romanesque, Romanesque, Gothic, Renaissance and baroque styles, which makes it a veritable catalogue of European architecture. What is more, it appears that the present stone building and the one before it were erected on the ruins of an even earlier wooden structure which is presumed to have been an ancient Slavic pagan temple. Fragments of its yew floor have been uncovered. St Adalbert himself complained in his journals that the Slavs worshipped stone and wood rather than his God, but this was the time of the conversions and the church here was obviously one of the first Christian buildings in this corner of the continent. It is built on a square plan with an elliptical dome over the nave which was added during eighteenth-century rebuilding. Small Romanesque windows survive and there is an exhibition in the cellars illustrating the history of the market square.

Close to St Adalbert's, embedded in the surface of the square, is a slab marking the place where in 1525 Albrecht Hohenzollern, duke of Prussia and last Grand Master of the Order of Teutonic Knights, knelt in public homage before King Zygmunt the Old in one of those crucial moments of Polish history recorded by Jan Matejko. The duke's act was part of a complex piece of politicking which revolved around Poland's access to the Baltic Sea, for centuries a region dominated by the Knights. As has already been mentioned, his giant canvas 'The Prussian Homage' hangs upstairs in the nearby Sukiennice. The Poles have a taste for marking such historic spots, real or imagined, and between the town hall tower and Szewska Street is a tablet supposedly at the place where Kościuszko raised his standard in 1794 and announced the uprising against the partitioning powers. Other plaques mark the homes of the famous, many of whom lived in the fine mansions which line the square.

Stanisław Wyspiański, a romantic Bohemian who was a painter, poet, dramatist and theatre-reformer, lived for some of his brief life at No. 9 on the east side of the square, a house which was originally Gothic but now has a Renaissance parapet. The house once belonged to the rich Boner family and, on the occassion of a royal wedding reception there, a hole was cut through to No. 8 next door to relieve the expected crush. All the houses on this side are much older than their façades suggest, No. 6 dating from the thirteenth century and others from the fifteenth and sixteenth. Once again they can be identified from their emblems; No. 8 is known as the Salamander House and No. 7 as the Montelupi or Italian House, having that family's crest as its ornament. It is claimed that a Montelupi instigated the first mail-coach service, the inaugural run to Vienna starting from outside this house in 1558.

No. 13 is a chemist's shop and has been so since the sixteenth century. The business was started by the apothecary Jan Pipan, who produced special incense, pastilles, mustard seed, rose-water, candles, confetti, spice, biscuits and other confections for the 1587 coronation of Zygmunt III Waza. Royal occasions, it seems, have always activated the entrepreneurial spirit. On the first floor is the headquarters of the interesting-sounding Society of Atheists and Freethinkers, although I cannot imagine why such people should feel the need for a society.

Where southbound Grodzka Street leaves the square there used to be a triumphal arch from which young girls sang pretty ballads and showered flowers on to the king whenever he came to town from Wawel. On the corner of Grodzka today is one of the best restaurants in Poland, the Wierzynek, named after the original owner of the house. Sadly, today's diners will not come away with the souvenirs presented to earlier guests. Way back in 1364, merchant Mikołaj Wierzynek threw a feast for the royal guests of Kazimierz the Great during a Congress of Monarchs held at Wawel, and after the event everyone received the gold plate off which they had eaten. Mind you, at the prices charged in certain countries today, some such scheme should perhaps be reintroduced.

The west side of the square now has many shops tacked on to the old houses, including a bookshop, a shoe shop, a busy wine store and a place that sells postcards, but on the north-west corner where Szczepańska Street joins the square, next to a cavernous and very good value restaurant, the **Krzysztofory Palace** remains intact, its first floor containing several galleries of the Kraków History Museum. The palace was created in the seventeenth century by the Crown Marshal Adam Kazanowski, who bought three adjoining burghers' houses and merged them behind a single façade to make a grand and luxurious town house.

From the north-east corner of the Rynek, Floriańska Street, with its tailors, jewellers and other smart shops, leads towards the tower of the Floriańska Gate which stands at the far end and marks the line of the old city wall. At a first glance there is little that bears witness to the great age of this street, many of the shops now having modern frontages, but the portals and arches and some fragments of wall betray the Gothic architecture buried beneath later fashions. Here, as throughout the town, there are still many of the old emblems which identified the occupants before the convenient anonymity of house numbering was introduced. And deep within some of these houses, restorers have uncovered beautiful murals, coffered ceilings and Gothic arched cellars.

On the corner of the long-scaffolded Solskiego Street, caught up in a never-ending process of restoration, is Kraków's oldest and most famous hotel, the **Pod Róża**, meaning 'under the rose', whose name refers to the emblem above the door. Tsars, dukes and Balzac have all stayed here, but the most glorious guest was surely Franz Liszt, who visited the hotel in 1843 during one of his wildly successful concert tours. He spread his custom by giving his recital in a rival hotel just around the corner. The Renaissance stone doorway is decorated with an inscription in Latin which reads 'May this house stand until the ant drinks the ocean and the tortoise circles the earth.' On the opposite corner the iron chains still hang which were used by the town authorities to close the streets in the event of enemy attack and more often to quell riots, particularly during the years of partition.

Farther up on the right, at **No. 41**, is the birthplace and lifelong home of Jan Matejko (1838–1893). The sixteenth-century house, now a branch of the National Museum, came to the artist from his mother's family, who operated a saddler's workshop here. Matejko was a Krakówian through and through, devoted to the city and all its monuments and active on committees formed to restore Wawel, the Sukiennice, Mariacki and many other buildings. He even found time to design a new façade for his own house. Two rooms on the first floor are kept as they were during his lifetime, and the front sitting-room contains extraordinary objects encrusted with marble mosaic which Matejko purchased in Venice. The visitor can also see the artist's studio and many memorabilia of his life, such as his collection of historical costumes, necessary research tools for his pictures, and many of his sketches and smaller paintings.

Next door but one at **No. 45** is a house which is equally famous, but far less stern. This is the coffee shop called Jama Michalikowa, meaning 'Michalik's Den', the home of a famous satirical cabaret called the 'Green Balloon', which was started in the early years of this century by a bunch of Bohemian artists and writers. Performances are somewhat irregular, so, if the language is no problem, check locally for times.

Now the **Floriańska Gate** stands straight ahead, a chunky, square tower built in 1300 and topped since 1651 with a baroque spire. On the south face is a bas-relief of St Florian himself. When the thick town walls were finally pulled down in 1806 and the surrounding moat filled in to form the Planty Gardens, a far-sighted local professor persuaded the authorities to retain a section of the defences for posterity. Thus the Floriańska Gate with a section of the wall on either side, together with three towers and the remarkable Barbican which lies beyond the gate, were saved.

The defences had evolved from a wooden stockade to the enormous double-wall system of the late thirteenth century, 10 metres high and 2.4 metres thick, with its moat fed by a diverted stream. There were 47 towers around the 3-kilometre length of wall, and during sieges, of which there were several, each was defended by a particular guild. The surviving towers are the Haberdashers (*Pasamoników*) to the east of the gate and the Joiners (*Stolarska*) and Carpenters (*Cieśli*) to the west. In between these last two is the building of the old city arsenal. There is a nice though scarcely credible story about one resourceful haberdasher who, having run out of ammunition during one siege, loaded his dress buttons into his musket and actually shot the enemy commander. This conjures up a comic image of all 47 towers spewing out the products of their defending guilds, from goldsmiths to fish merchants, bakers to furriers. Access can be obtained to the towers and the guards' gallery which links them.

Passing through the Floriańska Gate (and ignoring if possible the displays of awful acrylic 'art for the tourist' which usually hang on the inside of the old town wall there), you will notice that the road level in the gateway has been lowered. This dates from the time when trams were introduced at the end of the last century, when it was found that the newfangled machines could not pass under the arch. In keeping with the priorities of the day, it was proposed that the gate be demolished, but the strongly intellectual town objected once again, producing a bevy of professors who solved the problem by the simple expedient of scooping out some earth beneath the gateway.

Immediately beyond, interrupting the narrow park of the Planty, is the **Barbican,** known locally as the *rondel*, a Polish word for a stew-pan. Built around 1498, this is supposed to have been modelled on defence structures common in the Middle East, and by central European standards the design is unusual. It is round, with a tile-hung roof and spiky little turrets, and there are 130 embrasures piercing the walls, which are 3 metres thick. Originally it was linked to the town walls by a covered walkway which spanned the moat, but now it stands alone, one of the best preserved and most striking pieces of military architecture in Europe, looking for all the world like a lost toy fort or some background detail from a medieval painting; a miniature master-piece of the defence architect's art.

A busy ring road runs beyond the Planty, lined on its northern side with commonplace shops and offices, and a right turn here leads very quickly to the main railway and bus stations. Directly opposite the Barbican is **Plac Matejko**, where the painter's old art college stands on the corner and a monument to the Battle of Grunwald in the centre. At the far northern end of this square is **St Florian's Church,** which sits on the site of another early settlement and itself originated as a Romanesque structure which was built in 1184. A later Gothic church was destroyed in the Swedish wars of the 1650s and the present baroque building with the usual florid rococo interior was built at the end of the seventeenth century.

Back in the peace and security of the Old Town, where trams no longer run, a right turn inside Floriańska Gate takes you down the gloomy Pijarska Street to the top of Świętego Jana Street which leads back down to the market square. On the right and facing down Świętego Jana is the Piarist Monastery Church, a good example of Polish baroque, which is linked by an overhead passage both to the old arsenal and to the **Czartoryski Palace,** which is on the top left-hand corner of Świętego Jana Street. This latter building is an absolute must for visitors, for it contains one of the finest museums to be seen anywere. The star attractions are Rembrandt's 'Landscape Before a Storm' and Leonardo da Vinci's 'Lady with an Ermine', less elegantly described in the English guide as the 'Lady with a Weasel', which does not have quite the same resonance. But there is much, much more besides. A large part of the collection comes from Poland's oldest museum of history and art, which was established by the Czartoryski family at their Puławy base early in the nineteenth century mainly thanks to the efforts of the highly civilized Izabela Czartoryska. Following the uprisings of 1830 and 1831 the family was forced to move from the Russian-occupied portion of Poland and eventually the city of Kraków offered accommodation for the much-travelled collection.

The main building used today was converted at the turn of the century from three old burghers' houses and provides a relaxed and sympathetic atmosphere in which to browse amongst the wonders that took Izabela's eclectic fancy.

The department of **Antique Art** contains some 1,400 exhibits, the oldest of which are cylindrical seals, stone reliefs and inscribed tablets from Mesopotamia, although Egypt, Greece and Etruria are also well represented. The **Decorative Arts** section displays Venetian, Bohemian, Silesian, German and Polish glassware as well as Meissen and Sèvres porcelain, Limoges enamels, silverware, ivory carvings, Flemish tapestries and Persian carpets. Room follows room of these items, all well displayed.

In the galleries of **Paintings** there are about 550 pictures, miniatures and sculptures covering the period from the thirteenth to the eighteenth century and including a fascinating collection of so-called Sienese and Tuscan 'primitives'. There is Bellini's 'Madonna and Child' and Giordano's 'Flight into Egypt', as well as a large group of Flemish paintings of which the Rembrandt stands alone, spotlit on an easel. It is a typically moody and wonderful piece of work. And then there is Leonardo da Vinci's famous and luminously beautiful portrait. Well known as a reproduction, this is a great joy to see in the original, and not just for the hypnotic power of the painted image. The wooden frame is quite delightful in its simplicity and proportions and suits the picture perfectly. It is far preferable to all those elaborately moulded gold frames which seem to be mandatory in so many museums.

The Prints Cabinet contains some 35,000 prints, drawings and water colours and the Library more than 150,000 volumes, including 2,500 rare old Polish books. There is also a large family archive and manuscript collection, but probably of more interest to the non-specialist will be the **Armoury**, which is over the bridge in the old arsenal building. This is one of Poland's best military collections because of the great variety of objects on display. Thanks to Jan Sobieski's achievement at Vienna in 1683, all the Polish nobles seem to have oriental trophies which were taken from the defeated army and a goodly selection is on show here. All in all, this splendid museum is a credit to the Czartoryski family, who were intelligent and scholarly collectors for over 200 years, and to the city of Kraków, which had the sense to provide their collection with a permanent home.

On the opposite corner to the museum is the Francuski Hotel, whose restaurant may provide a welcome pause to those who have trekked thus far round the city. The hotel building is known as the Peacock House, again because of the emblem over the door. Świętego Jana Street contains many old town houses that once belonged to the nobility, **No. 12**, now housing a branch of the Kraków History Museum, being a good example with its baroque portal, carved beams and fine ceiling paintings. The museum itself describes the history of the city's defences and guilds with many objects, pictures and prints of old Kraków, the prize exhibit being the silver cockerel given to the town's Gun Cock Fraternity in 1565 by King Zygmunt August. This society, which still exists, is the oldest civic organization in the country, having been founded more than seven hundred years ago to train the town's guildsmen in the art of defence. Each year around Corpus Christi time, a colourful and traditional shooting match still takes place, the target being a wooden cockerel which is presented to the best shot, who becomes the King of the Gun Cock Fraternity for a year.

Świętego Jana Street leads back to the Rynek, from the south-west corner of which Świétej Anny Street leads to the Jagiellonian University which occupies many buildings on this western side of the Old Town. On the left, just across Jagiellonska Street, is the **Collegium Maius,** the red-brick Gothic heart of the university and another must for visitors. The origins of the university go back to the fourteenth century and Kazimierz the Great. Throughout Europe at that time there was an awareness that the newly consolidated states with their complex legal systems needed trained administrators, and it was with this in mind that Charles IV, king of Bohemia and emperor of Germany, founded a university in Prague in 1348. The Polish king, an enlightened ruler whose peaceful policies had led his country out of a troubled period, determined to follow the Prague example. The Act of Foundation is dated 12 May 1364, and states that the college should be 'a pearl of great learning producing men ripe in excellent council, illustrious in adornments of virtue and proficient in many branches of learning'.

Historians differ when it comes to the location of that earliest college, but it is known that after the death of Kazimierz, the last of the ancient Piast dynasty, in 1370, the place went into a decline. It was rescued in 1397 by the old king's grand-daughter, Queen Jadwiga, and her husband King Władysław Jagiełło, who obtained papal permission for an Act of Restoration to ensure the future of the university. At about the same time, the present Collegium Maius was taken over, and existing houses were adapted during the course of the fifteenth century to form the magnificent building seen today. The high and slightly forbidding street walls, surmounted with pinnacled Gothic gables, belie the interior, at the heart of which is a tranquil courtyard. A marble wellhead stands in its centre and arcades surround it, with pointed arches and chunky stone pillars. Entered by a vaulted passage from Jagiellonska Street, this is an ideal place to pass a few quiet minutes. It is inside the four wings, however, that the treasure lies, and the whole complex is now devoted to the Museum of the History of the Jagiellonian University, having been restored to its Gothic glory between 1949 and 1964.

The ground-floor rooms, once used for lectures, still retain the scientific, mathematical and geometrical murals which were formerly used as teaching aids. The **Alchemy Room** has a reconstruction of a clay stove, much in the style of those still to be seen in some village houses but here laden with oddly shaped glass containers and pots, a vivid reminder that magic, alchemy, astrology and good old-fashioned superstition were for many generations part of the curriculum in European universities. According to certain German and English texts, the sorcerer Dr Faustus is supposed to have studied here, and the famous Kraków magician Twardowski also prepared his potions in this room. Whether the suspended turtle, the human skull and the mummified cat were contemporaries of these historic characters I cannot say, but the cat was unearthed from beneath the 1516 library and appears to have been buried alive as an offering for protection against evil. A nasty habit, but not uncommon at the time. There are in the college many signs of these old superstitions, perhaps the strangest being the bricks which bear the imprint of dog's paws, believed to be the work of the devil. And next to a beautiful old lock on a wooden door is the obviously fake impression of a hand, again supposed to be the mark of that fallen angel — he was obviously kept busy in medieval Poland.

On the first floor, reached by a staircase in the courtyard, is a set of magnificent rooms restored to their sixteenth-century splendour with dark carved wooden panelling, exotic portals and elaborate ceilings, a testament to the skill of Polish craftsmen then and now. Most noble is the long and high **Jagiellonian Room,** also known as the **Aula** or **Assembly Hall.** The Renaissance coffered ceiling is decorated with a different carved rosette in each section, survivors from the time that the room was first completed some time around 1507, but the frieze directly below is, for the most part, a reconstruction based on surviving fragments. Another Renaissance survivor is the portal enscribed with the words *'plus ratio quam vis'* — 'Wisdom is greater than strength'. This surround and the intricately inlaid door, both dating from the end of the sixteenth century, were in fact rescued from the old town hall. The walls are covered with portraits large and small of monarchs, benefactors and the professors, whose wooden pew-like benches line the room.

The **Common Room** was the professors' daily meeting-place and served also as the refectory. It was the duty of each professor, in the order in which their degrees were granted, to read aloud during meals, the menu for which has survived. Although they were described at the time as modest, I would consider a meal of plain soup, meat, fish, a good portion of turnips and peas, followed by porridge or dumpling with poppy seed and honey, then fruit, all washed down with water or beer, to be quite sufficient for the average day. The room itself is large and simply furnished except for an ornate Gdańsk spiral staircase of the early eighteenth century which was transferred after the last war from an old palace, and an arched bay window in which there is a replica of a fourteenth-century statuette of Kazimierz the Great.

On display throughout the Collegium Maius are many precious items accumulated over the centuries by the university, and together these amount to a unique museum where art and science rightly merge. Many of the old lecture rooms now contain equipment used in the earliest days, a time of great new discoveries in both science and geography. There are about 150 astronomical instruments including an Arabian astrolabe dating from 1156 and a globe of the sky, both of which were in the building when Copernicus was a student and were no doubt used by him. Of the many globes on display, two are by the man with his name on so many school atlases, Mercator, the Flemish cartographer and mathematician. The so-called Jagiellonian Globe is, in fact, a small and very precise clock with a globe inside it on which is the earliest known marking of the American continent. These instruments are fascinating and many are quite beautiful. There are even pocket sundials, each complete with the necessary compass. One eighteenth-century model, made surprisingly in Dieppe, is set in a lovely little ivory box.

The collection of sculptures, reliefs, figures and altars, mostly from the Kraków region, includes some 80 woodcarvings. Several wooden Madonnas have survived from around 1300 and one is from the workshop of Wit Stwosz, but the most gruesomely realistic is a *pietà* from the 1480s which was probably carved in the Austrian Tyrol. This depicts a rather bemused, even embarrassed lady nursing a very dead male figure across her delicately carved robes. It is not a pretty sight.

In the treasury rooms are four rector's sceptres, the oldest from 1400, several maces, one of which features a likeness of Kazimierz the Great, and other objects of value such as gold chains and rings. There are also collections of tankards and clocks and an assortment of other relics.

The atmosphere of all the buildings grouped around the courtyard is softened by the many tapestries and carpets that are displayed, some from a priceless seventeenth-century French collection which somehow found its way here. The oldest, however, are the 100 specimens of ancient Coptic hangings from first- to third-century Egypt. Walking through these halls where the Polish Enlightenment was born, one is amazed that so very much has survived the vagaries of history; some, no doubt, by the skin of its teeth.

To continue the mood of quiet reflection it is necessary to cross the street to the **Church of St Anne** from which the street of Świętej Anny takes its name. It is a large baroque building, the third church on the site, and serves as the university's own house of worship. Modelled on a church in Rome and built in the form of a cross surmounted by a large dome, it marked the entrance into Kraków society of that workaholic architect Tylman of Gameren, who built, it would seem, half of Warsaw. Facing the church is another old university building, the Nowodworski Collegium, put up in the 1630s as the first Polish secondary school. A school, in fact, to prepare students for the neighbouring Collegium Maius. Many famous Poles attended here, including Jan Sobieski and the artists Matejko and Wyspianski.

Before leaving the university quarter it is worth knowing that behind the northern end of St Anne's Church, at the corner of Szewska Street and the Planty, there is a very agreeable café, the U Zalipianek — one of the few places in Poland which serves herbal teas, each with a tiny glass of warm honey. U Zalipianek is named after the tiny village of Zalipie 80 kilometres down the Vistula, which is famous for painting both the inside and outside walls of its cottages with floral designs; and the café is decorated in the same way.

Once you have walked back to the main square, the next route to explore follows Grodzka Street, in the south-east corner close to St Adalbert's Church. Visitors with strong Polish blood in their veins may like to know that one of the first buildings on the right is the Dom Polonia, the local headquarters of the Polish Diaspora. After the pedestrian-only Old Town centre there comes a rude awakening as Grodzka crosses a busy tramline at Plac Dominikanski. If you look to the left, you will see the large brick basilica of a Dominican monastery raised originally in the thirteenth century. A fire in 1850 unfortunately destroyed much of the interior, but the church is still a fine and impressive space, adorned by the chapels of the magnates who could not make it into Mariacki.

Following the tramlines in the other direction leads to the even larger and much plainer Franciscan monastery founded by Bolesław the Shy, also in the thirteenth century. The order seems to have got itself well and truly involved with affairs of both state and heart. Queen Jadwiga, wife of the founding Jagiellonian, is said to have held a secret tryst with her beloved Prince Wilhelm in the refectory here, close to the spot where her own husband was baptized in 1386. A hundred years earlier Władysław the Short, before becoming king, hid from attackers in the church and was lowered over the town walls disguised as a monk to make his escape. In 1461, the powerful noble Andrzej Tęczyński was either not so lucky or not so clever, for he was murdered here by a rebellious mob.

Grodzka continues through a narrow section of the Old Town which was one of those early settlements outside Wawel, this whole district funneling down to the great riverside rock. The houses here are lower than those in the main square, hiding ancient interiors and courtyards behind baroque façades. Above the door of No. 32 is a Gothic lion, the very oldest of Kraków's many house emblems. The next crossing is Poselska Street, which is of interest on several counts. Turning right from Grodzka, a few paces lead to a little turning into Senacka Street, on the corner of which is the dumpy fourteenth-century **Hebdowski House**, once the home of the ill-fated Tęzzyński and before that the residence of the abbot of Tyniec Monastery, just up the river. The house has a very picturesque courtyard and Gothic, Renaissance and baroque details have been preserved. Beyond the Senacka Street entrance and running out to the encircling Planty Gardens is a much larger but equally ancient ensemble of buildings now occupied by an excellent **Museum of Archaeology**. Various groups have occupied the site over the centuries, including the court of Tyniec Abbey and a group of Carmelite monks who were thrown out in the nineteenth century by the Austrians, who proceeded to turn the place into a prison and law court. Since the Second World War the museum has established itself as the most important of its type in the country, illustrating the history of man in the Polish lands from 150,000 BC to the early Middle Ages. One of the oldest Slavic exhibits is a famous stone statue of the god Światowid, whose four faces see everything, dating from the eighth or ninth century. The house at **No. 12 Poselska Street** has its own more recent story to tell. A wall tablet announces that 'In the house which stood on this site Józef Konrad Korzeniowski [Joseph Conrad], son of an exiled poet, lived in his youth around 1869. He infused something of the Polish spirit into English literature, which was embellished by his works.'

Turning back and then down the narrow Senacka Street, you come to the top of Kanonicza Street, known from documents dated 1401 as the residence of canons from Wawel Cathedral. Curving down towards Wawel, this is one of the most atmospheric streets of Kraków, perhaps because it is still largely unrestored, although detailed work is proceeding apace. But before you continue there is a group of notable churches back in Grodzka, themselves recently restored and visible from Kanonicza through the little Plac Wita Stwosza. Facing on to the main street are large statues of the apostles standing on columns, and behind them is the façade of the **Church of SS Peter and Paul**, the first baroque building in the town, started here in 1598 on the site of a Gothic basilica. It was built for the Jesuits who were brought to the city specifically to fight the Reformation, and beneath its great dome it has excellent acoustics, which must have been useful for such a sermoniz-

Kraków. The Market Square with its Cloth Hall and Town Hall Tower, viewed from the trumpeter's gallery of the Mariacki Church.

Kraków. Wawel Hill has been inhabited for millenia and for several centuries was the seat of the Polish monarchy and government. The mainly Gothic cathedral (*left*) is still perhaps the spiritual centre of the country, containing the tombs of most Polish monarchs and many national heroes as well as religious, architectural and decorative treasures. The neighbouring Royal Castle (*below*) evolved from a tenth-century wooden structure to the present Renaissance-styled palace, whose rich interiors can be visited.

Kraków. Statues of two of the Apostles outside the sixteenth–century church of SS Peter and Paul are amongst the many riches to be discovered in the town's ancient streets.

Above: Kraków. In Poland flowers accompany every social call. The flower-sellers outside the Cloth Hall in the Market Square are busy throughout the year.

Below: Kraków. To mark the hours, day and night, the famous trumpet call rings out across the town from the tower of Mariacki Church, seen here to the right of the Cloth Hall.

The Tatra mountains around the lovely resort town of Zakopane offer some of the most stunning scenery in the country. The peak shown here is Giewont, supposed to represent a sleeping knight.

The Podhale region of the Tatra foothills contains many villages built entirely of wood, such as Dzianisz, shown here, where life at 1000 metres can still be very hard.

Above: In the mountains, clothes richly embroidered with traditional local patterns are still commonly worn to church and for weddings and feast days.

Below: When the steep hayfields are ready for cutting the whole family does its share of the work in a landscape still dominated by horse-power and manual labour.

ing order. Behind this formal edifice there is an open area of rough grass and dirt complete with washing lines, hens and chained dog: a fragment of village life right in the city centre.

Next door are the twin white stone towers of **St Andrew's Church,** founded way back in 1086, the year of the English Domesday Book, by the then Duke Władysław Herman as a votive offering on the birth of his son Bolesław, later to be king of Poland and nicknamed 'Wrymouth'. It is a traditional, aisled Romanesque basilica, but the inevitable and overdone baroque decoration does not sit comfortably in such surroundings. The church treasury, however, does contain some of the oldest Nativity figures surviving in Europe, said to have been given to the church in the fourteenth century by the sister of Kazimierz the Great. Next door is the rleatively modest little church of St Martin, baroque once again. This was given in 1816 to the Lutheran community, which has been present in Kraków since 1555.

Wawel is very close now and can be approached either from the bottom of Grodzka, where it looms on the right, or better still by way of Kanonicza, where the silhouette of the castle hill appears above the rooftops of houses with carved stone windows and strange coats of arms above the doors. The last house on the right, quite literally in the shadow of the castle, used to contain the royal baths and after conversion became the house of the historian and royal tutor Jan Długosz, who wrote here his 'magnum opus' *Historia Polski, The History of Poland.* In the last century Stanisław Wyspiański's father had his sculptor's studio in the house and there is a wall tablet to commemorate the fact. The façade also displays a corner-stone dated 1480 and a seventeenth-century picture of the Virgin Mary, pockmarked with bullet holes, which is said to date from the Swedish Wars.

7

Kraków:
Wawel Cathedral and Castle

As you approach the gloomy north face of Wawel Hill, you will come to the foot of a long cobbled slope which leads to the north entrance, climbing beneath a wall inscribed with the names of contributors to the restoration fund and then past a large bronze statue of Tadeusz Kościuszko, leader of the 1794 insurrection. The original of this equestrian monument was erected only in 1921, but the Nazis demolished it and the present copy was presented to Kraków in 1960 by the citizens of Dresden, itself destroyed in the war, though by the Allies.

A left turn through the 1595 Waza Gate leads to the west door of the cathedral and beyond to the large open space which now occupies more than half of the hilltop – it was a tight-packed township before the Austrians cleared it to make a parade ground. Two million people a year come this way, mostly Poles paying homage to the spirit of their land and nation for, although it is 400 years since the country's head moved to Warsaw, its heart for many still beats here on Wawel.

The hill is a veritable palimpsest, every generation having left its mark for a thousand years and more, and to unravel in just a few pages even its architectural history is well nigh impossible. Even the several local guide-books available in English make complicated reading when it comes to the chronology of development here, but broadly speaking it falls into three periods: Romanesque, Gothic and Renaissance. There are four main exhibitions to see as well as the cathedral, and even if you miss a couple out it is necessary to allow two or three hours at Wawel simply because there is so much to see. The exhibitions are of the Castle Rooms; the Oriental Collection; the Crown Treasury and Armoury; and Lost Wawel. As at the castle in Warsaw, it is possible in the high season that after buying an entrance ticket you will have a little time to wait for a guide, and this will provide an opportunity to walk around the ramparts and admire the view over the river and country-side beyond.

Since the days of Bolesław the Brave, the first great Wawel developer of almost a thousand years ago, the **Cathedral** has been the most important building on the hill. Its foundation goes back to that resounding meeting at Gniezno in AD 1000 between Bolesław and the German Emperor Otto III which resulted in Poland's obtaining an organized Church. Christianity itself preceded this moment, as it is apparent that by the end of the ninth century there were several sacred buildings here including the Rotunda of the Virgin Mary and a mysterious church which was uncovered only in 1966 and whose stone foundations are now displayed in the courtyard. That which is considered to be the first cathedral was started in the 1020s. Frag-ments of it can be seen in the western wing of the castle and in a courtyard that lies between the castle and the present cathedral building, but how it came to be destroyed is not known. One of the few events of the late eleventh century recorded in any detail was the assassination in 1079 of the bishop of Kraków, Stanisław Szczepa-nowski, either by the king himself or at his command. Either way, Stanisław became the Thomas à Becket of the Polish Church and the king was forced into exile. Later on, the bishop was canonized and his tomb is now one of the glories of the cathedral.

A second cathedral was built in 1142 in the form of a basilica with a nave and two aisles, and a major section, the crypt of St Leonard, has survived to be incorporated in the present structure. The interesting thing about this crypt is that over the centuries it has somehow subsided until the window of the apse is below ground level, in spite of the fact that Wawel is a solid lump of limestone. The cathedral seen today is the third on this site, begun in 1320 during the reign of Władysław the Short. Its elaborate side chapels were added in the sixteenth century, when Kraków's power and glory were at their greatest.

From the west door it is difficult to see the tall and slender west façade with its typically Gothic gable and rose window, because lean-to chapels project far out into the yard forming a narrow passageway to the west door, which is reached by steps. On the left side of this

131

passage, hanging by heavy chains, are large prehistoric animal bones, reputed to be the shinbone of a mammoth, the rib of a whale and the skull of a hairy rhinoceros. Legend has it that the cathedral will stand for as long as they remain. It all sounds a bit pagan to me, but as the former archbishop here is now Pope, it must be all right with Rome.

Once you have passed through the heavy wooden doors the atmosphere is very different. The nave is tall and narrow with beautiful slender columns, and all the better for being constructed from a white sandstone which makes the most of what light comes through the high, truncated windows. Straight ahead in the Transept is a fabulous shrine which on a clear day can reflect shafts of sunlight from its golden roof and columns. This is the mausoleum of the martyred bishop St Stanisław, installed around 1630 and enclosing a silver coffin the like of which can surely exist nowhere else. Created in 1671 by the Gdańsk silversmith Peter van Rennen, it is a credit more to his skill than to his taste, or that of his age. Ornate is too mild a word to describe this last refuge for the murdered Stanisław. The sides of the coffin are adorned with five detailed scenes from the life, or rather the legend, of the saint, each as crowded as a Matejko canvas. Each is framed by chubby cherubs who swirl out of the silver in a great flurry of feathers, and the lid is smothered in vines and surmounted by more cherubs supporting a bishop's mitre and maces, the whole creation being held aloft from a pink marble plinth by four large angels. The whole thing is a bit over the top for my taste and completely blocks the nave, forcing any church procession to circumnavigate it, at great risk no doubt to robe and candle as well as to the dignity of the occasion.

For centuries the cathedral was the scene of great events in the nation's history, especially coronations and funerals. Writing in 1370, the chronicler known as Janko of Czarnków described the funeral that year of the much loved and greatly respected Kazimierz the Great: 'First there came four carriages with four beautiful horses harnessed to each of them, and everything — that is, the drivers, the horses and the carriages — was shrouded with black cloth. There were forty knights in full armour on horses covered with red cloth, followed by eleven carrying the banners of as many dukedoms and one with the banner of the Polish kingdom and each of them held a shield with the crest of one of the dukedoms. These were followed by a knight in golden robes on a beautiful royal steed covered in purple cloth and this one personified the deceased king.' Janko then describes the cortège of the new king, Louis of Hungary, and the great mass of clergy, princes and lords: 'and between them and the hearse there marched the courtiers of Kazimierz, more than a hundred of them all in black and all greatly moaning and weeping. One threw money left and right to the poor.'

This stream of glorious sorrow processing through the town and up the slope to the cathedral must have been very impressive and served several functions, not the least being to show that it took more than one man, however great, to run a kingdom. The civil service, as it were, remained in place. The sight of more than 50 armoured knights clanking and squeaking up the echoing nave, however, must have added a touch of levity to the occasion. The sarcophagus of the wise old Kazimierz sits at the eastern end of the right-hand aisle, a beautiful rectangular tomb of red Hungarian marble with slim columns supporting a canopy of Gothic tracery and pinnacles which is echoed at the base by the sculpted marble figures of court advisers. The effigy of the king stretched out on the tomb shows a serious, almost classical face; he is bearded and long-haired, wearing simple robes and a modest crown.

To reach this monument in the south aisle it is necessary to pass another dozen equally impressive tombs as well as six of the most exquisite chapels to be seen in any European cathedral. Only four of Poland's 45 monarchs are not buried on Wawel, and with bishops, poets and national heroes taken into account the total number of monuments in the cathedral is considerable. The first chapel on the right inside the west door is the **Holy Cross Chapel (Świętokrzyskie)**. Begun in 1447 for Kazimierz IV and his wife, it is a classic example of the Kraków Gothic style. On the walls and vaulted ceiling are golden, red and vivid green polychromes on a faded blue background which were painted around 1470 in the Byzantine-Ruthenian style, apparently by artists from Novgorod. But outshining even these are the only two Gothic altars to have survived here in their entirety, both beautifully carved and heavily gilded. The paintings on the side panels are both superb masterpieces in their own right; and the chorus of prophets on the Triptych of the Holy Trinity have strikingly knowing and worldly expressions. As if this were not enough for one chapel, the sarcophagus of the king was carved in his own lifetime by Wit Stwosz, and some of the canopy detailing was done by another great sculptor, Jorg Huber of Passau. As you would expect from Stwosz, the faces of the mourners around the base of the tomb show great individuality of expression. This chapel alone is a sumptuous feast for both eye and mind, but there are so many more of equal splendour that a mere sketch must suffice to describe them.

One chapel which must not be missed is the **Zygmunt** in the south aisle, which is the one with the gilded cupola that can be seen from the courtyard. This chapel is judged by many historians of art to be the finest piece of Renaissance architecture in central Europe. Designed around 1510 by the Florentine Bartolomeo Berrecci to the order of King Zygmunt the Old, it was planned as the mausoleum for the latter's Jagiellonian dynasty. Writing from Wilno to the castle administrator in 1517, the king commented, 'We have seen the Italian and his model of a chapel which he is to build for us and which we like.' In such a matter-of-fact way do kings discuss their eternal monuments. He continued with the instruction, 'Take care that he is supplied with as much Hungarian marble as he needs since, as he says, this is better to work than any other and more convenient to be brought over.'

The body of the chapel is hexagonal and made of sandstone which is intricately carved into floral patterns interwoven with fantastic animals and grotesque faces. The red Hungarian marble was used for the great double sarcophagus of the king and his son Zygmunt August and also for numerous medallions and figures that are set in alcoves. Another marble tomb features the sleeping figure of Queen Anna Jagiellonka and portraits of all three royal personages hang over the door, which is separated from the aisle by a large ornamental screen. There are also two sixteenth-century altars in the chapel, one with fourteen beautifully painted scenes, the other intricately worked in darkening silver.

The neighbouring **Waza Dynasty Chapel,** completed in 1676, celebrates the baroque, the interior being painted in dark colours set off by a great deal of gilding. The domed ceiling is a light yellow and white over quite crude alabaster moulding. The best-decorated domes seem to belong to the bishops; Jakub Zadzik's 1650 ceiling, further along the south aisle, is particularly spectacular. **St Mary's Chapel,** which houses King Stefan Batory's tomb, is behind the altar in the ambulatory and is linked to the castle by a passage. It was built in the late fourteenth century with a vaulted roof, but in 1595 it was clad in black marble and the king's tomb recreated in a combination of marble and sandstone by the royal architect Santi Gucci. The impressive things here, though, are the ebony and silver ciborium where the Eucharist is stored and a rather cold-looking royal pew carved from marble.

My personal favourite is the **Tomb of Władysław the Short** which is in the north aisle, balancing that of Kazimierz the Great in the south. Carved some time around 1333, it is the oldest royal tomb in the cathedral and has been executed entirely in cool white sandstone. The king's figure in coronation robes reclines on a sarcophagus sculpted with the figures of 28 mourners. The beautifully proportioned and very Gothic canopy is supported by slim, moulded columns, the whole giving an impression of elegance and dignity. Somewhat less dignified are the innumerable bishops in their wall-mounted tombs, perched precariously on narrow ledges like so many park-bench sleepers.

To give both the ladies and a more recent artist their due, the white marble **Tomb of Queen Jadwiga,** who died in 1399, was carved only in 1902 by Antoni Madeyski and is splendid in its simplicity. In the ambulatory the same queen has a dramatic crucifix from her own fourteenth century which appears to rise out of a barren, rocky landscape and has a silver skull and crossbones mounted below the feet of Christ.

Some of the finest features of the cathedral are the iron doors to the various chapels, once again the result of great craftsmanship and very varied in their design. But not all in the cathedral is elegance and beauty. One horror is the silver bas-relief copy of Matejko's painting of Sobieski entering Vienna in 1683. This melodramatic scene was presented to the cathedral on the bicentennial of the famous battle. Of much more interest is the **Cathedral Treasury,** located behind the sacristy in the north-east corner of the church. This has a collection of extremely valuable, interesting and beautiful items of religious art such as mitres, reliquaries, monstrances, chalices and crosses. The room itself dates from 1500, although the wonderful frieze and vault decorations were painted 400 years later by Józef Mehoffer. The oldest item on display is an eighth-century miniature showing the four Evangelists, and there are many illuminated texts from the eleventh to the fifteenth century. Even the spear of St Maurice, presented to Bolesław the Brave in AD 1000 by Emperor Otto, has survived, but by far the most shocking exhibits are the two gold boxes designed to receive the heads of St Florian and St Stanisław. Both are remarkable products of the goldsmith's craft and both were the gifts of queens, in the fifteenth and sixteenth centuries respectively. Other reliquaries can be pretty gruesome too. That of St Zygmunt appears to hold a bone in a glass cylinder, while the dismembered Florian and Stanisław also have arm-shaped receptacles containing bones. More moving, con-sidering his power, is the simple, even primitive crown of Kazimierz the Great, which looks for all the world like a long-discarded prop from a village *Macbeth*.

Before leaving the cathedral, there are more tombs downstairs in the **St Leonard's Crypt,** the oldest part of the building. These include the tombs of national heroes Prince Józef Poniatowski and Tadeusz Kościuszko and, in an adjoining crypt, that of the pre-war leader Józef Piłsudski. Also underground in a special crypt are the tombs of two of Poland's greatest poets, Adam Mickiewicz and Juliusz Slowacki.

The Polish nation's attitude to its heroes and its history is illustrated by an event which occurred in the cathedral during the nineteenth century. During conservation work in June 1869, stones around the tomb of Kazimierz the Great were accidentally dislodged, revealing the king's remains together with his crown, sceptre, orb and spurs. The painter Jan Matejko was called to make drawings of the grave goods, and after examination by many notables the tomb was closed in the presence of a special commission. It was then decided that a second funeral should be held for the old king, and when news of this became public knowledge it had a profound affect upon a nation enduring partition and with fresh memories of the failed January insurrection of 1863. The writer Józef Ignacy Kraszewski wrote of these events:

> The impression the news aroused in the whole country cannot be put down on paper. It stirred the hearts of all and the thought of a new funeral was born unanimously...Not for a long time have I seen such ardour, such general emotion-...This appearance of the ashes of the great king, law-giver and reformer, together with the Polish crown and sceptre, among the living, on the grave of a Poland torn asunder, had something mystical about it, as if awakening a faith in the future by memories of the past.

According to the local press, half the nation turned up for the funeral, lining the streets of the city as the bells tolled and thoughts of independence were aroused in many hearts. The ceremony, as it turned out, had a double significance, boosting both patriotic sentiments and the coffers of the cathedral; a large number of donations was received, which allowed further restoration work to be carried out.

I do not know what music was played at this second funeral, but I doubt that it matched that of the previous royal interment here in 1734 or of the subsequent coronation of August III, when special music was composed by one Johann Sebastian Bach. The last king of Poland was crowned in 1764 in the Church of St John in Warsaw, and from then on the importance of Wawel Cathedral waned somewhat under the influence of the partitions. But the beauty of the place continued to fascinate foreigners. Of his visit in 1847, Honoré de Balzac wrote:

> So I visited Kraków and saw the glory of the departed Poland, the famous cathedral of Kraków castle...it is full of chapels with tombs and an abundance of treasures which can hardly be matched except perhaps in Rome and some Belgian churches.

Finally, mention must be made of the church towers. Five bells hang in the Zygmunt Tower, including one huge one which is also named Zygmunt. With a diameter of 2.4 metres, it is the largest in Poland, sounded only on Easter Sunday and other special occasions. Legend has it that any girl who has touched the hammer of this bell will soon be married, but the day that I climbed the tower for a view of the city I saw nobody straining to reach it. Its beautiful deep sound travels far beyond the city and is said to be due to Bekwark, the court lutanist, who took his most golden-sounding string and threw it into the molten metal, which was prepared like all the best bells from captured cannon.

Fire seems to have played a more significant role than cannon in the shaping of the royal **Wawel Castle**. 1499 was a particularly disastrous year, followed by a succession of conflagrations a century later. The work done since 1945 is reckoned to be the 21st rebuilding of this royal residence in its long history. Chronicles mention a modest building here in the tenth century and remnants of a small stone structure from that time have been unearthed. Today the castle quite matches the cathedral in opulence, although the architectural splendour of the arcaded inner courtyard is somewhat diminished by the patina of dirt which clings to the white stone. As soon as this is cleaned, the entrance to the courtyard through the Renaissance gatehouse will have even more impact. Not that it is unimpressive now, having a larger courtyard than most of the Italian palaces on which the building is based. The three castle wings and southern curtain wall rise three storeys from the cobbled yard, each level adorned with gracefully columned arcades from which, no doubt, favours were tossed on feast days to jousting knights below. The columns of the first two levels are topped by semicircular arches, while those on the top floor are equally slender but of double height, running up to the eaves. The simple Ionic capitals on all the columns were originally painted.

Quite obviously the architects and builders brought from Italy by Zygmunt the Old in 1500 following the previous year's fire were faced with many problems that did not exist south of the Alps, such as the need for steep and strong snow-shedding roofs. And the quality of light here was more frequently grey than that of Florence — and it was therefore desirable that it should be allowed into the building rather than shut out as in Italy. In consequence, the building which evolved over 36 years on Wawel to replace the old Gothic palace was definitely Renaissance but also different from anything ever built in Italy. In such ways the Florentine style migrated, adapting itself to the circumstances of northern Europe, and was welcomed everywhere for its new lightness and charm. As the fashion spread, kings and nobles competed to have the grandest, most modern palace, and there is plenty of evidence in surviving journals and letters that Zygmunt's new contender created quite an impression upon the many visiting ambassadors and princes who watched it grow or attended its banquets. Considering the heavy Gothic halls to which they were used, that first moment must have been exhilarating, as their carriages pulled through the tunnelled entrance into the colourful courtyard with its pink crushed-brick surface, gallery walls painted with bright frescos and coloured roof tiles.

Today it is the interiors which are likely to cause most excitement, the rooms having been restored wherever possible to the atmosphere of the sixteenth and seventeenth centuries. The north wing, however, was damaged by yet another fire in 1595 and rebuilt by another Italian, Giovanni Trevano, in an early baroque style which gives a quite different feeling to the rooms there. Perhaps the worst days for Wawel were in the nineteenth century during the long Austrian occupation. While Poland was divided under the three partitioning powers, there is no doubt that life in Galicia, as the region was then known, was more relaxed than in the Prussian and Russian areas. There was also less suppression here of Polish culture and language, but this did not stop the military from erecting ugly barracks on the western end of the hill, some of which still remain, or from paying little heed to the precious interiors of the castle, which suffered accordingly.

Finally bowing to local pressure, the Emperor Franz Josef evacuated his troops from the hill in 1880 and allowed the Polish citizens to restore the castle, a slow process but one which speeded up enormously in 1918 when Poland regained her independence. It goes without saying that the years 1939 to 1945 were another low point, both physically and symbolically, when the castle became the seat of the hated Governor-General of the Polish territories, Hans Frank, who was later executed as a war criminal. Fortunately some of the most precious objects, including the tapestries and the coronation sword, were hustled out of the country as the War began, first to Romania, which then had a common border with Poland, and finally to Canada whence, after years of diplomatic pressure, they returned to Kraków in 1961. Many Polish citizens and emigrant Poles throughout the world have contributed valuable and interesting items to the castle, some of which turned up in the world's auction houses after being looted by the Nazis. Wawel's luck, and that of all Kraków, turned for the better in January 1945, when deliberate and intelligent tactics by Marshal Ivan Koniev of the Red Army enabled the town to be liberated without suffering the awful fate of Warsaw.

By my reckoning there are more than 60 rooms in the castle, many of which have been restored and are included on the guided tours. These rooms, including the various royal chambers on the first and second floors of the north and east wings, have been refurnished wherever possible in the original style and according to the function intended for them; Renaissance decoration represents the time of the last two Jagiellonian monarchs and baroque the succeeding Waza dynasty. Without doubt the most valuable and impressive furnishings are the collection of **Tapestries**, the majority commissioned or collected by King Zygmunt August between 1550 and 1565. Considering their history and that of Poland, it is remarkable that 136 of the original 356 tapestries have survived. During the partition period they disappeared into Imperial Russia, only to return in 1921, but even before then King Jan Kazimierz Waza, short of money to wage war in the late seventeenth century, sent them to Gdańsk as security for a loan, and it was nearly 50 years before they could be bought back.

The most gorgeous tapestries are those from the famous Brussels workshops, the main designer of these being the artist Michel Coxcie, who was known in his day as the Raphael of the North. There are three series of them. The first series, made up of eighteen tapestries, shows the stories of Eden, Noah and the Tower of Babel. Among the most stunning is a large tapestry of God blessing Noah and his family after the Flood, which is in wonderful condition, the colours still bright and the detail incredible.

139

The second series, composed of 45 tapestries, portrays landscapes and animals, both realistic and fantastic. One typical example shows a large griffin-like creature in the foreground of a forest, its teeth firmly fixed around the neck of a tigerish beast, while other animals look on from the safety of the trees. If you study the tapestry, you will see that flowers and plants are accurately rendered down to the smallest detail, and even degrees of shade are incorporated into the fabric.

The third series displays the coats of arms of Poland and Lithuania and the initials SA, representing the Latinized name of the king, Sigismund Augustus.

The tapestries, some an enormous nine by five metres, are scattered throughout the castle and dominate every room in which they appear. Goodness knows how many weavers were involved in producing these miracles of the craft, but they obviously represent many thousands of hours of painstaking work. At some stage in its history, at least one has had a door flap cut into it, this apparently being the only way of fitting it into a room.

Wawel's oldest tapestry is on the first floor in Zygmunt the Old's bedroom. It was woven around 1460 by one Pasquier Grenier of Tournai, and depicts the medieval French ballad, 'The Story of the Swan Knight'. This bedroom, together with its adjoining dressing room, has retained much of its original appearance, with splendid Renaissance doorframes, coffered ceilings and a frieze by Hans Dürer, brother of the great Albrecht but not quite in the same class as an artist. There are also many fine pictures and some good Italian furniture in the room but I found, to my surprise, that the dark and heavily carved oak four-poster bed was ordered from England in the latter part of the sixteenth century.

In the north-west corner of the first floor are the remnants of the earlier Gothic building, including a feature easily recognized from the outside, the so-called **Hen's Foot Tower,** a little watch-tower dating from the fourteenth century which contains two small rooms lined with eighteenth-century Cordovan leather from Spain, a common luxury at the time and no doubt valued as much for its insulating qualities as its luxurious appearance. Also in that corner is the later **Zygmunt III Waza Tower,** named after its founder and decorated in an early baroque style, but the thing to look out for here is the striking portrait of a woman by Nicolaes Maes, painted in 1679, which hangs just outside the tower rooms.

In the north wing there are five rooms which alone would furnish a palace or museum in a lesser town, and they illustrate just how rich Polish monarchs were in those long-lost but unforgotten days. One room is arranged in the style of an eighteenth-century palace drawing-room, with decoration and furnishings to suit. The next contains a collection of Meissen porcelain representing the earliest period of its manufacture in the first years of the eighteenth century through to the end of the nineteenth century. The very oldest piece, sensibly enough, is a teapot dating from the days of Böttger, the founder of the Meissen works which still operates in the little hilltop town near Dresden in the German Democratic Republic. Most interesting, though, are the rare figurines of Polish noblemen and women, of which this is by far the largest collection in the country.

The last chamber on the first floor of the north wing is known as the **Silver** or **Merlini Hall,** the latter name referring to Domenico Merlini, who also executed the designs for the Łazienki Palace in Warsaw. In 1786 he renovated the room in the newly fashionable classical style for a rare visit by King Stanisław-August Poniatowski, achieving a remarkable harmony between the new décor and the earlier architecture. It is hung with portraits of notable people of the period, the centrepiece being court painter Marcello Bacciarelli's imposing picture of the king in his coronation robes. Just for a change, all the furniture is Polish.

The most spectacular rooms of the castle all lie on the top floor, and a vivid impression of the fourteen chambers there has come down to us from the pen of the Italian poet Carmignano, who travelled to Poland in 1518 with the entourage of the new Queen Bona Sforza, who was Zygmunt the Old's second wife:

> Here is a great hall faced with wood lavishly sculpted and gilded. Adjacent to it is a room hung with arrases of silk and gold, and behind it another one whose walls are covered with brocade; in yet another hall there is red cloth on the floor and a golden curtain on the wall, reaching from the ceiling to the floor, a gold throne with an orb and a canopy. Nearby, four rooms one after another bedecked with brocade and silk tapestries, in two of them there were also gilded fireplaces and fine wooden doors in stone frames. Similarly furnished was the hall of the coronation feast; in this hall as well as all the others in which guests were entertained, stood a great cupboard on whose shelves was ranged all the silver tableware required for the feast.

141

These were the rooms in which all important state functions took place, and those in the east wing have retained their original wooden ceilings and wall paintings. The most impressive chamber is the **Audience Hall** at the south end of this wing, where the king received envoys and consulted his chief advisers. It no longer has red cloth on the floor, just a couple of precious rugs, but one glance will explain its informal name of **Heads Hall**. The elaborately coffered ceiling is set with handsomely carved heads, looking down from many of the deep lacunas, but sadly only 30 have survived out of 194 that were carved in the 1530s. Those remaining, however, are powerful faces, well known throughout Poland and even available as little plaster models and postcards. The painted heads represented people from all levels of society, from kings and nobles to maids and farmers, one inexplicably showing a woman with her mouth gagged. There is a legend which claims that once, when King Zygmunt August pronounced sentence upon a subject, one of the heads spoke the words '*Rex Auguste, indica iuste*' (King August, judge justly). A theory for this unusual decoration is that the heads were intended to represent the populace and former sovereigns looking down on the king, keeping an eye on him, to remind him that his primary role was that of servant to the people. It sounds a liberal concept for the period, but it must be remembered that for a brief but glorious time Poland was an enlightened society where such notions were commonplace.

The painted frieze below the ceiling is by Hans Dürer and shows man's life from the cradle to the grave in a sequence based upon the text of an ancient Greek story translated and published in Kraków in 1522. There are more of the magical tapestries in the Heads Hall, from the biblical series, showing the Garden of Eden. And there is also the usual ornate and ceiling-high porcelain stove, which was fired through a little door in the gallery wall outside so that neither dust nor soiled servant need enter the sumptuous apartments. Perhaps one of the missing ceiling heads depicted a child stoker — or did democracy not stretch that far? The original throne mentioned by Carmignano disappeared long ago and its place on the low dais has been taken by a simple but stylish armchair. Behind it hangs a heraldic tapestry, and enormous baroque Italian candlesticks stand on either side. All in all it is a splendid room.

Down the corridor is the old **Dining Room**, also known as the **Zodiac Room** because of its frieze of astrological signs, which was painted only in 1929 on the basis of a reference made by a renowned

Dutch mathematician who visited Wawel in the sixteenth century. The tapestries here are again from the biblical series, illustrating the story of the Tower of Babel, and especially remarkable are those showing the Confusion of Tongues and the Dispersion of Peoples. All the way round this floor, in the corridors as well as the chambers, there are quite beautiful pieces of furniture, many of them Italian, as well as fine pictures and many other precious ornaments. Among the pictures, look out in the next room, the **Planet Chamber,** for a portrait of Zygmunt August's goldsmith Caraglio, which is the work of Titian's pupil Bordone.

In the north-east corner towers are the royal Bedchamber, Study and Chapel, all set in the old Gothic portion of the castle. The little **Study** in the protruding Zygmunt Tower is one of the most exquisite and best-preserved rooms in the whole castle. The heavily embossed Cordovan leather wall-covering of the ante-room, the floor and the fine stucco decorations are all original, as are the pictures that crowd the walls. A total of 48 Dutch and Flemish paintings are hung in tight rows, the most notable being a Rubens sketch of 'Achilles Among the Daughters of Lycomedes' and the younger Breughel's 'May Day Festival', but there are many equally fine landscapes and portraits by less well-known artists. The little **Chapel** was built in 1602 during the restoration of the castle and has a window on to the royal bedchamber, perfect for a busy or lazy monarch. There is also a fine triptych which was painted by Kraków artists.

Next door in the north wing is the **Bird Room,** so named because at one time wooden birds were suspended from the ceiling, which sounds an exotic if not eccentric form of decoration. As a memento of this earlier form of display, a frieze and plafond featuring birds was painted by Felicjan Kowarski during the 1929 restoration. The marble doorframe designed by Trevano and the early baroque fireplace which bears the eagle emblem of Poland and the sheaf of the Waza family are, however, original, as is the Cordovan leather wall-covering. Further along the north wing in the **Eagle Room** is an imposing portrait of the young Prince Władysław Zygmunt Waza before he came to the throne, which was painted in the Rubens studio in 1624 when the prince was on tour. The experts have only recently agreed that this marvellous work is actually by the master himself, and it is in Kraków on more-or-less permanent loan from the Metropolitan Museum of Art in New York in exchange for some magnificent suits of armour, of which Wawel had enough to spare.

The final room that must be mentioned is the **Senators' Hall**, the largest in the castle and one of the most impressive rooms that I have ever been in. Its shiny checkerboard marble floor contrasts with an ornately coffered ceiling, each lacuna containing a carved rosette. At one end is a balustraded minstrels' gallery built in 1592, and on the two long walls are large tapestries depicting the Noah story, illustrating the Building of the Ark, the Embarking of the Animals, the Flood, Disembarking and Noah's Thank-offering. This fine space was designed for the meetings of the Senate, but was also used for important state and court ceremonies and even theatrical performances. Today, occasional concerts are given in the room. Incidentally, the reason many of the original marble floors throughout the castle are in such good condition is that, almost as soon as they were installed by the Italian architects, the Poles covered them with wooden floors which were far more practical for the northern climate.

As if all these treasures were not enough for one castle, there is a display in the west wing, the oldest part of the castle, that frequently astounds the uninitiated. Under the title of **The Orient at the Wawel** its stated aim is to 'show the role which was played by the Orient in the life and creative activity of the Polish nation'. Which sounds a bit highbrow considering that most of the exhibits come under the heading of good old-fashioned war booty. The prize exhibits and the ones which everyone comes to see are the truly sumptuous tents captured during the various seventeenth-century confrontations with the Turks, particularly Jan III Sobieski's famous victory at Vienna in 1683. They are quite astonishing in their beauty; truly the stuff of eastern legends, of Hollywood movies of harems and other such Turkish delights. Twelve tents are normally on show, some put up to display their full splendour. The largest of these is an oval three-poled affair which is basically red with finely detailed blue and gold decorations; these are based upon architectural and plant motifs which are typically oriental in form. My own favourite is the oval two-poled blue tent, again decorated in gold, which has the repeated message 'May you be happy and blessed' woven into it. Obviously not a sentiment that was extended to the infidel Christians of Europe. These tents are both high and wide with normal-sized doorways; visitors can walk through them and inspect the suits of Turkish armour that stand solitary guard, empty of the chieftains who were grand enough to take such luxury accommodation to war.

The whole oriental collection fills two floors of the west wing and, to be fair, not all of it is booty. There are many items collected by various monarchs and magnates or presented to them as gifts by eastern neighbours. The rest of the collection consists of Persian carpets and prayer rugs, a few examples of saddlery and swords for good measure, and a room full of glorious Islamic banners decorated in gold and silver thread, all of which were captured at Vienna. Pride of the carpets is the sixteenth-century Paris-Kraków Carpet, a name logically derived from the fact that one piece is in Paris and the other here in Kraków. When it arrived on Wawel in 1785, given by the descendant of a Vienna combatant, the carpet was complete and was used on the steps of the high altar before being vandalized by person or persons unknown. The other name for this product of the Shah's Tabriz workshops is the Paradise Carpet, because the design shows the Garden of Eden. The carpet was woven in the second quarter of the sixteenth century, and it is interesting to compare it with the Flemish tapestries which were produced at about the same time. The Persian style is less realistic in its portrayal of trees, flowers and animals; it is very decorative and altogether lighter in character, as one might expect from that very different climate. It is sensibly displayed so that its willows and cypresses, cherries, almonds and wildlife, both real and imaginary, all woven on to a ground of golden yellow, can be easily seen.

With two more exhibitions still to see, it is to be regretted that there is no café on Wawel where the visitor can pause and ponder one vivid experience before moving on to the next, but so be it. If you like beautifully crafted artifacts, you must not miss out on the **Crown Treasury and Armoury,** entered from the north-east corner of the inner courtyard, however weary you are. There was a treasury in this corner of the castle from the time of Władysław the Short's coronation in 1320 until 1795 when, on the order of the Prussian king, the coronation insignia were looted during the act of partition. Such was the Prussian desire to see an end of Poland for good that in 1809 the royal crowns were melted down to make gold coinage and the jewels were sold off.

By the time of partition, however, the once-rich treasury had already been reduced to a fraction of its former wealth, depleted by the expensive demands of both wars and marriage dowries. A few items were hidden from the Prussians but when in the 1920s historians set about the task of assembling a collection that matched at least the character of the old treasury they faced a difficult task. Much of what is on display today is material that was returned from the Soviet Union, having found its way there during the partitions. The most important of these items is the Sword of State, commonly known as *Szczerbiec*, meaning 'Jagged Sword'. But no sooner had the collection been assembled and put on public display than along came Hans Frank and his Nazi henchmen. The Poles, though, had learned from experience and the treasury was whisked away to Canada along with the tapestries. It was not until 1960 that a new treasury display was opened to view in the very rooms which had been assigned to it in the Renaissance rebuilding.

There are five exhibition rooms. The **Kazimierz the Great Room** has a Gothic ribbed vault supported on a single column which dwarfs the showcases. These contain the oldest relics on display. A ring inscribed MARTINVS and probably dating from the fifth century is obviously the odd man out although it was found near Kraków. It is pre-Slavic and perhaps connected with the ancient amber route down which the Romans traded. Most items date from the thirteenth and fourteenth centuries through to the eighteenth, and are mainly small objects such as enamelled crosses, golden chalices, rings, altar cloths and many miniature royal portraits. The coronation shoes of Zygmunt August, who was only ten years old at the time, are fascinating and a silver eagle made in Augsburg for King Jan Kazimierz is quite splendid. No doubt he could have bought such an item off the shelf; most nations of central Europe have an eagle as their emblem, some looking to the left, some to the right, and one, with very good reason, looking both ways at once.

The **Jadwiga and Jagiełło Room** is again Gothic, the keystones in the cross-ribbed vault bearing the double-cross emblem of Władysław Jagiełło and the Anjou arms of his wife's family. Only three items are displayed here, three priceless survivors of the old treasury. In a case supported by two Romanesque columns is *Szczerbiec*, the early thirteenth-century sword used at so many coronations from 1320 onwards. The hilt, decorated in gold with vines and images of the Evangelists, is a good example of the decorative arts of the period. In a corner of the room is Zygmunt I's sword, made in Kraków in the early sixteenth century and used mainly for dubbing knights. After partition it ended up in Berlin and was eventually purchased by Poles living in England who presented it to Wawel in 1963. The third exhibit in the room is the oldest surviving state banner, thought to have been made in 1553 for the coronation of Zygmunt August's third wife, Catherine of Habsburg. It is made of painted and gilded silk and decorated with the arms of Poland, Lithuania and the Habsburgs, together with provincial emblems.

The third room contains various items of honour connected with **Jan III Sobieski**, the 'Hammer of the Turks'. They include his mantle of the Knights of the Order of the Holy Ghost, made in black velvet with gold and silver embroidery, and his consecrated sword and hat, which were sent by the Pope in honour of his services in defence of Christendom — meaning his defeat of the Muslim Turks at Vienna. The barrel-vaulted fourth room contains horse equipment, banners and parade weapons of great beauty and fine craftsmanship, including round shields and handsome pointed helmets known as *zischagge,* which have a distinctly oriental look to them. The last room contains firearms, many richly decorated with silver or gold, a large display of hunting crossbows and even an eighteenth-century Viennese air-pistol. Strangest of all, though, is a late seventeenth-century Polish axe with a pistol built into it. Awfully ingenious are the ways of destruction, and ever have been.

The final stop on Wawel Hill, for those with the energy left, is the exhibition of **Lost Wawel** which is entered from the open area south of the cathedral. Here in the bowels of the west wing are the oldest Wawel structures, discovered during excavations carried out over the past hundred years. They are viewed from a catwalk which winds through the vaulted basement of what used to be the royal kitchens. Here, under a pavement of armoured glass, the foundations of Poland's oldest known church can be seen, the **Rotunda of the Virgin Mary** dating from the tenth century, with an open grave containing human bones nearby. The winding route continues into a former coach house where there is a collection of Waweliana from the Middle Ages including various everyday items of pottery, metal and bone and some coins found on the site. In the same building is the **Lapidarium** where fragments of Renaissance stonework which was not incorporated into the restored castle are displayed on pedestals. The most decorative items are the sixteenth- and seventeenth-century stove tiles which are all that remain of the original roomheaters, but are enough to show the styles and skills of the tile-makers of that time. They display a great variety of designs, from plants and their flowers through recognizable animals to images of kings, queens and saints, and many are known to have been made by the local tile-maker Bartosz.

All then that is left to do on Wawel is to stagger to the western end of the hill, admire the view over the river and contemplate one final legend. Although mentioned in every history book, this particular tall story first made an impression upon me via the medium of a children's comic-strip book published bilingually in Polish and English and presented to me by a group of Polish ten-year-olds. The legend concerns the beautiful Wanda (in my comic a blue-eyed and wet-lipped American-style blonde bombshell) who inherited the Polish throne at Kraków long, long ago. Of course she was beautiful and wise, but an invading army of Germans threatened the nation. Wanda led her army into the field and routed the Germans but their terrible leader swore he would return time and again until Wanda agreed to marry him and merge their lands. (At this point my comic-strip version has a weeping Wanda, crown on head, bubbling the words, 'Oh how unhappy I am. I will not marry a German.' Prophetic sentiments that have been echoed down the centuries by Polish women.) So she went by night to the edge of Wawel's rock and plunged to her death in the waters of the Vistula, thus saving her nation. Her distraught people poured soil over her tomb until the burial mound that is still visible today was formed. The antagonisms in this part of the world stretch back a very long way.

Wanda's mound, to the east of the city, is now overshadowed by the gigantic post-war steelworks and solid new town of Nowa Huta, a place recommended only to those addicted to 1950s socialist architecture, a distant relation of the 1930s school of British Brutalism. However there is an impressive new church here, built in the 'seventies with the help of Pope John Paul II when he was the local archbishop. There are better outings to be made from Kraków, some of which are explored in Chapter 8, but first there is one important section of the city to see.

If you descend Wawel Hill by way of the south slope and then turn right beyond the Bernardine monastery into Stradomska Street, you will come eventually to the suburb of **Kazimierz,** once a city in its own right that was surrounded by marshy tributaries of the Vistula. Named after Kazimierz the Great, who signed the charter of foundation on 27 February 1335, the new town boasted many assets, including a market place as large as that of Kraków, its own walls, water and sewage systems, and even its own Gun Cock Fraternity to organize defence. Towards the end of the fifteenth century King Jan Olbracht insisted that Kraków's Jews settle in Kazimierz, and this action was to determine the character of the district right up until the Second World

War. As always, there must have been a degree of racism in the king's decision but the immediate cause seems to have been a conflict between Kraków's local guilds and the Jews, many of whom were turning to the crafts for a living. The closed shop became the closed town, but at least in Kraków the Jews had another protected place to settle. At about the same time in Warsaw the Jews were also forced to live beyond the walls of the main town.

From that time Kazimierz developed as a predominantly Jewish town, coming in certain places to resemble a Middle Eastern city, with narrow, twisting streets and handsome synagogues. There was a non-Jewish element in the town, but this tended to be at the western end, up by the river where there are still two interesting churches to be seen, St Catherine's, built in 1363 and the so-called Church on the Cliff, a Pauline monastery. But away to the left of the main road, around the Żydowski cemetery, the inhabitants were all Jewish. In fact the size of the cemetery, which has some very interesting tombstones, and the six synagogues in the district are some indication of the density of the population in the few streets here.

Well worth seeking out is the **Old Synagogue** at No. 24 Szeroka Street, aptly named as it is the oldest example of religious Jewish architecture in the country. Begun at the end of the fifteenth century, it was modelled on other synagogues in central Europe such as those at Prague and Regensburg, but after a fire in 1557 the inevitable Italians were involved in the rebuilding and it is the Florentine Matteo Gucci's structure which stands today. Looted by the Nazis and bereft of its congregation, it is today a more than suitable home for a museum dedicated to the 'History and Culture of the Kraków Jews' with a special section dealing with the tragic wartime period. Needless to say, the Nazis deported pretty well the entire Jewish population to Auschwitz and other nearby camps, and when the peace finally came there were no Jews left to sit in the little workshops or pray at the synagogues. Today, in their place, a tape-recorder plays old religious songs.

Back in the main southbound street, Stradomska, just where it crosses Plac Wolnica, is the large former town hall of Kazimierz, a sixteenth-century building with a crenellated attic, leaning on a rather too large nineteenth-century extension. Today it is the **Ethnographic Museum**, Poland's oldest and largest collection of folk customs and crafts, which also includes items from other Slavic nations. The costume galleries are a feast of gorgeous colours and beautiful

149

hand-made fabrics, the most popular decoration being in the form of wild flowers, varying according to the region of origin. The decorative theme continues in the section of Rural Economy where various cottage interiors from southern Poland are displayed complete with their simple furniture and brightly painted walls. There are several rooms devoted to folk customs which include displays of musical instruments, Christmas cribs and strange animal masks which formed part of ancient rituals. The Folk Art department is another bright and attractive section, showing a rich collection of painting on glass, a speciality of the mountain region south of Kraków. These simple pictures usually show dancing or hunting scenes and are now very popular and widely available souvenirs. There are also fine examples of wood carving, including beehives in human shapes, dowry chests, oil paintings, ceramics, pottery and paper cut-outs. These last vary from region to region; those from the Kurpie Green Forest area of Mazovia are single-colour silhouettes while those from Łowicz and other regions are made up of several layers of different coloured paper.

For those unable to travel out into the villages this museum provides a splendid opportunity to see something of Polish rural life of not so long ago, along with the everyday tools used in the home and the art which decorated the wooden cottages. The beautifully painted 'hope chests' in which young girls stowed their dowries of linen, hand-embroidered table cloths and dresses are rarely seen today but small models, correctly painted, can be bought in any *Cepelia* shop and make attractive and useful containers. The old customs and beliefs illustrated in the museum may seem somewhat arcane to the outsider but many are still enacted today. Even in Kraków some customs have continued down the ages although in many cases it is obvious that the original meaning has become blurred and they are today mainly an excuse to have a good time.

One of these Kraków specialities is *Lajkonik*, which takes place on the day of Corpus Christi and is supposedly derived from a local raftsman's heroic action against the Tartars in the thirteenth century, although its modern popularity owes much to the brightly coloured costume for the central character which was designed in 1904 by Stanisław Wyspiański. In brief, a man dressed as a mounted Tartar, the imitation of a horse hung round his neck, leads a very loud parade from the nearby village of Zwierzyniec right into the old market square. Stops are made at a couple of restaurants for the usual Polish refreshment and at the town hall for a handful of symbolic coins. The

Lajkonik continues on his exuberant way, striking at the crowd with a wooden sceptre whose blow is supposed to bring luck. His path through the crowds is cleared by thirty colleagues in equally colourful dress, and the whole entourage is accompanied by a band playing old Kraków melodies.

Another nonreligious custom is *Sobotki*, which takes place on the shortest night of the year and involves the lighting of many bonfires. Since a great fire in 1850 this event has been banned from the city centre and is confined to Kraków's river bank where it is combined with another ceremony, *Wianki*, which has to do with the martyred Wanda. Processions of brightly lit boats sail past Wawel Hill, also decked out with lights, and girls cast flowered wreaths on to the water, each with a burning candle in the centre. If her wreath sinks, the unfortunate girl in question will die before too long. If it is carried quickly away by the current then marriage will be some time coming. If it floats to another wreath, this means that the caster of the flowers will find a faithful girlfriend. Only if a boy catches hold of the wreath does it mean that the girl will be married soon. This rather arbitrary, even distressing process may well date from the time that young men were so frequently called upon to do battle for their lord that the population of girls exceeded that of available menfolk.

Wreath-throwing in one form or another is still widespread throughout Poland but there are as many customs peculiar at Kraków as there are legends. Every two years in early June, for example, the Days of Kraków Festival commences with a trumpet call from the tower of the Mariacki Church followed by a fanfare from the town hall tower just across the square. A spectacular pageant then follows featuring the Guilds and the Gun Cock Fraternity. A make-believe wedding party enters the square in decorated wagons and a herald reads from a parchment the ritual opening speech, setting in motion revelries that can last for two weeks. The whole thing is an enjoyable arts jamboree with concerts, fairs, exhibitions and two film festivals, culminating in a grand fireworks display.

Of the local religious festivals, *Pucheroki* takes place on Palm Sunday and involves boys from villages around the city sporting inside-out sheepskin coats, tall conical hats and soot-blackened faces. Each with a mallet and a basket of chaff, they knock on doors, and when invited in recite from a large repertoire of set speeches, poems and hymns. Another strange tradition, no longer practised, was *Rękawka* on the second Sunday after Easter, when boiled eggs and honey cakes were hurled from the top of the ancient Krak burial mound to boys waiting below. These days the ceremony has been diluted to a fair held at the Krak mound on the Tuesday after Easter.

All these traditional events happen only once annually and may be missed by the visitor, but the famous Kraków Nativity scenes known as *szopki* can be found somewhere in Kraków at any time of the year. This custom of making a model of the Christmas Nativity scene goes back hundreds of years, some fourteenth-century examples surviving in St Andrew's Church in Grodzka Street. Although this was obviously a religious custom to start with, so many secular and even satirical figures had been introduced into the models by the eighteenth century that they were banned from the town's churches. Nowadays the *szopki* usually show nothing more contentious than Kraków landmarks, Mariacki being the favourite, and are decorated more often than not with coloured tin foil which makes them sparkle in the winter lights. In December new models are displayed in the market square and one is chosen as the year's best. Some of these creations are so beautiful that they are retained as permanent museum exhibits.

8

Tours from Kraków

It is quite normal for a venerable former capital city to be surrounded by old summer palaces, hunting forests and monasteries, all of which Kraków possesses, but this city is unique in having what is possibly the oldest continuously operating industrial site in the world. Just fifteen kilometres south-east of the city centre is the small town of **Wieliczka,** which has been a source of natural salt for at least 5,500 years. Long, long before the Poles arrived in the area, clay vessels were used to produce the highly prized salt by boiling water taken from brine springs and surface pools, a system which was continued until the medieval period, when larger iron pots allowed a great increase in productivity. As the surface deposits became exhausted, mines were dug into the rock salt below in a process which has continued to the present day, with the result that the ground beneath Wieliczka is now riddled with tunnels. The extent of these workings is quite staggering. It is difficult to believe that the tourist route through the mine, which itself takes about two and a half hours and treks through some four kilometres of dank grey tunnels, in fact represents a mere two per cent of the workings, which now descends through nine levels to a depth of 327 metres. New faces are still being opened up in the giant block of salt deposited some 20 million years ago by the warm Miocenic sea which once covered the land. It is estimated that Wieliczka salt extends for about ten kilometres from east to west, at a width which varies between 500 and 1,300 metres, and is up to 400 metres thick. Which is more than a pinch.

In the Middle Ages Wieliczka was a focal point for the European salt routes, boats and rafts carrying solid cylinders of the stuff downriver for export via Gdańsk and wagons hauling the heavy mineral overland, both eastwards and westwards. The salt industry was one of the first to have a strictly controlled system of regulations governing its extraction, and Kazimierz the Great's 'Mining Regulations' of 1368 were by no means the first. Traditionally all minerals belonged to the monarch, and in the thirteenth and fourteenth centuries revenue from Wieliczka accounted for a third of the royal treasury income, paying for wars and palaces alike. Magnates and nobles who were owed favours by the king received mining rights in ample satisfaction and thereby increased their wealth. Estimates suggest that medieval production peaked at about 40,000 tons a year, all hewn and raised to the surface by the muscle of man and horse, some 3,000 men work in the mine.

Visitors enter through a little painted building, not unlike a railway station, sitting over a shaft which was sunk in 1635 but no longer used for commercial extraction. Some 800,000 visitors every year safely descend the 394 winding wooden stairs to the first level of the mine, 64 metres below the surface. The return journey, I hasten to add, is by lift, albeit a clanking treble-decker one. If time allows, it is useful to scan the English-language guide-book beforehand or at least to take it with you, as all the guides are former miners and only a few of them speak English. This will provide you with all you need to know about the place. It is just a shame — and rather unusual in Poland — that the translation seems to have been done by someone with a very fine dictionary but no other knowledge of the language. But it can be disentangled, and it ill becomes an Englishman to mock when it comes to the abuse of a foreign language.

Once underground, the traveller spends much time traversing long, dismal passageways with floors which look like ice and are worn super-smooth by so many shuffling feet. Every few minutes wooden stairs plunge down to another level, and in the giant bell-shaped Weimar Chamber the stairs are fixed to the bare wall and end beside a shallow lake. The most spectacular of the many chambers visited is the **Blessed Kinga's Chapel,** a 50-metre long cavern carefully carved in the early years of this century and adorned with altars, figures, a pulpit, a bas-relief based on Leonardo's 'Last Supper', and even large chandeliers, all carved out of solid rock salt. Kinga was the daughter of a Hungarian king who married the Krakówian prince Bolesław the Shy in 1239, and her association with Wieliczka derives from a legend about a ring she is supposed to have dropped into a mine shaft as she left Hungary, which magically reappeared in a block of salt dug from the ground here in Poland. One of several chapels once used by miners who stayed underground for days at a time before there were lifts, it has incredible acoustics and is often used for choral and chamber concerts.

Tourism is no new thing here, having been well established by the end of the eighteenth century as one of the wonders of the European itinerary. And to ensure that the visitors keep coming, decoration of the mine has continued until quite recently; the place described in the guide-book as the **Brownies'Chamber** was cut in only 1962 by one of a long line of miner-sculptors. It features not little girls with badges on their sleeves but gnome-like characters engaged in the tasks of mining.

Half-way through the tour, when you have visited numerous caverns and gingerly edged around deep lakes, you will come to a subterranean Post Office, claimed to be the only one of its kind in the world. Here, picture postcards of the mine can be bought, franked with a copy of the seventeenth-century Wieliczka town crest and posted. There is also a fairly basic snack bar next to the adjoining **Warsaw Chamber,** a vast hall which serves as a sports arena for the miners as well as a venue for many other entertainments, including — and you must believe it — model-aircraft-flying events. It seems extraordinary that though surrounded by fine countryside the Wieliczkans should want to pursue their leisure activities a hundred metres underground. It is perhaps more understandable in the case of asthma sufferers, for whom the Warsaw Chamber is converted in the summer to a sanatorium. Since 1966 the mine has also housed a permanent hospital for people with respiratory diseases, who are helped by the salt-laden but otherwise pure air. During the war the giant **Staszic Chamber** was put to a more sinister use by the Germans as a secure factory for the manufacture of aircraft parts.

After the scuttling and burrowing, the ever-descending stairways and the pause at the Post Office, the most fascinating part of the whole subterranean tour is kept until last. Down at the third level, 135 metres from a surface which by this time beckons like a promised land, is the **Kraków Salt Works Museum,** which houses a large and splendid display of which the mine can be truly proud. It covers the history of the mine, from the geological formation of the salt beds in the ocean through the early evaporation system of recovering the salt to modern mining and processing techniques. Exhibits range from fossilized date palms and corals to all the mechanical contrivances necessary both to excavate and extricate the still highly valued mineral. Huge wooden windlasses which were worked by teams of horses; ancient installations for fire fighting, ventilation and pumping; a wide variety of tools and safety devices; all this equipment is fascinating, but the well laid-out historical sections are of particular interest. Here models, maps, drawings and documents describe the history of the salt trade, plot the routes taken as it travelled throughout Europe and show how trade fluctuated but never ceased, even in times of war. Documents displayed include ancient licences complete with royal seals and even a copperplate engraving of the mine taken from Diderot's *Encyclopédie*.

The atmosphere of the mine seems to be as conducive to the health of works of art as it is to that of human beings, because there are original portraits on show of many of the famous folk who have visited the place as well as paintings relevant to the history of Wieliczka. The most important visitor must have been the Emperor Franz Josef, who came in 1860 when the region was under Austrian rule, and for this esteemed gent a special horse-drawn rail carriage was built to haul him around the underground portion of his domain. The visitors' book was opened as far back as 1774. An early entry amongst the many eminent names was that of Goethe in 1790, and Balzac's name appears in 1847.

One museum chamber is devoted to the history of Wieliczka town, easily forgotten in the deep down-under. The town site seems to have been occupied for 10,000 years, reaching a peak in the fourteenth century under the patronage of Kazimierz the Great, when it was surrounded by a stout wall to protect the mine and its workers. There is a large and detailed model of the town based on a plan from the 1630s which shows that it was a fine and prosperous place. Sad to say, only a few of those buildings have survived to the present day.

Having spent the better part of three hours underground all that remains for the visitor is to rise in the creaking, clanking lift to the over-bright daylight and purchase the obligatory box of refined salt from a kiosk by the gate. If time permits, one of the surviving town buildings is certainly worth a visit. The wooden **Church of St Sebastian** was built in the sixteenth century but its exciting and colourful decoration was painted early in this century by Wlodzimierz Tetmajer in a style akin to art nouveau. Tetmajer was one of the leaders of a movement known as Young Poland which operated in many fields of artistic endeavour, taking inspiration from nature and the lives of the peasantry; in this it was somewhat similar to the arts and crafts movement of William Morris. Tetmajer carried his beliefs as far as marrying a peasant girl from the mountains, an occasion which inspired Wyspiański's famous play *Wesele (The Wedding)*.

The last place to be mentioned in relation to Kraków lies some 55 kilometres from the city. It is also the most difficult not only to describe but even to contemplate. It is as if all the most evil aspects of human nature that have accumulated since the world began were focused at one time and at this one place on the earth's surface. Perhaps that is why the Nazis called it a concentration camp. But as the world knows, Auschwitz – for which the Polish name is **Oświęcim**— was by no means the only death camp operated by the Nazis in the Second World War; just the biggest and perhaps the best organized. Exact figures are not known, but it is generally accepted that some three to four million people were put to death here on the outskirts of the little industrial town of Oświęcim.

A particular reaction is often expected when the subject of concentration camps is raised and yet we each have our own way of dealing with such horrors, not least those who lived in the vicinity of one. All visitors to Poland are expected to visit Auschwitz or at least one of the smaller camps, but I sympathize with those who are tempted to resist the pressures. In my experience it has been the private contemplation and study of the Nazi atrocities which has been the most revealing, profound and distressing. The actual remnants of the camp are disturbingly ordinary. Ordinary brick huts, ordinary gravel paths, ordinary grass, even ordinary barbed wire. Yet what occurred here during the last war was unspeakably awful. Perhaps if one were allowed to wander alone here in a February dawn one would hear the voices, the cries of children torn from their mothers, the curses of the exhausted and the starved, the cracks of the pistol; and the faces from the many photographs now mounted in the old cell blocks would be even more haunting. But for the visitor to Auschwitz today, it is hard to disassociate the camp from the coach parties, the guides calling groups to order, the crush of too many well-fed people in too small a space. Not that the mood is joyful. Sanitized as the place is, there are still plenty of reminders of what happened, and it is just as moving to see the occasional individuals searching the boards which list the victims, looking for the name of a father, grandparent or other relation, as it is to see the cramped punishment cells, the instruments of torture, the piles of wooden legs and human hair.

What is incredible is not only that some survived the ordeal and just a few managed to escape, but that these people have been able to live on as seemingly stable citizens in the world. As a child of the 'forties I was raised on a diet of newsreels showing the liberation of the camps, the emaciated inmates and the piles of bodies, and having absorbed the facts over a lifetime I still found it shocking when one evening some years ago in Warsaw the subject of the camps cropped up in conversation, and a friend rolled up her sleeve without a word to reveal the awful number tattooed on the inside of her forearm which meant that as a young girl she had been in Auschwitz.

Another camp close to Oświęcim, the remains of which can also be visited, was Brzezinka. Both camps are known to the world by their German names and are often linked as Auschwitz-Birkenau. The sites were carefully selected by the SS leader Himmler and his gang, who wanted somewhere away from prying eyes and yet convenient for the infamous closed trains. Oświęcim was a major rail junction in Silesia and there was a suitable flat, swampy and sparsely inhabited area nearby.

Something in my stomach which may well be cowardice tells me that it is unnecessary to describe in detail the operation of the camps and the lifestyle and suffering of the inmates. Such details should be known, I believe, and told to the generations to come, but much has already been published and the museum at Auschwitz has several publications in English, from a 20-page leaflet to a large book, which describe the two camps and how they operated in gruesome detail. The tour guides are usually camp survivors who feel a duty to the dead to come back and tell their story. For group visitors there will be interpreters on hand. Perhaps the weightiest experience is to sit through the one-hour film show at the Auschwitz Museum where documentary footage and interviews reinforce the horror of the experience. But beware: it is nightmarish stuff and not for the very young or the delicate.

One fact which is very often overshadowed by the enormity of the crimes against the Jewish people is that many others also died in the camps. Following a building programme which used the labour of local Jews and some prisoners from other camps, the first inmates in the 'Konzentrationslager Auschwitz' were 728 Polish political prisoners who had been held in Tarnów Prison. The commandant was Rudolf Höss, a former farm labourer who had served half of a ten-year sentence for murder. Beneath him was a group of SS guards and, at a lower level again, thuggish criminals were employed to keep discipline within each block. It was these last who were often the most cruel, brutal and perverted. As well as Poles, Jews and gypsies, all of whom Hitler had decided he could do without, those imprisoned and murdered under this régime included Austrians, Belgians, Bulgarians, Croats, Czechs, Dutch, French, Germans, Greeks, Hungarians, Italians, Letts, Lithuanians, Norwegians, Romanians, Russians, Serbs, Slovaks, Slovenes, Swiss and Turks. There were Americans and Britons in the camp at some stages of the war. No one was spared in Hitler's quest for *Lebensraum* — living space for his preposterous Reich.

Still to be seen in the Auschwitz camp are the gas chambers and ovens, the parade square, the watch-towers, and that awful entrance gate with its cynical slogan *Arbeit macht Frei*. Each brick hut where the prisoners slept is now labelled with the country from which its occupants came; many of these nations still contribute to the running costs of the museum and have installed their own memorials. Without a doubt the largest group of people imprisoned and destroyed here were Polish citizens, Jewish or otherwise. The fact that there were 35 buildings solely for the sorting and storing of belongings that were taken from prisoners as soon as they arrived will give some idea of the number of people who were 'processed' through Auschwitz. Although 29 of these stores were burnt before the camp was evacuated at the approach of the Red Army, the amount of personal property found in the remaining buildings was astounding. The poignant items included 348,820 men's suits, 836,255 women's outfits, 5,525 pairs of women's shoes, thousands of toothbrushes, shaving brushes and pairs of spectacles, kitchen utensils and even artificial limbs.

Do not visit Auschwitz – or Majdanek, Treblinka, Stutthof or Sobibor – lightly. Do not cram in a visit between a pilgrimage to the Pope's birthplace at nearby Wadowice and a trip into the lovely hills to the south. Look quietly around and retreat, grateful that you can, to read the guide-books and ponder the fragility of civilization. There are many other books to be read that a visit here may send you searching for. Those by survivors are the most revealing and moving; just one that comes to mind which will burn the Auschwitz message into the mind for ever is a dignified account by a Hungarian, Olga Lengyel, who lost her family in the camp but survived to escape as Soviet shells exploded nearby. Her account was published as a British paperback under the title *Five Chimneys*. But to quote Lord Russell, legal adviser at the Nuremberg War Crimes Tribunal and author of a standard work on the subject, *The Scourge of the Swastika:* 'Were everything to be written it would not be read. If read, it would not be believed.'

9

Zakopane and the Tatra Mountains

If palaces and princes have so far taken precedence over landscape on this journey around Poland, then now is the time to forget all the dates and the dynasties and revel in nature's own architecture. Having come as far south as Kraków, it would be folly not to travel just a little further and experience not just exquisite scenery but a region which amounts to a country within a country. The place to aim for, just 100 kilometres south of Kraków, is Zakopane, which despite being the most popular and famous mountain resort in the country is still a small and intimate town. With the exception of the Moravian Gap, the ancient route to the Danube, the whole of Poland's 600-kilometre southern frontier is mountainous. Each region has its charm and its sights, its characteristic architecture and folklore, but if one place is special above all others it is the Podhale region around Zakopane. The name Podhale means 'beneath high pastures' and refers to a small area of foothills running back from the Alpine peaks of the High Tatra Mountains towards the lower ridges of the Beskids, which run from east to west right across south-east Poland. It is an area of sharp green hills speckled with wooden villages which clamber high up the treeless ridges or trail the valley bottoms, at all times watched over by the rocky backdrop of the Tatra Mountains which rise, right on the Czechoslovak frontier, to 2,499 metres (8,200 feet), by far the highest point in Poland.

As Podhale and the Beskid ranges comprise the most accessible, most popular and arguably most beautiful upland region in the country, I will focus here first before following the hills eastwards to the lower and much more scantily populated Bieszczady Mountains, which have less charm but are favoured by those hardy outdoor types who like to nurse their blisters on lonely hilltops. The much older and

160

geologically separate mountain range which lies to the west of the Moravian Gap is a long way off and will be described in the next chapter.

It would be possible, though only just, to get a taste of the mountains on a day trip from Kraków, but this would entail an early start by car. The train is impossibly slow and follows a roundabout route, while the buses, although quicker, are uncomfortable and smoky and stop everywhere. The real problem, though, of allowing only a short time for these mountains is that once people have arrived there they seldom want to leave. The greatest joy of the region is that it has still not been spoilt by overdevelopment, its few hotels being concentrated in the few towns. Which does not mean that accommodation is a

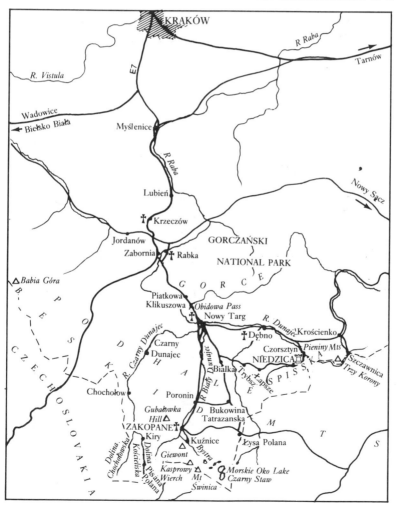

problem, because in every village there are beds to be let, an important contribution to the scanty income of many highland families. Look out for the equivalent of a bed and breadfast sign which reads *Noclegi*, meaning literally 'a night's rest'. This is normally all that you will get, as there is no tradition of serving breakfast in such places. Local PTTK and other tourist offices keep lists of families who take guests and they can arrange bookings, but the most rudimentary phrase-book Polish, or even just the word *Noclegi* by itself, will serve in most villages. And once you have set eyes on some of the wonderful log-built farmhouses, the luxury Kasprowy Hotel in Zakopane may not seem so appealing.

Zakopane, then, is our first destination and one of the easiest to find. The well signposted road heads due south from Kraków, sharing its route for the first sixteen kilometres with the international E7 road before the latter swings away westward to Bielsko Biala. Right from the Kraków suburbs, the road starts to climb through soft and well cultivated hills, and the first of the several ridges of the Beskid Mountains comes just after the town of Myślenice, 27 kilometres from the city. This little town, pleasantly situated on the Raba River and surrounded by hills, received its charter in 1342, and can proudly report that little has happened since. Being convenient for a dash from town, it is popular with Krakowians, offering rugged walking and rather cool bathing from the bank of a mountain river.

From Myślenice the rare dual carriageway reverts to a more appropriate single-lane road which follows the steep and stony Raba, a typical wide and shallow highland torrent, for some sixteen kilometres. After the spring thaw or a summer storm such a river becomes master of its valley, sweeping rocks against its fragile banks and changing course in an instant. The hills here rise to 700 or 800 metres, but you will see only their steep and heavily wooded flanks from the road until you reach Lubień, where the Raba is left behind, and the road climbs through a side valley, past the village of Krzeczów with its sixteenth-century wooden church, and crosses a bare ridge at 660 metres (2,165 feet) from which you can obtain the first distant but clear view of the Tatra peaks.

Far away to the west, the highest peak visible is Babia Góra in the western Beskids, and closer at hand to the east and south-east are the hills of the Gorczanski National Park, a wild area of truly tough terrain. During the last war, this region was the base for many partisan groups who harassed German troops or convoys venturing into the area. But their raids resulted in brutal reprisals against local villages, and it is always something of a shock in these splendid hills to come across memorial stones commemorating such recent conflicts. One would need to be a strategist to understand why the German army came to these parts at all, and had the Germans won their war I do not doubt that these tough highlanders would be fighting in their hills to this day, such is their proud and independent nature.

Some of the great attractions of the Beskids — indeed of Poland — are the little wooden churches which, when found in a complementary setting, can be breathtaking in their charm. Made entirely from local larch, inside and out, with wooden shingles on the roof, they traditionally do not include a single iron nail; everything is held together with wooden pegs and the sheer mass of the timber. Many of the tinier and less well preserved rural ones seem to have grown through the thin soil during some moist autumn night and stand behind their screen of trees looking as natural as yesterday's toad-stools. **Rabka** boasts a wooden church built in 1606 and, although the shingles will have been replaced over the years, the huge timbers of the basic frame are as good as new, seeming to suffer in this climate less than the oak frames of many an English house of the same age. It has an unusually sturdy bell tower whose steeply sloping sides are shingled right to the ground. The tower is capped by a wooden onion dome which itself is shingled, double curves included. Even the stone wall around the little churchyard is topped by rain-shedding shingles. Small as it is, Rabka with its barrel-vaulted ceiling is a cathedral amongst wooden churches. Today it serves a more fundamental deity: it is a regional museum with a rich collection of mountain folk-sculpture, paintings on glass, furniture, pottery and other household items which are traditional to the region.

Back on the main road, there is a restaurant at **Zabornia** which Krakowians recommend for the trout, served with a species of agaric mushroom which is supposed to be the tastiest of Poland's many edible fungi. From here the road climbs over the western end of a forested mountain ridge known as the Gorce, passing at Piatkowa a tiny and quite isolated wooden church. This is said to have been built in 1757 by a traveller who was miraculously delivered from the hands of one of the many gangs of robbers who lurked in these hills, no doubt regarding as fair game any merchant threading his way through to Hungary on the old trade road. The Gorce is a wild area of steep-sided valleys which for the most part can be penetrated only on foot. For those who brave the primal slopes, there is a hostel on the 1,310-metre (4,300-foot) high point which can be reached by way of marked trails, although signs in Rabka suggest that it is a five-hour slog through thick woods with only occasional views and probably more wild boar than people for company. In crossing this ridge the main road reaches a pass called **Obidowa** which is 812 metres (2,664 feet) above the Baltic and from the partisans' memorial here the view is once again stupendous: ridge upon ridge of hills receding through green and grey to a distant blue haze, with the Tatra peaks coming ever closer. At this height the winters can be imagined. In Warsaw the winter temperature commonly reaches $-20°C$. I shudder to think of the conditions up here in a January gale.There are nevertheless a few farms on the top here. It has been my good fortune to come this way many times, the most memorable being on a November day when the snow was already thick on the road and the view sparklingly clear. And there was a time in the late summer, when the valley bottoms were filled with the golden crowns of beech and we crossed Obidowa at sunset: a magical, subdued, red and purple sunset over a horizon of ridges that stretched for 60 or 70 kilometres. I have promised myself that one day I will be there for the sunrise, which must be equally wonderful.

From here the road swoops down to cross a little river at Klikuszowa and then very soon comes into the much wider and flatter valley of the Czarny Dunajec river, which here is more like an upland plain. This is the site of **Nowy Targ,** the capital if not the prettiest town of the Podhale region. Flat as the area seems, the altitude here is still 585 metres (1,920 feet), and the residents certainly consider themselves to be highlanders or, in Polish, *góral.* Much of Nowy Targ still has the atmosphere of a small and simple market town, especially on a Thursday when the roads are thick with horse-drawn carts taking farmers and their families, plus the odd colt or couple of pigs, to the market. This muddy yard may not be Harrods, but everything from a horseshoe to the giant workhorse himself is bought and sold here every week. This is not a place for plastic buckets and Hong Kong watches, but the hard bargaining centre for supplies essential to the *góral* farmers, many of whom will be dressed for the occasion in their best white flannel trousers embroidered with flowers and a skinny black hat, which is shaped like an upturned soup plate and decorated with the tiny white shells to be found in the local rock.

If you like the feel of handmade pots and pans, baskets and brass sheep bells or old-fashioned hand tools then **Nowy Targ Market** is the place to shop. Most luxurious of the bargains to be had is the thick hand-spun wool which is sold from big plastic bags by a line of talkative farmers' wives. It can be purchased in large creamy hanks or already made up into heavyweight sweaters adorned with traditional patterns around the neck. Still smelling sweetly of the sheep's natural lanolin, this wool performs just as efficiently on the back of a farmer or a Warsaw secretary as it did on its original four-legged owners. As well as one of these sweaters, my prize purchases here have included delightfully old-fashioned wooden toys and a solid brass bell. Along in the little town square, its cafés and restaurants packed solid on market day, there may seem to be an abundance of shoe shops. This is explained by the fact that in the woods outside the town is Poland's largest and newest shoe factory; the source, incidentally, of many of those desert boots which lurk at the back of British high-street window displays.

As well as having a market and producing seven million pairs of shoes a year, Nowy Targ has other claims to fame, such as being the ice-hockey capital of Poland and possessing a building where Lenin was held on charges of spying during the period he spent living down the road at the village of Poronin. Surprisingly for a place which before the railway came must have been very remote, Nowy Targ is an old town, first mentioned in the thirteenth century and with a town charter dated 1346. The reason for its existence is the familiar one: trade routes intersected here as they wound their way through the hills. Close to the market square, the nave of **St Catherine's Church** dates from 1606 and its presbytery from way back in 1364, while across the Czarny Dunajec river there is a larchwood church which has two Gothic pictures incorporated into the main altar. I am sure that many prayers were said and many candles lit in these two churches on the night of 29 January 1945, the day that the Red Army came into the town and engaged German troops in a fierce battle which left more than 1,200 Soviet soldiers in the local cemetery.

You may want to leave Nowy Targ for the return journey or a Thursday outing from Zakopane, for now that the mountains are so close the temptation is to press on those extra 20 kilometres and stare up at the great rock wall of the Tatras. The road, too, makes a beeline up the straight valley of the Biały Dunajec before curling westward around the great sheltering dome of Gubałówka Hill to end in the long and busy high street of **Zakopane**.

This town feels quite different to Nowy Targ, having no market place and nothing ancient, however fine its older wooden houses are. Until the middle of the nineteenth century, Zakopane was a small mountain village, a collection of timber farmhouses whose occupants scraped a living from small flocks of long-legged sheep which were driven up to the high pastures in summer and shut up for the winter in the large barns still built into every farmhouse. The only hint of industrial activity was some simple metal-working, using ores which were extracted from the mountains just to the south of the town. Its discovery as a healthy and attractive place for city folk to spend their holidays follows the usual pattern of a chance visit by a doctor who then recommended that tubercular and other patients come to stay in the clean, pine-scented atmosphere, a turning point coming with the arrival of the railway in 1899. At the end of the last century Zakopane and the Podhale region were taken up by artists, writers and musicians from the Austrian-controlled south of Poland, and many fine works were dedicated to or based upon the life and landscape of the area. Other notable residents were the poet Jan Kasprowicz and the composer Karol Szymanowski, whose villa is now a museum in his honour.

Today Zakopane is an all-year-round resort, peaking in summer, when the main street is clogged with the big boots and rucksacks of rock climbers and mountain walkers, and again in winter, when even the horse-cabs wear skis. There are several ski lifts in the area, as well as cable cars to the top of Gubałówka and to the rocky peak of Kasprowy Wierch, 1998 metres (6,522 feet) up in the High Tatras, from where there is a fantastic view back over the Beskid ranges and south to the even higher peaks of Slovakia. As is so often the case, late spring and early autumn are perhaps the best months to visit. In May the pastures and valley floors, untouched by agricultural chemicals, shimmer purple and violet with crocuses, while higher up the tall spruces give way to dwarf pines and edelweiss, fading into tough grasses and little saxifrages until, near the summit peaks and ridges, only mosses can survive on the bare rock.

If you have not booked in advance, the main hotels are likely to be full, so the first task upon arrival is to seek out a room, either directly or with the help of the PTTK office in the main Ulica Krupówki, just a few steps up the hill from the junction with Ulica Kościuszki. Then can you relax and enjoy the town. Zakopane is spread none too densely down its valley, and only the short Kościuszki Street and the long, sloping Krupówki have any of the feeling and architecture of an ordinary town. Krupówki is a pedestrian-only promenade and the place to go for cafés, restaurants and most of the town's shops, many of which sell a mixture of locally crafted goods and phoney souvenirs. When they are open, that is. Late opening, early closing and long lunch hours seem to be a speciality here, as elsewhere in Poland.

There are two places not to miss. One is the first café up the hill on the left, just past the PTTK office, a large, smoky and undistinguished room which in recent years has featured a succession of ageing Bohemian pianists adept at lazily throwing off a few jazzy improvizations before slipping off to rejoin the gossip and cards at a corner table. The fare here is limited to the usual black tea and over-rich cakes, but the cosmopolitan clientèle who mix city with mountain fashion gives the place a warm and friendly atmosphere which I once jeopardized by trying an experiment. It is the absurd custom in Poland when serving tea to deliver to the table a glass of hot water with a tea-bag neatly laid beside it in a saucer. The problem is that, Polish service being what it is, several minutes may have elapsed since the water met the glass, with the result that the tea-bag sinks but does not infuse. Poles are accustomed to this system, but I chose Zakopane as a place to complain, requesting that the waitress return to the kitchen and put the tea-bag in the glass before adding water which ideally should be boiling. To cut a long story short, I did eventually get my tea, but the fact is that much remains to be learned in this fascinating country about the niceties of catering.

The other epicurean high spot of the street is further up the hill on the right where, on a corner and overhung with trees, there is a rather seedy establishment with the international name of Cocktail Bar. Seedy it may be, with dreadful lampshades and chipped plates, but it does serve beautiful cakes and amazing ice-cream concoctions. Top of the range is *ambrozja*, a delightful indulgence consisting of four scoops of different-flavoured ice-cream garnished with nuts, cherries, frozen strawberries and sauce and served with a large wafer biscuit. Less exuberant, and less costly, confections are also available.

Krupówki continues up the slope towards the ever-present peaks, soon thinning to a tree-lined avenue of timber villas built in a rich turn-of-the-century style, but if you follow the street and its little parallel stream back downhill and past Ulica Kościuszki with its large hotels to right and left, you will come to the **Tatra Museum,** a large wooden building above the road just at the point where sad, patient horses wait in the sahfts of old *dorožkas*, the horse-cabs. Their drivers will doubtless be old, wizened and dressed in a rather grubby traditional outfit of white felt trousers with red pompons at the ankles and a flat *góralski* hat. For a fee, this team will transport you around the leafy town or up to the cable car at Kuźnice.

The museum is dedicated to Tytus Chałubinski, the doctor who first realized Zakopane's potential, and contains good ethnographic and natural history sections as well as an extensive library of the region. Here you can see the highland costumes at their pristine best and study the beautifully embroidered work which is still carried out by the highland women, young and old alike, during the claustrophobic winter months while the woodpile diminishes and the triple-glazed windows prove their worth.

I remember struggling in an old Morris Minor car to reach friends in a village high above Zakopane during the winter of 1981. I walked the final kilometre in finger-nipping cold, only to enter a hot fug of positively tropical humidity, generated by the one main clay stove in the kitchen which is used for both heating and cooking. Such is the insulating property of the tree-thick timber construction of these houses, every gap caulked with decoratively twisted pine bark, that no heat escapes. Fortunately the hills still provide a plentiful supply of firewood. On the day of my visit, a dozen village girls were assembled in the house to receive instruction in a certain stitching technique from a visiting expert employed by *Cepelia*. Thus do the tentacles of central planning reach deep into these hills, with the result that there has been a certain standardization of designs over recent years, although there is still scope for individual skills to shine and local patterns to survive.

When shopping for embroidery or other local items such as *kierpce*, the thin leather shoes with decorative brass buckles which are worn by the *góral* men and women and appear more suited to the Maghreb than to these mountains, the thing to watch for is a *Cepelia* shop that is closed when it should be open. This indicates that a new delivery of goodies has been received, for it is normal practice to shut out the customer whilst the shelves are restocked. The trick then is to be there early for the reopening in order to get the best choice of items which, being individually made, are often few in number.

Further down Krupówki from the museum and on the right-hand side is the main **Zakopane Church,** a strange grey stone building totally out of keeping with the traditional styles but no doubt representing the new wealth brought by tourism when it was erected early in the century. The older wooden church is in Ulica Kościeliska, which crosses the very bottom of Krupówki, and overlooks the place where village ladies sell vegetables and cheese. The latter is made from ewes' milk and is sold either as a soft paste or smoked and moulded by decorated wooden presses into little golden-brown barrel shapes: very decorative but salty. The little wooden church, although built only in 1847, is very traditional. Today it is visited mostly for its surrounding graveyard, where many of the writers and artists who took to the hills a century ago now lie. Fresh flowers still decorate many of the tombs, some of which are carved from wood by local sculptors.

Followed westwards, Kościeliska will lead you out of town past splendid wooden villas but, before making one of the many walking excusions into the mountains for which Zakopane is the ideal base, it is worthwhile to ascend **Gubałówka Hill** by way of the funicular railway, which departs from a station just beyond the cheese market. The top of this hill is a rounded ridge running from east to west at a height of more than 1,100 metres (3,600 feet) and provides a spectacular view back across the town to the broken peaks and ridges of the Tatra. The peak closest to Zakopane and the one which dominates the town is the famous **Giewont,** easily spotted because of its summit cross and its shape, always likened to a sleeping knight. This vantage point of Gubałówka is well served by a café and by locals selling souvenirs and sweaters. It is also conveniently situated opposite the centre of the Tatra range, thus presenting a panorama of the possibilities available to the walker or climber. The peaks to the west are predominantly limestone; those to the east, harder and higher, are granite. Even from here, the very topmost peaks of the range are just out of view, and these present many climbing challenges although they are lower than the Alps and have no glaciers. The winding frontier with Czechoslovakia has never been difficult for a determined person to cross and many times in the past people out of favour with the authorities have gone up the long high valleys and over the ridges to what was, until 1918, the Hungarian territory of the Habsburg Empire. In the last war, villages in the area acted as transfer points for couriers taking news of the Nazis' activities to a government in exile and a disbelieving world.

For those who do not want to penetrate the Tatra valleys, where the most dramatic walks lie, there are many hours of splendid walking to be had from Gubałówka itself, all within view of the main range. One well marked trail leads westwards down a soft ridge and through a long straggling village to the remarkable **Chochołów,** a long street of timber houses which is now a protected zone, a living exhibition of mountain architecture which includes No. 24, known as One Fir Tree Cottage. It must have been some tree: four and a half horizontal logs were enough to reach from the ground to the eaves. As with the churches, nails and glue are not necessary for these great balks of timber, which are cut to slot together rather like a children's building set. From here it is a 20-minute bus ride back to Zakopane.

Walking east from Gubałówka leads down to the main Kraków road close to the Lenin Museum at Poronin, where the great man's statue stares thoughtfully across a pond and from where it is but a short bus ride back to town. For the determined walker, however, one of the most fabulous views is to be had by continuing on the marked trail up the steep hill behind Poronin to the rolling hilltops, where scattered farmsteads litter the rich green slopes which in summer are speckled with tiny pyramids of drying hay. The hedgeless fields are cultivated in patches and strips, each a different shade depending upon the crop and the time of year. In the autumn, you will see brown patches where women in headscarves and children pick potatoes that have been turned up by a special horse-drawn contraption.

It is possible to reach this magical place by car, turning sharp left at the village of Bukowina Tatrzańska and following a narrow road up the bare hillside, from which there are breathtaking views in all directions. Right at the point where the hills start to fall away westward, seemingly miles from anywhere, a new church is being built by the old methods. I say 'being built' because on my last few visits it seems not to have progressed very far; so it may still be possible to catch the highland carpenters at work with their adzes and chisels, cutting large and beautiful joints in the honey-coloured timbers. Look especially at the doorframes for a fine example of large-scale and decorative dry jointing. The best thing about this church, though, is the fine silhouette it cuts, its little shingled spire seeming quite timeless against the sky.

Far less attractive is the new church down in the village of Bukowina Tatrzańska. This is a great white concrete and glass affair which quite dwarfs the old wooden church now being left to rot next door. The locals of course are proud of it, however incongruous it may appear to an outsider. Bukowina itself runs down a ridge and contains some splendid individual houses, many of which are very new, but it lacks much of the charm of the less tightly packed farmsteads on the hills all around. Nevertheless it is a good place to stay, having many private rooms available, a couple of shops and a restaurant which serves plain local dishes. It is also just fifteen minutes' drive from Zakopane.

Beautiful as this Podhale region is, the serious business of Zakopane is the High Tatras. For 30 years, or so, these mountains have been a National Park on both sides of the frontier and, in an effort to protect the natural flora and fauna which has survived so far, even the grazing of sheep has been banned on the high pastures, the *hala* from which the name Podhale derives. The many shepherds' huts which provided summer shelter through the ages now stand empty but although the bare peaks and wooded valleys may seem still and silent they are not devoid of life. For the skilled and patient naturalist there is the chance of seeing the chamois, marmot, lynx and golden eagle, and, preferably from a distance, the brown bear as well.

You can explore the Tatras from the top or the bottom. In order to start at the top, wandering along the high ridges with the whole world far below, yet escape the pain of actually climbing up there, the place to head for is **Kuźnice,** about three kilometres from the centre of Zakopane by way of Krupóski and into the valley of the little Bystra stream, called the Dolina Bystrej. Here there is a cable car, jam-packed in winter with skiers, which sails above the pine forest and up past rocky crags to the terminus which is close to the summit of Kasprowy Wierch (1,985 metres; 6,512 feet). The journey takes about 20 minutes and is carried out in two stages.

The summit of Kasprowy Wierch is right on the Czechoslovakian frontier and is the starting-point for several marked trails, all of which are clearly shown on the National Park map, a yellow folding affair called the *Tatrzański Park Narodowy.* This is widely available, as is a very useful guide-book called *Tatry Polskie,* which details individual routes in several languages. If you intend to walk in the mountains, take both these publications, for safety's sake. The different routes are colour-coded and the average times taken to reach various landmarks are given on signs. The toughest ridge walk, only for those with the footwear, clothing and experience to cope with the variable mountain weather, takes you eastwards and upwards to the peak of Mount Świnica and then along a difficult and spectacular rocky ridge known as the Orla Perć (Eagle Path) from which several descents are possible; some of them, however, reach the valley bottom quite some distance from Zakopane. It is a long but exciting and dramatic route over sharp granite peaks with sheer cliffs dropping several hundred metres to icy glacier lakes, the most famous of which is Morskie Oko (Eye of the Sea). From here there is a bus service back to town, some 20 kilometres away.

But there are easier routes from Kasprowy Wierch which any sensible and fit person can enjoy, the obvious ones being the yellow and green trails back down the mountain to Kuźnice. This way you have all the sensation of being on the open mountain without the uphill slog, but be warned: wear only sensible shoes and respect the weather. The mountain, after all, is quite high and subject to its own rapidly changing climate. Forecasts are readily available both in town and at the summit. The most popular choice for cable-car riders, of course, is simply to stay on the summit, admire the views from the restaurant and maybe trot along the nearby ridges for a few minutes before returning to base by the cable. From Kuźnice it is also possible to walk by a relatively easy route to the summit of Giewont, a trek of about three hours. From here there is a choice of several descents, down ridges or by way of lovely valleys.

For those who prefer mountains to be above rather than below them, there is an even greater choice of walking routes to explore. Many valleys run north out of the mountains and into the larger east-west valley which houses Zakopane, the two most accessible and beautiful being Dolina Chochołówska, in the extreme west of the National Park, and its eastern neighbour Dolina Kościeliska. Both can be reached by car or bus by way of Ulica Kościeliska, the entrances to the valleys being about six and eight kilometres respectively from town.

Dolina Chochołówska is the longest valley in the whole range, a narrow strip of meadow following a swift stream far back into the hills, and the advantage here is that there is a car park some way up it, providing splendid scenery for anyone unable or unwilling to walk very far. An hour's flat walking from the car park leads beneath high ridges to a mountain hostel and café set above a lovely meadow with dark pine forest all around it, out of which steep limestone crags emerge. Above the meadow is a tiny wooden chapel which adds a fairy-tale aspect to a scene which could have come from a children's story book. Beyond the hostel the path becomes steeper, rising eventually to the 2,000-metre (6,562-foot) ridges and summits of the western Tatra. Be careful not to descend beyond the ridges because in doing so you will be making an illegal entry into Czechoslovakia, and border guards patrol even at those heights.

There are several little side valleys before the hostel which provide a good stiff climb through the trees to the eastern ridge and it was half-way up one of these on a fine autumn day that I heard the unmistakable bellow of a brown bear come rolling down from the pines; a sound both thrilling and chilling, very *basso profondo*. Beyond that ridge is **Dolina Kościeliska,** long regarded as the loveliest of the Tatra valleys. This has the added interest of a vast network of deep limestone caves, including the Jaskinia Mroźna, Frosty Cave, whose walls are permanently covered in ice. No cars are allowed in this valley, but a horse-cab — or in winter a horse-drawn sled — can be taken from the entrance at the little village of Kiry, travelling the three kilometres to Pisana Polana, Pisana Glade. The track passes through the narrow rocky defile which made the upper valley an easily guarded hideaway for the robbers of old who, legend has it, played out their Robin Hood lives in these hills. According to one of these legends, the caves here are full of treasure left by the robbers, and sleeping knights are hidden nearby who will rise at an angel's signal to defend their country. This whole idea of treasure no doubt derives from the silver mining carried out in the hills centuries ago.

Beyond Pisana Polana the valley narrows again as it breaks through a craggy ridge into a magical upper valley which is now a strictly controlled nature reserve. Half an hour's walk here leads to a modern but traditionally styled hostel which is open all the year round and from which two marked trails lead out of the valley, one climbing south-east for a kilometre or so to a small lake trapped high on the slopes amidst pine forests, the other heading westwards over a high pass to the Chochołówska Valley.

A few hours devoted to the Kościeliska will leave many intense memories of the Tatras and, for the photographer, a feast of pictures showing high foaming waterfalls, fantastic rock outcrops and snow-capped summits, all with that special mood induced by rock, sky, pine and water. For the hardy walker there is at about 1,200 metres a long trail which travels from Kuźnice all the way along the contours to Chochołówska, winding its way up and down all the valleys and a stiff walk by any standards.

One final mountain outing from Zakopane has already been mentioned. The long and winding road to **Morskie Oko Lake** in the granite peaks of the eastern Tatra sees much traffic in the summer season, some of it branching off at Łysa Polana to cross the river which marks the frontier there, as remote a customs post as one could wish for. As an islander I still find it strange to travel along a forest road knowing that the unfenced far bank of a little stream just ten metres away belongs to another country, but that is how it is here before the road climbs through the trees to a car park beneath the highest peaks in Poland. From here it is a fifteen-minute walk to the shores of Morskie Oko lake, the largest of the hundred or so glacial pools trapped hereabouts. Lying beneath sheer rock cliffs which rise up a further thousand metres, this clear, deep lake will seem either frightening or exciting, according to the mood of the day. In summer it can be exhilarating, the fresh clean water spilling from the lake down into the forested valley. In winter the atmosphere is chilling; the lake dark and forbidding, the cliffs rimed with ice, and the road from the car park a trudge through deep snow. Experienced climbers use the hostel beside the lake as a base for some of the most difficult climbs in the Tatras, but there is one stiff little ascent which offers no technical problems in summer and is popular with ordinary mortals. This is the red route, which climbs up to a low ridge from which there is a view down on to an even higher lake, Czarny Staw or the Black Pond.

The Tatra Mountains, then, really do offer delights for most tastes and abilities. Some people get no farther than the hotel verandah or the ice-cream parlour, while others stay on the hills for weeks carrying all they need on their backs, but there are many wonderful walks which fall between these two extremes. Although these are the highest mountains in the country, and the only range with truly Alpine qualities, there is plenty more rugged country in the south. Just a short distance away, to the east of Nowy Targ, are the **Pieniny Mountains,** which make up another protected National Park and are long established as a holiday haunt. Never having been scoured by glaciers, the Pieniny has richer and more varied flora than the Tatras and many little plants and even some animals which in Poland are unique to the region. The highest point, **Three Crowns Peak (Trzy Korony)** is less than 1,000 metres high, which is lower than some of the villages around Zakopane, but provides a marvellous view back across Podhale to the high mountains just 30 kilometres away. The best centre is the resort town of Krościenko or its neighbour Szczawnica on the Czarny Dunajec river, and the obvious route from Zakopane is back up the main Kraków road to Nowy Targ and then east along the broad and pleasant Dunajec valley. There are, however, a couple of alternative routes and both involve following the road through the village of Bukowina Tatrzańska as it curves northward past the old houses of the straggling village of Białka and cuts across to Nowy Targ, entering, as it were, by the tradesman's entrance. If you are not planning to visit Nowy Targ, there is a fascinating road for the adventurous driver which turns off beyond Bialka and heads east through the hamlets of Trybsz and Łapsze, where tourism has yet to encroach and the road belongs more to children, geese and hens than to any through traffic. This road meets the Dunajec at Niedzica, where a fourteenth-century castle is poised romantically above the river.

A strange tale is told of **Niedzica Castle** which, though it may be hard to believe, concerns the lost Inca people of South America. It is said that the widow of the last descendant of the Inca rulers lived in the castle in the eighteenth century and in 1797 hid here their last will and testament, which contained information about the legendary treasure supposedly deposited in Lake Titicaca. It is also said that a document in a strange script was found in 1946 but what happened to it after that I have been unable to discover. The castle stands in a suitably remote spot for such a tale, but its site was also critical for reasons of defence, for this has long been a frontier zone, the present Czech frontier being just two kilometres down the road. As if one castle were not enough, there are the remains of another across the river and back upstream a little way at Czorsztyn, where the road to Krościenko turns off and climbs over the hills.

To reach this same spot by way of Nowy Targ does have one great advantage, however, in that it passes through the village of **Dębno**, just twelve kilometres west of Czorsztyn. This is worth a diversion at any price because its church is one of Poland's most precious monuments of wooden architecture, with an interior of unrivalled exuberance for a country church. The building itself dates from the fifteenth century and is typical of the region, a charming wooden structure protected by trees and a timber stockade. Delightful as its external appearance is, its real treasure is the painted interior decoration done around 1500. Every square centimetre of the ceiling and walls, it seems, is covered with a bewildering variety of patterns, creating a quite breathtaking effect which is augmented by a large and eccentric chandelier, a monstrance out of which stares a single eye, ornate wooden crosses, Gothic sculptures and a golden sixteenth-century triptych. It is a unique place, miraculously preserved. When newly done, its colours shinier and brighter than they are today, the little church must have represented a fragment of heaven on earth for those scratching a living in what has always been one of the poorest regions of the country.

Before leaving this valley, those brave enough to make the famous journey by water through the limestone gorge carved in the Pieniny by the Czarny Dunajec river must go to the landing stage below Niedzica castle and book a place on a raft, if this has not been done in advance from a hotel or local tourist office. Exciting as the nine-kilometre descent of the swift waters is, the raftsmen are experts and the dangers negligible. The river twists and turns so much in cutting its course that it seems the raft will be dashed against the rock walls towering overhead, but the current always carries the raft safely on to the next dramatic corner. The rafts are sturdy affairs with seats, each controlled by two men, one at either end, with long poles which serve as both oar and rudder. For most of the journey the right bank is Czech territory and, in the first few kilometres before the gorge closes in, the river flows past several little villages which are the homes of Slovak farmers, although this region, known as Spisska, was for many centuries the subject of dispute between Poland and Hungary, which was then its neighbour. No doubt this see-sawing of political mastery left the independent-minded locals unmoved, the structure of village and family outweighing any influence from a distant capital, north or south.

10

The Beskid and Bieszczady Mountains

The long chain of the Beskid Mountains was not colonized to any great extent until the fourteenth and fifteenth centuries and then it was inhabited as much by people from the south as from the north, a significant number being Wallachians, whose natural domicile was, and still is, the hills and plains of southern Romania. Scholars maintain that their influence can still be detected in dialect as well as architecture and folk design, similar patterns emerging right along the serpentine range of the Carpathian Mountains. Later settlers included Hungarians, Slovaks and Germans, reflecting the fact that until modern times frontiers have been an imprecise and flexible phenomenon, and also that mountain people often have more in common with each other than with their compatriots from the city and the plain.

It is not easy for the traveller passing through to get a true flavour of the seasonal grind of mountain life, but neither is it too difficult to imagine. Work hard to survive, play hard towards an early grave; this seems on the surface to be the name of the game. The problem is that most of the social activities, especially in the long winters, revolve around the bottle, and it is quite common for a village wedding party to last for a week, the supply of vodka seeming never to dry up, the fiddle band playing on and the table of cooked meats and cakes being continually replenished. I have survived the early hours of Podhale weddings, watched the leaping dancers, often men together, marvelled at the brilliance of the embroidered clothes and seen the bride crowned with flowers in an age-old ceremony. The best chance of seeing mountain folk in all their finery is to watch out for a church that shows signs of great activity on a Saturday and wait for the

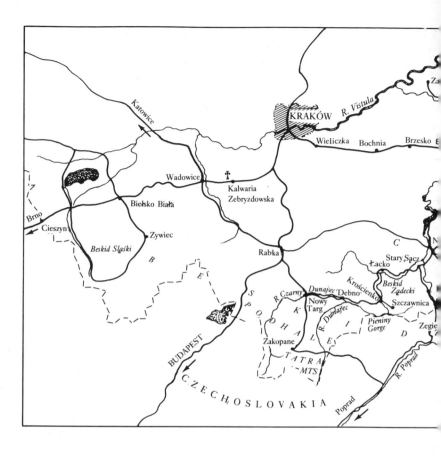

wedding group to emerge. In many villages the whole party will then walk in procession to one or other of the family homes, where the tables will be creaking under the combined weight of food and bottles.

When the Czarny Dunajec river, including the whole length of the Pieniny gorge, became an international frontier, it inevitably made life complicated for those locals who had land or traditional grazing rights on both banks, and a traveller in the area 50 years ago reported that each horse and cow had its own passport, only the geese and dogs going back and forth unchecked. I like to think that each of these

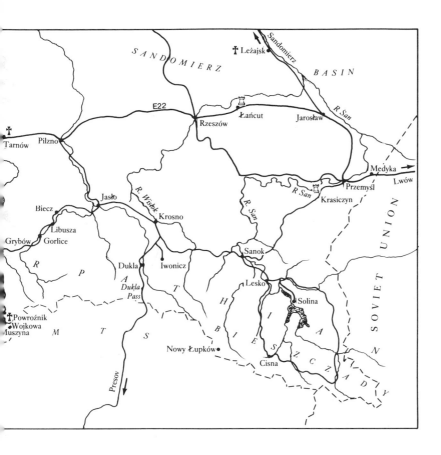

farmyard passports bore the usual unflattering photograph of the holder.

Once through its dramatic gorge the Dunajec flows north, past the holiday centres of Szczawnica and Krościenko, and then around the western end of another ridge of the outer Carpathian chain. This ridge is known as the Beskid Sądecki, a tangle of deeply incised valleys and thick forests which are scantily populated and have very few roads. Those roads that do exist here follow the routes carved by rivers, and from Krościenko it is a lovely drive along the left bank of the Dunajec, beneath green hills and past many small villages such as Ochotnica where a fierce battle was fought in October 1944 between Nazi troops and partisans living in the surrounding hills; a monument records the details. A few kilometres on and the river turns right into a broader valley with lower and more densely populated hills rolling away to the north behind the little town of Lącko which, surprisingly at this altitude, is one of the famous orchard centres of Poland and also a centre of folk art and dance, something best seen in mid-May during the local festival of Apple Blossom Days.

The main town of this area is Nowy Sącz, 28 kilometres further down the ever broadening valley, but ten kilometres before you reach it is the much smaller **Stary Sącz**, situated just before the Dunajec river is joined by the Poprad which cuts through the centre of the Beskid Sądecki Hills from the south. As its name implies, Stary Sącz is the older of the two settlements, being first mentioned in 1163, but the charm of the place lies today in its smallness and in the complete lack of architectural pretension in its market square. The prevailing atmosphere is of somewhere the past couple of centuries have passed by without leaving a trace. Even now few concessions have been made to the present age, although I cannot believe that the surface of the market square will stay as it is for very much longer. It is metalled with giant river pebbles, many as big as a man's head. Twisted ankles apart, the problem is that this is the designated town car park and, to be frank, Stary Sącz would not be my favourite place to suffer a collapsed suspension. The simple and open atmosphere of this square is due to the fact that all the surrounding houses are both old and low, the whole ensemble having the autumnal patina of somewhere recently deserted, which in a sense is what has happened — all recent development has taken place down the valley in Nowy Sącz. Perhaps fittingly, the fortified Gothic church and its neighbouring convent just to the east of the square are dedicated to 'Poor Clare'. The parish church, to the south, is also Gothic, dating from the thirteenth century, but, interesting as these edifices are, a few minutes spent absorbing the atmosphere of the eighteenth-century houses in the cobbled square is likely to leave a deeper impression.

As for Nowy Sącz, I am going to suggest that you take the pretty route there, even though it is ten times longer than the direct way. This road and a railway line follow the long narrow valley of the Poprad river as it squeezes between thousand-metre peaks. There are several health centres here and seventy mineral springs, providing plenty of opportunities to take the waters. And for the disgustingly fit there are hiking trails disappearing into the trees at every turn, one of the best being from the very first resort of Rytro, where a long ridge path leads up through a nature reserve to the 1,262-metre (4,140-foot) peak of Radziejowa. Most sensible folk, though, will be content with a view of Rytro's castle ruins from the safety of the valley floor, before moving on to the larger resort of Piwniczna where it is important to cross to the east bank of the river to avoid the embarrassment of finding yourself at the Czechoslovak frontier with neither the appropriate documentation nor indeed the desire to cross. Piwniczna has turned its carbonated spring water into a small industry and has several large holiday centres for children; so too has Łomnica-Zdrój, which lies up the next side valley to the left. The word *zdrój* means a spring or well and when affixed to a place-name is a good indication that a health resort is to hand.

For the next 25 kilometres the river, now to the right of the road, constitutes what must be one of the most picturesque frontiers in Europe, twisting and turning in the steep valley which narrows to a gorge at Żegiestów-Zdrój. Set amongst the trees, this spa is regarded as one of the prettiest in the country, and the old village of Żegiestów is worth a visit; stuck up in a side valley, it consists of a long straggle of wooden farmhouses and cottages with a church for each end of the settlement. This is the southernmost point of the excursion; the road now leaves the frontier and the Poprad behind, turning east and then north along a fast-flowing tributary river. At the confluence of the two rivers lies the town of **Muszyna**, a resort with sixteen mineral springs and all the trappings of a modern health centre, as well as a baroque church which houses inherited statues dating back to the fifteenth century. And the hilltop ruin here of a castle built in 1301 is an indication that this valley was yet another through which the merchants of yore made their way to Hungary.

A careful look at the village architecture and any traditional costumes that may be spotted hereabouts will reveal that an ethnic frontier has been crossed, if not a frontier of state. This was just about the western limit of settlement for Orthodox Christian highlanders of Ruthenian origin, and the Muszyna regional museum, housed in a seventeenth-century inn, has examples of the local arts and costumes for comparison. One speciality of the hills is wood-carving and many specimens can be found locally, not least in the churches. From here eastwards, the wooden temples of the Orthodox Christian Church are to be found, distinguished by their double crosses and pronounced onion domes. The first of these is just five kilometres up the road at the village of Powroźnik, where there is also a prominent wayside shrine, one of the most common sights in the whole of Poland. Travelling eastwards from here through the hills right to the Soviet frontier, the avid church-hunter will find numerous wooden Orthodox churches, some very ancient and many hidden away up remote tracks in tiny hamlets whose very existence is a shock. But one man's wilderness is another's universe. Far up a little valley above Powroźnik, for example, close to the Czech frontier, the dozen cottages of Wojkowa support three shrines and two churches, one Catholic and the other Orthodox. The latter is used today by Catholics, the original worshippers having died or moved away during the last war.

The road from Muszyna now travels north, accompanied still by the railway which terminates at the next town, **Krynica**. One of the oldest and most famous of Polish spas, Krynica sits in a lovely spot some 600 metres (1,968 feet) up at the top of a valley, surrounded by the inevitable wooded peaks. The combination here of a gentle micro-climate which is protected from the north wind and a great variety of mineral springs became known to city people as far back as the eighteenth century and over the years all the usual spa facilities have developed, including the promenade where consumptive girls once tottered beneath parasols, a traditional pump room, a century-old therapeutic centre and a concert hall which is crowded every night. In summer the funicular to a local hilltop operates until midnight, allowing romantic descents from spectacular sunsets. Beautiful as it is for holidays all the year round, Krynica is also a serious medical centre famed far beyond Poland for its treatments, and boasts, I am assured, a spring containing the most concentrated mineral water in Europe. This contains 24 grammes of solid matter per litre, which may not sound healthy but brought fame to a certain Professor Zuber who discovered it in 1914. There is also a large medical academy, a clinical sanatorium, fourteen other sanatoria and three physiotherapy centres. There cannot be a nicer place to have a mud bath or even, dangerous as it sounds, a dry bath in fumes of carbon dioxide which are emitted under great pressure from a natural shaft.

So visitors to Krynica are divided between those who come for treatment and those who are on holiday, perhaps sent by their factory or institute. I have friends who have been regular visitors for years: the wife has been referred by her doctor for specific treatments while her husband, strong as an ox, goes along for the air, the massages and the high life of late-night drinking and dancing in the cafés. The waters are freely available to any visitor, although without a guide or knowledge of the language it may be a question of potluck which fluid is imbibed. A rather charming tradition of the pump rooms is that alongside the woman who checks the hats there is another who takes the spouted drinking mugs of regulars, who buy season tickets in order to keep their mug hanging conveniently to hand, much as certain Englishmen keep a tankard in their local pub. All this excitement goes on throughout the year; skis replace shoes in the winter and the skating rink takes over from the promenade as the place to see and be seen. The casual visitor who has not booked ahead may have trouble with accommodation but, as at Zakopane, local people take in paying guests. The information centre at the southern end of the promenade should be able to help with this.

North of Krynica the road climbs a pass before following the little Kamienica river for the 30 kilometres or so north-west to Nowy Sącz. An alternative for those heading directly eastwards towards the Bieszczady Mountains and their foothills is a road that turns off at the top of the pass and travels down a lovely valley containing at least three Orthodox churches to the town of Grybów where it joins the main 208 road, parallel to the main mountain ridges. But before heading towards that remotest part of Poland, a word about **Nowy Sącz** itself. Founded in 1292 and recently expanded to house some 65,000 people, the town enjoyed its cultural climax during the years 1440 to 1460, when a group of painters established themselves here and produced what is recognized as the first clearly definable school of purely Polish painting. Most of their works have by now made their way to the larger national collections, but the regional museum has some on display together with sacred paintings and sculptures from the Orthodox churches of the hills. The largest collection is of some 400 primitive paintings by the Krynica artist Nikifor who died in 1968. The museum is also a good place to study the ethnic differentiation within the Beskid Sądecki region, and the antiquity of the local valleys as trade routes is confirmed by the gold Roman coin dated AD 275 which was found nearby.

As for the town itself, the best place, as so often, is the **Rynek,** the old market place in the town centre, although it is spoiled by a monstrous 1893 town hall which is stuck in the middle and should be removed post-haste. But for once a good meal can be guaranteed at the Staropolska Restaurant in the Rynek which is sponsored by a college devoted to the culinary arts. Students do a share of the cooking and serving and traditional dishes are the speciality. Behind the restaurant is the Gothic parish church, built in 1446 and reconstructed in the eighteenth century, a process which the Renaissance altars survived. The adjoining canonical house with its two fine Gothic portals houses the museum mentioned above. This northern and oldest part of the town is sited on a promontory overlooking a valley where several routes through the hills meet, and the remains of a medieval castle ruined by German mines in 1945, can be found here. Heroic as those days were, with their mass arrests and executions, Nowy Sącz's greatest military moment was in December of 1655 when an army of local peasants seized the town from its Swedish occupiers and thus began the process of rolling back the deluge of invaders from the north.

The next town on this road is **Gorlice,** famed for a most unexpected reason. Here it was in 1853 that the local pharmacist Ignacy Łuka-siewicz made the world's first experiments in refining the crude oil which still flows from the ground in this part of the country. His initiative resulted in the first dug-out wells being sunk and the birth of an industry which has changed every society on earth, a fact of which little Gorlice is proud, dedicating its museum both to its most famous son and the local petroleum industry. Otherwise Gorlice has little to offer except a reminder of a battle in 1915 between the Russian and Austrian armies which left some 20,000 new graves in the local cemetery. For the ardent seeker of the beautiful wooden Orthodox churches, a word of warning: one of the most famous was at Libusza, off to the right just ten kilometres past Gorlice, but I have to report that a recent visit revealed only a few fire-blackened sticks of wood.

The purpose of this eastward push is to reach the Bieszczady Mountains in the farthest corner of the country but, attractive as many of the side roads and villages are, there is nothing of great beauty or import along this route, particularly after Jaslo where the international E22 road joins it from the north. Before then, credit must be given to a splendid little museum at the ancient town of Biecz, on record as far back as 1023. This museum is at the far western end of the town on the south side in a building that for years was the old pharmacy and still shows its *Apteka* sign today. This locally assembled and slightly eccentric collection of pharmacy equipment, musical instruments and other odds and ends provides a delightful diversion and is displayed in a lovely old house which once formed part of the town's fortifications. The museum was opened, as the curator proudly explained, on the very day in 1978 that Cardinal Karol Wojtyła was proclaimed Pope.

The apothecary's equipment on show dates from the sixteenth century, much of it coming from the local pharmacist who was obviously a bit of a magpie. There are prescriptions, textbooks, microscopes, herbs and all the paraphernalia of the profession from the days of leeches and long-forgotten remedies. The musical section has a fascinating array of fiddles, clavichords, hurdy-gurdies and cymbalons as well as some more primitive folk instruments including one that resembles a giant football rattle. There is even a musical dressing-table mirror and fragments of a music manuscript from the thirteenth century.

The house itself is fascinating, the main room having decorated beams from which arrowheads were removed during recent restoration work. Here, amongst the furniture and other knick-knacks, there is a handsome, obviously ancient wooden figure of Kazimierz the Great and an Odessa secretaire while in an adjoining room devoted to religious objects you will find an embossed leather triptych. Part of the museum is in one of the seventeen towers that used to protect the town; each, as at Kraków, defended by a local guild. Here there is a motley collection of looms, wine presses, weighing balances, wooden locks, and the contents of both a carpenter's and a boot-maker's workshop.

The museum is an altogether charming and fascinating place, all the better for being assembled and run by enthusiastic amateurs. And whilst you are there, it is worth crossing the road to the big church, where there is a wonderfully carved pulpit featuring scenes from musical life and rows of Gothic and Renaissance pews. In the town centre the town hall is also a Gothic-Renaissance structure with a 50-metre tower, but there is otherwise little sign of the wealth and glory of the Middle Ages, when Biecz had a school of public executioners who enjoyed the special privilege of executing convicted persons. The records show that 120 public executions took place here in 1614 alone.

Jasło, 20 kilometres east, is another old town, but it was almost completely destroyed by the Nazis and is today a manufacturing centre, supplying equipment for boring to the local oil industry. Twenty-five kilometres further on, Krosno apears as the valley widens. The mainroad bypasses the town centre, but this is not a great loss to the visitor; the surviving arcaded houses have been overwhelmed by the industrial atmosphere of the town, which has factories connected with the oil industry as well as glass and textile plants. It is known, for its sins, as the petroleum capital of Poland, and proudly displays a large statue of Ignacy Łukasiewicz, 'inventor of the paraffin lamp'. The local museum contains a large number of unusual oil lamps.

Just beyond Krosno some of the heavy traffic will turn off our route and head south towards the Dukla Pass, now a frontier with Czechoslovakia and for centuries one of the main crossing points over the hills to Hungary; at 500 metres it is the lowest pass in the Carpathian range. As is inevitable in this part of the world, it has been the scene of many battles, culminating in the autumn of 1944 in a fierce struggle in which 20,000 Soviet soldiers died, along with 6,500 members of the Czechoslovak 1st Army. The gentle green valley had been made into a lethal trap by German troops defending the pass, with mines, tank traps and gun emplacements littering the landscape and the manpower on the pass doubled to an amazing six infantry and two Panzer divisions. All this proved too much even for the Red Army, who were attempting to enter Slovakia to assist a rising against the German occupiers.

Back on the main route the road rolls on through the broad valley of the Wisłok River, a turning to the right leading to the lovely old spa of Iwonicz. Then it enters low hills and comes to the little town of **Sanok**, perched on a hill above the San river and best known in Poland for its bus and rubber factories. From here the main road turns north-east towards Przemyśl, but Sanok is an ideal base for the exploration of the Bieszczady Mountains, the wildest part of the country which is tucked away on a promontory that extends between the hills of Slovakia and those of the Soviet Republic of Ukraine — thereby hangs a tale which I shall come to in a moment. But the little town has charms of its own, the best of which are the fourteenth-century church where King Władysław Jagiełło took his marriage vows and a large and very naturalistic *skansen* down on the river bank. This last is one of the best in the country, laid out along riverside meadows and up into the neighbouring woods, where little churches and highland houses brought in from the neighbouring mountains sit looking out over the rather too tidily assembled village street. As at Nowy Sącz and most other skansens, the idea has been to make a working village with people living in many of the cottages and crops growing in the back yards; there was a wood-carver hard at work on a large figure during my visit. The main ethnic groups living in the area in the recent past were the Bojkowie, who inhabited the higher mountains, and the Łemkowie, who occupied the lower Beskid hills, and both groups are represented with a comprehensive range of buildings.

There is still more to see in Sanok. In the rebuilt castle on the eastern slopes of the town is the second largest hoard of Ruthenian icons in existence, the largest of all being in Moscow. And a fabulous display it is, most of the icons having been taken from the little Orthodox churches which still dot the remotest regions of the Bieszczady — raising the question of where all the believers can have gone. This is still a sensitive subject, as the following brief outline shows.

The redrawing of international frontiers is a difficult enough job at any time and, after the cataclysmic war of 1939-45, the task proved to be particularly tricky in an area as ethnically complex yet sparsely inhabited as the eastern Carpathians, where it was obvious that few would be satisfied. After the War, the whole Polish frontier with the Soviet Union was moved bodily westward, displacing those not already disturbed by the fighting. Predictably, given the independent nature of mountain folk, many objected, and in essence the war continued in the Bieszczady, the last shot being fired only in 1947. It is a complicated story but, briefly, when the War officially ended there were still many armed factions operating independently in Poland, representing all political colours. Many were determined to make trouble for the new Socialist government which already had enough troubles trying to establish some sort of order in a devastated land. One such group, the National Armed Forces (NSZ), was active in the Holy Cross Mountains but by the end of 1945 had fought its way south to meet up with US army units then in Czechoslovakia. The Ukrainian Insurrectionist Army (UPA), however, was trapped in this far south-east corner, surrounded by Polish, Czech and Soviet forces, their rallying call after earlier flirtations with the Nazis being 'Neither Hitler nor Stalin'. The Polish Deputy Minister of Defence, General Karol Świerczewski, once Commander-in-Chief of the International Brigade in the Spanish Civil War, was sent to put an end to the fighting, but in March 1947 his convoy was ambushed and he was killed. Finally the UPA was routed and many of the Ukrainian-Ruthenian inhabitants were uprooted and resettled, either in the northern and western territories regained from Germany or in the Soviet Union.

For many years the area was desolate, its villages empty and its churchyards overgrown and it was at this time that the icons were collected and placed in the museum at Sanok. Slowly life returned to the Bieszczady, greatly helped by the construction of a 140-kilometre road, the Bieszczady Loop, which encloses the area, and by the trend for wilderness holidays — this region is popular with the rucksack and woolly-hat brigade, of which Poland has many members. And there is certainly plenty of wilderness here to get lost in, so anyone tempted to go off the road in search of bear, wolf or lynx, beautiful lost valleys or the dramatic steppe-like tops that lie above the forests of oak and spruce, must be well prepared. Hotels, restaurants, even shops, are few and far between, and mostly concentrated around the newly formed lake at Solina, the spectacular view of which is spoilt by the unsympathetic block design of the new holiday homes perched around the shore.

The best way to see the hills is to drive around the loop road, making occasional forays up side roads by car or on foot. The local map makes everything very clear and even marks the Orthodox churches separately from other wooden ones. An even more leisurely way to see the south-western corner of the range is from the narrow-gauge forest railway which runs between the villages of Nowy Łupków and Majdan (near Cisna) where there is a forest railway museum. This 25-kilometre journey takes over two hours and includes a wild, trackless valley which climbs to a 700-metre (2,300-foot) plateau hard by the Czechoslovak frontier. It is not quite as spectacular as some of the Alpine railways but a good trip none the less and a chance for railway fans to see old wood-burning locomotives at the museum. Diesel locomotives, I am sad to say, have recently replaced the old 'Samovar' steamers for actual haulage duties.

Another little place that would be a good base for exploring the area is **Lesko,** further into the hills than Sanok, but also on a hill above the San river. It is interesting for its seventeenth-century synagogue, once fortified and one of the few left standing after the war. A nearby Jewish cemetery, with some of its tombstones dating from the fifteenth century, gives a clue to the numbers who used to live in the area.

The Bieszczady are not as spectacular as the Tatras, nor are they as richly endowed with picturesque villages as the Podhale region, and the visitor who is not a naturalist or a church historian may want to pass directly from Sanok to Przemyśl, a lovely run of 60 kilometres which twists up and down low hills and through beech forests. In autumn, these forests display a gorgeous range of browns and golds with views varying from leafy tunnels to distant blue peaks.

Just ten kilometres before Przemyśl and easy to miss amongst trees on the left of the road is **Krasiczyn Castle**, which is more splendid than ever, following recent restoration work. It is a shame that Krasiczyn is so far from the main centres of interest in Poland, because it is one of the most attractive and interesting buildings in the country, perfectly set in a natural, almost English park of rare trees, facing a lake which reflects two of its shiny white towers. The present castle was built between 1592 and 1618 on a long-established site by the Italian Gallazzo Appiani for the powerful Krasicki family. It is based on a square inner courtyard with a massive round tower at each corner, each with a differently styled crown. These towers are named after God, the Pope, the King and the Nobility, which certainly makes clear the social pecking order in the days of elected monarchs before it was deemed either just, necessary or politic to flatter the proletariat. The walls facing into the courtyard are decorated with *trompe-l'oeil* frescos depicting a variety of saints, Polish kings and scenes from the history of Ancient Rome and the Bible. The outer walls, rising from a now dry moat which was once fed by the nearby San river, are painted in white with a stoneblock effect picked out in grey, and a frieze above the second floor shows detailed hunting scenes. The complete roof line, with one of the towers, is topped with ornamental parapets. Another tower, containing a chapel, is domed, while a third is topped with little bartizans, small turrets of the type often seen on fairy-tale castles. It is a splendid place, best seen from across the lake so that the full glory of the western façade glows in a frame of high trees.

The cultural, business and shopping centre for this corner of the country is **Przemyśl,** built long ago to guard the crossing of the San river, but the town seems not to have recovered from the shock of losing much of its traditional hinterland when the frontier was moved after the Second World War. Now it is just ten kilometres from the Soviet border and cut off from the old regional capital and university city of Lwów, less than a hundred kilometres to the east. The trade route to the Ukraine, however, is busier than ever, huge amounts of goods travelling in both directions, but instead of passing through Przemyśl market place as they did in the old days, they bypass the town centre in trucks which congregate for clearance at a massive, so-called dry port at Medyka to the east of the town. Przemyśl itself has some industry, including a famous sewing-machine factory, and development continues, but the appearance of the old town, established more than a thousand years ago, should survive, built as it is on a steep hillside on the right bank of the river. Some restoration work seems to be in hand, including that of the hilltop castle where remains have been unearthed of buildings dating from the time of the first Piast dynasty and almost all succeeding periods.

I cannot recall any other town of this size with quite so many large churches in the centre. Six or seven towers rise above the narrow slightly grubby streets of the old town, and it seems that the various religious orders competed to construct the most dominant house of worship, moving up the hill to gain a natural advantage. Religious activity seems not to have dwindled; the black garb of priests and nuns appears in every street, giving the impression that a loud noise such as a ringing bell would bring dozens more scurrying from their hidden cells like foraging ants. Beside one convent I came across some nuns engaged in heavy gardening work whilst still wearing the regulation gowns and hoods, which, to say the least, must have been inconvenient.

At the top of the town are two massive structures; one a Jesuit church now under repair, containing a crazy pulpit in silver which is shaped like a boat complete with its rigging, and the other a regional museum with, as always, an interesting ethnographic section including beautiful costumes, painted Easter eggs, wood-carving and unusual green and brown pottery. Three rooms are devoted to Ruthenian icons, one of which features a sixteenth-century Prince Charles look-alike, even down to the ears.

Down the slope from the museum, on the corner of the square, is a late baroque Franciscan church with the usual over-rich interior. A similar fate has overtaken the nearby **Cathedral,** in whose vaults are the remnants of a twelfth-century Romanesque rotunda. The most elaborate décor here belongs to the chapel of the Fredro family, in contrast to a rather fine Renaissance alabaster *pietà* within the main altar. The separate bell tower, at 71 metres (233 feet), outclimbs all the other towers but is itself diminished by the proximity of the castle hill in whose shadow it sits. Far from dominating the town, however, the castle itself, or what is left of it, is a low affair by the same architect who built Krasiczyn. Hidden amongst trees, it is home now to a local theatre, so interval promenaders have the benefit of a splendid view across the San Valley and out to the rolling plains to the north.

The hills of this chapter end at Przemyśl, and the San breaks out to wander across the wooded Sandomierz basin for 150 kilometres before joining the Vistula just downstream from Sandomierz town. Just beyond these foothills, however, and on or close to the main Kraków-Przemyśl road, are several places which must be mentioned.

The **Castle of Łańcut** is no longer fortified and is now simply a very large mansion, except that 'simply' is not really the word to use. It possesses one of the finest collections of pictures, furniture and *objets d'art* in the country, all assembled in the many chambers as if in daily use and a real joy to wander amongst. The richness of the collection is all the more remarkable because the last private owner, Alfred Potocki, who was reckoned to be the richest man in pre-war Poland, removed himself on 23 July 1944 to the sanctuary of Liechtenstein, having sent ahead eleven railway carriages containing some 600 crates of the most valuable objects from the castle. Seven days later, the Red Army arrived to find a sign on the gates, written in Russian and placed there by Potocki's secretary, stating simply, 'Polish National Museum'. The ruse worked: the Soviet General Pavel Kurochkin appointed a special guard on the castle and it escaped without a scratch. Later the same year the place was opened to the public and the present collection has been accumulated since from many sources.

The origins of the castle stretch way back into the past. The foundation deed is believed to have been signed by Kazimierz the Great in the fourteenth century and several great and noble families have owned the place, as well as one that was famous for being ignoble. In 1586 ownership passed to Stanisław Stadnicki (1551-1610), who became known throughout the kingdom as 'the devil from Łańcut', partly because of his fierce performances on the battlefield but mainly because of his habit of robbing merchants who passed his door and then cocking a snook at the legal authorities when they subsequently indicted him. He became an outlaw, at war with the Crown, until in 1608 an army raised by another aristocrat attacked Łańcut and burned the place down. Stadnicki just escaped, only to be killed two years later in battle against the same troops. Łańcut then passed to the illustrious Lubomirski dynasty, one of the greatest of Polish families, who rebuilt and fortified the castle in the 1630s. Living in stormy times, Stanisław Lubomirski demanded the most modern and impregnable fortifications for his investment, and scholars presume that the five-pointed star plan used, the so-called bastion system of Dutch origin, derives from a book called *Architecture Militaris*, written by Adam Freytag, the leading theoretician of the day, and had recently been published. It was a sort of Ideal Home book of defence systems, which conjures up an image of the nobleman and his wife sitting by the fire skimming the pages for a suitable design. A seventeenth-century plan of Łańcut shows the large palace lost in the midst of an enormous system of earthworks, dry moats, curtain walls and bastions which housed 80 cannon; these precautions proved their worth, withstanding sieges in 1657 and 1702.

Safe behind this insulation, the Lubomirskis created a sumptuous and elegant residence, with stucco work by the great Giovanni Battista Falconi. It was a suitable place to entertain the noble and mighty during the two centuries that Łańcut remained in the family. Stanisław's son Jerzy Sebastian became Grand Marshal of the Crown, as did his grandson Stanisław Herakliusz; and kings of Poland, future kings of France and sundry lesser mortals were guests here at one time or another. The last resident in the Lubomirski line was another Stanisław, also Grand Marshal, and his wisest move was to marry Izabela Czartoryska, famed for her patronage of the arts and her avidity as a collector. Under her guidance the eighteenth century saw Łańcut at its most glorious. The ramparts were levelled and a park complete with orangery and mock-Romantic castle was laid out in their place. Artists came from all over Europe to contribute to the interior design, to add wings and turn the palace into the rococo and neo-classical building that, with few changes, has survived until today.

One of the loveliest interiors of a palace full of delights is the little theatre, the only one to have survived from a palace of the period. It is equipped with a proscenium arch, fully working stage machinery and seats for 80 in the stalls and gallery, and still displays an original romantic backdrop of the 'moonlight on the terrace' school. Izabela was blessed with a son-in-law after her own heart, Jan Potocki, who was gifted enough to satisfy her intellectual demands. He was a pioneer in the science of archaeology and the history of the Slavonic countries, a great traveller who even visited China, and a distinguished man of letters as well, writing several plays for the family theatre. Eventually his children inherited the estate and the Potocki family maintained control until that fateful day in 1944 when Alfred disappeared with his treasure.

The last great rebuilding work was done by Alfred's parents, Roman and Elzbieta, who came from the equally powerful Radziwiłł family, and it was they who gave the castle its present exterior style, reshaping the elevations in the French neo-baroque fashion but retaining the most precious interiors.

Once inside the main doors, a different world envelops one. The entrance hall, with its vaulted ceiling supported on a single stone pillar, was designed to allow carriages to drive in, offload their passengers and exit by another set of doors at the rear. From this hall, corridors and stairways lead to the 40 or so rooms which are open to the public, laid out around a green courtyard. One of the first rooms on the ground floor contains a richly decorated chapel with a folding triptych, and nearby guest apartments are equally sumptuous in their décor especially the **Views Room** which has two oval pictures of Łańcut showing the castle before and after the levelling of the ramparts. The fascinating thing about this house is that so many interiors have survived with their original decoration, from the eighteenth century right through to the 1930s, thereby tracing the evolution of styles favoured by the wealthy of three centuries. On a mantelpiece in the owner's study there is a clue to the way in which European royals moved in a society of their own: two photographs of the Greek Princess Marina and her husband George, Duke of Kent, who visited Łańcut in 1937.

The **Turkish Apartment** is decorated in a suitably exotic manner, complete with a portrait of Izabela in a turban, but its parlour has a collection of English-style furniture from around 1800. This was obviously a favourite fashion here, for one of many pieces of English furniture is a neo-Gothic clock, whose chimes imitate those of Westminster's Big Ben. The best rooms, as usual, are upstairs, and contain a veritable cornucopia of wonderful furniture, pictures and decoration, even if there are still a few gaps left from 1944, most obviously the specially shaped ceiling paintings in a couple of rooms. It is difficult to single out particular rooms for comment; they all have unique features and contents. The Dining-Room and Ballroom are suitably capacious and grand, and the Sculpture Gallery and Column Hall contain well rendered copies of classical sculptures and originals by Antonia Canova which were commissioned by Izabela. But for my money it is the smaller rooms which have the most charm, the **Corner Salon** with its pale blue walls and tall, fancy porcelain stove being an especial delight. Two rooms retain their original Renaissance ceilings complete with decorated beams and the Bedroom of the Lady of the House will be the envy of many. In the north-west tower is the Zodiac Room which still has a domed ceiling decorated with Falconi's original and elaborate stucco work from the middle of the seventeenth century, but beyond this lies my own favourite chamber, the **Library**. This is still chock-full of books — 22,000 of them — and was decorated by the last owner as a man's room with heavy leather armchairs and little tables which convert at a touch into steps for climbing to the top shelves. As is my wont, I could not resist a quick scan for English titles. *Vile Bodies* and *Breakfast in Bed* seemed appropriate fare for a plutocrat, but *Spying in Russia* and *The Fall of Tsardom* were, I thought, more revealing. Old copies of *Country Life* and *The Field* magazines lay unread in racks.

Finally, do not leave without visiting the old **Stable Block** and coach house in the park, where there is a large display of carriages: 64 from the Potocki collection and many more acquired since. The term 'stable block' is rather demeaning, for this was a luxury palace built at the turn of the century to house the famous thoroughbred racehorses of Roman Potocki. Only four carriages on show are of Polish manufacture; it seems that the demanding aristocrats preferred to order from work-shops in Paris and Vienna, although also on show are two of English make. The star exhibits are a huge fourteen-person carriage and a sleeper which enabled the occupant to travel in a horizontal position and which was even heated, though I cannot imagine sleep came easily to a traveller bouncing down Europe's rough roads, prone inside a closed box and hauled by horses clattering, jingling and panting their way through the night.

One of Łańcut's specialities these days is to hold music recitals by an array of international performers. It is worth enquiring beforehand about these and trying to book into the hotel which occupies some of the castle rooms — this also has a restaurant and café which are accessible from the courtyard. And before proceeding westwards on the main road, both music-lovers and admirers of the baroque may like to make a detour 28 kilometres to the north-east, where the little old town of **Lezajsk** sits in the San Valley.

Pleasant as the town is, the reason for stopping here is the early seventeenth-century **Bernardine Church and Monastery,** still with defensive walls, which was built as a votive offering after the defeat of our friend 'the devil from Łańcut'. The interior is as tasteful as the baroque style allows and many works of art adorn the building, including wall paintings illustrating a hundred religious scenes and various richly sculpted and gilded altar pieces, but the unavoidable focus of attention is the organ, whose banks of pipes, rising to the ceiling, are smothered with gilded figures and elaborate decoration. The machine beneath all the gold is a masterpiece of the organ-builder's craft and one of the best known instruments in Europe.

Famed for its clear, strong tone, it is frequently used for recitals and recordings. Once again, enquiries will provide concert dates.

Back on the main road **Rzeszów**, like Przemyśl, is an old county town beside the Beskid foothills, but it is not, I must admit, a favourite place of mine, the old town centre having been swamped by the industrial town rapidly growing up around it. This is a great improvement, I imagine, on the decaying pre-war town, but only the area around the old market place and the museum attract visitors here today. Close to the market, two synagogues have somehow survived all that the twentieth century has thrown at them, one a fine Renaissance building from the end of the sixteenth century and the other dating from 1705. Also surviving is the seventeenth-century castle sitting on its massive defensive bastions, and a former Piarist monastery. The latter now houses the regional museum which has archaeological and ethnographic sections, paintings, products of artistic craftsmanship, including Polish furniture, and mementoes of the old guilds such as a 1662 beaker belonging to the Shoemakers' Guild.

West again, and the main road to Kraków crosses a pleasant but undramatic landscape with many of its old trade-route towns industrialized during the past 40 years after suffering badly in two world wars. **Tarnów**, however, large as it now is and complete with its fertilizer and machinery factories, is still worth a call, for its centre has survived with something of its old atmosphere. Although the town did not have a charter until 1300, it was a well known stop-over on the Kraków-Lwów route for several hundred years before that, and equally convenient for a route to and from Hungary. At the end of the fifteenth century much of the town was destroyed by fire, a not uncommon experience at the time, and it was not until the end of the seventeenth century that the Tarnówski family, owners of the region, saw fit to restore it to something of its former splendour. But they did a good job, importing Italian architects and craftsmen according to the fashion of the day.

The most noticeable building today is the **Town Hall,** plumb in the middle of the large Rynek as usual and somewhat lacking the grace such a position deserves. But it is an interesting building; the first two floors are rather plain and, with the tower, date from the fourteenth-century Gothic period, while the upper floor is a more decorative Renaissance addition. Since the last war, the town museum has been housed here, and it has a very good collection of European paintings and drawings, including fascinating architectural plans from the eighteenth and nineteenth centuries. The craft section has a rich array of glass tableware from the seventeenth century, including many German and Bohemian specimens, European and Far Eastern porcelain, clocks, pistols, saddlery, tapestries and furniture. There is also the inevitable folklore section featuring local costumes and customs. The museum spills over into two of the old merchants' houses around the partly arcaded square.

The north-east exit from the square leads directly to the **Cathedral,** the unusual spire of which is visible above the roof-tops. It is a rather fine sixteenth-century Gothic basilica, impressively sited on one of the town's higher points and not too disfigured by remodelling. Inside there are several Renaissance tombs, perhaps the best being that of Barbara Tarnowska, built in 1520, and that of the Grand Hetman Jan Tarnowski, from the 1560s, which has bas-reliefs illustrating the occupant's military victories and other sculptures by various Italian artists. There are also several early baroque tombs and all the usual splendid fitments of Catholicism. The tower can be climbed and the reward for your effort is a view over the town and neighbourhood.

The little cathedral square is crammed with old houses, the best, Dom Mikołajowski, dating from 1524 and now containing a diocesan **Museum** with over a hundred sacred paintings, many well known to art historians. There are about 4,000 items of Gothic art in the museum, though they are not all on show at any one time, some 400 examples of weaving from many countries, dating from the Gothic period to the present century, and a large collection of folk paintings on glass from most countries of central Europe. In the southern suburbs of the town there are two wooden churches, one of which was built before 1460 and is thought to be one of the oldest wooden structures surviving in the country.

Country roads which follow the Dunajec river north from Tarnów lead eventually to a unique village, stranded amongst back lanes close to the Vistula and well worth a diversion for anyone interested in folk designs. Mention was made of an attractive new café in Kraków, the U Zalipianek, which is named after this village of Zalipie. The old tradition of folk painting here had all but died out by the 1930s but, led by the remarkable Felicja Curyłowa, the village women resurrected the custom of covering their cottages inside and out with elaborate and wonderfully executed flower designs. A room in Felicja's own cottage is preserved as a memorial to her and a display of her art; even the white painted clay stove is decorated in the green, red and white floral designs. Every September the village holds a contest for floral painting which has become a great attraction within the region.

The long circuit from Kraków around the mountains and back is now almost complete, Tarnów being some 80 kilometres from the old capital city. The main road between the two places takes in the little towns of Dębno — which holds concerts of ancient music in its Gothic castle — Brzesko, and Bochnia, which lies at the eastern end of the Wieliczka salt deposits and has its own mine. The road then passes Wieliczka itself on its way into Kraków.

Some 30 kilometres west from Kraków on the main E7 road, the tiny town of **Kalwaria Zebrzydowska** is, as its name implies, a site of pilgrimage; and has been so since 1609 when the construction of a massive Bernardine church and monastery was started by the land-owning Zebrzydowski family. During Holy Week when the Passion plays are performed, and again in August, pilgrims from all parts of the country make this the most visited shrine in Poland after Częstochowa. The interior of the church is baroque, with a large silver Italian Virgin mounted on the high altar, but the real fascination of the place is the 42 chapels representing Stations of the Cross which dot the local hillsides. Linked by narrow roads, the system is modelled on that of ancient Jerusalem, many of the chapels being replicas in miniature of buildings in the Holy City. Most of them are the work of the Antwerp artist Paul Bandarth who worked in a baroque and mannerist style. The town beneath these extravagant hillsides is famed also for its production of high-quality furniture and hosts an annual trade fair. It is a shame that furniture is so cumbersome to transport, because it is possible in Poland to buy handsome items, bearing the stamp of authentic craftsmanship and often decorated with traditional designs but which are also very functional. The *Cepelia* shops for example, are full of fine cupboards, chests and tables.

Just fourteen kilometres further west is **Wadowice**, unknown to the world, and no doubt to many Poles, before that October day in 1978 when a Polish Pope was proclaimed in Rome. On 18 May 1920, Karol Wojtyła, now Pope John Paul II, was born here into a modest family. His father was a junior officer in the Austrian Army who transferred to the new Polish Army when independence finally arrived at the end of the First World War. The child could not have chosen a more traumatic year to be born. After 125 years of partition and legal non-existence, Poland's transition to autonomous statehood was not an easy affair, and in 1920 Jozef Piłsudski, the new chief-of-state and a professional soldier, took direct action in an attempt to settle once and for all with the equally new and troubled Soviet state the position of their common frontier. This military expedition was saved from disaster only by the gallantry of Warsaw's defence in the face of the counter-attacking Red Army. This complicated episode is well worth studying in detail.

The man who became Pope, then, grew up with the modern Polish state and, like it, was tempered in the furnace of the Second World War. Opinions on his abilities as a Church leader may vary world-wide but he is undoubtedly an intelligent, interesting and charismatic man who in his time has worked in a quarry and written stage plays which are still performed. His election in 1978 contributed towards the atmosphere that led to the founding of the Solidarity movement in Poland during 1980, and it is interesting to speculate what course events might have taken if he had been elevated to head the Church not in Rome but in his own country. Needless to say, Wadowice has become a site of pilgrimage, and the Pope is a blessing to the souvenir industry here, as elsewhere in Poland. Although industrialized, this is a pleasant enough town and the small flat where Karol Wojtyła was born can be visited; it is behind the market square, in the shadow of the parish church which proudly holds the baptismal record of its greatest son.

South-west of Wadowice, in the very heart of the hills, Żywiec is the main centre for exploring the landscape of the region. For Poles it is also synonymous with the finest beer, brewed in the valley since 1856; Żywiec boasts an annual output in excess of 30 million litres (8 million gallons). These Beskid Śląski hills, host to the Vistula river's source have their devotees and claim to provide the best skiing in the country, but I think most visitors will find more delights further east.

11

Silesia and Wrocław

On the surface, the historical region of Silesia (Śląsk) divides easily into an area of high rounded hills and a rolling foreland, but in reality its geology is almost as complex as its history. The hills are known as the Sudety Mountains and are part of the ancient Bohemian massif which was folded and crushed into its present position by the same intercontinental collision as forced up the great Alpine chain. Would that the human history of the area could be so easily summarized. In the early Middle Ages the region was settled by some of the founding tribes of the Polish state and today it is the most industrialized part of the country, crucial to its economic future. In between these periods, however, the political management of Silesia has changed hands many times. Bohemia, Austria, Prussia and Poland have shared the honours with local princes, which explains why this corner of Europe has suffered as much destruction over the centuries as anywhere else; probably a lot more, given the catastrophe of the last War. Despite all this there are notable and even magnificent things to be seen here.

To start at the beginning, this south-western corner of the country provided natural conditions favourable for human settlement and, being close to central Europe and only a short hop from the Danube Valley with its Balkan connections, it was extensively peopled by the time of the palaeolithic period. Agriculture began to be practised here in neolithic times, and early civilization reached its peak with the development of the highly organized Lusatian culture, which left its mark over a great swathe of the north European plain. In 500 BC the Scythians invaded and a century later it was the turn of the Celtic tribes, who were the first to leave traces of iron smelting. Although Silesia was only on the fringes of the Empire, iron-working quickly

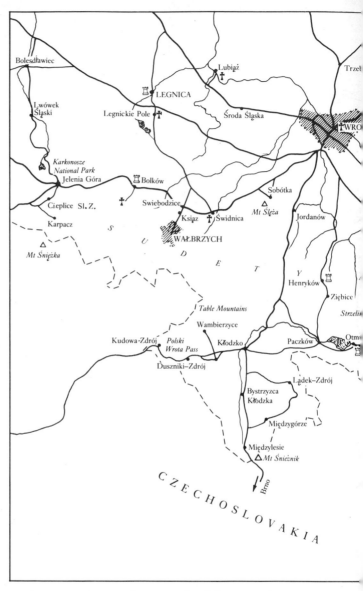

developed in the area during the period of Roman domination and trade routes which passed through it, such as the amber road from the Baltic and Jutland to the Danube, were consolidated.

It is not clear exactly when it was that the Slavic tribes appeared on the scene but by the ninth century they were well established around Wrocław, developing the site into a fortified town which was incorpo-

200

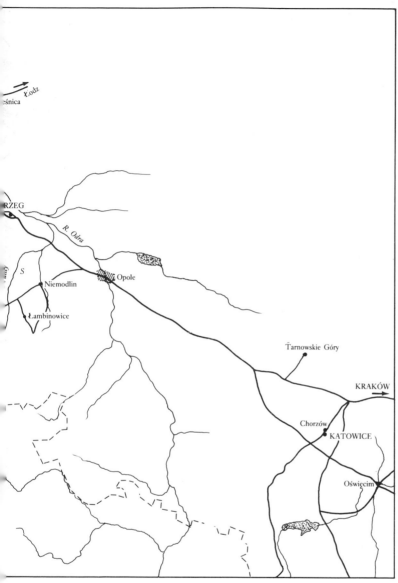

rated into the fledgling Polish state in the tenth century. Within a few years, however, the region became the scene of fighting between Polish and German tribes, and it was then that a chain of castles was erected along both the German and the Bohemian frontiers, many of which have survived until today.

From this time until the end of the last war, Silesia came under the influence of those cultures based to the west. When pressure was exerted by Bohemia, even Kazimierz the Great was forced to recognize its supremacy. The population nevertheless retained a strong Polish identity until 1526 when the Habsburgs came in and set about Germanizing both the towns and the local rulers.

Development here was slowed down by the Thirty Years War (1618–1648), which caused great devastation and reduced the population by more than 30 per cent, resulting in the decline of towns and in land lying fallow for long periods. For the doggedly Polish groups hanging on in the region, matters became even worse in 1742 when Silesia was incorporated into Prussia; from that time they were actively suppressed. But pressure often confirms and hardens the will and, despite the centuries of foreign rule and the German-controlled industrialization which had turned the eastern region of Upper Silesia into one of the workshops of Europe, literary and scientific books were still being published in Polish and there was enough support to make three uprisings against the Germans possible.

When Poland was shifted westward in 1945 the whole of Silesia returned at last to direct Polish rule and, despite centuries of Germanization and the worst efforts of the Nazis, an incredible 860,000 Silesians declared themselves to be of Polish nationality.

In 1946 some 1.4 million German nationals from Silesia were repatriated to one or other sector of the new Germany, while Poles uprooted from the lost eastern borderlands and those unsettled by the war moved in and started life afresh. I mention all this because for many nations it would be inconceivable that frontiers should be moved around in this manner, people simply being ordered to move by the townful. The many published stories of the period make it plain that this caused wholesale confusion and created great problems for the new Polish régime — which, heaven knows, already had problems enough trying to establish its authority under such circumstances. But time and nature, together with a lot of hard work, have healed many wounds and rebuilt many cities. A Polish name has been allocated to every village and farm and only an odd assortment of architectural remains today bears witness to the region's past.

Travelling westward from Kraków the worst of Silesia comes first. The Upper Silesian Industrial District is an agglomeration of thirteen autonomous towns with a population of around two million which has developed around Poland's most valuable mineral resource, a great deposit of prime coal. 'Ugly houses line the monotonous streets, discoloured by the factory smoke, dust and soot. Even the green areas have lost their green colour.' These are the words of a Polish guide-book published in the 1970s and frankly there is not much more to be said about this region. It is very like any other old industrial area of Europe, the main difference being that raw coal is still burned in Poland, and the air has an almost nostalgic aroma as the acrid smoke drifts around the streets. Unfortunately, the region still pushes a lot of its waste products into the atmosphere, a large steelworks outside the chief town, Katowice, being the main culprit, and the recipient of much of this pollution is Kraków, just 80 kilometres downwind. Much of the gilding on the roofs and spires of Wawel has been dissolved away and considerable damage done to the softer stones of the old buildings themselves by this unwelcome addition to the air. But the picture is not all unremitting gloom. Katowice has its own culture, including theatres and a symphony orchestra, although with eight coal mines beneath its streets the industrial image prevails. To an industrial historian, of course, this may well present a joyful patchwork, a living museum of manufacturing and mining. For such enthusiasts there is a Museum of Mining at **Tarnowskie Góry** on the northern fringes of the region, where it all started back in the thirteenth century, when local ores were first extracted.

The first coal-mining charter in Poland was granted to Tarnowskie Góry in 1528 and by the seventeenth century there were estimated to be 7,000 shafts in the neighbourhood. For those who developed a taste for the underworld in the Wieliczka salt mine, the ultimate subterranean journey must be through the eighteenth-century mining galleries of Tarnowskie Góry, which are open to the public. The climax of the visit is a journey by boat down the underground river known as the Black Trout Gallery, part of an 150-kilometre system of tunnels. The people here, who spend most of their waking hours underground and quite deservedly are the country's highest paid workers, know how to relax. In the autumn the region celebrates a series of festivities called Days of the Miners, when the many local folk-music and dance groups go through their paces.

Developed as the area is, it is still possible in many places to glimpse the landscape as it once was. Large pine forests reach even to the suburbs of Katowice and a large park at Chorzów contains among its lakes and sports stadiums a *skansen* museum showing old regional houses. At Będzin a fourteenth-century castle still stands, poking its tower above the nearby smokestacks. But it cannot be denied that there is much more of interest further west, and from Oświęcim (Auschwitz), for example, most of the industrialization can be by-passed by taking a more southerly route and heading eventually for Opole and Wrocław, passing on the way through Pszczyna where, in an eighteenth-century palace set in old parkland, there is a superb museum of interior furnishing from the Renaissance to the present century.

Opole was for many centuries an important junction on two trade routes and a crossing point on the Odra river. This strategic position led to the town's centre being almost completely destroyed in the last war, although great efforts have been made to recreate the old market-town atmosphere by rebuilding on the medieval street layout. The name 'Opole' indicates the antiquity of the place, coming as it does from the word for a type of early Slavic settlement. No doubt it derives from the same root as the name 'Polska', namely the word *pole* meaning 'field'. It is known that there was an organized community here in the seventh century which was fortified by the tenth and became the capital of a principality in 1202. From 1327 the town came under Bohemian rule along with most of Silesia but it returned to Poland very briefly from 1645 to 1666. The Polish King Jan Kazimierz took refuge here during the Swedish invasion of 1655. From the end of the Seven Years War in 1763, it was Prussia's turn to rule and Opole remained in German hands until 1945. Through it all, a Polish population hung on here, as is evident from the customs and crafts of the area, and today the town has some delightful features, not the least of which is that many of the restored houses rise directly from the waters of the river.

The medieval town is on the northern, right bank of the Odra but the earliest settlement was on an island where the tower of an early fourteenth-century castle still remains, the rest of the building having been pulled down in the 1930s by the Germans to make room for an administrative block. On the ground floor of this office block there is now an **Archaeological Museum** with relics from the Palaeolithic, Neolithic and Bronze Ages as well as from the Hallstatt, La Tène, Roman and early medieval cultures. All of these have been excavated on the island site and provide further proof of the antiquity and importance of those old trade routes. Many of the items discovered were found during excavations marking the Polish millennium in 1961, the nature of the soil having preserved such things as footwear, furniture and what is thought to be the oldest violin-like instrument found in Europe. In the Old Town itself, the **Market Place** is as usual the centre of attention, the old baroque and rococo houses having been carefully rebuilt. The town hall here is an oddity, a modern construction completed just before the War as a replica of the Palazzo Vecchio in Florence, but it is better, I am sure, than any contemporary design of the 1930s would have been.

Continuing on the E22 road towards Wrocław, the density of ancient monuments increases as you reach the old region of Lower Silesia (Dolny Śląsk), where good black soils on the left bank of the Odra encouraged early settlement. Not far beyond an open-air museum a turning to the left leads for fifteen kilometres to **Niemod-lin**, a small town with a big castle. Set in the forest and surrounded by parkland, the site was first developed early in the fourteenth century by Prince Bolko, while the present imposing structure dates from after the Thirty Years War, during which the old castle had been badly knocked about. The entrance to the courtyard is set beneath an unusual octagonal tower, but the building operates today as a college and there are no noteworthy interiors to see.

A little further down this side road is the village of **Łambinowice** which, known by its German name of Lamsdorf, was the site of Stalag VIII B, a prisoner-of-war camp where thousands of British, French, Canadian, Russian and Polish soldiers were interned. More than 100,000 of them died and a monument has been erected in their memory.

Another 20 kilometres south is an area of the Nysa-Kłodzka Valley which was occupied in the Middle Ages by a string of fortified towns, all but one of which suffered badly in the war.

First comes **Nysa**, where tradition has it that the first Silesian church was established some time before 1015. Later, in the twelfth century, the town was the capital of its own duchy and it owes its enormous shed of a church to this period. Although some individual buildings have been restored, much of the market place and most of the rest of the town is grey post-war concrete, devoid of charm and character. Only the monumental parish church and a Jesuit college and church complex hint at Nysa's former days of glory, when the town was renowned as an educational centre. Two Polish kings were students here: Michal Korybut Wiśniowiecki (1669–73), and the better known Jan III Sobieski (1674–96), forever dubbed the Saviour of Vienna. The baroque Jesuit buildings survive together with the remains of a bishop's palace and two towers of the old city wall. Sw.

Jakuba (St Jacob's) Church in the market place was put up originally in 1430 and again in 1950, when much use was made of the old material, including an interesting double portal and a remarkable sixteenth-century altar which sits in the heart of the cavernous interior. Oddest of all is a most decorative bit of street furniture which sits next to a pedestrian crossing in the town centre. It appears to be an old well head protected by a tall and intricate wrought-iron cage which is itself a masterly piece of work.

West of Nysa the river is dammed to create two lakes, each about ten kilometres long, and on a little hill in between the two is **Otmuchów**, smaller, prettier and better preserved than its neighbour. Built around AD 1000 by King Bolesław the Brave to protect his southern frontier, it is a pleasant place to stop for a break; so pleasant in fact that several holiday homes for children have settled on the nearby lake shore. What makes the town so different from Nysa is the fact that the last German army to destroy the town was that of Wallenstein in 1627. There is not much more to it than the market place and a hill, upon which sits a Gothic and Renaissance castle. From here there is a wide view of the smooth plain to the north and of the high, wooded Sudety Mountains over the border in Czechoslovakia, now just ten kilometres away. Larger than the castle, though, is the baroque church, whose high gable and twin towers are prominent for miles around. The town hall stands just down the slope, the body of the building dating from 1538 and its Renaissance tower from 1608. On the south-east corner of this tower is a lovely gilded sundial.

Personally, I prefer Otmuchów to its more famous neighbour **Paczków**, which is situated at the western end of the second lake. Someone, it seems, once attached to Paczków the sobriquet 'The Carcassonne of Poland', and it has stuck for no other reason than that the town walls with their four gates and numerous towers have survived intact. I warn you that it is no Carcassonne, although with a bit of spit and a lot of polish it would be a much nicer place than it now is. It looks as if not a penny has been spent so far on the restoration of what is obviously an interesting little place, but maybe that will change and Paczków will one day be worth a visit. Briefly, then, the defence walls date from 1350 and the town hall from 1552, whilst behind the market place is another great brick box of a church, built in 1382 and rebuilt in the sixteenth century as a fortified church with very little decoration on its massive walls.

At Paczków the road splits; the traveller can turn right towards

Wrocław or go straight on for 30 kilometres to the lovely spa town of Kłodzko, which is described later. But there are still some places to see back on the main Opole to Wrocław road, and an interesting way of getting back there through the rich, rolling countryside goes by way of Ziębice, where there is a late thirteenth-century Romanesque and Gothic church, and **Henryków**, famous out of all proportion to its size. Sitting below the Strzelin Hills, source of much of Poland's best building granite, Henryków developed around a Cistercian abbey where, at the end of the thirteenth century, the abbey chronicler wrote the first known sentences in the Polish language in a book known simply as *The Book of Henryków*, the original of which is now in Wrocław.

Back on the main Wrocław road is the town of **Brzeg**, another riverside settlement which in the sixteenth century was the centre for Renaissance activities in Silesia, much of its wealth coming from the production of woollen cloth and tapestries. Brzeg took a terrible beating as the German armies retreated early in 1945, pausing to make a stand at many such towns, but once again the tight grid pattern of the old street plan survives, as well as many of the more interesting buildings.

The Old Town is on the left bank of the Odra and is dominated by the **Castle**, first built by the Piast dynasty in the thirteenth century and reconstructed in a Renaissance style between 1535 and 1560, with a fine arcaded courtyard very similar to that of the castle on Kraków's Wawel Hill. The main arched entrance is adorned to its third-storey parapet with some remarkable stone carvings. The pillars and window-frames are ornately cut with vines and floral forms, and the full-length figures of a Piast prince and his lady, together with three coats of arms, runs above the archway. One floor higher, the frieze consists of a double row of figures depicting Polish kings and Silesian princes. A good cleaning would greatly enhance this remarkable entrance. Inside the surviving castle wings there is a museum dedicated to the activities of the Piast dynasty throughout Silesia; it also has the usual collection of paintings and prints of the town and an ethnographic department.

Just up the road, the last stop before Wrocław, is yet another old town, **Oława**. This has a faint connection with Britain, because at the beginning of the eighteenth century the town belonged to the son of Jan Sobieski and his daughter Marie Clementine was born here; she married James, the Stuart pretender to the English throne. Oława was another casualty of the last war and the only interesting survival here is the 1718 town hall clock which produces prancing figures on the hour.

On 15 February 1945, Soviet Army Commander Zhadov's 5th Guards joined up with their colleagues of the 6th Army to the west of the city then known as Breslau, an action which encircled 40,000 German troops and sealed the fate of the rich and ancient Silesian capital. For three months the battle raged, whole districts being shattered by Soviet shells, the defenders clearing buildings to improve their field of fire and even demolishing several streets and a monastery to make an airstrip from which their German commander could escape, as he eventually did. The town and many of its inhabitants did not. Of the large city spread over several islands and both banks of the Odra River, roughly 70 per cent was destroyed and the rest was jammed with barricades, burned-out tanks and all the awful débris of such street fighting. In 1939 the population had been 621,000 but at the end of 1945 there were only 35,000 people in the city, all but a handful of the old German inhabitants who survived the siege having fled or been transported westward into the new Germany. It is only in recent years that the population has regained its pre-war level.

Today, rechristened **Wrocław**, it is a busy industrial, commercial and educational centre, its ruins restored, its streets busy and parking a problem. However, despite the reconstruction of the churches and many of the old houses around its two market places, Wrocław does not have the magical quality of Kraków, Warsaw or Gdańsk, which may be partly because more traffic is allowed right into the town centre and partly because it could all do with a coat of paint. But if Wrocław has lost its crown, several of its jewels have survived, including a dozen churches, one of the best Gothic town halls in Central Europe and a University building which is a quite astonishing temple of the baroque. It has regained its position as a provincial capital and can boast a lively culture with opera - and operetta - houses, a philharmonic society, four theatres including the world-famous Mime Theatre and Actors' Laboratory, a big publishing house and six museums. The presence of some 40,000 students at the university and various colleges constantly refuels this creative life, as well as providing fertile soil for all the usual political arguments.

As at Kraków, the medieval city grew up away from the original settlement which here was on several easily defended islands around some of which the Odra river still flows. The most dramatic evidence that this was an important site on the old trade routes was the discovery in a Wrocław suburb of a hoard of three tonnes of high quality amber, already graded for size. It was buried, no doubt for safekeeping, in the first century AD, a common practice at the time, but presumably either the merchant or the town itself met with some misfortune which prevented it from being collected. In the year AD 1000 Bolesław the Brave founded on the island known as Ostrów Tumski one of the three episcopates subject to the newly created Archbishop of Gniezno, and fortified both the township and the new church. Wrocław was always within a frontier zone. In 1109 Bolesław Wrymouth led an army which fought off the German Emperor Henry V who had designs on the area, and this victory was followed by a period of peace and prosperity which saw the erection of many substantial Romanesque buildings in the town. That great battle took place just to the north-east of Wrocław at a place still known as Psie Pole, meaning Dog's Field, so called, legend has it, because the fighting was so fierce and the defeat so thorough that the Germans had no time to collect their dead, a task subsequently performed by the local hounds. Gruesome but not impossible.

During the twelfth century the town expanded to the southern left bank of the river, but no sooner was it established there than in 1241 the Tartars arrived and burned it down. Far from being abandoned, the town was quickly rebuilt, acquiring municipal status under the recently introduced system known as the Magdeburg Laws and taking on the layout which survives to this day: a grid of streets centred on a market place with a defensive wall and moat around the outside. One of the first buildings of this new town was the **Town Hall** which also served as home to a hereditary bailiff who governed the town on behalf of the ruling prince. As it was to be the centre of social and political life, an imposing building was called for, and it was frequently enlarged and modified as the town prospered and the rich burghers dispensed their patronage. The original one-storey structure had an upper floor added in the mid-fifteenth century as the town reached the peak of its medieval power and authority. By 1500, with the addition of a south aisle, the building had the basic form and decoration that is seen in today's post-war restoration. During the Renaissance and baroque periods the all too familiar details of those times were added, including a Renaissance spire on top of the Gothic tower.

Today the town hall is a historical museum, but before you go in it is well worth studying the exterior, for the south and east faces comprise a rich collection of architectural details. The east façade is crowned with a Gothic gable from 1500, embellished with decorative pinnacles

209

above a border of intricate stone tracery which is echoed inside the gable triangle with terracotta decorations. In the centre of this elevation is a large astronomical clock made in 1580 and decorated in blue and red with gold numerals, a truly splendid time-keeper which has a golden-faced sun in its centre and displays the phases of the moon. The south side is even more decorative, giving a chronicle in stone of the city's fifteenth-century inhabitants, from jousting knights to ancient crones and many small grotesque figures, the whole group set in a maze of intricately carved stone. An entrance in this wall leads down to the Piwnica Świdnicka, an old wine cellar which now houses a café, its ancient doors decorated with a description of the tavern in an old script.

The town hall itself is entered beneath the tower on the plainer west side. The main item of note in the vestibule is a fragment of Renaissance wall painting which was uncovered during pre-war preservation work. From the vestibule an archway leads to the long **Burghers' Hall (Sala Mieszczańska)** which is the oldest part of the building. It is a two-aisled hall divided by five pointed arcades, each resting on a large square pillar. Erected in the 1270s as a chamber for meetings and feasts, it also served as a covered market up until the seventeenth century. At the far end of the hall a door leads to the Bailiff's Room (Izba Wójtowska) which was added in 1299 as an office and a court. It has ribbed stellar vaults of stone and steps up to a door leading to other rooms. This is a sturdy, wooden door, simple and bold, but its stone portal, added in 1528, is a highly decorated affair, apparently a reduced copy of a giant portal that once existed in the town walls. A portal a century older, complete with a metal-plated door, connects the Councillor's Room with the Town Clerk's Office in the north-east corner of the ground floor. The late Gothic vault of the latter room has polychrome keystones representing the letter W, the head of St John the Baptist, the Silesian eagle and the Bohemian lion, all components of Wrocław's early coat of arms.

If the ground floor is splendid and handsome, the first floor rooms are no less noble. The only shock is the broad nineteenth-century marble staircase which connects the two levels and delivers you to the largest and most beautiful room in the building. This is the **Refectory**, also known as the **Knights' Hall,** which is as long as the ground-floor hall but this time has three aisles. The south aisle provides a particularly striking aspect, with the light from the oriel windows slanting on to the polished floor and illuminating a great deal of sculptured ornamentation on the way. The middle oriel is the loveliest: protected by a carved parapet and arched with stone tracery, it has fully detailed armoured knights standing on either side. The bay window itself has a coffered ceiling, but the gilded rosettes which once decorated it were lost in the last war.

Next in size and splendour is the **Prince's Room (Sala Książęca)**, built initially in the mid-fourteenth century as a chapel, but used from the seventeenth century for conferences of Silesian princes as they juggled with the complex power politics of the day. The ribbed cross-vault of the ceiling is supported by a single pillar, the slender stone ribs resting on a capital which displays a variety of carved heads and a band of delicately sculpted oak leaves.

In the **Aldermen's Room** there is an excellent example of metal-work from around 1500 in the form of a strong-room door which seems more than adequate for the job. This studded door is patterned in a diamond grid of iron which is decorated with lions and eagles. Inside the strong room was the customs department, which had a vital part to play in the raising of revenue at a time when most towns imposed a toll on passing merchants.

The town hall stands together with several other old buildings, including the Grotowski Theatre, as an island in a market place ringed by medieval houses with Renaissance or baroque fronts, all rebuilt since the last war. The last 40 years have not been kind to their painted exteriors and they once again give the impression of having stood unmolested for centuries. Perhaps the best building on the square is the **Griffin House (Dom Pod Gryfami)**, the largest patrician house in the town and designed in a Flemish Renaissance style. Part of the house was completely demolished in the war and, during the clearance of the site prior to rebuilding, the remains of a twelfth-century wooden house were found under the foundations. Unlike those of Kraków and Warsaw this square is used by traffic and is busier with local people than with visitors. There is a bookshop on one corner where guide-books and maps can be obtained, to be studied at your leisure while you wait to be served in any one of the several cafés and restaurants which face on to the spires and gables of the town hall.

It is difficult to plan a tour of the city because the many places of interest are scattered far and wide and the streets *en route* are not always attractive. The nearest church is visible beyond the north-west corner of the square and is reached by passing between two little Gothic houses, linked by a baroque gate, which have long been associated with the Hansel and Gretel legend. This **Church of St Elizabeth**, like others in this previously German city, was Protestant until the war but was rebuilt as a Catholic institution. Sadly, a fire has since damaged St Elizabeth's and restoration work is only now being completed. Continuing past the church and northwards along Odrzańska Street, you will come to the river bank where it will be immediately obvious why the site was chosen for settlement so many centuries ago. Within a short distance of turning right there are nine islands in the Odra and this is only one branch of the river, for what seems to be the far bank is itself an even larger island upon which sits a great chunk of the modern city. It is a very watery view from here as one island is glimpsed beyond another and there are said to be something like 80 bridges within the city limits, including those over the old defensive moat which still surrounds the town on its southern side and links up with the river.

Walking upstream one very soon comes to a huge building facing out over the river which is the seat of the **University**; and huge is not an overstatement. It is 171 metres long, a monumental baroque edifice built to a design by the Italian Domenico Martinelli. It was founded in 1702 by Emperor Leopold I and completed by 1741 on a site once occupied by a castle. Its destruction in 1945 was only the latest and worst indignity suffered by this building, which previously had survived inundation by the Odra, broken windows when the city gunpowder tower exploded in 1749 and occupation by various armies, one of which used the college and its neighbouring church for the storage of corn.

One room alone was spared from these storage duties and that was the **Aula Leopoldina**, an extraordinary long and narrow hall whose proportions and decorations remind me of those old photographs which show the interiors of railway carriages designed for tsars, shahs and maharajas. Even the ceiling curves down to meet the walls, as in a train, and a spectacular ceiling it is, smothered in *trompe-l'oeil* paintings which fuse with the frescos adorning the walls and deep window recesses. The room serves as the main assembly hall of the university and above the raised dais which occupies one end there is a painted figure of the Emperor Leopold, floating amidst biblical and mythological images. At the opposite end is a music gallery under which there are five plafonds showing an angelic choir and orchestra, and the ceiling between these two extremes is equally exuberant, incorporating portraits of famous men and great scholars of history, from Moses and Solomon through Thomas à Kempis and Aristotle to Livy, Ovid and Virgil. The wall space between the windows is decorated with a gallery of portraits honouring the rulers and officials who encouraged the Jesuits to set up their college in Wrocław.

Beyond the university the river channel narrows and a short bridge, the Most Piaskowy, leads to Wyspa Piaskowa or Sandy Island. This is an apposite name, for the island is nothing more than a stabilized sandbank, which explains why the church here is called **Our Lady of the Sand (Marii na Piasku)**. This church is well known for its beautiful high vaulting. It also contains fragments of a Romanesque temple thought to have been founded in 1150 and a tympanum from that original building. Next door is a huge baroque building, put up in the eighteenth century as an Augustinian monastery but now serving a wider audience as the University Library, and opposite this, maintaining the ecclesiastical atmosphere, are the fourteenth-century Gothic buildings of a convent and hospital. But the necessities of life can never be far off. Hard by the convent are two ancient water-mill buildings, one each from the thirteenth and fourteenth centuries.

There are two ways off this island. Walking north leads across a little island of parkland to the northern suburbs, while a right turn leads to the oldest part of the city, **Ostrów Tumski**, once its own island but long since a part of that larger island which makes up the north bank here. It is easy enough to find the place; the two great stumps of the cathedral towers are visible from far away across town. This is the most attractive part of the whole city, with narrow cobbled lanes and old houses, many connected with the cathedral, which create an area of calm far removed from the bustle of the rest of Wrocław. Church administration is definitely big business here. Priests are forever scuttling around the streets, nuns popping in and out of doorways beyond which all is mystery, the realm of Catholic bureaucracy. I did once enter a building in Katredralna Street with a friend who worked there editing a church newspaper: the atmosphere bore no resemblance at all to any newspaper office of my acquaintance. The gloomy rooms and corridors conveyed just the mood I had expected of such an ecclesiastical institution, with only the pink faces of black-frocked priests visible in the eternal gloaming.

The **Cathedral** first commands your attention here, its massive red brick towers looming above the far end of Katredralna Street, its portico an elaborate stone affair with a pointed gable and many carved figures. The present building is the fourth cathedral on the site since the bishopric was founded in AD 1000, or the fifth if an explosion which occurred during the 1945 siege is taken into account. The Germans used it as a dump for explosives but, sanctified or not, the whole lot went up, leaving yet another restoration job to be done. Amazingly for such a large building, it was pieced together again by 1951, during a period when so much else also had to be rebuilt. Churches and other historic monuments came fairly high on the list of priorities, absorbing a lot of scarce labour, money and materials. The original cathedral was built soon after the destructive raids of the Tartars in 1241 and represented some of the earliest purely Gothic architecture in Poland. The slender towering vaults of the interior impose that special and slightly obsequious atmosphere which is unique to large holy establishments and lends an ethereal air to decorations which might otherwise appear frivolous. Here I am thinking in particular of the two baroque chapels in the north-east corner, the **St Elizabeth Chapel** and the Corpus Christi or Elector's Chapel. The first was built by Giacomo Scianzi in the 1680s to the order of Cardinal Frederick, Elector of Hesse, a convert to Catholicism who obviously wanted to leave no doubts as to his faith. The fresco in the oval dome is also by Scianzi, while the kneeling figure of Frederick and his bust are by Ercole Ferrara and Domenico Guidi, both pupils of the great Bernini. The **Corpus Christi Chapel** is even more extravagant, being, like much else in the Habsburg lands, the work of the architect of Vienna's Schönbrunn Palace and St Charles's Church, one Johann Bernhard Fischer von Erlach. The elector for whom this space was reserved was Franz Ludwig Neuborg, who combined his position as Archbishop of Wrocław with that of Elector of Trier, far away in the west Rhineland. Behind the high altar there is a Gothic Chapel of the Virgin containing an interesting sarcophagus, while the magnificent altarpiece itself was inspired if not created by Wit Stwosz. All the stained glass in the choir was lost in 1945 and the present windows are the work of several modern Polish artists.

To the north of the cathedral, on the corner of the curving Ulica Kanonia, is the **Archdiocesan Museum**, which has a large collection of Silesian sacred art, much of it from the Gothic period. Outstanding are a Romanesque chalice and paten together with liturgical garments from the thirteenth century and a sculpture of St John the Baptist from the twelfth. There is also a group of beautifully crafted Gothic altarpieces from the region, as well as some document cabinets from 1455 which are claimed to be the world's oldest filing cabinets. What competition there is for this title I do not profess to know. Ulica Kanonia itself curls around and heads back towards the Tumski Bridge, passing the end of the pleasant and popular Botanical Gardens with their Natural History Museum on the right and emerging beneath one of the most beautiful Gothic buildings in the country, the **Church of the Holy Cross (Sw. Krzyza)**.

Unmistakable beneath its slender blue-green spire, this church is much more exciting than the rather sombre cathedral. The best view of it is across the water from the west, a view which also encompasses a modern statue of Pope John XXIII and the tiny eleventh-century church of St Mark (Sw. Marcin), whose stumpy hexagonal tower contrasts with the soaring gables and spire behind. The most extraordinary thing about the Holy Cross Church is that it is two churches, one above the other, the upper floor being dedicated to the Holy Cross and the lower to St Bartholomew. It was begun in 1288 under the auspices of Henry IV Probus, Duke of Silesia, who with his wife Mathilde is preserved in stone in the upper church, the duke's tomb itself having been removed to Wrocław National Museum. As if the little islands and ancient areas of the city did not possess enough churches, there is a fifteenth-century temple dedicated to SS Peter and Paul (Sw. Piotr i Pawla) just across the road beside the Tumski Bridge.

The joy of this part of Wrocław is that one is away from the traffic. Thanks to the miracle of the restorer's craft, it is easy to while away the hours amidst these atmospheric streets, and the several little green islands, linked by foot-bridges, all provide views of the city. However, for the seeker of all things interesting and beautiful this tour is only half-way through and to reach the next port of call the left bank of the Odra can be regained either by the way we came, then turning left along the river bank, or by continuing beyond the cathedral and crossing by the busy Peace Bridge (Most Pokoju). Both routes lead to the large nineteenth-century **National Museum** building which houses several important collections.

The section of **Medieval Silesian Art** contains some precious and beautiful survivors from the early centuries of this millennium, none more entrancing than the 'Madonna Enthroned on Lions', also known as the 'Skarbimierz Madonna'. This wood sculpture from some time around 1360 shows a chubby-faced and smiling Mary supporting a precocious baby Jesus, who stands on his mother's knee with his right hand to his temple as if in salute. Mary sits on a bench and, while supporting angels stand on the backs of a pair of none-too-pleased lions, the silkily polished wood of her dress folds and falls between the animals. Fine as the workmanship is, it is the happy smiling face of the Madonna which lingers in the memory, in such contrast to the poker-faced portrayals one so often finds. In fact, some of the painted madonnas in this very same gallery are none too cheerful, but one example from 1410, painted on wood, shows a very pretty Mary set in a wonderful gold frame. Another, from 1450, also tempera on wood, shows the scene set in a chamber with a distinctively Dutch feel to it. The picture is dominated by huge folds of dark velvet so wonderfully painted that the temptation is to reach out and touch them. This section also contains stone sculptures from old Silesia, including the previously mentioned tomb of Henry IV Probus. This limestone sarcophagus was made locally in around 1320. The duke lies full-length on top, resplendent with sword and crown and a shield showing the Piast eagle, while around the sides are the carved figures of mourners, regarded as the first example in central Europe of what are known as 'weepers'. It is interesting to compare the Silesian art of the fourteenth and fifteenth centuries with work from the same period further east, that of Kraków, Lublin or Przemyśl, for example, where the stylistic influence from the East shows itself so strongly. Here in Silesia the traditional connection was with Prague and Germanic Europe and this is evident throughout the region.

The permanent exhibition of paintings is divided into **Silesian Modern Art** – actually from the sixteenth and seventeenth centuries – **Foreign Painting** and **Polish Painting**. Within these rooms is a feast of pictures, from the grand gestures of the inescapable Matejko, which here include a moving portrait of Konrad Wallenrod, and Bellotto (Canaletto), with his vastly peopled scene of Chancellor Jerzy Ossolinski entering Rome in 1633, to the introverted images of Malczewski, whose pictures I find particularly haunting, and the gentle documentary landscapes of Dębicki. The foreign paintings are few in number but of great merit; there are examples from fifteenth-century Siena and other Italian schools as well as Dutch and Flemish pictures, found everywhere in northern Europe. The nucleus of this collection was originally held by the museum in Lwów when it was the regional capital of south-east Poland but after the Second World War, with that city absorbed into the USSR, the Soviet authorities turned the pictures over to Wrocław, where many Lwów people had settled.

Many exhibits in the section devoted to **Artistic Craftsmanship** also derive from Lwów and include ceramics, glassware, metalwork and textiles. There are fourth-century earthenware figures from China and some of the first porcelain from Meissen together with a large collection of Italian, Dutch and Slovak faience. Glassware is well represented by engraved and cut Silesian items, painted guild cups from the sixteenth century and some beautiful *art nouveau* glass. Finally, the textiles, again from Lwów, include oriental work as well as Polish *kilim* rugs and a large group of costumes from the eighteenth and nineteenth centuries. The museum has much more under its control, including collections of photographs, graphic art and coins, but these are shown only at occasional exhibitions or by appointment to scholars. All in all, it is a rich museum and well worth a visit.

Back in the open air, there is a welcome area of park opposite the museum. As you turn right into it, a strange object may be seen lurking amongst the trees, remarkably like a concrete gasholder. This is the **Racławice Panorama**, the **Rotunda Panoramy Racławickiej**. It contains a single painting 15 metres high and 114 metres long, wrapped around the inside of the cylindrical building, which illustrates in great detail a famous battle of 1794. This was the year that Tadeusz Kościuszko led his peasant army of insurrection northwards from Kraków, defeating a Russian army on the way at the village of Racławice, an event much celebrated in Polish history. A hundred years later a committee was formed in partitioned Poland to consider a suitable memorial and this great picture was the result. It was a popular attraction for many years at its original site in Lwów.

The main painters involved were Jan Styka and Wojciech Kossak, with other artists adding specialized detail, and although competently painted it is a bit like a comic strip, redolent of illustrations from old-fashioned school history books. The unfolding battle is shown in all its stages; the two artists travelled illegally to Racławice, then in the Russian zone, to study the battlefield. Astonishingly, the whole thing was completed in nine months, the two painters working towards each other from either end of the scene. By a brilliant control of perspective and the addition of a well-balanced three-dimensional foreground, the painting achieves an illusion of great depth. It is very popular with Polish tourists and school groups, for whom the battle is one of the great moments of modern Polish history, even though the end result of the insurrection was a failure and led to the total partition of the country the very next year. Explanatory cassettes are available in several languages including English, French and German.

Heading from here back towards the city centre, a right turn into Ulica Bernardyńska leads to the **Museum of Architecture** which, as well as describing general styles and their history, covers the post-war reconstruction of Silesia in detail, with dramatic photographs showing the awful damage which was inherited by the new Wrocławians. The museum is also a last resting place for decorative fragments of buildings which were never restored. This was almost the fate of the museum itself, a complex of fifteenth- and sixteenth-century structures which was built as a Bernardine monastery but gutted by fire in 1945.

As you continue down the main Ulica Wita Stwosza, back towards the market place, a little green space opens on the left, and beyond it is the fourteenth-century **Church of Maria Magdalena** which has a twelfth-century Romanesque portal set into the south wall. The tympanum from this is in the National Museum, and is highly regarded by art historians for the quality of its sculpted figures. It originally decorated the nearby Abbey of Ołbin, which was demolished in the sixteenth century.

Once you are back in the Rynek, I suggest a left turn into Ulica Świdnicka which is the main shopping street of the city and is for pedestrians only. This leads via an underpass to the nineteenth-century Opera House and one of the theatres, but also to a very interesting **Archaeological and Ethnographic Museum**, reached by turning right at the underpass and down the busy inner ring road known as Kazimierz Wielkiego. The museum is a storehouse of Silesian history going back to the earliest days of man's settlement in the region, but as usual the ethnographic department is the most fun. I especially liked the amazing wooden beehives, some as big as the tree trunks from which they were carved. Their ornate shapes include life-size noblemen and bishops in full rig and they underline the importance of honey throughout history. It is a pity that the square modern boxes, of which Europe must contain millions, are so efficient, because before this century beehive construction was more interesting, as much art as science.

One very Polish tradition displayed here is that of decorating such commonplace items as cupboards and wardrobes with sometimes rather garish flower patterns, which must have provided a welcome splash of colour in dim, pre-electric cottages. Wood-carving is still very much alive in Poland, the favourite secular subject being folk musicians both singly and in groups, and there are many of these on display here. There are also several complex if only decorative machines featuring groups of figures which dance as the wind turns a simple propeller.

On the way back towards Świdnicka Street, a little turning on the right leads to the **Church of St Dorothy (Sw. Doroty)**, an imposing building in the familiar red-brick Gothic style, which was founded in 1351 to mark the meeting in Wrocław between Kazimierz the Great and the German Emperor Charles IV. This otherwise unexceptional church recalls for me one of my rare encounters with the Catholic faith in practice, for it was here that I first witnessed the special ceremony for the blessing of Easter eggs. This is still an important event for most Polish families, the idea being that the food to be eaten on Easter Sunday must first be blessed by the sprinkling of holy water. On the Saturday morning that I went with friends who live nearby, the little strip of park opposite the church marking the line of the old town walls was full of smartly dressed families. Each one carried a little basket in which, prettily displayed on a napkin, were a few eggs and something to represent the other food to be eaten on the most important feast day of the year. Usually this includes a piece of dry sausage, some bread and a pinch of salt. During the short ceremony in the packed church, hymns were sung and prayers spoken, then a procession of priests moved down the nave sprinkling water first to one side and then to the other. It is a tradition that eggs for Easter are painted with a floral pattern which varies from region to region but, although wooden eggs decorated in this way can be bought in *Cepelia* shops and seen in museums, few will be found in church these days. My father-in-law, a country boy from the forests north of Lublin, has his own technique for enhancing the natural colour of eggs for Easter. This entails boiling them with the outer skins of onions, which leaves the eggs with a wonderful rich reddish-brown sheen.

This more or less covers the historical aspects of Wrocław, because, once beyond the old moat, Ulica Świdnica comes to the post-war buildings, the first of which is the main department store (Dom Handlowy Centrum), which overlooks Plac Kościuszko, a square of 1950s offices and shops from which other shopping streets emanate. As usual, bookshops are plentiful and local guide-books and maps may suggest other places of interest in or around the town. With such a history, Lower Silesia has plenty to offer to the curious but after a spell in the city I shall make, as is my wont, for the hills.

12

The South-West

South from Wrocław the international E12 road heads for the Czechoslovakian frontier and on to Brno or Prague but, visible from the city although some 40 kilometres away across the smooth, rich plain, the symmetrical cone of a hill emerges from the haze and this is the first target. A right turn at the village of Jordanów leads through lanes to the small town of Sobótka, sitting below the hill which rises 500 metres from the surrounding plain. This isolated outcrop is called **Ślęza** and is a place of great mystery and fascination for historians and archaeologists as well as an attraction for tourists, not least because of the view from its 718-metre (2,154-foot) summit, which can be reached either by road or after a couple of hours of steady plodding up a footpath. The mystery starts in Sobótka where, beside a fifteenth-century church, there is a carved stone known as the Mushroom. A twelfth-century carved lion and other carved stones, including one of a headless woman carrying a fish, are found on the way up the hill, but these can be seen only from the footpath and not from the summit road. The top of the hill, as well as sporting a television mast and hostel of more recent vintage, is surrounded by stone ramparts.

The accepted theory for all of this is that in the late fourth and early third centuries BC the Celts expanded from their lands along the Danube, settling in the hills of Bohemia and as far north as Silesia, where this mountain became a major centre of worship. The site was then inherited by other people including the Ślężanic, one of five Slavic tribal groups known to have settled in Silesia by the ninth century and the one from which the name Silesia (**Śląsk**) is thought to have derived. Such are the legends surrounding this hill and so evocative is the atmosphere created by the sculptures scattered around its slopes that, if it were in England, I am certain it would have the cult attraction of a Stonehenge or a Glastonbury. As it is, the Catholic faith in Poland is still strong enough to minimize the numbers of such extremist worshippers and so the hill remains just an archaeological oddity and a picnic site.

Back on the main road, the spa town of **Kłodzko** is some 50 kilometres south of Ślęża in the largest basin in the Sudety Mountains, a beautiful valley of spas, springs and forests which has attracted the rich and famous since the seventeenth century. The combination of a mild climate, lovely countryside and natural mineral water is always a winner and has provided Kłodzko with a living since its importance as a trade-route frontier town diminished. It was known as a settlement as far back as AD 981 and until the mid-fourteenth century was controlled by the Piast dynasty before following the rest of Silesia into foreign hands. After the Thirty Years War the Austrians built a fortress in the town which the Prussians later strengthened — obviously to good effect, because in 1807 it withstood an attack by Napoleon. It was less lucky in the last war but has since been well repaired and today it is a handsome town on the right bank of the young Nysa-Kłodzka river, its medieval layout recognizable and even its thirteenth-century Gothic river bridge still standing, although this is now adorned after the style of the Charles Bridge in Prague with statues of saints, put there during the baroque period which could never leave well alone.

A greater act of vandalism occurred in the sloping market place during the nineteenth century, when the old town hall was rebuilt in the rather heavy-handed style of the time, leaving just the tall Renaissance tower built in 1654 as a reminder of a more elegant if less capacious building. An eighteenth-century palace on the south side of the square houses a museum which tells the long story of life in the valley and the streets close by contain numerous baroque and Renaissance mansions as well as the twin-towered parish church, which has baroque ornamentation on its earlier frame. A Gothic tomb plate of a fourteenth-century bishop of Prague survives here, as does a rather nice statue of the Madonna with a songbird from the same period. The best view of the town is from either of the two fortresses; there is one on each side of the valley immediately south of the town. There are two hotels in Kłodzko as well as the usual private accommodation but, although the town is a good centre for the valley and its surrounding hills, there are plenty of places to stay in the resorts which abound in the neighbourhood.

East from Kłodzko the road heads towards Paczków and Nysa, which we visited earlier, while to the west this same road continues for some 37 kilometres before reaching the Czechoslovakian frontier, passing several spas on the way and climbing out of the valley into wooded hill country. The first town on this road is Polanica-Zdrój, a twentieth-century spa whose waters are recommended for those with circulatory or digestive problems and whose park is a mass of rhododendrons and azaleas in the spring.

Ten kilometres further into the hills, **Duszniki-Zdrój** is altogether different; known as a spa since the fifteenth century, it has three warm and mineral-rich springs and modern medical facilities. There is an old market place lined with the familiar baroque houses, one of which bears a plaque announcing that both Felix Mendelssohn and Fryderyk Chopin rested within during the 1820s. The sixteen-year-old Chopin was there for treatment, but was persuaded to give two recitals in the eighteenth-century theatre in aid of orphaned children. The theatre has survived and today is the scene of a Chopin piano festival every August, for which, I would imagine, it is necessary to book in advance. Duszniki is an altogether pleasant place, surrounded by hills with well marked trails and offering a couple of real curiosities. In the 1708 church there is a pulpit in the form of a whale, for reasons which I have not fathomed but presume to be connected with Jonah. On the little river which tumbles through the town, there is an old paper mill of the most striking appearance, built in 1605, which now houses a museum of paper-making. This details the development of the industry and shows how such processes as the watermarking and handmaking of paper are carried out.

From Duszniki the road climbs the Polskie Wrota Pass (670 metres, 2,110 feet), above which stand the ruins of a thirteenth-century frontier castle, and then falls down a slope into a high basin in which sits **Kudowa-Zdrój**, another ancient spa which was developed several hundred years ago and was once host to a certain Mr Winston Churchill. With a mild climate, plenty of mineral springs and medicinal mud, it is a popular place and competes musically with Duszniki by hosting an annual festival dedicated to the music of Stanisław Moniuszko, a nineteenth-century composer known as the father of Polish opera. On the west side of the hill which rises above the town, in the village of Czermna, there is a most extraordinary eighteenth-century chapel. Its walls are lined with some 3,000 human skulls and there are a further 20,000 in the vaults, all supposed to be victims of epidemics and wars. Hardly a reassuring sight at a health resort.

North-east of the town is a favourite rambling region amongst the rocky sandstone outcrops of the Table Mountains (Góry Stołowe). Some geomorphological oddity has left these pillars of bare rock, formed by the weather into labyrinths of weird and wonderful shapes, protruding from the pine forest. An exciting walk from Kudowa Zdrój could include these hills with their magnificent views and then descend to the village of Wambierzyce, which has a most enormous basilica built in the 1720s in a late-Renaissance style. Reached by a broad, steep flight of steps, the pale-yellow and white church with its rich interior dwarfs everything around it in the samll village. It was built for the celebration of religious festivals and is the last and most important of a line of chapels which form the Way of the Cross.

In the hills on the opposite side of the main valley, sixteen kilometres south-east of Kłodzko, is yet another old spa town, **Lądek-Zdrój**, which is protected from the north winds by hills known as the Golden Mountains. This spot was known for its mineral waters as far back as the thirteenth century, although its most venerable remnant is a stone river-bridge built in 1596. It has one of the nicest market places in the region, where the ornate attics of the arcaded burghers' houses are silhouetted against the dark hillside. As elsewhere in this 'Valley of Health', as the Poles call it, there are many modern sanatoriums here. Although less attractive than the older buildings, they are for the most part well hidden amongst the trees, and I have no doubt that earlier visitors here, who included Goethe and Turgenev, would still recognize the place.

From Kłodzko the main valley runs south for some 40 kilometres before rising to pass over the frontier. Only citizens of Eastern European countries may cross over here, incidentally; a constraint which applies to many of the smaller frontier posts. Half-way up the valley is the old town of **Bystrzyca Kłodzka**, yet another place which earned its living from the old trade routes. In the market square there is a pillory dating from 1556, while nearby one of the three remaining towers from the almost completely destroyed town wall has been turned into a belfry. The most interesting building is the parish church with two naves, built at the turn of the fourteenth century, and perhaps the oddest local attraction is the **Philumenistic** (*sic*) **Museum** which is housed in a former Protestant church in the small market place

(Mały Rynek). This is devoted to the history of fire-making, displaying everything from medieval flint lighters to safety matches from the past century and fully explaining the modern process of match manufacture. A central exhibit — and a must for those few specialists in the subject — is the huge collection of matchbox labels, with a special emphasis on graphic design since 1945. The building also contains the regional museum.

Right up at the head of the valley is the neat little thirteenth-century town of **Międzylesie**, which still has several lovely wooden houses in its centre, each with a porch and high gable, as well as baroque houses. Up here, though, it is the hills on the east side of the valley, amongst which the dome of Śnieznik Mountain rises to 1,425 metres (4,675 feet), which attract most Poles. At the foot of Śnieznik and hidden among steep, tree-clad slopes is the village of **Międzygórze**, a place I have visited only in early winter when the snow was deep but the skiers still in the cities. The scene then was quite magical — the stuff of which Christmas cards are made — down to the children pulling toboggans and the horse-carts having their wheels replaced with skis, a common practice in the Polish countryside. The waterfall was still tumbling through the snow down its 28 rocky metres (84 feet), a bridge across the top providing a dizzy view straight down. During my visit I spent several hours in the cottage of a large extended family who somehow eke a living out of the hills. The large combined kitchen and living room was baking hot from the old stove and its endless supply of logs, but there were precious few luxuries or modern conveniences up on this snowy slope. As is quite typical, three generations shared the house and all the duties although only two people seemed to have a regular income: the son of the house was the village postman, and some other money came from the operation of a rather short ski lift which rose from one of the family's fields. But what impressed me in that muggy room, one of the simplest I have ever been in, was its inhabitants' wide knowledge of international current affairs and the ferocity of their opinions; both of these attributes, I have to say, are quite typically Polish.

In the winter and summer seasons, the Kłodzko Valley is a favourite haunt of Wrocławians for weekend outings, but there are other hills in the south-west which are equally bracing, their main centre being Jelenia Góra, 95 kilometres west of Wrocław. This can be reached directly from Kłodzko, but the route goes by way of the large industrial and mining town of Wałbrzych which, despite having an interesting history, is not a pretty sight today. Coal-mining began there even

Wooden churches still abound in southern Poland. This splendid eighteenth-century example can be found in the large open-air museum of folk architecture at Sanok on the edge of the Bieszczady Mountains.

The interior of the wooden church at Sanok exhibits a typical combination of rustic architecture and exuberant Catholic decoration.

Although this cottage is now in the Sanok open-air museum, many such simple and seemingly precarious houses survive in the southern hills.

The Renaissance style of architecture reached deep into eastern Europe. Krasiczyn Castle, in the far south-east corner of the country, was started in 1592 by one of the many Italian architects employed by the wealthy nobility.

Niedzica Castle stands above the fast-flowing Czarny Dunajec river on an old trade route through the mountains. Close by is the starting point for raft trips through the dramatic Pieniny gorge.

Until the Second World War, the Bieszczady Mountains were home to many Orthodox Christians, whose easily identifiable wooden churches can still be found in the remote valleys, as here at Turzańsk. The plains of central Poland, however, were Christianized from the west and the church at Tum (*below*) is a fine example of the Romanesque style to be found in that region.

Wrocław. The ancient Silesian capital contains many Gothic buildings, the fifteenth-century Town Hall shown here being one of its best. The splendid interior now houses a museum.

Above left: Wrocław. A charming sixteenth-century detail from the richly decorated façade of the Town Hall.

Above right: An ice-cream seller, a common sight in most Polish towns.

Below: Wrocław. The old Salt Market (Plac Solny), with its ornately gabled merchants' houses, adjoins the main square and is still an active market.

earlier than in Upper Silesia. Prince Bolko of nearby Świdnica granted extraction privileges to several of his courtiers in 1366 and surviving documents tell of mines operating on a large scale in the sixteenth century.

There are, however, several interesting towns and one spectacular castle in the area, which can be conveniently visited coming either from Kłodzko or directly from Wrocław. On the Wrocław road, some 40 kilometres from the city, is **Świdnica**, an ancient trade-route town which became the seat of a castellan in the twelfth century and was the centre of the largest of the Piast principalities in Silesia from 1314 until the take-over by the Bohemians in 1392. In the later Middle Ages the town was second only to Wrocław as a manufacturing and trading centre in the region and was well known for the quality of its beers, which were exported as far as Kraków and Toruń. In 1747, Frederick the Great turned the place into a fortress, as was his wont, and the town was besieged four times during the Seven Years War.

The centre of Świdnica has retained its ancient character, although most of the Gothic houses have had the usual baroque frontages tacked on to them. In the market place there are still fragments of the 1329 town hall within the later structure and the **Parish Church**, again with surviving fourteenth-century features including a magnificent Gothic portal, has the highest tower in Silesia, climbing 103 metres (309 feet) above the streets. Almost buried beneath the baroque décor of the interior are a 1492 triptych inspired by Wit Stwosz's Kraków altar, a fourteenth-century painting of the Virgin Mary and a 1410 *pietà*. More unusual than the parish church is the extraordinary, half-timbered Protestant Church, of a multi-storey baroque affair not entirely dissimilar to a Black Forest *Gasthaus* or even a nineteenth-century German railway shed — both of which can be handsome structures, I hasten to add. Built in the years 1656–8 to a Greek-cross ground-plan, the towerless church has a wreath of little chapels which protrude like carbuncles from the outside walls. It is like nothing other than itself, a genuine and splendid curiosity for students of architecture.

Just thirteen kilometres west of Świdnica, at the small industrial town of Świebodzice, turn left and follow the Wałbrzych road for no more than a kilometre to arrive at **Książ**, a tiny place with a monumental castle which towers over it, rising out of beech woods and, in spring, glorious clumps of rhododendrons. This is the largest medieval stronghold in Lower Silesia and a museum of all architectural styles from the Romanesque to the modern. The oldest parts, around the central tower, are the remains of the Romanesque castle started in 1292 by Prince Bolko, which was regularly enlarged and altered right up until the time of the Second World War when the last private owner, descended from relatives of the Piasts, fled to Britain. Had the war turned out differently, Książ would surely be much better known than it is, because Hitler chose it to be one of his seats within the enlarged Reich. Huge caverns were cut out of the rock beneath the castle to protect the little man from bombardment. The work done for Hitler almost did for the castle, so brutalized were the interiors, but conservation and restoration work in recent years has returned many chambers to their gilt and marble best. And this splendid red-roofed pile provides a dramatic backdrop for a nearby equestrian centre which has a stud farm and a riding school where you can spend a holiday in the saddle. Book in advance, of course.

Back up on the Jelenia Góra road, it is 20 kilometres from here to Bolków, a picturesque town which was once, as its name implies, the property of Prince Bolko, whose castle dominates it. Both Bolko and his son Bolko II, by the way, are buried in the magnificent former Benedictine **Abbey of Krzeszów** which is in the hills 27 kilometres to the south. Founded by Henry the Pious in 1242 and later enlarged, the abbey is one of the most beautiful baroque buildings in Silesia, with a magnificent twin-towered façade and rich rococo decorations.

There is much less remaining of **Bolków Castle** but it does provide a good view over the country ahead and the rooftops below, while the castle museum tells the prince's story and explains the conditions of the time which made the building of castles a necessary part of self-preservation for a local ruler. Bolko's protective walls were a massive 4.5 metres (14.75 feet) thick.

From here Jelenia Góra is only 30 kilometres away, the road passing through the densely forested hills of Kaczawskie before dropping down into the wide basin to which the town gives its name.

Jelenia Góra has the best of both economic worlds together with a fine location on the Bóbr river. It is the tourist base for the western Sudety Mountains, including the Karkonosze National Park, and is an old industrial town which planners have managed to modernize without destroying the atmosphere of its attractive old streets and market place. Legend has it that King Bolesław the Brave founded a castle here, but it was not until the twelfth century, during the reign of Bolesław Wrymouth, that a significant settlement grew up. It was granted a borough charter in 1288 and by the fourteenth and fifteenth centuries mining, iron smelting and glass production were well established. Weaving took over as the predominant activity from the sixteenth century. The town's fame as a weaving centre was based on production of the very highest quality fabrics which reached distant markets by way of an annual textile fair in the town. Prussian control in the eighteenth century brought the usual depression but by the end of the last century large mechanical textile mills had brought renewed wealth to the town which escaped serious damage during the Second World War.

The heart of the town with its narrow streets and market square is encircled by roads built along the line of the old defensive walls, which skirted the river bank to the north. The town hall, built in 1748, is a little large for the otherwise elegant and still arcaded market place of white-painted mansions. The parish church is the usual mixture of styles: a high baroque tower rising from fourteenth-century foundations and Renaissance tombs, stalls and pulpit inside.

The town's proximity to the hills is reflected in the local museum, a modern building at 28 Matejki Street, which was founded in 1889 by the Tourist Society. Although it is now called the Museum of Glassware because of its comprehensive displays of artistic glass, the weaving industry and the culture of the region are also well covered. There is even an old mountain hut erected next to the museum, part of an ethnographic display which includes a section on herb-gathering in the Sudety Mountains. Pleasant as the town is, most visitors use Jelenia Góra as a base for exploring the Karkonosze Hills which rise to the south. The summit of Mount Śnieżka, just 20 kilometres away, is 1,602 metres (4,806 feet) high.

This is the highest point of the whole Sudety range, which is a granite outcrop of great age stretching for 300 kilometres on an east-west axis. The area around Śnieżka became a national park in 1959 and parallels a park on the Czechoslovakian side of the border. Most of the lower slopes are managed spruce forests, but natural spruce takes over higher up, giving way at about 1,450 metres to typical species of dwarf mountain pine and tough grasses with many heavily eroded outcrops of rock on the summits. There is none of the Alpine crags or sheer faces of the Tatra Mountains nor the picturesque wooden villages of the Podhale. The western Sudety, like the Bieszczady, are for the determined hill-walker or naturalist who is prepared to trudge uphill for hours through dense pine woods to gain a summit view back over those very same trees or beyond to the blue haze of the faraway plain. But there are several pleasant resort centres in the area that are much favoured by Poles and many schools and factories have hostels and holiday homes here, the main centres being Cieplice Śląskie Zdrój, Karpacz, Szlarska Poręba, and Sobieszów. **Cieplice** is one of the most famous resorts in Poland, providing special treatment 'for rehabilitating the organs of movement' among a long list of therapies. The knowledgeable and the privileged have been going to Cieplice for centuries, where the waters were watched over by the Cistercians from 1404 up until 1810. It seems sad that those days have gone, because the idea of taking six-hour baths, wearing a long linen shirt and singing hymns all the while, sounds like the perfect therapy for modern man.

Karpacz lies directly beneath Śnieżka and is another popular centre, perhaps just as busy with skiers in winter as it is with walkers and holiday-makers in the summer. A 30-minute walk from the resort along the blue trail leads to a natural terrace at Bierutowice on which, to the astonishment of many, stands a complete and splendid early thirteenth-century Norwegian wooden church known as the **Wang Chapel**. This unique and elaborately carved example of Nordic Romanesque architecture from the Middle Ages, with the proportions and silhouette of a Buddhist temple, was moved here lock, stock, and barrel by the Prussian King Frederick Wilhelm IV from Lake Wang in Norway in 1847. As to Śnieżka itself, the ski slopes at the summit where snow lies for a hundred days each year are topped with a weather station and a hostel upon which trails converge from both the Polish and Czechoslovakian sides of the mountain.

Leaving the mountains for the very last time, there is a roundabout route from Jelenia Góra back to Wrocław which takes in most of those places which have survived the centuries to tell an interesting part of the Silesian story. The largest town is **Legnica** which, although heavily industrialized, has a long history, being first mentioned in the chronicles back in 1149. At the turn of the twelfth century a new stronghold was built overlooking the Kaczawa river, and this was one of the few places which withstood the Tartar raids of 1241. This led in the following year to its establishment as a seat of the Legnica princes, a role it maintained until 1675 when, after the death of the last Silesian Piast, the territory passed into Habsburg hands. Always an important trading town, in the sixteenth century it could also claim to be one of the most important centres of printing in central Europe. From the nineteenth century, Legnica developed rapidly as an industrial town before being badly damaged in the Second World War. The great Piast castle was burned down, and all that remains today are two towers and the richly carved Renaissance east gate which was built in 1532 and which, with its massive columns, has something of the Hollywood epic about it.

The rebuilt market place has a baroque town hall and a Neptune fountain from 1731, while the south-eastern part of the town is dominated by a parish church which dates back to the fourteenth century but was largely rebuilt in 1894. Two fine Gothic portals have survived and, inside, a sixteenth-century stone pulpit, the sarcophagus of the Legnica Prince Wacław who died in the 1360s, and a rare bronze font with relief decorations from the thirteenth century. There is also an interesting circular baroque church to the north of the market place which incorporates a Gothic chancel. In the seventeenth century this was made into a mausoleum for the Piast dynasty and is adorned with frescos showing the apotheosis of the Piasts, and statues of some of the princes. The industrial heritage of Legnica is celebrated in a Museum of Copper which traces the history of copper-working in the area over the centuries; huge opencast mines are still being worked in the region.

There is a spectacular riverside building to be seen some 20 kilometres north-east of Legnica, but a place well worth a visit first is **Legnickie Pole**, just a few kilometres south-east of the city and quite close to the *autobahn*. The village's name means 'Legnica Field' and refers to the site of the great battle on 9 April 1241 in which the combined forces of the princes of Silesia and Wielkopolska clashed with the Tartar hordes. Although the Polish armies were defeated and their leader, Prince Henryk the Pious, killed, the Tartars must have learned something from this fierce struggle, for after besieging the survivors at Legnica castle they gave up their destructive westward drive and turned south towards Hungary in search of easier pickings.

In the market place of the little town which developed on the site of the battle, there is a church founded by Prince Henryk's mother, St Jadwiga, in memory of her son whose body, legend has it, was decapitated by the Tartars and identified by Jadwiga only because he had six toes on one foot. The original chapel was superseded in the fourteenth century by the larger Gothic church which now houses a Battle of Legnica Museum, but a more impressive piece of architecture exists in this tiny place, for the present parish church was once a great **Benedictine Abbey** built around 1730 on an elliptical ground plan by the youngest of a famous family of Austrian architects with the splendid name of Kilian Ignaz Dientzenhofer (1689–1751). His father, uncle and grandfather all left their mark on the Habsburg lands with impressive buildings. Kilian himself settled in Prague, where he became the leading exponent of the baroque style, with several churches and palaces to his name. He can have created no building more perfectly proportioned than this abbey church, which he decorated with the work of equally renowned artists including Cosmas Asam, a Bavarian who painted the ceilings with frescos showing the discovery of the prince's body after the battle as well as various activities of the Benedictines.

One of the great joys of travelling around the chaotic palimpsest of Europe is the discovery in remote places of references which provide odd insights into history. Legnickie Pole can add to its historic battlefield the story that when the abbey was closed in 1810 by the Prussians it was turned into an army cadet school where, later in the century, none other than Hindenburg, the man who appointed Hitler as Chancellor of the Reich in 1933, received his army education.

Now to that riverside building mentioned earlier. This is at Lubiąż over on the right bank of the Odra river, just at the point where it makes a sharp turn to the north. A little road crosses here providing a view along the river to one of the largest buildings in Poland, a former **Cistercian Abbey** which was founded in 1163 by monks especially imported by Prince Bolesław the Tall. Little of the original abbey remains; its present massive baroque form dates from the 1690s onwards, following the devastation of the Thirty Years War. The main elevation is 223 metres long and the wings are not much shorter but, big as it is, the impression of the abbey's size is greatly increased by the fact that it stands virtually alone in a vast flat landscape of forest, dwarfing the few village buildings. In the old days it must have presented a powerful sight to anyone travelling on the river, as barges still do, but the best view is from a riverside rise just a kilometre or so west on the same bank, from which the great block with its twin towers shines in the light, almost the only artifact in a great panorama of water and forest. Unfortunately, the interiors were damaged in 1945, but restoration has been in progress for several years and some of the 1,000 cells as well as the surviving Gothic church with its tombstones of Piast princes, wall paintings and baroque sculptures can be visited.

From Lubiąż, once you have crossed back over the river, it is but a straight 50-kilometre run back to Wrocław through the little old town of Środa Śląska, a name derived, like so many in Poland, from the day of the week that a market was held in the place; *Środa* meaning Wednesday. The main road passes through the long market place with its baroque-spired Gothic town hall which now houses a museum, and church lovers may want to investigate both a late Romanesque and a Gothic church, both of which have been remodelled over the years.

Although most of Lower Silesia lies to the south and west of Wrocław, there are a couple of historic sites just to the north of the city towards the ancient borders with the province of Greater Poland (Wielkopolska). To the north-east of the town, 30 kilometres along the main E12 road which leads to Łódź and Warsaw, is the town of **Oleśnica** which was the capital of its own principality during the period of the thirteenth and fourteenth centuries when the unified Polish state crumbled into feudal duchies. In the sixteenth century it was a vital centre of the Polish Reformation Movement, there being a large Polish population in Silesia despite the years of foreign control, and many tracts were printed at Oleśnica in the Polish language until the Thirty Years War caused devastation from which the town never recovered. The surviving ducal castle, however, is a suitable symbol of former splendours, a handsome golden-coloured building with an octagonal tower which was enlarged into a Renaissance-style residence by the grandson of King George of Bohemia. The arcaded courtyard is reached by way of a gateway decorated with various coats of arms and a covered walkway leads from it to the originally Gothic church which contains the tombstones of several Oleśnica dukes. Its proportions, detailing and site in the flat plain make this one of the best-looking grand houses in Poland, and well worth a visit.

The final call in Silesia is **Trzebnica**, 24 kilometres from Wrocław on the main Poznań road. This is another ancient site, long ago settled by the Slavic Trzebowian tribes who lived amongst the low morainic hills that mark the northern extent of the region. The town was another victim of the last war, but its most valuable building survives, the former **Abbey** which was founded in 1207 by Henryk the Bearded and his wife, who endowed it with great wealth as the first Cistercian establishment in Silesia. Queen Jadwiga died in the abbey in 1243 and was canonized only 24 years later, after which her grave became a focus for pilgrims throughout Poland. Up until the sixteenth century all the abbesses were members of the extensive Piast dynasty; a total of 118 Piasts have been buried in the church, the last in the eighteenth century. As at Legnickie Pole, the building was secularized when the Order was abolished in 1810, becoming first a cloth factory and then, more appropriately, a hospital.

The large abbey church was begun in 1203 and is one of the oldest brick structures in Silesia. Two Romanesque doorways lead to a nave with two aisles and a large three-nave crypt. All the Romanesque carving, including that of the columns and capitals, is beautifully done; the tympanum over the west door shows King David playing a lute-like instrument to Bathsheba, and that over the north door the adoration of the Virgin Mary by angels. Fire damaged much of the building in the fifteenth century and baroque decorations were added when that fashion came in. A marble sarcophagus of Henryk the Bearded was added in 1680, the same year that a similar tomb of St Jadwiga was installed in her chapel as an addition to the original Gothic sepulchral slab which was laid at the end of the thirteenth century. There is also a 1409 slab commemorating the Silesian Prince Konrad II. The monastery building, in its early eighteenth-century form with two internal courtyards, adjoins the church on the south side.

At Trzebnica the main road north divides, both directions eventually arriving at Poznań yet neither offering much other than an ever-smoothening landscape interrupted by gaps in the forest and the occasional line of sandy hillocks which were deposited by the ice sheet as it retreated after the last cold snap. After 25 or 30 kilometres, depending upon which road you take, there is a belt of wet, marshy ground with scattered lakes, again the result of the geologically recent ice. This natural frontier zone marks the traditional boundary between Silesia and Wielkopolska and it is a wilderness which is home to dozens of species of bird including heron, black stork, crane and goose. Which of these two roads you follow depends as much upon the mood of the moment as upon sideways excursions which may tempt you, but both travel through territory described in the next chapter.

13

Wielkopolska

It is customary in books about Poland, academic or popular, to refer to Wielkopolska as the cradle of the Polish state and, hazy as our vision is of those days of more than a thousand years ago when the Slavic tribes were organizing themselves into ever larger units, there is plenty of evidence that something special was happening here. Today's landscape is often monotonous — except, that is, to geomorphologists, for whom it is a youthful region with fascinating stories to tell of the behaviour of the ice sheets whose stuttering retreat shaped the land, planned the rivers and deposited the soil and stones, sands and lakes which make up Wielkopolska. The conditions seem to have suited man who, for thousands of years, did much more than scratch a living. Rich and successful cultures developed here, the best known of which was the Lusatian which spread its influence over a large area of the European Plain, eastwards from the watery land which is now Berlin to well beyond the Vistula river, leaving many traces that tell of a highly organized and sophisticated society. One of the most illuminating survivals from this period, and now a popular as well as a scholarly attraction, is **Biskupin** near Gniezno, a 2,500-year-old village where people cultivated the land with iron tools, fished in the lakes and traded with their neighbours.

Little is known of life here in the first centuries of the Christian era. It is assumed that the great migrations and invasions of the period held development back, but from the eighth century a picture clearly emerges of Slavic tribes such as the Polanie occupying fortified settlements between the Warta and Vistula rivers which became a nucleus for the Polish state. The earliest detailed information comes from a ninth-century chronicle by an author known only as the

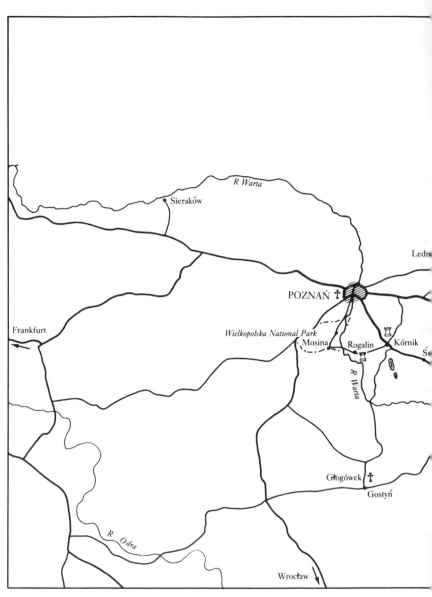

Bavarian Geographer, who estimated there to have been about 50 tribes in the Polish lands. From the same period come the earliest legends purporting to describe the origins of the first Polish state amongst these jostling groups. The Polanie, who were settled in the Poznań and Gniezno area, were the great rivals of their eastern

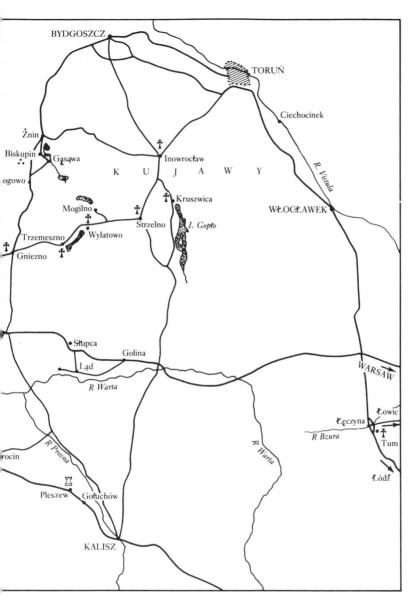

neighbours the Goplanie, whose defeated leader Popiel, imprisoned in a tower at Kruszwica, is supposed to have been eaten by mice. This sort of story abounded in the Middle Ages, when the names Piast and Ziemowit were given to the probably legendary founders of the dynasty which came to dominate Polish history for so many centuries.

235

The first identifiable leader of the united tribes of Wielkopolska was Mieszko I. His capital was Gniezno, where he accepted the Christian faith in AD 966, but during this period a fortified island in the nearby Warta was expanding and also became a seat of power in the first kingdom. This was **Poznań**, which today considerably outweighs Gniezno in size and importance; it is one of the major industrial and cultural cities in the country and the undisputed capital of western Poland.

Poznań's origin is the familiar one of a settlement developing where a trade route crosses a river, and in the tenth century, with a population of 4,000, the original island site of Ostrów Tumski was made into a powerful fortress, sharing with Gniezno the functions of capital. After Mieszko's conversion and the establishment of an archbishopric at Gniezno, Poznań soon had its own bishop. In 968 a church was built on the island, to be followed in 1058 by a Romanesque cathedral which in turn was replaced by a Gothic building founded in 1346. Those early kings may have felt that Poznań, surrounded by water, was easier to defend than Gniezno on its rolling hills, but the river was certainly not enough to stop the Bohemian ruler Bratislav who, after the death of Mieszko I's son, Bolesław the Brave, invaded Poland in 1039 and destroyed both Poznań and Gniezno as well as other settlements in the area. After this attack the political capital was moved to Kraków. Gniezno has never since regained its position of power but Poznań was soon rebuilt and flourishing, expanding beyond its island with suburbs first on the east bank at Środka, which despite gaining municipal status in 1230 never really prospered, and then on the west bank, where the local prince, Przemysław I, built a new market and township with its own defensive walls which is today the heart of the modern city.

Evidence that Poznań flourished in the centuries that followed is there for all to see in the market place and surrounding streets of the Old Town. Colourful and richly decorated merchants' houses line the square, but the magnificent and much photographed **Town Hall** holds pride of place. First mentioned in 1310, it was enlarged to its present form in 1550 by Giovanni Battista Quadro from Lugano. It is a beautiful building, its façade adorned with a three-storey loggia surmounted by a tall decorative parapet with octagonal turrets at the corners and a central turret framing a large clock from 1782. Emerging from the centre of the almost cubic building is a square brick tower surmounted by a pinnacled belfry as tall again as the main building.

This tower also features a clock, but each noon it is the lower timepiece which is the focus of attention, for then a door above it opens and two metal goats emerge, knock their heads together and disappear back into the building. The ritual is supposed to commemorate two such creatures who entered the town hall from the market and proceeded to use the sumptuous chambers as a personal battlefield. Legend has it that the local people, roused by the din, spotted a nearby fire and were therefore able to save the town. It may not be a very convincing tale but the goats have featured on the city's arms ever since. Running across the attic façade beneath the clock is a colourful frieze featuring eight Polish kings in full regalia which, together with the warm colours of the walls behind the loggia arches, makes for an altogether delightful effect. These days the cobbled square is reserved for pedestrians, so it is possible to wander freely, eyeing the building first from the front and then perhaps from the south, where it appears above a line of a dozen or more little arcaded houses, each painted a different pastel shade. These were the homes of market stall-holders, built in the sixteenth century on the site of a row of fish stalls.

The town hall is entered by the steps once trod by the immortalized goats, and the splendid interior is a rival to Wrocław and Gdańsk. The most impressive room is the **Renaissance Chamber** or **Sala Renesansów** on the first floor. This has a truly spectacular vaulted ceiling featuring a highly intricate design of white twisting plants on a black background, and inset with golden coats of arms, portraits and mythological scenes. Decorated in 1555, it survived the bombardment of 1945 without too much damage — unlike the rest of the building, which needed careful reassembly. Most rooms are now used as a museum of Poznań's history and contain a wide variety of objects, all refugees from the town's rich past. In the cellar is the original pillory, a copy of which stands outside in the square, which was apparently paid for by the fines imposed upon women who were deemed to be improperly dressed. I do not know who judged them, but it seems to me that this system could raise a fortune from both sexes on many of today's streets. Also on show are fragments of thirteenth-century stone decoration from the earlier Gothic building and other monumental stone sculptures, including a church keystone which bears an image supposed to be that of Prince Przemysław I. Other products of medieval craftsmanship include a beautiful wrought-iron lattice screen made in Toruń in around 1400, the head of a bishop's crosier made in

Limoges in the first half of the thirteenth century, and the signet ring of Bishop Boguła II from 1255.

Upstairs there is a model of the fortified settlement on Ostrów Tumski and various items from excavations there, such as bone tools, bronze stirrups and cooking pots, while many documents and drawings provide backward glances to previous centuries; one engraving from 1618 shows the town crouching low behind its great walls with only the towers of innumerable churches and the town hall protruding. In the sixteenth and seventeenth centuries, Poznań was one of the largest trading towns in Europe, its merchants travelling from the Atlantic to China, its crafts and printing industries flourishing, and this period is illustrated by a fascinating collection of pictures showing guild members at work. There are shoemakers, foundrymen, bakers and a potter, and in one picture four merchants sit deep in discussion while an artist beyond paints frescos on a wall. Then there is a 1525 map which clearly shows the main east-west trade route as well as many other roads converging on the town.

The second floor is devoted to the city under partition when, under Prussian rule, it was actively Germanized, and to more recent days when Poznań was taken into the Reich. Following five years of repression and deportations in the last War, the city, like Wrocław, was turned by the Germans into a fortress in a vain attempt to stop the Soviet armies in their push to Berlin, and half of the city and most of the Old Town were left in ruins. So, like Warsaw, Gdańsk and many smaller places, Poznań today is a reproduction of its former self, with old stones reassembled, new paint on new plaster and church spires laboriously hauled into place. The museum's photographic gallery tells this story through images of the burnt-out and collapsed buildings and the restoration work in progress.

After this, the friendly square appears in a new light. It is here that visitors pass most of their time, for it houses other museums and many cafés and restaurants, including a well run Indian-style tea room where, at last, you can obtain a decent brew. There are also the usual souvenir shops and the inevitable *Cepelia* store crammed with hand-crafted goodies and, in the south-east corner, a fine second-hand bookshop (*antykwariat*) where old prints and books in many languages can be found. In the Rynek, opposite the front door of the town hall, beyond the elaborate baroque fountain, No. 45 is an essential stopping place for musicians. This is the **Museum of Musical Instruments**, a rare collection in an intimate setting which is based on the private hoard of one local enthusiast and now has more than 750 instruments from all over the world, although the heart of the displays is a selection of Polish stringed instruments from the sixteenth to the twentieth century. There is also a Chopin room with wooden busts, a marble hand and a life mask of the composer, two of his pianos and a large 1829 engraving of him playing to a crowded salon. Most memorable, though, are the odd instruments of folk origin which never graduated to the modern orchestra; a seventeenth-century Italian *surdynka*, for example, which is an eight-stringed bodyless fiddle, long and thin like a fish, its fingerboard plated with an ivory chequerboard pattern. There is a 1700 baroque harpsichord elaborately decorated with gilt carvings and an eighteenth-century zitherlike instrument which has a charming landscape painted under its lid. There are glass harmonicas and hurdy-gurdies, strange contraptions made up of goatskin bellows and brass horns, and a pedal-pumped accordion which is unique to the Kurpie region of Mazovia and which I myself have recorded in action there in recent years. Altogether there are five rooms of folk instruments, the simplest items being earthenware whistles in the shape of rabbits, hens and ducks, copies of which can be found in many *Cepelia* shops. On the top floor there are strange objects from India and Africa and an amazing dragon-shaped rhythm stick from China. It is a good place to spend half an hour.

Behind the town hall and the row of little houses, the centre of the square is occupied by more buildings. The largest is a concrete structure which is entirely out of place and incorporates the flower market and the loveliest is the Renaissance municipal weighing house, an essential facility in any market. This adjoins the **Wielkopolska Military Museum** which contains beautiful ceremonial armour and the eleventh-century boat full of weapons which was found at the bottom of Lednickie Lake, just up the road on the way to Gniezno. There is also a helmet from the time of the earliest Piasts and the usual collection of patriotic banners from the many insurgences and uprisings of the nineteenth century. Also here, in a classicist guardhouse, is the Marcin Kasprzak Museum of the History of the Working Class Movement. Kasprzak, born in 1860, was one of a group who founded the first Polish Social Democratic Party, for which he was hanged in 1905 by the partitioning powers, and the large collection of photographs here gives an interesting picture of the town with its factories and inhabitants both before and after the turn of the century. Outside the museum is a statue of St Jan Nepomuk, a medieval Czech cleric who chose martyrdom in the waters of Prague's Vltava river rather than reveal the secrets of his confessional. The Looking around for a candidate for the job of anti-flood saint, the Church somewhat ironically chose this one, but placed his image here in Poznań only after the great flood of 1736, when the river spilled into the town and floated coffins out of church crypts. On the lower eastern side of the square a mark two metres up a wall shows the level that the waters reached.

Beyond the *antykwariat* in the south-east corner of the square, Ulica Świętosławska is closed at its far end by the bulk of the **Parish Church**, which was designed in 1651 by a group of Italian architects. Together with the neighbouring college, this was a Jesuit building until the Order was temporarily banned in 1773. The school now teaches ballet rather than liturgy. Perhaps it has never recovered from the shock of housing Napoleon for the night in 1812. The church is perhaps the finest baroque edifice in Poznań, with large side chapels, rich stucco decorations by Giovanni Bianco and, on the high altar, a large painting of Lazarus by the Polish painter Szymon Czechowicz, who himself studied in Rome. The oldest object in the church is a sculpture of Christ from 1435 which sits in a side aisle. Close by at No. 27, Ulica Wodna is the Archaeological Museum, which comprehensively describes the evolution of early society in Wielkopolska with artifacts from the Stone Age to the early medieval period.

There are plenty more churches around the town, of course, another baroque example being the **Franciscan Temple** which can be found behind the west side of the square, at the foot of the little hill on which the remains of a castle stand. The temple is now home to an Arts and Crafts Museum displaying Venetian glass, Chinese vases and Meissen porcelain. It was decorated by the brothers Szwach, Adam doing the paintings and Anthony carving the stalls and the altar piece in the Virgin's Chapel. Above the entrance to one chapel there is a line of coffin paintings of Polish nobles painted on hexagonal tinplate which it was the custom to fix to coffins — not, I presume, for the purpose of identification. There are more of these peculiarly Polish items up the sloping Ulica Paderewskiego and round the corner at the bottom of the long Liberty Square (Plac Wolności), where the large nineteenth-century building of the **National Museum**, as well as a library, can be found.

Serious students of painting must allow plenty of time — days even — for this large museum which is among the most important in the country. It has departments of Medieval Art, Polish Painting, Foreign

Painting and Contemporary Polish Art, a Cabinet of Prints and a large library. It is a spacious, purpose-built museum. The main ground-floor gallery is lit by high skylights and devoted to modern **Polish Painting and Sculpture** which shows wide European influences, with a preference by some artists for muted, even gloomy colours which, it is tempting to think, is a reflection of modern Polish history. The moody, melting forms of a Parisian street at night (1927) by Stanisław Eleskiewicz took my fancy, as did a little pine landscape by Kubicki, but the main attractions are upstairs, reached by a marble staircase at the top of which stands the usual box of *pantofle*, the felt slippers that must be worn in most museums in order to protect the marble floors. The great problem with this commendable system is that the most popular sizes very often have no tie-strings attached, so one is forced to shuffle around in fear of the wrath of the stern female guardians, who will descend if one of these loose contraptions is accidentally shed.

On the first floor, of **Medieval Art**, more rows of coffin portraits stare down, vividly and often rather crudely painted; one character looks very much like Jack Lemmon, even down to the blue chin. Beyond are the strange Malczewski self-portraits so familiar from other galleries, their pastel shades belying the painter's obsession with death. Above those of all other local artists I think that his works deserve to be better known abroad, perhaps reproduced in book form, for which they would be eminently suitable.

There is something uniquely Polish about the work of the earlier artists upstairs, most of whom, if not in exile, were caught up in the many nineteenth-century struggles for independence from the smothering control of Prussia, Russia and Austria; but perhaps it is too easy to interpret their work in this light. The **Eighteenth-century Pictures** — that is, from before the partitions — are more contention-al: formal portraits of the rich and powerful, scenes of public buildings and events, and pictures of private country estates. Franciszek Smug-lewicz and Bernardo Bellotto are well represented here. Bellotto's vast picture of the election of Stanisław-August is difficult to avoid, as is the Bacciarelli portrait of the same monarch. Historically interesting is the canvas of Warsaw in its heyday by the immigrant Frenchman Jean-Pierre Norblin, a pupil of Watteau who came to Poland as a court painter for the Czartoryskis and stayed for most of his long life (1745–1830), a devoted painter of Polish people and places. The soil of Wielkopolska shows itself in many works, none more so than in the dynamic images of man and horse by Józef Brandt (1841–1915). One of his largest works also reveals a nationalistic flavour, as a Polish horseman pulls a Tartar from his galloping horse by means of a whip around the neck. Józef Chełmoński's huge pictures are also devoted to the earth, but his native soil was the Polish Ukraine, which he painted throughout his long exile in France.

Also prominent on the upper floor is the work of the so-called **Young Poland (Młoda Polska) Movement**. This developed at the end of the last century in the Lwów and Kraków territories which were ruled from Vienna under the name of Galicia. In this movement the Polish language was encouraged and both the past and the peasantry were romantically viewed by young artists and writers. The person who proved to have the widest appeal was Stanisław Wyspiański, whose life was bound up with Kraków and the mountains, and Poznań has a fine collection of the soft pastel portraits through which he introduced the sinuous *art nouveau* lines of Paris.

The **Foreign Painting Gallery** possesses some 2,000 works. Many of them are displayed in the palaces of Rogalin and Goluchów, both of which will be visited later, but the rich nucleus of the collection is on display here. Italian and Spanish pictures from the eighteenth century are dominant, but Massys's tender madonna from the fifteenth century is one of the several Dutch and Flemish masterpieces here which include many landscapes. The Italian pictures include works by Daddi and Monaco, Bellini and Veronese, Strozzi and Bronzino, while the Spanish circle of Velasquez is represented by Antolonez's 'Blind Woman'. It is safe to say that a feast of European history hangs on these walls, all the more interesting for being so little known outside Poland.

The windows of the museum face up the length of Plac Wolności to the high-rise blocks of the modern city, about which there is little to say except that the shopping here is much the same as elsewhere in Poland and the streets have the atmosphere of any modern city. One of the main shopping streets, Ulica 27 Grudnia (27 December Street), continues westward from the top of the square and, facing down it from the far end, just across the street from a new circular office block, is the international bookshop where volumes in several foreign languages can be bought. A left and then a right turn from here lead to the Adam Mickiewicz University, built in 1910 in a rather incongruous style known as Dutch Renaissance, and from here the road crosses the railway line close to the station and meets the western arm of a ring road which boxes in the town centre. This area will be well known to many in the engineering world because to the left are the buildings of the **Poznań Trade Fair**. This is an international market place where manufacturers from many countries set up shop, intent upon selling pumps and pistons, trucks and tractors and these days probably computers too.

The fair maintains Poznań's long history as a trading city and is now a vital part of the local economy. Hotels have been especially built to cope with the rush which now comes twice a year; the June fair specializes in industrial products while the September exhibition caters for consumer goods. Both these times are to be avoided if you need a bed without booking in advance. The atmosphere of the fair spills over into the town where temporary exhibitions spring up all over the place, and on Saturday and Sunday nights the market place is crowded for *son et lumière* spectaculars. Since 1976, St John's Market (Jamark Świętojański) has also been held in the square during the fairs as a deliberate attempt to jolly things along for the visitors. This features a noisy and colourful folk pageant with stalls and booths, music and dancing, reaching a climax on Midsummer Day with the traditional tossing of wreathes of flowers into the river.

And it is to the river that you must now go to see the original island site upon which Poznań was born. Cut back through the Old Town, perhaps this time to the north of the market place and past the **Dominican Church** which is the modern home of the Jesuits. Although this has a baroque appearance, there lurks beneath the gold and stucco icing an ancient Gothic church built in the 1240s. Still visible from earlier days are the Rosary Chapel from 1500 with its lovely stellar vault and the Renaissance Chapel of St Jacek from 1622. When it was built, this church was close to the river which then flowed just beyond what is now Ulica Garbary, the eastern arm of the ring road, but now is at least 200 metres further east, and the only way to reach Ostrów Tumski is to trudge across the new and long Bolesław the Brave Bridge (Most Bolesława Chrobrego) which carries the main Warsaw road. The river here looks shallow and tame enough but the wide berth given to it by buildings on both sides indicates that in certain seasons the waters have their own way despite the best efforts of St Nepomuk.

The great red-brick towers of the **Cathedral** will have been visible from the moment that the buildings of the west bank were left behind and immediately beyond the bridge a left turn leads past the little Mariacki Church into the cathedral close. Although trapped between the main road and the railway to the north, this is now a peaceful place of trees and fine old houses which are occupied by canons and various officers of the Church. It was in AD 968, just two years after his baptism, that Mieszko I founded a church here, a pre-Romanesque basilica which was enlarged just in time to be destroyed in 1039 by the Bohemians, who merely cleared a site for the first Romanesque structure, completed by 1075. This church seems to have served the community well and it was not until 1347 that it was replaced by a large Gothic building made from the recently introduced red brick. This was an altogether richer affair, a three-nave basilica with ambulatories and a ring of chapels and, although today's cathedral is still a large Gothic structure, its fortunes have risen and fallen since the fourteenth century along with those of the nation; it has been burned down or blown up on more than one occasion. At each rebuilding current styles were incorporated until, on the cathedral of 1939, most of the brickwork had been plastered over with baroque and classicist decorations.

The Nazis as usual did their worst, using the cathedral as a store and ammunition dump, which led to the holy building going up in smoke in 1945. Once Poznań was back in Polish hands, a decision was made to recreate the cathedral in all its Gothic glory, leaving just the spires on the great towers and some other details from later periods. The problem of furnishing was overcome by collecting items from some of the many smaller churches of the region which had been destroyed. The late baroque pulpit and the font, for example, came from the small town of Milicz on the Wrocław road and the stalls from the western frontier town of Zgorzelec, although the great bronze west doors were made as recently as 1980. At the point of the rather lop-sided east end, beyond the high altar, is the **Gold Chapel**, the only one to survive the war intact. Its unusually rich decoration of gold, red and blue with twisted columns and painted scenes dates from 1837, when it was rebuilt in a supposedly Byzantine style as a mausoleum for the first two Polish kings, whose remains had always been in the cathedral. Tragic as the war was for Poland at every level, the destruction of so many ancient buildings did give the archaeologists the opportunity to dig. Beneath the crypt at Poznań they found the remains of both the Romanesque and pre-Romanesque churches of the tenth and eleventh centuries, fragments of tombs thought to be the original burial places of Mieszko I and his son Bolesław the Brave and a tenth-century baptistry.

The first impression one has upon entering the cathedral today is of height, the plain brick soaring to a slender spray of ribs across the white vaulted ceiling, which is lit by high windows. Some scholars trace the style to the French Gothic which came eastwards by way of Lübeck and in spite of the extensive rebuilding it is still possible to marvel at the ability of the medieval craftsmen to erect such a structure at a time when most towns were still made of wood. After the Gold Chapel, the richest is that of the Górka family, but apart from a 1512 polyptych above the high altar, very much in the style of Wit Stwosz, the main interior is simple and quite bare, unlike that of the little **Mariacki Church** which sits across the close from the west door of the cathedral.

Built in the 1430s, this is a short-hall church of beautiful proportions, widely regarded as one of Poland's loveliest fifteenth-century buildings. The post-war restorers bravely allowed the local artist Wacław Taranczewski to cover the walls with new frescos, and these contrast well with the Gothic portal and sculptures. Also in the tree-lined and atmospheric close are several old canons' houses, an interesting 1508 *Psalteria* where the cathedral psalmists lived and the Lubrański Academy, a Renaissance building from around 1520 which now houses the **Archdiocesan Museum**.

This is certainly worth a visit, its exhibition of medieval art being one of the best outside Warsaw and Kraków. The collection was started in 1893 by the then archbishop and continued with enthusiastic acquisitions by later churchmen, although the Second World War did see the disappearance of 70 paintings and 150 sculptures. Especially beautiful are the early sculptures such as the 1430 'Madonna and Child' which represents that Polish school known simply as 'The Beautiful Madonnas', while the 'Madonna Enthroned' is a century older and came from the church at the village of Obłok. The late-Gothic figures include many from a now lost high altar from somewhere near Leszno, to the south of Poznań. The paintings include a triptych of 'Jesus at the Well' from 1500 as well as surviving panels from other triptychs of the same period, and also on show are baptism bowls from the fifteenth and sixteenth centuries, a Romanesque candlestick base from the early 1200s and a number of embroidered Gothic chasubles, those ornate vests worn by a priest during mass. Then there are coffin portraits, Renaissance and baroque textiles, the waist sashes of Polish noblemen, and two items of Spanish art: a seventeenth-century wooden sculpture of St Ignatius Loyola and, from the same century, a richly embroidered banner.

Beyond Ostrów Tumski on the east bank of the Warta river it is still possible to trace the layout of that earliest suburb of Śródka, trapped today between the main road and a sports ground, and the persistent pursuer of sacred relics will here be rewarded with three places worth visiting: a late fifteenth-century Gothic church which incorporates a Romanesque building, a former monastery and a baroque Reformist church. The truly dedicated, however, will push east a few hundred metres further, past the new Novotel Hotel, to a locality known as Komandoria, which means 'command post' and was the site of a settlement attached to the Knights of St John of Jerusalem who were brought to Poznań in the eleventh century. Still standing here is a brick and stone Romanesque church dating from 1187, which was restored after the war.

Today Poznań is a fully fledged regional capital with its own distinctive cultural activities, influenced, as always, by a large student population at the university and the many specialist colleges. There are six theatres, a well travelled Polish Dance Theatre, a State Philharmonic Orchestra and two good choirs, and every fifth year an event occurs in the town of great significance to all violinists and violin-makers: the international contest and seminar dedicated to Henryk Wieniawski, one of the greatest of nineteenth-century virtuosi.

For business visitors to the Trade Fairs there are several parks and palaces in the district which are handy for day trips and, for the insatiable technocrat, there is even a museum in the south of the city which celebrates the history of Poznań's largest and most famous employer, the engineering works of Hipolit Cegielski, founded in 1846 to make agricultural equipment and today producing railway carriages, diesel engines and machine tools among much else.

The easiest and most pleasant excursion from Poznań is a triangular out-and-back journey to the south of the city which takes in the wooded ridges and lakes of the **Wielkopolska National Park** and two interesting country houses, both of which are now fine museums. Starting some 20 kilometres from the city, the 10,000-hectare (25,000-acre) park covers an area of terminal moraine and post-glacial gullies which are typical of the region as a whole but are here condensed into a small area which is cut through by the Warta river. Man removed most of the hardwoods long ago, leaving forests of pine fringed with birch trees where they drop to the edges of lakes, some of them large but several hundred of them small, often little more than woodland pools. In the village of Puszczykowo there is a natural history museum which gives a detailed picture of the landscape. Needless to say, the area is a favourite playground for Poznań people, but it is not at all overdeveloped, for example, the little town of Mosina having a quite remote feel about it.

Seven kilometres east of Mosina, across on the east bank of the Warta at a point where the river has left a host of little oxbow lakes, is the large country palace of **Rogalin** which was built in 1770 for Kazimierz Raczyński, then Marshal of the Kingdom. The main body of the building is typically baroque with later rococo and classicist titivations, and long single-storey wings curve around the wide entrance courtyard. The main rooms overlook an orderly French garden with a pavilion which is a copy of the Roman temple at Nîmes, but beyond this the formal layout merges into a more naturalistic English style of parkland which ends on a bluff overlooking the wide and marshy riverbed. Here, as great an attraction for many as the palace itself, are groves of ancient oaks which were middle-aged when Kazimierz the Great was a boy. Altogether there are over 900 oaks, many reckoned to be a thousand years old and the largest a massive 9 metres (27 feet) around the trunk. This venerable botanical creature looks like one of God's own gargoyles or one of those speaking trees in the illustrations which accompany children's stories. It and the two next largest have been given the names Lech, Czech and Rus after the legendary brothers who were supposed to have founded the Slavic nations of Poland, Czechoslovakia and Russia. These trees can be every bit as evocative as any cathedral or castle ruin, for they were here, shedding leaves and sprouting acorns, while everything in Poland's busy thousand-year history was actually happening.

The estate is now managed by the National Museum in Poznań and the palace contains several valuable collections, although the hoard of paintings which was here before the last war was pillaged by the Nazis and never seen again in Poland. From that pre-war treasure chest, several portraits of the Raczyńskis and a huge Meissen porcelain chandelier from the eighteenth century do remain, but a marvellous display of pictures and furnishings has been built up since the war. The plan was to create whole rooms, each with a functional setting from a particular period. Especially successful is the baroque salon with Italian and Dutch furniture from the sixteenth and seventeenth centuries and a tapestry based upon the Rubens drawing of the fight between Hector and Achilles. The ballroom is dressed in nineteenth-century romantic garb with Italian rococo furniture, but looked its best, I am sure, when crammed with ladies in crinolines and starched young officers. Other rooms in the main house are furnished with Polish objects and hung with paintings from the Age of Enlightenment, including Bacciarelli's shining portrait of Stanisław-August Poniatowski, the last king, in his coronation robes. Look out for the bust of Napoleon and the full-length sculpture of Zofia Cieszkowska by Antonio Canova, who was the favourite of more than one pope and also produced two large marble statues of a naked Napoleon, brave fellow.

Alongside the main palace there is a building erected in 1910 which houses a **Gallery** of Polish and foreign painting and acts as an overspill to Poznań Museum. Although Monet's 'Landscape from Pourville' is a prize exhibit here, it is overwhelmed by some powerful Polish works, particularly Matejko's gigantic 'Joan of Arc', as awe-inspiring as any of his large canvases. And Malczewski's 'Melancholy' is one of his most moving and distinguished creations. Some of these pictures are rotated with others from the Poznań Museum, so between them these two places represent a good spectrum of Polish painting.

Continuing eastwards for thirteen kilometres, the little road comes to a string of narrow lakes through which a tributary of the Warta flows and on the far shore is a quiet, dusty little town with a broad market place, a large red-brick church and little else. This is **Kórnik**, and hidden just around the bend at the bottom of the high street is a building whose architecture is so singular that I can describe it only as a residential folly. To tell the truth, the first impression it gives is disappointing. Its fame and the many published booklets and pictures of it lead one to expect something more dramatic, more imposing. Singular it may be, even eccentric, but from the outside it is also a little drab.

The interiors are a delight. The site is an old one, for Kórnik was the seat of the powerful Górka family — they of the luxurious chapel in Poznań cathedral — who built a castle here back in 1426. From 1675 until 1880, however, it was the property of the equally strong Działyński family and it was they, in the last years of their tenure, who set about embellishing the existing building with an exuberance typical of the nineteenth century. The trade magnate Tytus Działyński was the moving spirit behind this, a great patriot and patron of the arts who accumulated a vast collection of *objets d'art*, old manuscripts, books,

248

pictures and armour. The Działyńskis were always an interesting family, on several occasions supporting popular insurrections when other aristocrats fought shy. Back in 1597 a Paul Działyński was sent to London on a diplomatic mission where, when presented to Queen Elizabeth I, he had the nerve to make a 'long oration in Latin complaining of the wars between the English and Spaniards, whereby he asserted that the commerce of Poland was seriously injured'. The queen, it seems, was not amused. She angrily replied in excellent Latin and, according to the chronicler Speed, 'lion-like rising, she daunted the malapert orator, no less with her stately port and majestical deporture than with the tartness of her princely checks'. But the Działyńskis, it seems, did not stay daunted for long; they even borrowed various Tudor and neo-Gothic forms from England for their mid-nineteenth century rebuilding programme. This building was designed specifically to accommodate their existing collection, and created to be not a house so much as a museum with living quarters attached, which it has remained to this day, having been presented to the nation in 1924 by Tytus's nephew Władysław Zamoyski. The collection of 150,000 books was found to be so valuable that in 1953 the management was taken over by the Polish Academy of Sciences, which also uses the park as an arboretum for the study and acclimatization of trees.

Both floors of the square-towered and crenellated **Castle** are open to the public and, as so often in these palaces, the visitor is first impressed by the wonderful floors of walnut and other hardwoods with their inlaid rosettes and geometric patterns. One of the first pictures to be seen is a fine photograph of Zamoyski in cape and beard, and four small Bacciarelli historical scenes hang over a fireplace nearby. The atmosphere is intimate, the furnishings a mixture of the exquisite and the ponderous, a large Gdańsk wardrobe fitting this latter category. I think this is the first mention I have made so far of a Gdańsk wardrobe, though they are ubiquitous in Poland. This one is a monster of a thing, huge and heavy, with deeply and elaborately carved doors, supported by fat spherical feet and surmounted by a large crested entablature. A fanfare of trumpets and I would not be surprised if the doors were slowly to open and a royal procession emerge. It is just the kind of wardrobe out of which D'Artagnan or Douglas Fairbanks might leap, sword swishing, before disappearing over the nearest balcony.

The large, heavily framed Działyński portraits show Jan with a lean and hungry look and his father Tytus looking like the successful industrialist he was, and many another strong-featured face also stares down at visitors to the house. It would seem that the branch of the Zamoyski family, founders of the lovely town of Zamość, who took over here a century ago, spawned one of those adventurous daughters so beloved of today's feminist publishers. Despite, or perhaps because of, her wide travelling, Zofia Zamoyska survived from 1831, a year of violent insurrection against the occupying Russians, until 1923, when Poland was coming to terms with its newly granted independence. Her travels are represented at Kórnik by several of her landscape paintings, including an 1854 panorama of Constantinople resplendent in an oval gold frame. The large garden rooms on the ground floor are lit by tall lancet windows, making a lovely showcase for the pictures, the assorted furniture and the gruesome trophy room. This last is stuffed with animal heads, antlers, Polynesian masks and even an anonymous human skull. Its ceiling is coffered and features 71 coats of arms, one in the corner being missing. Amongst the family portraits here are paintings by Smuglewicz and a 1938 painting of one Jadwiga Zamoyska, taken from a photograph, which shows a straight-backed old lady standing in a hilly landscape, a coat over her arm and holding a furled umbrella; she looks typical of her breed and definitely not a lady to tangle with.

The real surprise and delight of Kórnik is upstairs, where the main south-facing room, again with tall arched windows, is decorated in a delicious mock-Moorish style taken from the Alcazar in Seville, with receding scalloped arches supported by slender pillars, all glowing white alabaster. This room contains armour and cannon, Turkish saddles, sabres and helmets, Greek vases, a case of beautiful miniature portraits, a seventeenth-century silver altar, a carved wooden triptych and a chest, the whole lid of which is filled with an intricate wooden locking mechanism. Several rooms upstairs are devoted to the library and cabinet of prints, which between them contain some 13,500 items of graphic art.

In the farther reaches of south-eastern Wielkolpoksa, some 90 kilometres down the No. 38 road from Kópnik, is another gem of a museum to be sought out if passing in that direction. Just eleven kilometres beyond the town of Pleszew, at the village of Gołuchów, a little turning to the left leads to the entrance of an old estate where there is a mansion about the same size as Kórnik and at first glance equally unimpressive. Its grey slate roofs are rather reminiscent of the villas built by Victorian shop-keepers and factory-owners from Harrogate to Hastings; a style, in fact, which was borrowed from nineteenth-century France. It is only when one goes round to the north-facing main entrance that Gołuchów starts to reveal itself, for here steps lead to a Renaissance courtyard with an arcaded loggia which hints at something earlier buried beneath.

The present house, in fact, is the third on a site first developed in 1560 when the local magistrate, or *starosta*, Rafal Leszczyński built a fortified manor house with octagonal towers at each corner. Fifty years later the family fortunes had improved. Wacław Leszczyński became Grand Crown Chancellor and it was he who added the Renaissance courtyard and generally enlarged the place to its present dimensions. During the eighteenth century the house was abandoned and slowly dissolved into one of those romantic ruins so beloved of nineteenth-century painters and engravers, a decline which may have been a direct result of the chaos of the early 1700s which history has neatly labelled 'the Wars of the Polish Succession'. This is a fair description except that beyond the battles and further invasions by the Swedes there was some ruthless politicking which seems to have involved every ruling house from Lisbon to Petrograd. The loser in all this, besides the country as a whole, was the admirable monarch Stanisław Leszczyński who was forced into exile in 1710. He made a fleeting comeback in 1733 but spent the rest of his life an exile in France, where he was a popular and enlightened ruler of Lorraine, benefiting greatly from the marriage of his daughter to King Louis XV. France's gain was Poland's profound loss, for Stanisław's successor, the Saxon Augustus II, odious son of a loathsome father who as elected Polish king had been at the heart of the whole trouble, did nothing to arrest the country's progress down the slippery slope which would end in partition.

All of this is a long way from the present tranquillity of Gołuchów but essential for an understanding of the period. In 1853 the village and house were bought by Jan Działyński of Kórnik and it was his wife Izabela, daughter of the mighty Prince Adam Czartoryski, who fell in love with Gołuchów and set about turning it into a summer house and a home for her great collections. They remained just as Izabela had created them until 1939 when the Nazi connoisseurs came and took their pick, but some of the contents were recovered after the war and the house today, once again filled with splendid treasures, is yet another branch of the Poznań National Museum.

It is as much a **Museum** of interior deisgn and architectural detailing as of *objets d'art*, the floors and ceilings, doors and fireplaces being particularly impressive. It is arranged as a series of room settings typical of each period represented, with busts, vases, tables and chairs just as a wealthy family might have had them for everyday use. The wood-carving on the doors, ceilings and staircases is very rich; the Royal Chamber on the first floor has a roof covered with various symbols and faces quite obviously carved from life. Wherever they are visible behind the paintings, tapestries and four-poster beds, the wall coverings in all the rooms are both beautiful and luxurious. But they are not all old, many having been especially created by the Fine Art College in Sopot, near Gdańsk, in the early 1960s.

The most valuable items in the collection include a group of Greek vases from the fifth century BC, one of which is in the form of an armoured head with two surprised eyes staring out, and several French bas-reliefs of the sixteenth century which have been incorporated into the walls. Amongst the furniture there is a rare Gothic chessboard table from the fifteenth century. Flemish weaving is represented by four mythological scenes from a seventeenth-century Brussels work-shop and there are Polish and Armenian rugs from the sixteenth century, oriental fabrics, a collection of Chinese figurative art in bronze and several products of the goldsmith's art.

As at Rogalin, some paintings are rotated with others at Poznań, but fixtures here include many portraits of the Leszczyński and Działyński dynasties, including a picture of the future Queen of France and one of her future husband in all the pampered finery of an eight-year-old who had already been on the throne three years. There are also religious pictures from fifteenth-century Germany and sixteenth-century Italy, secular works from Holland and Spain and fascinating oddments such as a seventeenth-century composite picture illustrating various kinds of Polish costumery and saddlery. The rambling layout of the house means that there are many surprises as you twist and turn around the corridors, climb up and down stairs or step into a charming little turret room which has a view across the park. All in all, it is one of my favourite places in Poland, and its interiors are on a human scale so that it is just possible to imagine living here. The park, too, is very pleasant and, like the park at Kórnik, has always had a scientific function. Research into tree growth still continues here and one area is set aside as a nature reserve where a small group of bison wander among the trees.

After Gołuchów the ancient town of **Kalisz** just down the road comes as a bit of an anticlimax. Reputedly the place marked as Calisia on Ptolemy's map of the second century AD, it was yet another trading post at the junction of two trade routes, the more glamorous one being the north-south amber road which ended up at the Adriatic coast. Today it is an industrial town with a population of more than 100,000 and, although the old street layout is still there, destruction in the First World War led to much rebuilding and the overall impression now is of a grubby place where high buildings press down upon narrow streets. There are no attractive corners or vistas and even the market square suffers, as at Lublin, from an unsympathetically designed and over-large town hall. But maybe it looks better in the sunshine, something with which I have never coincided at Kalisz.

Because of the town's obvious antiquity, archaeologists have done a lot of digging in the vicinity and have been able to paint a picture of a region which was economically very active from at least the first century BC. Some 200 homesteads and burial sites from that time have been discovered within a fifteen-kilometre radius of the town and, among the many objects unearthed, Roman silver denarii, found both singly and in hoards, prove that, even if the Romans themselves rarely ventured this far, goods from the north were certainly traded down the line to their colonies on the Danube. There is, of course, the well known story told by Pliny of the 'Roman equestrian' sent by Nero to collect amber who, returning with an enormous load, reported that its source lay some 600,000 paces from Carnuntum, the crossing point of the Danube which lay between Vienna and modern Bratislava. The details of his route were not recorded but it could be that he passed Kalisz, buying security, sustenance and guidance from the local chiefs.

Although it seems that agriculture and livestock were the basis of that early economy, remains of foundry furnaces and blacksmiths' forges have been found, along with evidence of horn and bronze workshops; all of which gives the lie to the widely held belief that beyond the Roman Empire all was primitive barbarism in eastern Europe. A later hoard contained only Arabic coins, demonstrating another influence beside the Roman. All of these were from the end of the ninth century and further evidence of the east-west trade route which has already been mentioned in connection with Kraków and the south-east. It is known that Kalisz at that time was one of the biggest strongholds of the Polane tribe of Slavs who were among those who gave allegiance to the first kingdom.

The main area of historic interest in Wielkopolska is normally approached from Poznań, taking the Gniezno road from the city. After 35 kilometres of rolling fields and woodland several old wooden windmills appear on the horizon as the road runs down to the village of Lednogóra, where a large wooden sign points to **The Museum of the First Piasts at Lednica**, the **Pierwszych Museum**. This is proof that one is now embarked upon what the tourist authorities have dubbed the Piast Way (Szlak Piastowski), which connects Poznań with Gniezno and other settlements to the east, crossing lands where innumerable Polish legends were born. From the main road here a narrow lake extends northwards, later disappearing along the bottom of a long, shallow and typically subglacial channel. There are three islands visible from the road and the largest of these is **Lednica**, where both evidence and legend suggest that the earliest leaders of the united Polish tribes had their base. It is reached from the eastern shore, where a ferryman can be found in one of the museum cottages.

The legends tell that Bolesław the Brave was born here to Mieszki I and his Czech princess, and according to the German chronicler Thietmar of Meresburgh it was here that the German Otto III came in 1025 and put his own crown on the head of Bolesław, acknowledging the independence of the Polish throne. Otto was on a pilgrimage to Gniezno to pay homage at the tomb of St Adalbert who had been killed whilst carrying out missionary work among the tribes living in what is now Mazuria, in Poland's north-east. The chronicle says that the road from Poznań to Gniezno, 50 kilometres long, was covered in rich fabrics for the emperor; several points up, surely, on Raleigh's cloak. Another legend has it that during a fierce battle here a knight and his retinue went to the bottom of the lake; this has been lent credibility by recent archaeological work which discovered the remains of a body in full armour, a horse and a long boat carved from an oak log all deep in the lake mud. Archaeologists also discovered the sunken piles of bridges which linked the two large islands to both shores of the lake. This explains how enough stone was carried to the islands to build the large castle and the church, which was thought to have been founded by Mieszko I in the middle of the tenth century.

Both were destroyed by the invasion of the Bohemian Bretislav in 1039, but the partly restored church remained in use until the fifteenth century before being left to become a ruin, most of the stones remaining where they fell until, during the partitions, the German leaseholder of the land moved many of them to the west bank as raw material for farm buildings. Most of what was left survived only to be used for road building by the Nazis, who removed some 900 cartloads of stone — which gives some idea of the size of the buildings and the effort involved in their original construction. From the fragments remaining it has been possible to learn that the church was built in the form of a Greek cross and four solid pillars remain which must have supported a stone dome; all indications that the building conformed to the known rules of the early Christian rites and rituals. In 1962 the foundations of another temple were found on a hillock within earth ramparts which occupy the northern half of the island. One of the most revealing discoveries made at that time (and a strong argument in favour of untidiness) was a bag of rubbish which contained the remains of liturgical objects including an ornamental book- or casket-cover made of horn, an ornamental comb and, still in its leather case, an archbishop's gilded pectoral cross. The remains of various craftsmen's workshops were also found on the site.

In recognition of the significance of all this, a museum was created to allow the remains to be seen and a scientific department set up to continue the research work and preserve what was found. It was then decided that an open-air museum should also be located at Lednica, and over the past few years a *skansen* has slowly taken shape on the site where a complete Wielkopolska village will eventually be built. Already some 30 or so buildings have been assembled, including cottages, granaries, an eighteenth-century inn and four of a proposed eleven windmills. Many facilities already exist and it is well worth a visit. An interesting little guide-book to the site called *The Lednickie Stronghold* has been published in English.

Given the proximity of Lednica to **Gniezno**, just eighteen kilometres further east, the question of which of these townships had precedence in those early years of the state is a little confusing, although it may not have been relevant at a time when tribal chiefs tended to maintain a moving court. What is generally believed, though, is that Gniezno was the seat of the leaders who, probably over a period of a century or more, consolidated in the face of the rising power of the Germanic states to the west. The name Gniezno is presumed to be derived from the Polish word *gniazdo*, meaning nest, which itself is connected with the legend of the eagle's nest found by Lech, common founder of the Polish tribes; the eagle, of course, is still a national symbol. Whether Otto crowned Bolesław at Lednica or Gniezno is an academic point, but it is clear from all the chronicles that crown him he did. Most importantly, he also consented to the new Archbishop of

Gniezno's reporting directly to Rome rather than being subservient to the German Church. This would seem to indicate, among other things, that, although it was only a few years since Mieszko I's baptism in 966, Christianity was already widely accepted amongst the Polish tribes. Following the raids of Bretislav in 1039 the capital was moved to Kraków in the south, far away from the conflict, but to this day Gniezno has remained the seat of the Church in Poland.

The cathedral itself, where Polish kings were crowned until the thirteenth century, may seem to be the best place to start a tour of Gniezno, but I would suggest that a visit be made first to the **Regional Museum,** a new building just five minutes' walk around the northern end of Lake Jelonek which skirts the town to the west. Not only does the museum's site provide the best view of the town with its dominating cathedral reflected in the water, but it also has amongst its other attractions a very good slide show describing the history of the region, with an English soundtrack on request.

From the museum you will see that the **Cathedral** is very similar to the one at Poznań, a large and plain brick structure with a high roof and twin square towers each topped with a baroque spire. And its history is also familiar. First there was a pre-Romanesque church here where, in 973, Mieszko's wife Dobrava was buried. This was burnt down twice in 1018 and a Romanesque building rose in its place which gave way between 1342 and 1372 to a large Gothic cathedral. This survived more or less unchanged until the seventeenth century when fashion caught up with it, adding chapels and baroque decorations, and the whole lot was then destroyed in 1945, the Germans having first used it not this time as an ammunition store but as a concert hall. Once again the policy was to rebuild according to the Gothic form, and this has left a plain nave with high cruciform vaults and twin aisles lined with chapels. The best of these are the 1610 Baranowski family chapel, which is in a late-Renaissance style; the Potocki, which has an elliptical dome constructed in 1727 by Pompeo Ferrari and a wonderfully exuberant iron screen; and the Lubieński, built 50 years later at the time that neo-classicism was making an appearance in Poland.

Following Adalbert's death amongst the Pruthenians, Boleslaw the Brave is thought to have paid the missionary's own weight in gold for the return of his body, the remains of which now rest in a splendid silver sarcophagus featuring the reclining figure of the saint, a masterpiece executed in Gdańsk by Peter van der Rennen in 1662. High above the nave is a very naturalistic crucifix carved from lime

Poznań. Built in 1550 by an Italian architect, the Town Hall, with its spectacular interior, is one of the finest Renaissance buildings in northern Europe. The arcaded houses were once the homes of market stallholders.

Frombork. Not much in this Baltic view can have changed since Copernicus lived here in the early sixteenth century, working for the cathedral authorities and writing his revolutionary book, the first to describe a heliocentric planetary system.

Frombork. The cathedral is one of Poland's
best examples of Gothic architecture;
its slender brick vaulting soars above
the mostly Baroque interior decorations,
such as the main altar and carved Virgin
shown here.

Gdańsk. One of the features of a fascinating city waterfront is the fifteenth-century Crane Tower and Gate, which was used to unload ships and mount their masts.

Gdańsk was one of the richest trading cities in northern Europe; even its lesser streets sport grand doorways such as this, which now leads to a shop.

Gdańsk. The view from the Green Gate up the Long Market to the spire of
the Town Hall is one of the best townscapes of northern Europe. The Town
Hall is now a museum and features some quite spectacular interior decoration.

Gdańsk. The Artus Mansion and Neptune Fountain in the Long Market. The mansion was the headquarters of the international merchants who lived here in the late medieval period; its façade dates from the sixteenth century and the fountain from the early seventeenth.

Gdańsk. The fourteenth-century St Catherine's Church stands above the ancient Radunia Canal in the Old Town with the steep roof of the Great Mill, also from the fourteenth century, showing on the left.

wood in around 1430 and at the west end of the cathedral is the finely carved marble tombstone of Archbishop Zbigniew Oleśnicki, which is thought by many experts to be the work of Wit Stwosz, and a bronze memorial to one Jakób of Siena from the workshop of another Nuremberg craftsman, Peter Vischer. But the real treasure of Gniezno is the pair of **Bronze Doors** which are now mounted inside the south door. Made in the 1170s, these are amongst the oldest and most important examples of Romanesque metalwork surviving in Europe. Going up one door and down the other, eighteen pictures in relief tell the story of St Adalbert from his cradle to his ultimate grave here in the cathedral, the whole series cast within a framework of sinuous foliage. Time has brought a rich polish to the darkened bronze but every detail of the exceptional workmanship is clearly visible. These doors alone provide many people with reason enough to visit Gniezno. While you are in the cathedral, though, take a look into the Treasury, whose collection of Gothic, Renaissance and baroque work in gold is one of Poland's richest.

The east end of the cathedral points up the rise of Ulica Tumska to the main market square, which is an undistinguished place these days; the busy shop-lined centre of a fast-growing town which is dominated by parked cars and bus queues. A narrow street in the southern corner of the square leads to the late Gothic parish church built in the 1420s and a monastery which has been rebuilt in baroque but which still contains an interesting late fourteenth-century wall painting in the chancel. Despite the fact that this covers more or less all of Gniezno's specific attractions, there is something likeable about the place.

Before continuing eastwards along the Piast route there is another detour to be made, this time north by way of the main E83 road to Bydgoszcz, turning right after 20 kilometres at the village of Rogowo and left after another ten kilometres at Gąsawa where there should be a sign for **Biskupin**, one of the most famous ancient sites in Europe. For many years it was known that this region had been settled 8,000 or even 10,000 years ago and in this immediate vicinity many traces of Stone- and Bronze-Age peoples had been recovered, but it was only in 1933 that a local schoolmaster noticed some obviously hand-worked oak stakes protruding from a lake when the water level was down. He informed the museum at Poznań, whereupon scientists descended upon this remote place and soon declared that it was a fortified Iron Age village of the Lusatian culture dating from 500 BC, much of it preserved in the mud of the lake. Today the fortifications and some of the houses have been reconstructed on their original sites and, with the help of the especially established museum, the farming, fishing and hunting lifestyles of 2,500 years ago can be imagined. Amongst items in the museum that were found locally there are digging hoes made from antlers, spearheads and arrowheads of horn, decorated clay pots, bronze knives and pins and axes, the clay figure of a bird, and even a spoked wheel made of clay.

Today the ancient village itself stands on a little peninsula which juts out from the south-east corner of the lake and was originally an island site connected to the shore by a wooden causeway. If you want to see it from the water, there are boat rides available. There is also a narrow-gauge train which can be taken from Biskupin around the lake shore to the village of Wenecja where there is a museum of steam locomotives. The steam-powered train ride lasts ten minutes and provides a long view across the water to the wooden towers and walls of the old village before stopping right by the museum entrance.

The oval-shaped settlement itself is reached by a path through the trees which emerges almost at water level and right beside the high wooden palisade which surrounds the place. The idea of sticking wooden posts into the ground might seem to be a primitive building technique but, as old photographs of the foundations when first uncovered and close scrutiny of the reconstruction will show, Biskupin was a sophisticated piece of work. Literally thousands of timbers were laid in an intricate web to form a base upon which to build, and complex, carefully designed structures projected into the lake to break up ice and thus ease pressure on the village during the winter freeze-up. The single-storey houses were built in terraces along eleven parallel streets which were orientated to make the best use of the sun, and a ring road inside the palisade surrounded all the buildings. All the street surfaces were made of what is known as corduroy road, that is logs bound tightly together to form a solid surface. The whole site is about 200 metres by 160 and it is estimated that with a family in each house a thousand people could have lived here, which is a sizeable population to live cheek by jowl and implies a well regulated tribal structure. One street has been reconstructed with its row of low houses, each with a stone-based fireplace in the centre and a raised platform for sleeping. Privacy, it seems, was not a concern in such a community. At the southern end of this street is the gateway with its stout wooden towers which would have served both as look-out posts and as defensive positions.

Although it seems to have been abandoned at various times in the distant past, careful examination has revealed that the site was occupied continuously from the fourth to the ninth century AD, and valuable Avar ornaments from Hungary have been found from this period. The history of the present village of Biskupin, which is nearby, is known and documented from the twelfth century, so it is quite likely that this quiet and misty lakeside corner of Europe has been continuously occupied for at least 2,500 years, new villages rising on the ruins of the old. The young and enlightened museum management seems keen to keep it alive for a while longer and has plans to assemble other buildings found nearby, including a late Stone Age long house and an early Bronze Age animal enclosure. A compound already exists where that re-bred and rather primitive horse, the tarpan, is kept and it is hoped to expand this into a working farm using ancient methods to raise pigs, cattle and horses and cultivate the fields. Biskupin is one of those rare places where a fragment of ancient Europe can be seen close up; somewhere to stimulate one's imagination and certainly to increase one's knowledge, because the patterns of progress perceived here would have applied throughout the continent and even today have their parallels in other parts of the world.

It may be worth noting that just ten kilometres north at the little town of Żnin there are hotels, motels and campsites beside another lake, but be warned: if the sound of perpetually amorous bullfrogs offends you, give it a miss and head back to the Piast route which lies along the 165 road running east from Gniezno. Passing the large new shoe factory and the spreading blocks of flats, this road heads into a bare rolling landscape of brown open fields offering distant glimpses of forest and lake. The first few kilometres are bleak and having visited a farmer friend hereabouts during the winter I can only advise others not to do so. At that time of year the east wind races across the treeless plateau, battering the little brick farmyards which understandably turn in upon themselves, protecting the family cow and pigs in an enclosed yard. This enforced self-sufficiency means that old ways persist, even though most people are post-war settlers. Three or four generations commonly live together and the home-prepared hams and cooked meats beat anything from a shop, every part of every pig being put to good use.

The first town along this stretch is **Trzemeszno**, sixteen kilometres from Gniezno. It is a small and typically unpretentious place which was first mentioned in the late tenth century when a Benedictine abbey was founded here. The townspeople seem always to have been a political bunch, taking part in several national uprisings and no doubt proud of their most famous son, Jan Kiliński, the shoemaker who was a hero of the Kościuszko insurrection of 1794 and has his statue outside the old walls of Warsaw. The **Church**, like everything else here, dates from the early years of the state and local tradition has it that it was founded by St Adalbert himself. Originally a stone basilica and crypt built some time before 966, it was rebuilt in around 1130 by churchmen who regularly came to Poland from Arrovaise in Flanders. Having passed through a Gothic stage, it stands today as one of the many buildings inspired by St Peter's in Rome, its baroque dome decorated with frescos by the renowned eighteenth-century painter Franciszek Smuglewicz. The walls and floor of the church are lined with variously coloured ceramic tiles which somehow survived the havoc wrought by the last War, when it was first used as a warehouse and later burnt, and recent restoration has revealed fragments from all its previous incarnations, including the original crypt. Worth a glance is a nearby former school building going by the name of the Kosmowski Seminary, which was built in the 1170s in the Gothic style.

Next comes Wylatowo where there is a wooden church from 1761, and several turnings hereabouts go north for five or six kilometres to Mogilno, nicely situated at the head of a long, narrow finger lake. The Benedictines were here too, but this time not before 1665, and more interesting than their monastery is the Gothic church which has two eleventh-century Romanesque crypts that are among the oldest in the country.

A glance at a good map shows that the area north and east of Mogilno is covered by a network of tiny roads any of which will lead to an ancient village or the overgrown ramparts of an old fortified farm or church. It is obvious that the region was both densely populated and highly organized long before Christianity arrived, attaching itself to the existing society and replacing or absorbing a less abstract system of worship. A rare insight is to be gleaned from the ancient annals, where the Polish tribes are accused of worshipping wood and water rather than God — but perhaps if our gods had remained closer to the tangible earth then the fabric of our planet would not have suffered as it has. After that contentious suggestion let us return to the main road south of Mogilno and travel the eleven kilometres to **Strzelno**, which has two of the most famous and best preserved churches on the Piast route.

The smaller of the two is **St Procopius**, a little red-stone rotunda in the Romanesque style built around 1160 and having a rectangular chancel and round tower. The interior is very fine, with a medieval statue of a sorrowing Christ beneath the low, domed ceiling. Right next door is the former Premonstratensian **Abbey Church of the Holy Trinity**, also Romanesque and built of stone, with a transept and two towers which were built in around 1175. It followed the usual progression through Gothic, which saw the addition of side gables and vaults, then emerged after 1750 with a baroque façade, southern chapels and much interior incrustation, but during post-war restoration the side walls to the nave were removed to reveal four of the most splendid Romanesque columns ever seen: one plain, one with a bold twisting form and two bearing beautiful and deeply carved figurative scenes. Each scene contains characters such as Virtue and Vice, framed in sculpted arches with each layer of the design separated by a different foliage. All the columns have large carved capitals supporting simple arches. Other Romanesque survivors include various tympana and a holy water stoup and, given what has been revealed beneath the baroque décor here, it is interesting to speculate about the hidden treasure of many another church. In St Procopius and Holy Trinity, together with the nearby Church of St Barbara which has a late Romanesque tympanum, Strzelno boasts one of the most precious ensembles of early church architecture in Poland, much studied and photographed by art historians.

The area between Strzelno and the Vistula, now only 60 kilometres away, is historically a subdivision of Wielkopolska called Kujawy or, in Latin, Cuyavia. It is a plain of fertile black earth, striped with the finger lakes which are a feature of the region, and in the fourteenth century it was a frontier zone facing the lands across the Vistula which were occupied by the Teutonic Knights; they occupied Kujawy itself for thirteen years before being thrown out by Kazimierz the Great in 1345. From Strzelno, the way east is blocked by Lake Gopło, the longest local stretch of water. After you have followed the No. 165 road north towards Inowrocław for a short distance, a little road turns off to the right and travels through flat fields of sugar beet to end fifteen kilometres later in **Kruszwica** at the northern end of Lake Gopło, itself a link in the amber route which allowed a 25-kilometre stretch to be covered on the water. It is difficult to separate myths about this lake from reality. Stories passed down to the chroniclers of the Middle Ages told of the legendary leaders Popiel and Piast who ruled from a lakeside castle here; the evil Popiel was eaten by mice, leaving the righteous Piast free to rule alone. On the shore there is an octagonal brick tower from which the view south reveals a misty, almost primeval landscape of flat green land merging with water in mudbanks and reedy peninsulas, but although known as the Mouse Tower this is the remains of a stronghold built by Kazimierz the Great.

The oldest Polish chronicle, from the twelfth century, describes Kruszwica as 'abounding in riches and knighthood' and it is known that under Bolesław the Brave it was the seat of the heir to the throne and later of a castellan and bishop, but the riches have survived less well than the legends. The town today, consisting of just a market square and a few surrounding streets, depends upon agriculture to feed its canning factory and sugar refinery. Its story is that of yet another old town which never recovered its political or economic importance after being devastated in the Swedish wars of the seventeenth century. The former cathedral is today a **Collegiate Church,** a stone basilica with a Romanesque transept built between 1120 and 1140 and a tower dating from a rebuilding programme in 1586. As in the case of so many churches, the baroque decorations were largely removed in the 1950s and the interior restored to its original Romanesque style. Many of the unwanted objects were relegated to the church treasury where items from the fifteenth to the eighteenth century can be seen. Kruszwica is an important, if now somewhat spartan, fragment of the distant past; in the early morning or late evening, the view from the Mouse Tower will give you a feeling for the landscape in which the Polish nation was born.

The river flowing north out of Lake Gopło is the Noteć which, after narrowly avoiding the Vistula at Bydgoszcz, turns west and flows right across Wielkopolska to join the Warta just before they both flow into the Odra. Today the major centre for this area is **Inowrocław,** twelve kilometres north of Kruszwica. It is an industrialized town with a large chemical industry based upon underground salt beds which feed a dozen hot salt springs. These have the largest concentration of iodine and bromine in Poland and have long been used for rejuvenation treatments. The spas are as popular today as they ever were. The street layout retains its medieval form and for those who want to learn more about both the town and its region there is in the market place a historical museum named after Jan Kasprowicz (1860–1926). Born of peasant stock, this great poet combined in his work those vital and often inflammatory themes of Polish life: an uncompromising patriotism, a romantic passion for the mountains and a vision of the end of civilization. As usual, it is the churches which have survived here to provide clues to the past. The rich Romanesque vein which distinguishes the Piast route is represented by **St Mary's Church**, a stone building from the twelfth and thirteenth centuries. On its outside walls are strange stone masks which date back to the foundation of the church — even stranger is the fact that the original Romanesque altar from here is in the British Museum in London. The parish church of St Nicholas is a late Gothic basilica with a baroque interior and a Renaissance pulpit, but four kilometres to the west in the village of Kościelec there is another thirteenth-century Romanesque church with a Renaissance chapel by the Italian who built Poznań Town Hall, Giovanni Battista Quadro, and sculptures by his compatriot Giovanni Maria Padovano. The tourist version of the Piast route continues west from here, describing a figure of eight as it returns to Poznań by way of Żnin, Gniezno, Września and Giecz, where there is a remote little church which is still surrounded by earth ramparts and was once a royal residence.

From Inowrocław, the temptation is to dash north-east to Toruń, just 36 kilometres away on the east bank of the Vistula, but that famous town is being saved for the next chapter; our route heads first to the Vistula further south at **Włocławek**, although if one decides to visit this town it may well be more convenient to do so while travelling from Warsaw to the north. It is one of the oldest sites in Kujawy and flourished in great prosperity in the fifteenth and sixteenth centuries. Today the town is a grim industrial place with a large paper mill fed by the surrounding forest. Its redeeming feature is its position on the river bank beside one of the oldest crossing points. In the tenth and eleventh centuries it was the stronghold of local princes, increasing its power after Bolesław Wrymouth's death in 1138 when, with predictably disastrous results, the country was divided into duchies ruled by the king's five sons, the eldest of whom was to be the Grand Duke and rule from Kraków. Kujawy and Mazovia were held by the second son, Bolesław the Curly, who consolidated his power base in Płock and Wrocławek. The Church also moved to the river, transferring the bishopric here from Kruszwica and starting work in 1340 on a new **cathedral**, which was extended in the late fifteenth century with late Renaissance chapels, only to be diminished in the 1890s by neo-Gothic remodelling. Inside, it is a Gothic basilica with radial vaults, a nave and two aisles, and a stained-glass window which has somehow

survived since the 1360s. Amongst numerous ornate tombstones of
bishops and nobles there is in the Chapel of St Joseph the tomb of
Bishop Moszyński, carved most wonderfully by that genius Wit
Stwosz. The cathedral also has many fine paintings, a rich treasury and
an interesting diocesan museum, as well as a sundial designed by
Copernicus who studied here in the 1480s.

Not much else has survived here. There is a parish church from
1538 but this is now heavily baroque, as is a nearby Franciscan
monastery and church. There is, though, a good museum of the
Kujawy region in Ulica Słowackiego, which has exhibits going back to
the neolithic period, mementoes of the 1331 Battle of nearby Płowce
where the Teutonic Knights came off the worse, and a folk department
with old costumes, pottery and painting. The Włocławek Cup, however, is missing: this most famous and valuable object ever found in the
town is now in the National Museum in Warsaw. Found in 1909, the
twelfth-century silver cup embossed with biblical scenes reveals a style
almost as oriental as it is western.

Włocławek also has one of those odd but fascinating little museums
which are sometimes more fun than the more official institutions. The
Museum of Weights and Measures is in an apartment at No. 29
Ulica Świerczewskiego, and is a reminder of the chaos that can rule
when systems of measurement differ. It has about a thousand exhibits
which describe the history of the subject, including balances; cali-
brated containers; weights of brass, iron, glass, porcelain and alumi-
nium; various measuring rods and rulers; clocks driven by springs,
pendulums, even sand; and a variety of thermometers and other
instruments. As you might guess, the museum is based on a private
collection, and it also has a library of books and photographs on the
subject of metrology.

Today Włocławek is best known for its crockery, producing a range
of glazed earthenware, typically with brown hand-painted floral designs, which is often used for wall decoration. It can be found in most
Cepelia shops throughout the country.

Before moving downriver, there is one very important place to
mention that does not easily fit into any itinerary. This is Łęczyca,
which lies 70 kilometres south of Włocławek, beyond the Poznań to
Warsaw road, on the way towards Łódź. Yet another trade-route town,
it was relocated to its present site beside the river Bzura in 1331 from
Tum, a couple of kilometres to the east, where it had been the centre
of a significant group of settlements way back in the first centuries AD.

The period from the twelfth to the fourteenth century was a time of much town building and very often a new site, considered more suitable for a larger town, was founded by charter some distance from an existing settlement. In the case of Łęczyca, this move enabled the local lord to move from his wooden buildings behind earth ramparts, which had only recently been damaged by the marauding Teutonic Knights, to a stone castle within new defensive walls. The walls were removed in the nineteenth century but a large fragment of the red-brick castle remains, today housing a regional museum with models showing the evolution of the town on its different sites.

Łęczyca's great attraction today, and the reason for its fame, lies out at Tum in the wide marshy valley of the River Bzura. As you travel east on the road to Łowicz, you will see the Romanesque church of **Tum** standing in bold silhouette a few hundred metres to the south, alone in the empty landscape but for a little wooden chapel and a couple of cottages. This splendid church is one of the most complete and interesting examples of Romanesque architecture in the country. It was bombed in 1939, the subsequent fire causing great damage, but since the war it has been fully restored, the hard grey stone and sharp-edged square towers giving the impression of a building much younger than it is. That the church as originally built in the 1140s had a defensive as well as a religious purpose is still clear from the massive walls and the embrasures in the towers; small round towers at the east end as well as the larger square ones at the west.

A Benedictine abbey had previously existed on the site, and during restoration work baptismal fonts were found in the crypt which apparently predate Mieszko's baptism in 966 and are further evidence that missionaries had made some impact here before the historic date of Poland's birth as a Christian nation. Also discovered were some fragments of Renaissance polychromy which can be seen in the chancel. The main door retains its original, beautifully carved and typically Romanesque portal which leads into a simple interior with balconies, late-Gothic stalls, baroque altars and Romanesque tomb-stones. From the square towers there is an extensive view, as was the builder's intention, and the windows are decorated with original arches and columns. One advantage of Tum over many town churches is that its isolated situation allows one to look at it from all angles, although seeing its best and most photographed view from the south-west entails standing in the middle of someone's onion patch.

Back to Włocławek and 30 kilometres downstream, just off the main road and well on the way to Toruń, is the spa town of **Ciechocinek** which has built a career for itself on the basis of its abundant saline springs. These are used for drinking and medicinal baths but are best known for the manner in which their waters are evaporated, in huge and quite extraordinary graduation towers which dominate the flat landscape and must be amongst the largest wooden structures ever built. The first two were erected in 1829, the third a few years later; and, lest it be thought that I exaggerate, the largest is by my calculations more than a kilometre long and three or four storeys high. The principle is that salt water is pumped to the top from where it trickles down through a great wall of blackthorn twigs, which both concentrates the salt and produces an oceanic atmosphere through which patients wander, breathing deeply. These enormous contraptions have produced a local climate which is almost maritime, and a nearby park supports a host of salt-loving flora. The town itself is purpose-built for the spa with a series of parks and typical hotel and sanatorium buildings; but those towers just have to be seen to be believed.

14

The Lower Vistula

The short distance from the region of the Piast route to Toruń on the Vistula river marks a vivid change of style and atmosphere. The small towns and ancient villages are replaced by large commercial centres feeding off the sluggish artery of the river which, unsuitable as it is for most modern shipping, still has the occasional barge churning up and down it from the sea at Gdańsk to Warsaw and beyond, just as grain and timber once flowed this way from the heart of the country.

One of Poland's problems has been that this corridor for exports has also been open to an influx of people. Sometimes these were peaceable traders who would later dominate many of the towns they settled in but on one fateful occasion the visitors were invited mercenaries who turned on their host with a savagery which has echoed down the centuries. These were the Teutonic Knights, mainly Germanic warriors from the crusades zealously looking for a new cause and territory on which to establish their own strict Christian state. Faced with regular invasions from the Baltic tribes to the north-east, Prince Konrad of Mazovia invited the Knights to Poland in 1226 to defend his frontier and carry Christianity to those pagan Pruthenian, Sudovian and Lithuanian tribes who were troubling him. This invitation was a classic example of political short-sightedness, for the cure was far worse than the original complaint. Over the following half century the Knights brutally exterminated or converted the Baltic people and then claimed all the conquered land as their own. In 1308 they took Gdańsk and by 1332 had occupied Kujawy, forcing Poland to link up with the Lithuanians to present a common front against this warrior state. By this time the Teutonic Knights occupied territory that spread from the Niemen river in the far north-east to a position 100 kilometres west of

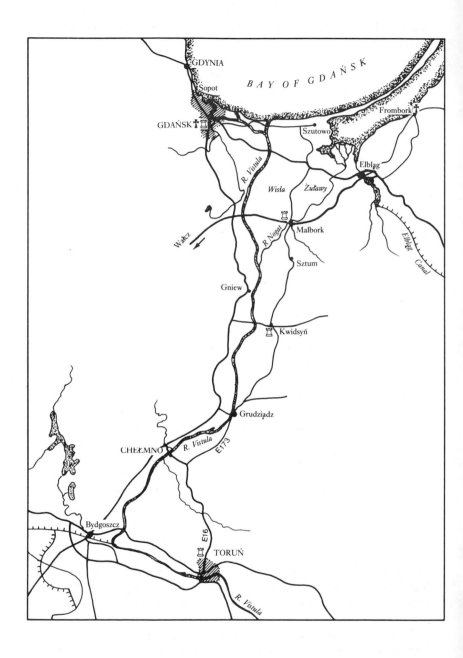

the Vistula, an expansion which was finally reversed in 1410 at the momentous Battle of Grunwald.

The influence of the foreign traders was more benign but, if anything, more long-lasting. The still German population of the so-called Free City of Gdańsk was used by Hitler as one of the reasons for unleashing the *blitzkrieg* of 1939. At that time much of the Knights' former land went by the name of East Prussia and was a part of the Reich which since 1918 had been isolated by the infamous Polish Corridor which embraced the lower Vistula and gave Poland her only access to the sea. Nowadays the ethnic map of northern Europe is much tidier, though at a price nobody should have been asked to pay, but the restored towns in the area still betray their past in every street. The high red-brick façades of the buildings have more in common with those of Brugge or Antwerp than those of Kraków, for the very good reason that they were built in the days of the Hanseatic League, a federation of North Sea and Baltic trading cities, by Flemings and Germans who colonized the region, often under the protection of the Knights. Gdańsk itself is the prime example of such a town, its old centre being almost indistinguishable from the streets of Amsterdam or Lübeck, but the style reached up the river to embrace **Toruń** and it is here in the city of Copernicus that our exploration will begin.

As one approaches from the south over the river bridge the stumpy brick towers of St John's Church and the town hall rise above the old roofscape, itself underlined by fragments of the defence wall which still stand on the river bank. As at Warsaw, the medieval area of the town is comprised of the Old Town and a New Town, each with its market square and town hall although only a few hundred metres separates the two centres. Toruń escaped destruction in the last war and its narrow streets of high buildings, including some fine examples of Gothic and Renaissance houses, bear witness to a past prosperity which has never quite been regained, despite the modern factories and the ranks of white apartment blocks which stand beyond the wall like an encamped army. The Old Town Market Place (Rynek Staromiejski), the more westerly of the two markets, is the focal point of the medieval city, and it is not a bad idea to climb the tower of the **town hall** here to make an aerial survey of the place, picking out the main streets and buildings and looking out across the river to the flat green plain that fills the southern horizon.

This town hall, considered to be amongst the finest Gothic buildings of northern Europe, was built in 1393 and somewhat remodelled in the Renaissance. It is a large, almost square structure of three floors and a high red roof laid out around a central courtyard and has an elegant portico in the west side and the square tower rising from the south-east corner. The brickwork is beautifully done. Each vertical set of windows is framed by a lancet-like arched recess rising to the eaves and there are delicate little octagonal turrets on three of the corners. As one looks out from the tower, four churches rise above the jumbled roofscape: two on the west side of the market place, a large barn of a place broadside on to the south, and another further east, beyond the New Town market place.

Before exploring the churches and the town in general, it is well worth visiting the rest of the town hall, which contains a regional museum with sections devoted to medieval art, modern painting and sculpture, artistic craftsmanship, graphic art and archaeology. This last section has some of the best specimens in the country, with thousands of neolithic items, some very exciting military and decorative objects from the Bronze Age, including a treasure-trove of bronze decorations from the village of Kuźnice, and a display of Roman relics which managed to travel this far north along the old trade routes. The other departments are equally rich and interesting. The medieval stained glass is particularly valuable, while an early sixteenth-century likeness of Copernicus not surprisingly holds pride of place in a portrait gallery which boasts 25 pictures of Polish kings. It is Copernicus too who stands in the market place beneath the town hall tower, staring out over the heads of the university students (for whom his statue is a meeting place) and down Ulica Żeglarska to the river.

The market square itself is flanked by old Hanseatic-type mansions with façades in a variety of styles. The baroque stucco of No. 35 fronts an unusual display of Far Eastern art based on the private collection of a local citizen who presented it to the city in 1966. **St Mary's Church**, just beyond the north-west corner of the market place, is a rather odd-looking building with an elegant Gothic chancel protruding from a much larger box of a nave. Inside it has delicate radial vaults and Gothic stalls and some late fourteenth-century polychromy. The organ is a splendid Renaissance affair from 1609, while the altars are baroque and rococo.

The east-west street which runs across the front of the town hall is the main shopping centre of the town and runs from the line of the west wall all the way through to the New Town. At its western extremity it is called Ulica Różana, and amongst the old shops here there is a bakery producing Toruń's most famous product, ginger-bread in ornate shapes, some produced from the original seventeenth- and eighteenth-century moulds. The most popular shapes are of hearts, richly dressed figures, animals and even horse-drawn coaches, and they are so splendid that they are very often not eaten but end up hanging on a wall as stale but decorative souvenirs of a visit to Toruń. Recently someone has had the clever idea of producing clay decorations from the same moulds, so that it is now possible to buy one shape to eat and one to display.

Several hundred people are employed today in the town's ginger-bread business and many local people make their own to private and well guarded recipes, a main ingredient of which is always honey. Perhaps the strangest tradition relating to this delicacy is that the dough should be made on the day of your daughter's birth and brought up from a cool cellar for baking only a few days before she is wed. Somehow I cannot believe that a 20-year-old dough is going to be suitable for anything but hanging on the wall, but so the story goes. I always buy a bag of the smaller, less artistic shapes and eat them the same day, having found it difficult to transport the large, fragile and temptingly edible souvenir editions.

If you turn off this street at the market square and go down Ulica Żeglarska, you will come to the large Gothic edifice of **St John's**, a church in the form of a hall, with its chancel from the late thirteenth century and its nave and aisles from the 1370s. Both in the presbytery and in the great rose window there are fragments of original Gothic stained glass, and fourteenth-century frescos can be seen in the choir, but otherwise the interior is heavily baroque — in great contrast to the stark brick exterior — with only a 1505 triptych on the high altar and a fourteenth-century crucifix surviving from earlier periods. In the monumental hip-roofed tower, built in the fifteenth century, is the Tuba Dei Bell, which was cast in 1500 and is second in size only to the Zygmunt Bell in Kraków.

Directly opposite St John's is the narrow Ulica Kopernika where, at No. 17, flanked by equally old but less impressive houses, the fifteenth-century **birthplace of Copernicus** (1473-1543) is entered by a simple yet elegant arched brick doorway. Careful restoration has recreated the atmosphere of a merchant's home in the late Gothic period, the father of Mikołaj Kopernik, to give him his Polish name, having been a wholesale trader who settled in Toruń.

The family was prosperous and well connected. Mikołaj's mother

271

came from another rich merchant family and her brother, as bishop of Warmia, (an old region to the north of Toruń) was greatly to influence the young boy. This uncle took charge of his education and after school in Toruń and university in Kraków went to Bologna and Padua, absorbing the fresh ideas of the Renaissance whilst studying medicine and canon law as well as science and philosophy before going on to Rome in 1500 where he lectured on mathematics. In that wonderful age of non-specialization he became at one stage a deputy to the Polish parliament before moving north to Warmia, first to Olsztyn and finally to the coastal town of Frombork. Here, as canon of the cathedral, he also practised medicine and continued to work on his great and profound theories about the working of the planets which were later to cause so much trouble within the Church but which opened the way for Kepler and Newton. He became a rather grumpy and reclusive figure, working away on his own in Frombork, but towards the end of his life he was tracked down by other astronomers and persuaded to allow his great work, *De Revolutionibus Orbium Coelestium*, to be published, the first edition being shown to him on his deathbed. Given the fate of thinkers such as Galileo whose theories also seemed to oppose the teachings of the Bible, it is all the more remarkable that the work was published by the Church authorities in Nuremberg. Copernicus covered himself both by dedicating the book to the Pope and stating clearly in the introduction that it was all theory anyway. Some years later, of course, it was banned by the Church and remained so until the nineteenth century, but the cat was out of the bag and the concept of a heliocentric galaxy firmly established.

The old family home in Toruń, together with its neighbour, now contains memorabilia from the life of Copernicus which includes several editions of *De Revolutionibus*, portraits, astronomical models and instruments, as well as the everyday objects of a fifteenth-century merchant's home such as furniture, books and ornaments. This house and the famous tower at Frombork, which will be visited later, are two fine monuments to one of the truly splendid, original and independent minds in history.

East of the town hall the main street goes by the name of Ulica Szeroka and is a narrow, pedestrian-only road flanked by tall buildings, the ground floors of which are occupied by the usual variety of shops and cafés where mothers gossip and children drink colas on the way home from school. At the far end of Szeroka the road forks left to the New Town market place and right to the far end of the district, but a sharp right turn just before this junction leads down Ulica Przed-zamcze to the ruins of the **Teutonic Castle**, built to overlook the ancient crossing point of the Vistula. One of the first of the Knights' castles in the region, it was rebuilt in 1233 and later enlarged as the confidence and authority of the Order grew.

Although its wings were clipped at Grunwald in 1410, the Teutonic Order retained its power over a large area of the north until the restless Polish citizenry of Toruń rose against it in 1454, destroying the castle and driving the Knights out of the town. The New Town, which had been set up by the Knights in 1264 to compete with the old one, and granted special privileges, was then joined with the Old Town under one authority and the combination of these events led to a thirteen-year war with the Knights which was ended in 1466 by the Treaty of Toruń. Under this treaty, and against the orders of the Pope, territory which included Gdańsk and the Pomeranian lands west of the Vistula as well as some other territories reverted to Poland.

Another event of profound and international moment occurred in Toruń in 1724 when, following a riot between Jesuit and Protestant students, several leading Protestant citizens were accused of sacrilege and sentenced to execution. Prince Lubomirski arrived in the town to supervise the event and the city president and several others were beheaded, although a few were either pardoned or decided that this was a good time to repent and embrace Rome. But the damage was done. The Protestant countries of northern Europe protested and the British Ambassador even threatened English Catholics in retaliation; all to no avail. Persecution of the so-called dissidents merely increased with the Polish nobles, like their French counterparts before the Revolution, failing to see that they were playing into the hands of their enemies. In 1733 a law was introduced which barred Protestants from any office or position of social dignity and although the worthless Polish King Augustus II died the same year, there followed only a period of confusion and power-mongering between rivals for the throne, each supported by a different European power. The seeds of the partitions which were to begin in 1772 were sown and sprouting.

Today there is little left of the Teutonic castle but there is a museum in the vaults outlining the history of the building and a walk around the surviving fragments is enough to make one wonder how the townspeo-ple were able to destroy such a massive fortress. Across the river from here, one can see the remains of another and smaller castle and a customs house, which once guarded the far end of the ford.

The next port of call is the **Rynek Nowomiejski**, reached by going back to the fork in the road at the end of Ulica Szeroka and taking the left-hand branch. The most impressive building in the square is the Gothic **Basilica of St James**, which dates from the first half of the fourteenth century. This has colourful ceramic ornamentation on the portal and several friezes as well as Gothic frescos and sculptures, while the mostly baroque interior incorporates a beautiful organ which was installed in 1611. The imposing iron gates to the churchyard are Gothic originals from the end of the fourteenth century.

The market place itself is flanked by fine old mansions, No. 13 housing a late Gothic pharmacy (*Apteka pod Lwem*) and No. 8 the fifteenth-century Blue Apron Inn (*Gospoda pod Modrym Fartuchem*), which is now a café. No. 17 is well worth a visit; this contains a gallery of children's art from Poland and abroad which is run in conjunction with the Copernicus University as a research institute studying children's creative activities.

From the New Town it is possible to find a way back to the area of the town hall by way of back streets which lie to the north of Ulica Szeroka. In a nineteenth-century arsenal at No. 13 Wały Sikorskiego, a road which runs along the line of the old northern wall, there is an **Ethnographic Museum** which covers most of northern Poland including the Baltic coast. As well as the usual exhibits illustrating country life, customs and costumes, there is a department devoted to fishing, from primitive spears to casting nets which are still employed today. Another section reveals some of the turmoil of recent Polish history through a display of items collected from the cultures of displaced groups who settled in the Toruń district after the Second World War. The work of contemporary folk artists is encouraged by the museum, which also collects oral folklore material and studies local folk dancing, making a record of all the region's dance steps. It must be said that, although Toruń is a fascinating place, it is a great pity that a fraction of the money and labour which rebuilt Warsaw and Gdańsk cannot be found to give the town a facelift, restoring and redecorating the houses of the Old Town which today are crumbling and shabby. Toruń has the potential to be a splendid attraction, but its jewels are set in a decaying mount.

From Toruń the river flows westwards for 30 kilometres before making a sharp turn towards the sea and just a few kilometres west of this bend, on the smaller Brda river, is the town of Bydgoszcz. Apart from a Gothic cathedral and some large old timber-framed granaries picturesquely situated along the river bank there is not much of historical interest left in this city, which was transformed between the Wars into a large industrial centre. At the outbreak of war in 1939, Nazi troops arrived to seize the town but were met by an armed population and detachments of the Polish army. After some fierce fighting might inevitably conquered, but a bloody revenge was taken on the town in the form of mass executions of Poles in the old market place. It is estimated that by the end of the occupation some 50,000 citizens died, with many more deported to labour camps and worse. Unless there is a particular reason to visit Bydgoszcz I suggest that you take the northbound E16 road from Toruń. This meets up again with the Vistula 40 kilometres away at the very beautiful and largely unspoilt town of **Chełmno,** which sits on a high bluff overlooking the river and its broad plain.

If anywhere has to be called the 'Carcassonne of Poland' I would select Chełmno rather than that present holder of the title, Paczków in Silesia. The main road passes below the little town and industry too seems to have given it a miss, leaving it to a dignified quietude, aloof on its hill. The easily defended site was known as a stronghold back in the tenth century, later becoming the seat of a Piast castellan and, in 1215, the base for an early missionary bishopric, but its crucial year was 1228 when the local lands were granted to the Teutonic Knights as part of their deal with Duke Konrad. Chełmno became their first Polish headquarters, joining the Hanseatic League and prospering as a trade centre before being returned to Poland after the Treaty of Toruń. It continued to thrive with a lively cultural and academic life right up until the first partition of 1772 when it was incorporated into Prussia but by some miracle the town stands today virtually undamaged, complete with its surrounding wall, seventeen towers and the lovely **Grudziadz Gate** on its north-east side. At the heart of the grid of streets, which is punctuated by five churches, is the market place. Here in the corner is a beautifully proportioned and quite charming white-painted Renaissance **Town Hall,** complete with a tower and attics and looking rather like an iced wedding cake. Remodelled on the previous Gothic building, it was completed in around 1570 and its old courthouse now contains a local museum.

Around the corner from the town hall is the largest of the churches, a red-brick Gothic building with twin towers and two aisles which was started in the late thirteenth century. It has an impressive doorway and retains much of its original interior, including carved pillars and other ornamentation and the fragments of a fresco. The granite Romanesque font is thought to be from an earlier church on the same site. On the western side of the town there is a group of Gothic monastery buildings from the early fourteenth century which housed first a Cistercian and later a Benedictine group and the church here has an unusual two-level nave, a tombstone from 1275 and more Gothic polychromy. Each of the other churches, although smaller, has its interesting features. If time allows one can take a walk around the outside of the virtually intact walls of this charming town, enjoying a distant view from the high bluff out across the Vistula which can have seen little change since the Knights first came here in the thirteenth century.

The castles of the Teutonic Knights dominate most of the riverside towns on the route downstream, increasing in size until you reach the massive fortress of Malbork, 100 kilometres away on the edge of the Vistula delta. But the next interesting place on the way there is **Grudziądz**, yet another town which grew rich from the old Vistula trade, which can be reached from Chełmno either by the 173 road or by a more daring route along a narrow country lane which cuts under the old river cliff. The latter makes a picturesque 20-kilometre journey back in time, through the villages of Klamry and Nowa Wieś where cottagers farm on the edge of the river plain. The modern approach to the hilltop town of Grudziądz which guards the next river crossing is not impressive. A great deal of industry has been located here in recent years and most of the town's streets are rather tatty. But those prepared to brave the appalling road surface inside the town (a common enough phenomenon in Poland) and seek out the old town centre will discover a Gothic market place and church and many large old granaries which look out over the river. Even this section of town can best be appreciated by avoiding the centre completely and crossing the river to look back from the west bank to a wonderful view of the backs of the old mansions and buttressed granaries. These seem to grow out of the top of the Vistula escarpment, looking as formidable as any fortification, while the chunky cathedral towers above them.

To reach **Kwidzyń**, the next fortified town, 35 kilometres downstream, it is necessary to return to the right bank and follow the quiet country road north. Founded by the Knights in 1233, Kwidzyń is smaller than Grudziądz although modern industry is causing it to expand in the usual less than elegant manner. The original castle was demolished back in the sixteenth century and the rest of the town met the same fate in 1945, but the extraordinary complex of the later castle and the cathedral somehow survived unharmed. It is worth a visit if only to see the strange tower which rises from the bed of the little Liwa river and is connected to the main buildings by a five-arched and red-roofed footbridge which looks like a section of railway viaduct. The effect of this so-called *dansker* construction is of a bridge which ends in mid-air rather like the famous Pont d'Avignon. The bridge emerges from the side of the great square castle itself which, with its central courtyard, is contiguous with the large cathedral. The whole complex dates from the fourteenth century. The cathedral has many interesting details including a 1380 mosaic over the southern vestibule, a fresco from the same time, various Gothic tombstones and a late-Gothic bishop's throne, while the castle houses an extensive regional museum illustrating the history of man's settlement along the lower Vistula as well as all the usual sections on local folklore and natural history. Once again the best view of this red-brick pile is from across the little valley, Kwidzyń now lying some four kilometres back from the modern course of the Vistula.

The next fort actually on the Vistula is a dozen kilometres down-stream at the much more charming town of Gniew, a quiet, agricultural place set amongst lush water meadows, where the large square Teutonic castle has been built from the now ubiquitous red brick. But this town is over on the west bank beside the main E16 road to Gdańsk and our next objective, Malbork, is reached more easily by the east-bank route through the town of Sztum, now a tiny place though once the site of another castle. Sztum stands some distance away from the river on a rolling plateau where tobacco-growing dominates and the yellowing leaves, hanging beneath their plastic shelters, line the road in the autumn. From here the road slowly descends back to river level and after another fifteen kilometres the massive towers and walls of **Malbork Castle** appear on the bank of what is no longer the main Vistula channel but the Nogat, an eastern arm which now wanders across the flat delta for another 40 kilometres before entering the Bay of Gdańsk. Malbork town is a medium-sized and uninteresting place but the fortress, itself as large as many a town, is one of Poland's great attractions, and the exploration of the different exhibitions buried within its vast complex of corridors and courtyards will easily absorb several hours.

There is a car park right behind the castle, reached from the town, but as so often the best initial view is to be had from across the river, where one can appreciate the enormous size of what is one of Europe's largest strongholds. As well as the road bridge, there is a wooden foot bridge from the northern end of the castle giving access to the quiet and grassy west bank, from which fishermen or even a grazing horse may be set against the formidable backdrop. And formidable is the word. It is an education to stand on the far shore and cast one's mind back over the centuries, imagining the impact such a place would have made on an approaching army or a passing peasant. The Nobel Prize-winner Henryk Sienkiewicz, in his novel *The Teutonic Knights*, describes the visit of Polish envoys to the Grand Master: 'The very sight of Malbork Castle was enough to strike terror into the heart of every Pole, for this fortress, with its upper, middle and lower castles, was something that was absolutely incomparable with any other in the world. In its sheer immensity it surpassed anything the Polish knights had seen in their lives. The buildings seemed to grow out of each other, forming a sort of mountain rising from the surrounding lowlands.'

Construction of the castle started in 1274 and two years later the Knights granted municipal status to the settlement which was growing up around it, enlarging the whole site when the headquarters of the Grand Master was moved here from Venice in 1309. The first castle became known as the Upper Castle; the Middle and Lower Castles being added during the fourteenth century. By 1350 granaries had been built along the river bank and a second ring of defence walls erected, and at the end of that century a magnificent palace for the Grand Master was built between the Upper and Middle Castles. Even after defeating the Knights at Grünwald in 1410, the combined Polish and Lithuanian forces were unable to break in here and it was not until 1465, the last year of the Thirteen Years War, that the castle was taken. The Grand Master then moved his base to Königsberg (now Kaliningrad in the Soviet Republic of Lithuania) on the Baltic coast from where he was forced to pay homage to the Polish king. For many people elsewhere in Europe, though, the Knights' cause had been seen as a continuation of the crusades against heathens and many young nobles joined the campaigns, including, as Chaucer noted in his *Canterbury Tales*, Henry Bolingbroke, who later became King Henry IV of England.

In the heyday of the Knights' power the town, known to them as Marienburg was a bustling place with a long market parallel to the river and, according to old records, 174 houses within the walls. In the fourteenth century there were butchers, bakers, cobblers, tanners, armourers, goldsmiths, painters and sculptors operating in the town, many of them already formed into guilds, and there was trading in wood, hides, furs, grain, cloth and horses, all products of the rich and forested Vistula hinterland. During the unsuccessful siege of 1410, however, the Knights set fire to their own town as part of their defensive strategy and 200 years later the rebuilt town was destroyed again during the Swedish wars. Like so many other Polish towns the place then slowly declined and only with the advent of the modern tourist age has it emerged in its new role as an essential museum for Poles and visitors alike. During the partitions the Prussians used the castle as a barracks and were on the point of pulling it down, an enormous task in itself, when an early pressure group was formed after the publication of a letter on the subject in Berlin and in 1804 the demolition was forbidden. Unfortunately, the houses of the old town have not survived and, in their place, magnificently sited along the river bank to the south of the castle, are a group of lacklustre post-war apartment blocks.

The castle is entered from the northern side by way of a dark gateway with a portcullis, a moat bridge and a tunnel which emerges into the large courtyard of the Middle Castle, a suitably dramatic setting for the *son et lumière* displays which are staged there on summer evenings. Outside the gate at the ticket office or inside at a souvenir kiosk, several guide-books are available; one has a good selection of photographs but only a brief summary in English, while another slimmer booklet is in English alone and contains a lot of interesting historical information as well as descriptions of what can be seen today. Coming close to the castle, one's first impression is of the sheer brutal mass of the towering walls; this is followed, after one has clattered through the cobbled tunnel, by the tranquillity and security of the courtyard with its trees and grass. Visitors on organized tours have a guide who speaks their own language, but unless you can tag along with such a group there is little alternative but to wander through the vast complex at will. A passage at the top of the first courtyard leads to the upper castle whose smaller courtyard contains an ancient well, but be careful not to lose yourself in the labyrinthine corridors beyond here which, on several floors, disappear darkly into the interior, some leading to splendid exhibitions of armour, amber or local history, others to the dead ends of dungeons or towers where slit windows provide spectacular views over the castle roofs or down to the river.

279

Some of these fragmentary vistas are quite magical, with nothing modern being visible; just a little round turret, perhaps, set against a golden tree, or a vast pantiled roof against the sky.

So rambling and capacious is this Teutonic complex, and so abounding in interesting architectural detail, that you need to keep a close watch on the signs to find some of the many separate exhibitions. Two of these are accessible from the main courtyard. In chambers on the left side is a large display of Baltic amber, both in its raw state, where it comes in a host of shades and forms, and in finished objects from ancient amulets to modern abstract jewellery. The most fascinating exhibits are perhaps the transparent lumps with insects or plants suspended inside, while the most spectacular are the sculpted caskets and miniature altars assembled from amber pieces which vary in colour from a pale cream through to the rich reddish-brown to which amber has given its name. Inevitably, the baroque era produced objects in amber which were every bit as ornate as the palaces and churches of the period and were often created in the long established workshops of Gdańsk where the craft continues to this day. The displays here include many items of exquisite jewellery both ancient and modern, and an accompanying exhibition details the knowledge, use and trading of amber since neolithic times.

Across the courtyard in the Middle Castle an entrance leads down to the cellars of the adjoining palace where a large exhibition of maps, models, artifacts and photographs describes the history of the Lower Vistula lands from the most ancient times. Upstairs are the main chambers of the former **Grand Master's Palace**, a six-storey box which projects from the castle towards the river, two of its ornate corner turrets almost overhanging the outer defence walls. One of the large rooms has intricate foliage designs painted on its vaulted ceiling while others contain examples of the sumptuous furniture which would have filled them during their long past days of glory. The most impressive room at Malbork is probably the **Great Refectory** in the Middle Castle, a huge chamber with a polished stone floor and slender columns supporting high and delicate vaulting. The walls are lined with cases of armour, swords and pistols, some of which date from the fourteenth century, but the focus of attention is Jan Matejko's famous and gigantic canvas of 'The Battle of Grunwald', typically crammed to the edges with violent action.

Deep within the Upper Castle there is a collection of medieval sculpture dramatically displayed in a cool dark chamber where spotlights pick out individual items, including a kneeling Christ carved in wood in 1390 and yet another of Poland's many beautiful triptychs, the right-hand panel of which features a character very reminiscent of a pantomime pirate. Elsewhere in the castle there are exhibitions of contemporary glassware and ceramics. But what impresses itself on the mind and memory at Malbork is not so much the beauty of particular exhibits or the fascination of details of its architecture as the great bulk of the place. It must have required a vast amount of money and millions of hours of labour to construct; and what is more, the Upper and Middle Castles represent only half of the original fortress. As you wander around inside the ultimately claustrophobic courtyards, you need little imagination to fill the scene with the stereotypical and romanticized figures of medieval history, but officially there were no lutes and flutes here, nor flaxen-haired ladies waving their knights off to battle from high windows, for the original statutes of the Order required all entrants to swear an oath of chastity. It was, of course a religious Order, intended to create an austere society in which people subsisted on a simple diet and slept on beds of straw but, as is the way of things, success and plundered riches led to complacency and decaying standards within the Order, all of which must have contributed to the unexpected defeat of the Knights at Grunwald. But if ever a place was tailor-made for a Hollywood movie it is Malbork and viewed from the river bank on a sullen day it is still an awesome sight.

Between Malbork and the sea there is a great flat area of low-lying marshland, the **Żuławy Wiślane**, some of which although below the level of the Baltic is today drained and rich farmland. This is the delta of the Vistula, a moody land criss-crossed by tiny tracks which connect its few villages and many isolated hamlets. Some fine old Prussian houses have survived out on these marshes; the best of them are large and arcaded, with the typically German diamond pattern of timber framing. They are stout and well made in contrast to the often more humble Polish dwellings. Malbork itself lies on a crossroads and before travelling to Gdańsk, which is only 50 kilometres to the north-west, I propose travelling the same distance in a north-easterly direction, through the once handsome city of Elbląg and over the low rolling hills to the tiny coastal town of **Frombork**, a remote place of great charm and peace, perfect for contemplation, artistic endeavour and feats of intellectual engineering. Had Copernicus been posted to a busy city diocese he would no doubt still have produced his great revolutionary work, but a feeling that in some way this place contributed to it is inescapable.

The town, now reduced in stature to little more than a village, sits at the edge of a vast sea lagoon which stretches for some 90 kilometres north-east from the mouth of the Nogat river to Kaliningrad, near the only sea exit. Clearly visible ten kilometres out is the long thread of dunes which separates the lagoon from the Baltic and for centuries this has been one of the main collecting areas for amber, which is dredged up and thrown on to the shore by stormy seas. From the Frombork road the lagoon shimmers beyond the pine forest but upon entering the town one's attention is taken by the red-brick cathedral on its fortified hill to the right. Inside and out, this is one of the very loveliest buildings in Poland. It completely dominates the little town huddled under its north side which, founded by colonists from Lübeck in 1310, occupies the few hundred metres between the hill and the normally placid lagoon, where in summer fishing boats and windsurfers weave their separate ways.

Started in 1328 and completed sixty years later, the **Cathedral** is a large hall-type building without a tower but it has a high decorated gable and there are little octagonal turrets with spires at each corner of the great red roof. Several paths go up the hill from the former market square, the easiest route being by way of the steps behind the large bronze statue of Copernicus which was erected in 1973 to commemorate the 500th anniversary of his birth. This leads eventually to the rounded towers of the south gate, behind which lies the large tree-filled courtyard with the cathedral, bishop's palace and canonries set around it. Having never served as a major fortress the place has a lighter, more wholesome and altogether less forbidding atmosphere than Malbork. Before you dive into the museum or cathedral I suggest that five minutes be spent beneath the ancient trees, which are themselves listed as historic monuments, before you tackle the stiff climb up the stairs of the **Radziejowski Tower** in the south-west corner. This not only contains an exhibition of ancient and modern astronomical equipment but also provides a fabulous view. From high above the cathedral roof the town shrinks in the perspective of the long sweep of coast and countryside; the wild and wooded shore of the lagoon disappears into the haze of Soviet Lithuania, less than 20 kilometres away, while to the south, small-scale farmland rolls to the horizon. With little traffic passing through, Frombork today gives one the feeling of being somewhere at the farther reaches of society and even in its heyday it never had more than a few thousand inhabitants. Fortunately the cathedral hill escaped devastation during the war; unlike the town, where the few restored buildings stand out among the post-war replacements.

The tower provides as good a view as any of the elegant west front of the cathedral, the high gable decorated with a fine terracotta frieze and blind arches. The equally elegant porch extension contains a portal of Gotland limestone carved with animal and plant forms, but it is the church interior which is most exquisite, its narrow brick ribs extending from the tops of sixteen columns to the high stellar vaulting. The columns themselves are octagonal with each white face trimmed with reddish-brown, and the plain capitals are painted with a delightful pattern of different-coloured geometric shapes. Together with the matching patterns inside the arches, this decoration was added only in 1890 and, as is usual in these cases, has always provoked controversy. To my eye the effect is very good and just a touch oriental. According to a surviving document from the early years of the fifteenth century there was then an altar at the foot of each of the columns and this arrangement remains today. Each of the altars is different but they are all rich, golden affairs dating from soon after the destruction caused during the first Swedish war in 1626, and some incorporate Italian paintings. The only Gothic altar to survive the years is a former high altar made in Gdańsk in 1504. Now in the north aisle, this is an object of great devotion, surrounded by hundreds of badges fixed there by visiting school groups.

The present high altar is an ornate baroque affair created by Francis Placidi in the style of the one at Kraków's Wawel Cathedral and installed here in 1751. The pride of the cathedral is the **organ**, built by Daniel Nitrowski of Gdańsk in 1683 and painted the following year by the very unPolish-sounding George Piper. This gorgeous instrument was damaged during the last war but in its rebuilt state it is considered amongst the richest-toned instruments in the country and the Sunday afternoon recitals held in summer here are very popular. The side aisles are crammed with memorial plaques and tombstones, many to the bishops of Warmia whose seat this was. Three in particular stick in my mind. One is a recent sculpture of a cardinal who died back in 1579 which has a flowing, Rodinesque quality, its vaguely triangular form calling to mind a drawing of Chesterton by Beerbohm. The other two are much older tombstones in brown marble, each bearing the image of a skeleton leaning comfortably on a scythe and engraved with a warning note about life's perils. Less morbid is the gold-framed memorial plaque and portrait of Copernicus, who is supposed to be buried here, although the exact spot is not known.

Copernicus, of course, is the main attraction of Frombork. He moved here as deacon in 1510 and, apart from a few journeys, stayed until his death in 1543. Beyond the west front of the cathedral the lower corner tower bears his name. Custom has it that he lived and worked there, but this is unlikely as the tower is purely a defensive structure and I doubt that the sergeant of the guard would want a philosopher with his library and telescopes cluttering up the place. The great man lived and worked in a house on the neighbouring hill immediately to the west of this tower and the confusion may have arisen out of a system whereby each important citizen was designated a storage place for his goods within the walls in the case of an attack. An exhibition devoted to his life and work can be found in the restored palace at the eastern end of the walled hill where some remarkable and rare items can be seen. There are several early copies of his *De Revolutionibus*, including the Amsterdam edition published in 1617 which belonged to the great Gdańsk astronomer Hevelius (1611–87), whose signature it bears. One extraordinary volume on display is a book by one Aulus Cornelius Celsus, a Roman writer living at the time of Christ, which contains details of all known medical problems of the time. This edition, published in 1497 in Venice, is a reminder that Copernicus also practised as a doctor. A name familiar to all who doodled in their school atlases is Mercator, he of the famous projection, and the museum here has a precious volume of his own atlas which was published in Duisberg in 1595. There are many more books on display along with portraits of Copernicus, including a copy of one by Matejko, and details of the many and varied projects he was called upon to tackle; the oddest of these, perhaps, being his treatise on monetary reform which was commissioned by the king. He was, of course, a prime example of that now tired cliché, the Renaissance man, who may be described as a workaholic if Copernicus's life is typical. His astronomical achievements tend to overshadow the rest of his work so that one does not recognize his strong character, never more clearly shown than in 1521 when, as administrator to the chapterhouse at Olsztyn in southern Warmia, he helped to defend the castle against siege by the Teutonic Knights. Do not pass this exhibition by, for it celebrates the life of a great man.

There is a little hotel in Frombork for those needing to stay overnight but it is finally time now to head west to that last great city of Poland, Gdańsk. The road heads back over the gentle green hills to Elbląg, today a nondescript industrial town distinguished only by the red roof of the restored parish church. This is a sad legacy from 1945 when this ancient and once-rich port town was devastated. In fact the old Pruthenian port here, described in his journals by the ninth-century sailor Wulstan, was one of the earliest places documented in the eastern Baltic. It prospered under the Teutonic Knights after they had conquered the territory in 1237 and settled a colony from Lübeck here which led to the town's joining the Hanseatic League. Although Elbląg town may no longer be interesting it nevertheless provides an escape route down a very peculiar canal system which makes for a wonderful journey deep into the lake district of Warmia and Mazuria; more of this later.

15

Gdańsk

As you stand on the steps of Gdańsk's famous town hall, with the Royal Way stretching left and right to distant gateways, you can be in no doubt that this is a city which grew fat on trade. And from the style of the richly façaded merchants' houses which line these and neighbouring streets it would be easy to believe that this was a German port such as Lübeck or Hamburg. In a sense this is so because, although Gdańsk was in Polish hands from 1454 until the second partition of 1793, its character was established both by its membership of the Hanseatic League, which brought merchants from all the Baltic and North Sea countries to the town, and by its 125 years under Prussian control which ended only in 1918, and even then only partially. It will come as no surprise that the political history of Poland's largest port is a bit of a Chinese puzzle, although the main skeleton of its past can be laid out in fairly simple terms.

Modern excavations have uncovered an early Slavic fishing village beneath the Old Town and it is known that trade with Germany, Flanders and even England was going on as early as the ninth century. Indeed, it is even possible that the greatest of the Greek sailors, Pytheas of Massalia, travelled along this coast during his epic voyage in the fourth century BC. In this millennium the town first became a power base for the dukes of Pomerania and received municipal status in the thirteenth century. By an act of blatant treachery in 1308 the fortified town fell into the hands of the Teutonic Knights who, commissioned to defend it during a local power struggle, turned on their hosts and slaughtered them. They held the town until 1454 and, during the ensuing Thirteen Years War with the Knights, Gdańsk remained remarkably loyal to the Polish king. It was rewarded with

286

many privileges which contributed to its period of greatest prosperity as exporter of the huge amounts of grain that were shipped down the Vistula. From the end of the fifteenth century Gdańsk experienced more than 150 years of unbridled prosperity as one of Europe's richest towns and it was then that the great building boom took place which produced so many fine houses and churches, extended the formidable network of fortifications and caused a burgeoning of the craft guilds. Although remaining a part of Poland, such was Gdańsk's power that it operated almost as a city state and, despite losing certain privileges when its burghers rebelled against the king over their support for the Reformation movement in the Church, it took the Swedish wars of the seventeenth century to send the port into a decline, further accelerated by the 1793 partition which left Gdańsk cut off from its Vistula hinterland. There could be no better indication of the town's declining prosperity than its population, which in 1800 was smaller than it had been 300 years before.

In 1797 Polish and German citizens united in revolt against Prussian rule and repression was the inevitable reaction, but then in 1807 came one of the most dramatic moments in the city's history. Its complex and carefully designed defences, lately uncared for, were put to the ultimate test by the combined armies of France and Poland which laid siege to Gdańsk on 1 February. Despite heroic defensive fighting and attempts at reinforcement from the sea, the city capitulated on 24 May, no doubt to the great relief of the townspeople. Like others before them, they expected great things of Napoleon, but instead of a united Poland all that the Emperor created was a short-lived duchy of Warsaw and the Free City of Gdańsk, which was encumbered with a large military base. This return to self-government was of little use to the merchants as the British Navy was still blockading the European mainland, making trading very difficult. By that time the whole of Poland, and Gdańsk in particular, was a political football, and following Napoleon's inglorious retreat from Moscow the city found itself once again under siege in 1813; this time the Franco-Polish troops were the defenders and the besiegers included the British fleet.

At the 1815 Congress of Vienna the European cake was again sliced by the people at the top table and Gdańsk found itself back in Prussian hands. Because it was still cut off from many of its traditional sources of supply, business was not good, and it took the coming of the railway in 1852 to bring new life to the port. The traditional water-mills which had been a feature of the town for centuries were replaced by new sources of energy, but as a part of the German Empire Gdańsk remained a heavily garrisoned fortress. Seven new barracks, new forts and modern gun emplacements were all added before the First World War, by which time the population had grown to around 180,000. At this time, of course, Poland as a state did not exist; the Polish people were citizens of the three partitioning powers. But they are never ones to let the world forget their plight and, for the Allies fighting the First World War, Poland was a bit of an embarrassment. Much has been written about the complex negotiations at Versailles in 1919, but the upshot was that a new and independent Polish state came into being, with a vital outlet to the sea by way of the Vistula corridor guaranteed; much to the chagrin of the Germans, through whose territory the corridor cut. Gdańsk and the Vistula delta attained the peculiar status of a Free City governed by a senate and under the protection of the League of Nations, who had a High Commissioner in residence. The majority of the inhabitants were German but Poland had its own Commissioner there to look after the new state's interests, most importantly its right to use the port.

Without superhuman goodwill on both sides, such a scheme was doomed to eventual self-destruction which, in the event, was hastened by the arrival on the scene of Adolf Hitler and the subsequent Nazification of many of the Gdańsk authorities. The 'thirties were not a happy time in Europe, least of all in the Free City of Gdańsk, or Danzig, as the rest of the world knew the town. And what followed is writ large in history. The first shots of World War II were fired on the city by the German battleship *Schleswig-Holstein*, ostensibly on a goodwill visit at the time. Despite the heroics of the tiny group of Polish defenders at their Westerplatte station, across the river from the city, and in the main post office, the city was once again occupied and in 1945 it was reduced to rubble.

Just as in the case of Warsaw, the 1945 photographs of the city centre show breathatkingly awful scenes but also give one a measure of the stupendous effort and skill of the restorers who, out of those skeletons of houses and heaps of broken bricks, had by the 1960s recreated one of northern Europe's greatest cities in most of its old glory. Coming back to the town-hall steps, it is almost impossible to believe that all these highly decorated and solid houses have not stood for centuries or that the nearby waterfront, punctuated by spires and towers, is not the same one as merchantmen looked upon as they negotiated the sluggish river four hundred years ago. For the visitor, Gdańsk's great charm lies in this combination of town and waterscape for, although the modern port and shipyards are to the north, the old docks are right alongside the heart of the city. To understand the place and appreciate the complexity of the old defences it is well worth getting a town map (*plan miasta*); these are widely available and fully indexed, but the map on p. 000 should help.

The focal point for any visit is the **Main Town (Główne Miasto)**, as distinct from the Old Town (Stare Miasto) which lies immediately to the north beyond the Radunia Canal and was the original settlement site. It is in the Main Town that most of the historic buildings are located and modern intrusions are least visible. The main thoroughfare of Ulica Długa, which means Long Street, and Długi Targ, Long Market, slices through the district from the Golden Gate at the west end to the Green Gate and waterfront at the east. There is no mistaking this street because a little over half-way along it is the slender tower of the town hall, startling in its proportions and with a glittering golden statue of King Zygmunt August on the tip of its tall Renaissance spire. This was the route taken by Polish kings on their annual visit to the town, for which reason it is known as the Royal Way. It actually commences just beyond the Golden Gate (Brama Złota) at the **Upland Gate (Brama Wyżynna)**, which was constructed in 1574 as a part of a new defence system. This arched gateway, as befits its original function, is a simple enough structure — too plain perhaps for the local sophisticates, because in 1588 a richly decorated frieze was wrapped around the upper portion, lending it some sort of grandeur. Today this building stands alone but when it was constructed an earth rampart ringing the town reached to the height of the frieze and immediately outside it there was a wide, deep moat spanned by a drawbridge which was filled in and levelled in the nineteenth century.

As the main land entrance to the town, this western gate was the most strongly fortified and three separate gateways still exist here. The second is the so-called **Prison Gate (Brama Więzienna)**, a formidable building which served as a barbican, complete with its own torture chamber and prison tower, which latter still soars high above the street. This Gothic structure started life in 1410 and was heightened in 1507, although the later Renaissance spire which shows in old photographs has not been restored to the high hipped roof. Thirdly comes the **Golden Gate** itself, built in 1612 by Abraham van den Blocke, one of two brothers working in Gdańsk at the time. The richly columned style is Italian Renaissance but the decorations are typically Dutch, which is not surprising considering the origins of the architect. This is quite obviously not a defensive building but a triumphal arch through which royalty and visiting dignitaries would process, presumably to the obligatory cheers of the populace. The lightness of this large windowed gateway with its classically virtuous ladies perched on top is perfectly suited to close the end of the elegant Ulica Długa and softens the solemnity of the prison tower which, from most angles, still manages to appear above it.

Adjoining the north side of the Golden Gate and somewhat dominating it when viewed from the outside is the much older and more substantial **Mansion of the Fraternity of St George**, which was completed for this patrician society in 1494. The building, a beautiful example of Gothic brick architecture and a tribute to its craftsmen-creators, is square in plan. Its pitched roof is topped by a later lantern which has a figure of St George on its pinnacle. Every country, it would seem, claims George as one of its own and this version has the white Polish eagle on his helmet, which can better be seen on the original which is kept in the local museum. Once through the Golden Gate, Ulica Długa stretches out for perhaps 200 metres towards the town hall, whereupon, now rid of its trams as a pedestrian precinct, it widens to become Długi Targ where the old market used to be held. The tightly packed houses, many now with shops at street level, follow the pattern of other northern European towns where space was at a premium. Typically they are five storeys high but only three narrow windows wide, giving the streets the look of a venerable library, the rows of pastel-painted houses packed like so many time-worn tomes on a shelf. Much of the decoration is high up on the ornate Dutch gables, calling for much neck-stretching to appreciate, but there are enough highly detailed doorways and windows lower down to keep the eyes busy. In Ulica Długa the house fronts now drop directly to the street, but originally the main doors were reached from low terraces such as those still to be seen in Długi Targ and some other streets in the Main Town. These terraces are splendid creations and allow an improved perspective for both contemplation and photography, the extreme height of the town-hall spire being the bane of all snapshooters who daily can be seen twisting, leaning and backpedalling in an attempt to include all of it in their pictures. These actions have replaced an earlier custom amongst the city's merchants, who used to doff their hats every time they passed the town hall as a sign of respect for a city council which went to great pains to maintain their wealth.

There are many interesting houses in Ulica Długa. No. 35, for example, is particularly elegant and decorated with carved lions, but the focal point of the whole Royal Way is the **Town Hall** itself and its setting of Długi Targ, where the houses are more grand and the extra width and few trees create a more open atmosphere. The town hall projects across the end of the old market place and has an interior which simply must be seen. The extraordinary thing about it is the overall architectural harmony of a building which was constructed in layers, each in a different style and period. The original Gothic structure, rising to three storeys, was completed in 1382 and a tower was added a century later. Then, in the second half of the sixteenth century, the rather plain Gothic eastern façade was crowned with an elegant Renaissance stone attic with delightful open turrets at the corners and the interiors were refurbished in a similarly sumptuous style. Today, the idea of the tower without its spire is inconceivable and yet this slender multi-storeyed Renaissance confection was like-wise added only in 1560, complete with its gilded statue of Zygmunt August, the king who granted so many privileges to the city, standing 84 metres (252 feet) above the street.

Along with most of the town centre, the town hall ended the War gutted and partially collapsed, and its reconstruction was one of the most complicated and skilful that the Polish restorers had to under-take. Today all is well again and the miracle complete. Now the town hall operates as a museum of the city's history, with many artifacts and displays, but the most impressive exhibit is the interior decoration itself. The entrance with its elaborately carved twin flights of stairs rising to a terraced portal complete with columns and a large heraldic carving is quite dull compared with the **Red Room (Sala Czerwona)**. The warm red wall coverings are perfectly attuned to the rich paintings and furniture around the walls, the enormous, gilded white marble fireplace and, literally above all, the spectacular ceiling which is smothered with paintings set in gilded frames. There are even golden baskets of fruit hanging from this ceiling, looking for all the world like heavenly sprinkler heads.

Most of the decoration as restored dates from the end of the sixteenth century and is in the Dutch Mannerist style; again a reflection of close links with the Low Countries. All the artists whose work is seen here had Dutch or Flemish names; Willem Bart carved the fireplace in 1593, Simon Herle did most of the woodcarving, and Johan Verberman de Vries produced the allegorical wall paintings. Just for once, each room is clearly labelled in several languages including English, so it is possible to learn that the central oval ceiling painting by Isaac van den Blocke, entitled 'The Glorification of the Unity of Gdańsk with Poland'; is an 'artistic representation of the function of Poland', with the Polish eagle spreading its protective wings over a panorama of the city. The Latin inscription is interpreted as 'Joined with the rainbow of the heavenly arch', which is surely something of an exaggeration. This whole incredible ceiling, I hasten to add, was removed from the buuilding and safely hidden away during the war, as were most of the town hall's other decorations. Nice local touches on the marble fireplace are the typically Polish bushy moustaches of the two supporting figures, although all that was actually in the fireplace when I last looked was a large modern candelabrum. Craftsmen in metal also contributed to the Red Room, in the form of two finely decorated iron-clad doors; the larger has no fewer than five locking devices, and the more lavish has fluted wooden columns, rich inlay work and elaborate carving.

Leaving the room by way of the three steps which lead to the smaller door, the officially ordained circuit of the building leads first to the Winter Assembly Room, which is little more than a gallery overlooking a small central courtyard but was apparently easier to heat than the Red Room. In 1950, when this section was being cleared of rubble, an unexploded bomb which had passed right through this room was found in the cellar, but now all is calm perfection once again. This mood is not maintained in the following room or many of those on the upper floors. The **Little Court Room** is also known as the Fireplace Room because of its extraordinary mantel and surround which were created in 1611 by the same gentleman as carved the front door. Its other decorations consist of a large selection of photographs showing the town in 1945 and, however many times such pictures are seen, they still have the ability to shock; gaunt shells and stumps of houses and churches emerge from the drifts of rubble and one moving image shows a man and woman picking their way through this scene of utter desolation.

The most glamorous route to the upper floors is now closed to protect it from the interminable tread of tourists, but this remarkable spiral **staircase** which winds up from the main entrance hall is yet another superb example of the wood-carver's art, assembled around a slender and gently twisting newel. The doorway beside this stairway is also a marvellous piece of work, with carved nymphs on the pillars, a great crest above and a trailing vine pattern on the door itself. They were certainly not shy of parading their wealth, those merchants of old. Once you have made your way upstairs by a more mundane route, there follows a sequence of rooms containing an exhibition of photographs of pre-war Gdańsk and the surrounding region, some from the nineteenth century clearly showing the German character of the town at that time in shop signs, advertising hoardings and hotel names. There are several pictures of Długi Targ with the town hall and these show a busy street lined with horse carriages and packed with fashionable ladies in striped blouses and straw hats. The oldest photographs show the massive old earthworks and fortifications and there is one lovely waterfront scene which is full of small boats, restaurants, shops and ship's chandlers — a stark contrast to today's quiet promenade.

Many aspects of the town's trading history come to life in a richly decorated front room which was once the office of the Municipal Board of Finance and now houses a display of coinage and paper money amongst the heavy furniture. On the landing there is a large tapestry which seems to sum up much of the city's history. It shows ships at sea and men fighting on the shore. The top floor is given over to war-time Gdańsk, with photographs, flags, newspapers and other material secretly produced by the Polish minority during the years of occupation. And finally a tip for the first-time visitor: beware of the signs which lead you to the way out. The trick is to entice you to descend somewhere at the back of the building by way of an echoing empty stairwell, but it is quite possible to move back through the exhibition rooms against the direction of the arrows, enjoying a second look or spotting something you missed the first time around. Before moving on from the town hall, too, make a note that one of the best cafés in town is downstairs in the ancient vaulted cellar.

Hard by the town hall in Długi Targ are the famous Neptune Fountain and the two finest houses in the street. The **Artus Court (Dwór Artus)** is unmistakable and quite extraordinary. In fact when I first set eyes upon it I was convinced that the façade was from early in this century, so clean and simple are its lines, so huge its three-storey arched windows, but this stone frontage was added to the existing Gothic brick mansion in 1617, when it must have been the talk of the town and was no doubt condemned by many aesthetes. The basic house was built in the fourteenth century but only the rear still shows the wonderful brickwork of the time, with a gable surmounted by nine slim, pointed turrets which look like cartoon sky rockets waiting to be lit. The building was created as a meeting-place for the local merchants and in its day was probably akin to a mixture of the Stock Exchange, Lloyds and a gentlemen's club. One thing is for certain: it was very exclusive, as the magnificent and recently restored interiors testify. All the fittings, with the exception of a 1485 statue of St George and the Dragon and a likeness of King Kazimierz IV the Jagiellon, the fifteenth-century monarch, were destroyed during the last war, but once again the restorers' magic has been hard at work. The magnificent main hall, spanned by a stellar-vaulted ceiling, is supported on just four thin, granite columns and the main doorway is decorated with medallions showing two more Polish kings. A little flattery could bring many privileges. Six life-size statues liven up the upper floors of the imposing façade, which somewhat overshadows the fountain below.

The **Neptune Fountain** with its statue of the mythological ruler of the seas was first installed outside the Artus Court in the 1630s and, although the stonework beneath the bemuscled bronze figure was replaced in the eighteenth century, the original barrier around the whole thing is a marvellous example of old wrought-iron work, resplendent with both Polish eagles and the Gdańsk coat of arms. Almost next door to the Artus mansion is the **Golden House**, with another stone façade which stands out amongst the town's brick and plaster, this time with sculpted Renaissance decoration from 1610 which includes a battle scene and the heads of two monarchs over the door, and four figures high up on the parapet who seem to be waving to the people below. On this north side of the market place there is an open terrace outside the houses, whereas each house on the opposite side has its own steps and private terrace, often trimmed with an ornately carved stone balustrade (the rural scene at No. 43 is my favourite). Many of the iron handrails slope down to rest on huge stone spheres and most houses have rainwater spouts which protrude from the front of the building and end in a dragon's head, or some other exotic form. Some façades have medallions, musical instruments and other designs picked out on their walls as well as richly carved window surrounds; No. 6 is a fine example of all this. The high, narrow gables, so reminiscent of Dutch city houses, are as various as they are decorative. Nos. 14, 15 and 16 present a particularly happy trio, No. 16 being richly painted with a floral wreath and eight figures in period costume. The view from the bottom of Długi Targ back towards the town hall is one of the most splendid and elegant townscapes in Europe, all the more interesting for being seen almost as new; most of the houses have been rebuilt from the ground up since the war.

All the main streets of the Main Town emerge at right angles on the bank of the Motlawa river, which goes on to join an old arm of the Vistula within the city boundaries and has long provided safe harbouring. Each of these eight streets ends at a water gate where goods were unloaded according to their type, but the old fortified gate at the end of Długi Targ was replaced in 1568 by the present **Green Gate (Zielona Brama)**, which was fitted out by the citizens as a residence for the king during his annual visit. The architects were Jan Kramer from Dresden and Regnier from Amsterdam and influences from both those cities are evident in a building which is a trifle heavy for its situation. Its archways lead directly to the Motlawa quays and the old Klonowicz Bridge, which provides the best view of the harbour, with the old granaries away on the right bank and the long and architecturally varied town waterfront on the left. The cranes of the modern shipyard loom over distant rooftops but the scores of triple-masted schooners seen in the old photographs and prints are gone, as are the crates of produce heaped along the quay and the hundreds of bustling porters, sailors and merchants. Today this quiet stretch is one of the town's popular promenades, where commercial life is represented only by a cake shop, some small amber workshops and a couple of cafés, although a waterbus can be taken from here which potters down the river, past the shipyards and out to the Westerplatte Memorial at the sea's edge.

As the town hall dominates the market place, the commanding presence on the waterfront is the combined gate and crane, the Żuraw Gdański, an inelegant and rather elephantine structure which hangs over the quay. The main bulk of the building is a twin-towered brick gateway capped with steep pantiled roofs; a large, unsubtle but not untypical Gothic fortification. The novelty is the timber addition which rises above the gate towers to its own hipped roof and originally enclosed a series of hoists, used to unload heavy cargoes and fit ships' masts. Built in 1443, an indication of the busy trade of that time, it was damaged in 1945, but the great mass of the towers withstood the firestorm and the whole thing looks today much as it must have done for most of its 500 plus years. Appropriately enough, it now contains a maritime museum which is dedicated to recording the history of

Gdańsk port. This has a large collection of ship models, including those sailed on by Joseph Conrad in his youth, and a complete set of models of every type of ship produced at Gdańsk since the war. As you stroll along this quayside, any turning will lead through an impressive water gate and back into the narrow streets of the town.

Moving northwards from the Green Gate, you will come next to the mid-fifteenth-century Brama Chlebnicka which leads by way of Ulica Chlebnicka (Bread Street) to the brooding bulk of the **Church of the Holy Virgin Mary**, the largest church in Poland and, it is claimed, the largest brick-built church in the world, with space for 25,000 worshippers. The original church here, a small basilica with a tower, was begun in 1343 and took about 160 years to evolve into the monster of today. I do not mean that word unkindly, but from most angles it is more impressive than elegant. For the visitor who is willing to make the climb, it is most useful as a perch from which a bird's-eye view of the town and surrounding sea and landscape can be had. But be warned: time and effort are called for to ascend the 75 metres (245 feet) of winding wooden stairs which climb the inside of the otherwise empty brick tower, passing on their way to the sky nothing but bells and pigeons. On a clear day you will be rewarded with a panorama which reduces even this city to a visually manageable size. The complex of canals and rivers shines away to the north, past the dockyard cranes, the ships of the modern port and the Westerplatte Memorial, to the open sea. The equally flat Vistula delta fades away to the east while westward the hills of Kaszubia rise amongst the outer suburbs. Directly below spreads the huge cruciform mass of the church, 105 metres long and 66 metres wide in the transept. The only decorative feature visible is the pinnacled gable of the east end, which rises above the narrow streets and jumbled rooftops. It is a church which seems as proud of its statistics as it is of its saints. In the Middle Ages, for example, we are told that it was ministered by a priest, 6 curates and 128 lesser priests who conducted mass in the 31 chapels.

Returning to ground level, the interior of the church is, at first sight, just a vast empty shell with 26 massive columns supporting the high vaulted ceiling, most of the decorations having been destroyed in 1945. Far away is the main altar, and a large crucifix hangs above the nave, but apart from those, a few statues and a bell which is embedded in the south wall, the walls, columns and ceiling show only bare white paint. The **Great Altar**, however, is a masterpiece, completed in 1517 by the Augsburg artist Michael Schwartz. Maybe it is the habit of Gdańsk's mercantile past which contributes to the flow of statistics provided; a leaflet produced by the church reveals that this altar cost 13,550 ancient monetary units, each worth 185 grams of pure silver, at a time when a lower priest took home the equivalent of 25 units a year. A very expensive altar, sadly damaged in the war, but now fully restored. It is in the form of a triptych depicting the coronation of Mary in the centre panel and with two painted scenes on each wing, while on the reverse side there is a stone relief of Christ at Gethsemane which was originally in polychrome. Rising gloriously behind the altar is one of the largest windows in Europe, in which bright new stained glass was installed in 1980.

There are other treasures here but they are hidden away in the side chapels, one of which, the **Chapel of 11,000 Virgins**, has a Gothic crucifix upon which the features of Christ are carved with a painful realism; this is attributed to the fact that the sculptor nailed his own son-in-law to a cross in order to capture the agony of the situation. Many other chapels contain furniture, fittings and paintings of great interest and value. The **Chapel of the Cross** in the north transept contains a crucifixion altar from Antwerp which was made in around 1520 for the Guild of Butchers and has many finely carved scenes, while opposite there is the marble Renaissance tomb of Simon Bahr, a broker to King Zygmunt III Waza, and his wife Judith, which is the work of Willem, one of the van den Blocke brothers who did so much work around the town. **St George's Chapel** contains two Gothic tombstones and its cornice is decorated with a figure of the saint on horseback which dates from about 1400, while nearby is **St Anne's Chapel** with its 'Beautiful Madonna of Gdańsk', carved in around 1420 by an unknown hand. Like the wooden madonnas of southern Poland, this is a wonderfully simple and sympathetic figure, topped by a large crown and encumbered by an oversized legend which claims that the statue was carved overnight by a young man who was due to die the next day for a murder he had not committed. So startled were the authorities by his creation that he was proclaimed innocent and set free. Far more prosaic is the neighbouring chapel which belonged to the Shoemakers' Guild. This contains a fifteenth-century polyptych and is decorated with a plate depicting the very last word in seventeenth-century footwear.

A final masterpiece which must be mentioned before returning to the streets is in the **St Raynold Chapel,** once home to the Memling 'Last Judgement' which we will find later in the museum. This remarkable work has been replaced by another, the 'Gdańsk *Pietà*', which is thought to be by the same unknown carver as the 'Beautiful Madonna of Gdańsk'. It is also spoken of as one of the loveliest Gothic sculptures in Europe, but I would choose the word powerful, rather, because the gaunt figure of Christ's disproportionately large body cradled in the lap of his fragile and sorrowing mother, though exquisitely carved, is hardly an image of beauty. Finally, beside a black-and-gold madonna in one of the chapels there is a wooden confessional which announces that both English and German are spoken within. Within the mixed fortunes of Gdańsk's history, the British are not blameless, but perhaps the Germans have more need of the service offered.

Immediately to the north of the church, facing on to Ulica Sw. Ducha, is a piece of baroque architecture by our old friend Tylman of Gameren, the man who built so many of Warsaw's palaces. In the face of creeping Protestantism, King Jan III Sobieski commissioned a royal chapel here in which the true faith would be practised, and Tylman called on his colleague Andreas Schluter, decorator of the Wilanów summer palace, to execute the fine façade. From this side the great mass of the main church can be appreciated, rising like a brick cliff.

But now to more earthly delights, reached by cutting back past the west door of the Church of the Holy Virgin Mary and into Ulica Piwna, a westward continuation of Chlebnicka. (Thus Bread Street becomes Beer Street.) Piwna is another street of tall merchants' houses with stepped terraces to the doors, but there are fewer shops here; just a couple of art galleries and antique shops, although one basement is now a pizza house. Facing the top of Piwna, on a street which confusingly changes its name every hundred metres, is the splendid **Great Arsenal (Wielka Zbrojownia)** which was built between 1602 and 1609 and is considered locally to be one of the best buildings of the Gdańsk Renaissance style. Once again, this is a product of the Low Countries, with the florid ornamentation of the Antwerp school showing strongly. The arsenal was built by Anthonis van Opberghen along the line of the original town wall and facing on to the Coal Market (Targ Węglowy), from where the best view of it is obtained. Today the upper floors are occupied by an art school but the ground floor contains a sort of indoor market with a variety of little state-run shops. Young men queue for hi-fi components next to a display of hardware, while opposite there is a selection of the beautiful but expensive woollen wall-hangings which are among Poland's loveliest products. And inevitably there is the sign of *Pewex*, the hard-currency shop which sells imported products for dollars, marks, pounds or whatever you happen to have. A strange use for an arsenal, but then anything is better than weaponry.

Heading north from the coal market across the wide open spaces that lie between the old city and a modern dual carriageway, one can follow various towers and fragments of the old town wall until they turn east towards the river. At this point Ulica Podmłyńska, a street of modern shops and offices which belie the age of the district, will take you north into the Old Town (Stare Miasto). But although few ancient buildings have survived here and the atmosphere at first is rather ordinary, two of Gdańsk's finest structures have been restored where the road crosses the Radunia Canal. On the left is one of the most remarkable industrial buildings I have ever seen: a great seven-storey mill, triangular in section, with its steep roof reaching almost to the ground. The functional style is reminiscent of mills and warehouses from the early days of the Industrial Revolution, but this mill was put up in the middle of the fourteenth century on an island in the newly cut canal which brought water to the city from eleven kilometres away — in itself a substantial engineering project. Many enterprises were built along the canal, including forges, a tannery, presses and sawmills, but the **Great Mill (Wielki Młyn)** was the most imposing of them all. It had undershot wheels on each side of the island, two tiers of millstones, six floors of granaries and a large bakehouse and chimney at one end. A mighty operation for its day which says much for the importance of the grain trade to Gdańsk and the organization of the town under the Teutonic Knights. Today the mill is used for offices, with the exception of the basement where there is yet another *Pewex* shop.

Directly opposite is **St Catherine's Church**, known locally as Katarzynka, Little Catherine. It was built in the fourteenth century and is one of Gdańsk's oldest churches, an impressive brick building with a Gothic interior and superb vaulting. Survivals include interesting old sculptures, a fifteenth-century fresco depicting the death of Bishop Szczepański in Kraków, a Gothic altar and paintings by the seventeenth-century local artist Anton Moeller, one of whose religious works shows a typical city street of the day. Next door to the church is a building which has survived not only the war but generations of town planners, for it looks suspiciously like a country cottage, complete with front garden. Either it was brought here for some post-war purpose or it is a genuine survivor; if the latter, long may it stand.

Just beyond the canal bridge there is a smaller but equally ancient mill, but the main interest of the surrounding streets, forgetting for a moment the curtain walling of the new Heweliusz Hotel and the international bookshop, are the half a dozen surviving churches and the **Old Town Town Hall,** younger and smaller than its Main Town equivalent. You can be reach this through the little park which lies immediately to the north of the Great Mill, turning left and following the canal until you come face to face with the typical Renaissance building. Just two floors and a steep roof topped by an elegant spire, it was the first important project of Anthonis van Opberghen and replaced a Gothic town hall on the same site. Around the door, there is a frieze of Polish eagles and the coat of arms of Zygmunt III Waza and, in the entrance hall, a bronze bas-relief of Jan Heweliusz, the Gdańsk astronomer of the seventeenth century who was a member of learned societies in Paris and London, an investigator of comets and the discoverer of several constellations which he named after his royal patrons.

Behind the town hall, on the corner of north-bound streets which lead to the main railway station and the Orbis-Monopol Hotel, are the Gothic Churches of St Elizabeth and St Joseph, and a Carmelite monastery which was rebuilt in a baroque style in the 1690s. The main road and railway-station area is not attractive and much of the Old Town, in fact, consists of post-war buildings including many offices, the largest of which is a great green block containing the shipyard design offices. And if you have made it this far you are only a stone's throw from the main gates of the **Lenin Shipyard (Stocznia Lenina),** which since the events of 1980 has hit the world's headlines and television screens more than most shipyards. Back in the Solidarity days of 1980 and 1981, foreign reporters and camera crews were thick on the ground here, snatching interviews with anyone who would talk to them. Now that the drama has gone from the situation the view is mundane in the extreme, but for the soaring steel crosses erected near the gates in memory of the workers who died here in the 1970 disturbances.

The oldest surviving document which mentions the building or repairing of ships at Gdańsk is a thirteenth-century letter from the local prince, Świętopelk II, to the good burghers of Lübeck, and it is known that by the fourteenth century there were two shipbuilding yards here. As trade grew so did the need for ships to carry the enormous cargoes of grain, though the Gdańsk craftsmen built not only for their own fleets but, just as they do today, for any friendly buyer. Dutch, Flemish and English traders all ordered ships from Gdańsk, which was well supplied with suitable timber and had a reputation for sound craftsmanship. The familiar slump came with the wars of the seventeenth century, but during the years of partition modern shipyards developed as steam and steel replaced sail and wood. Gdańsk was a major builder for the expanding Prussian Navy, slackening only after 1866 when Kiel was taken from Denmark and became the home port for the German fleet. Later, as the Imperial Shipyard, Gdańsk produced Germany's first submarines and then the city's equivocal position between the two World Wars gave rise to the bizarre situation whereby the yards were run by a company which was owned 30 per cent by Britain, 30 per cent by France, 20 per cent by Poland and 20 per cent by the Free City of Gdańsk. Unfortunately, the German managing director became a devoted Hitlerite and, despite the international shareholding and the guarantees of the League of Nations, the Germans used the yards for their own ends. Although the company constitution forbade the production of warships it has been estimated that by 1937 some 80 per cent of output was for the German military machine. In other words, a company in which France and Britain were the majority shareholders was producing warships destined to be used against those countries in the Atlantic war. When the British finally gave up their holding in 1937 they sold to the Nazi-run Free City rather than to the independent Polish state which desperately wanted to buy. Poland's chances, therefore, of building up its naval strength for the confrontation which it saw as inevitable were dealt a severe blow.

From the modern and busy shipyard and its cranes, the long Ulica Łagiewniki runs all the way back to the walls of the Main Town, meeting them just where the largest fragments survive. A left turn here down Podwale Staromiejskie goes back to the waterfront, in the area where the early Slav village was excavated, and this in turn is close to the post office building, remembered for the heroism of its small Polish guard in September 1939. Attacked by artillery and armoured vehicles and armed only with rifles, they held out until their commander was killed. Four managed to escape but the rest were shot after surrendering, giving Poland a taste of what was to come during the years of occupation. Today a jagged and shiny steel memorial stands outside the Poczta Polska as a memorial to those men.

The Swan Tower (Baszta Labędz) sits where the north wall meets the river. It is one of many such towers which still surround the Main Town and can be sought out by the eager fan of military architecture, for whom Gdańsk still has much to offer. Huge sections of earthworks and bastions survive outside the town, both on the hills to the west and in the southern suburbs, where the Motława river still feeds water into a huge defensive ditch surmounted by more bastions. Likewise, forts sit on either side of the channel used by shipping entering and leaving the port for the open sea and these can be seen from the Westerplatte Monument. The defensive structure to look out for now, though, is the Baszta Jacek at the western end of the Main Town's north wall, just at the point where we earlier headed north towards the Great Mill. This is a fine, octagonal tower with a pointed roof, but more interesting is **St Nicholas's Church**, a few steps away in Ulica Pańska. This was a Domenican church, the presbytery dating back to the thirteenth century and the main hall structure with its late Gothic chapels to about 1487. Together with the nearby St John's Church, it is the oldest building in the town which survived the war relatively unscathed. St Nicholas's is a long, handsome and unpretentious church with an unusual octagonal tower, fine stellar vaulting, a marvellous late Renaissance high altar covered with wonderful carving which completely fills the east end and many other details worthy of attention. It is certainly one of the best churches in these parts and difficult to miss, being right alongside the main outdoor vegetable and flower market — always crowded as Poles buy flowers, which are not cheap, at every opportunity.

Unless this town is toured with military discipline, there will always be things missed the first time around, and there are still interesting places on the waterfront and in the neighbouring streets that have not been described. One delightful little street is Ulica Mariacka, which is approached under its own impressive gate. The view up this narrow, once prosperous street of merchants' houses is blocked at the far end by the east façade of St Mary's Church, which increases the slightly gloomy atmosphere, but the restored houses are a delight with their familiar terraces, stone steps, open balustrades and ornate ironwork. The essential attraction of Mariacka is the late Renaissance **Naturalist's House (Dom Przyrodników)**, built in 1597, which adjoins the fifteenth-century Brama Mariacka and contains the regional Archaeological Museum.

And when all the streets have been tramped, the cafés sampled and all possible towers climbed, there still remains the great artistic treasures of Gdańsk to be savoured in the main **Pomeranian Museum** which occupies a former Franciscan monastery beyond the old southern walls of the Main Town and the modern dual carriageway, at No. 1 Torúnska Street.

There are a total of twelve permanent exhibitions, ranging from Pomeranian Gothic art of the fourteenth to sixteenth centuries which includes sculptures, paintings, fabrics, embroidery and goldplate to a gallery of children's art. The ground-floor rooms are in the old Gothic cloisters, refectory and chapter-rooms of the monastery and impress with their polished floors, white-painted vaults and good natural lighting, particularly in the cloisters, where Dutch and Gdańsk furniture line the walls. Of the paintings, those produced in the various Gdańsk workshops are especially noteworthy for their insight into the life of the town, the portraits of local patricians showing people as rich and sophisticated as any in northern Europe at the time. The earlier medieval pictures and sculptures produced locally were usually religious in nature and include altarpieces, *pietàs*, a remarkable wooden Christ on the Cross, and the most valuable work in the museum, the Dutch artist Hans Memling's triptych of 'The Last Judgement' which was completed in 1473. This is a remarkable work, showing the transition from a gruesomely detailed hell-fire through the vagaries of life on earch, where one poor soul is in the familiar position of being grabbed by both angel and devil, to an ordered, peaceful and slightly orange afterlife where Christ sits on a rainbow. When closed, the triptych's two front panels show the kneeling figures of the donor, Angelo di Jacopo Tani, and his wife Caterina with statues of the Madonna and child and St Michael above them.

Simply displayed in a plain wooden frame, it is a virtuoso piece of painting whose history is itself a drama worthy of a novel. Angelo Tani was the representative in Brugge of the Medici Bank and the triptych was intended for a church in his home town of Florence, but in the spring of 1473 the English ship carrying it to Italy was involved in a sea battle off the English coast and captured by Paul Benecke, captain of the caravel *Peter of Gdańsk*, who repaired to his home port with the spoils. Whether he sold the triptych or it became the property of his master is not mentioned in the chronicles which relate the story, but it ended up on the altar of the St George's Fraternity Chapel in St Mary's church, despite the protests not only of the city of Florence but of the Duke of Burgundy and Pope Sixtus IV himself. But it remained

303

in Gdańsk, through war and fire, until 1716 when Peter the Great, passing through the city, demanded the painting as part of a settlement he was negotiating at the time. Again the town council refused and it was Napoleon who finally purloined the piece in 1807, installing it in his own Paris museum. In 1815, with Napoleon fallen, the Prussians carried it to Berlin which then offered to Gdańsk a copy of the Sistine Madonna and three painting scholarships in compensation, but again the city, now a Prussian town, held firm and finally got its Memling back in 1816. It does not take a genius to guess that the next time the painting travelled it was in the hands of the Nazis, who took the picture to the depths of the Thuringian Hills. It was discovered there by the Red Army who in their turn took it to Leningrad, where experts at the Hermitage ensured that it was in good repair before returning it to Gdańsk in 1956. Where it deserves to rest in peace; Florence, I presume, having long since lost interest.

Other foreign art in the museum includes much else of Flemish or Dutch origin, often from the sixteenth and seventeenth centuries and including works by Frans Floris, the so-called Raphael of Flanders, the younger Breughel, Rembrandt, Van Dyck, Teniers, Cuyp, and many others, all reinforcing the picture of Gdańsk as almost a Dutch and Flemish outpost in the Baltic. I particularly recall a fine portrait of a gentleman by Albert Cuyp and a long-haired, effete boy, looking much like a contemporary English pop star, by Nicolaes Maes. The Polish artists, of course, are not ignored here. Matejko, for a change, is represented not by a vast historical scene but by a very striking portrait of a stout man. A 1610 picture by Jan Krieg has in the background a detailed view of Gdańsk which is worth studying as a historical document, for all the defensive works, the church towers and houses have been meticulously painted.

For the lover of textiles there is always something to see in a Polish museum and here there are gorgeous fourteenth-century brocades from Asia Minor, silks and cloth of gold from Lucca and Venice, and locally woven linens from the fourteenth and fifteenth centuries. The decorative arts sections display an abundance of ornate Gdańsk goldsmithery, silverware and some startling wrought-ironwork, as well as a collection of 1545 stove tiles from the Artus Court, each painted with the image of a local merchant, and an assortment of those large and deeply carved Gdańsk wardrobes. Two items which always appeal to me and are here in plenty are large wooden chests with intricate locks and heavy carved doors, one of which on the ground floor is quite spectacular. And living in an old, cold English farmhouse, I have become obsessed with the wonderful ceramic tiled stoves of central Europe which are lit in the autumn and simmer away all the winter, large, warm and decorative. One such stove here is crowned with arches which rise to the ceiling much in the manner of a tiered wedding cake, and another, which comes from the Artus Court, was originally twelve metres high. There is also plenty of Meissen (which is not to my taste) and Delftware (which is), and several complete rococo room settings containing such wonders as a scenically embellished longcase clock amongst their rich furnishings. But I was as impressed by some modern fabric pictures here as by anything else. Hidden away in a corner of the second floor along with the art nouveau ceramics and post-war pots, these are big abstract concoctions in rich glowing colours just crying out to be touched, and they are all by a contemporary artist called Urszula Strzelecka. One of her creations, well over two metres high, has extremely fine stitched detail and is adorned with golden birds.

This national museum has another branch nine kilometres north of Oliwa. Although surrounded by suburbs and reached by way of the less than handsome modern city, this is a delightful spot, where there is a beautiful old church set in a park with lakes, waterfalls, grottoes and a botanical garden. It was way back in 1186 that Prince Sambor of Pomerania first brought the Cistercians to his territory, and they built their monastery here, close both to the sea and to Gdańsk and taking full advantage of their rights to income from the port and the local fisheries. The first monastery church, built in around 1200, was destroyed after only twenty years or so by the Teutonic Knights and rebuilt at the end of the same century in a Gothic style. By the end of the eighteenth century, several fires later, it had a rococo façade squeezed between its two slim octagonal brick towers, and this combination of plain red brick and white-painted plaster works a treat: the full frontal view of the church, now classified as a cathedral, is an absolute delight. The gable is crowned with a fancy top, there is an elaborate portal, and the Gothic towers are capped by Renaissance spires; a combination which by luck or design manages to achieve great harmony. The secret, perhaps, is that the central section is hardly wider than the towers themselves, leaving little room for ornate decoration. The pride of the interior is the eighteenth-century organ built by one John Wulf, upon which wooden stars and suns rotate, angels raise their trumpets, and bells tinkle whenever the instrument is played, which it often is for recitals. Nowadays this complex mechanism of levers and wheels is operated by electric motors but originally it took seven people pumping bellows to animate the celestial apparatus. The high altar is from 1606 and other Renaissance decorations include the tomb of the Kosów family, which is by one of the van den Blocke brothers, marvellously carved choir stalls, and frescos showing both Polish kings and Pomeranian princes.

Alongside the church is the former monastery with its arcades and chapter houses; this dates back to the thirteenth century and contains some interesting Gothic and Renaissance polychromy. Behind the church is the **Museum**, housed in an eighteenth-century palace which was built by the same abbot as laid out the park; in recent years the latter has become an outdoor gallery for modern sculpture, from angular metal to soft stone, from the abstract to the classically representational, from the absurd to the sublime. The palace now houses the regional ethnographic collection which covers the period from the eighteenth to the twentieth century, including many lovely textiles, rugs and wall-hangings and plenty of basic but dignified rural furniture. There is also an exhibition of interior decoration and furnishings and a large gallery of contemporary art which is a showcase for local talent. The park itself makes a pleasant change from tramping the streets of the city, but the main road which led here continues northward first to the resort of Sopot and then to the modern port of **Gdynia**, both of which offer lungfuls of ozone to those in need of fresh air.

Gdynia boasts an excellent Oceanographic Museum and a **Naval Museum** with over 1,000 exhibits, including a 1697 model of a Gdańsk ship which came from the Artus Court and another of an early eighteenth-century galley with oars and sails which was used by King August II for cruising on the Vistula. The museum covers the history of Poland's access, and lack of access, to the sea, and the history of naval warfare, displaying gun barrels from the seventeenth to the nineteenth century, but by far the largest and most popular exhibit is the old destroyer *Burza*, which had a distinguished record of action with the Allied navies in the Second World War. So for both seafarers and sea-lovers Gdynia should be an interesting place to spend a day. If you want actually to get out on the briny there are ferries and hydrofoils that tour the bay or take you on the 20-kilometre trip to the tip of the Hel Peninsula, a long sand bar separating the Bay of Gdańsk from the main Baltic Sea. Hel is a popular place amongst the locals, with its long sandy beaches, small resorts and fishing harbour, and it was there, in the home of a local fisherman, that I ate the very best fried fish of my life. But I have to admit that there is not very much for the foreign visitor to tempt him on such a journey.

Dedicated landlubbers may want to miss Sopot and Gdynia completely and head into that other Gdańsk playground, the Kaszubian Hills, which rise to the west of the city and into which the suburbs are slowly spreading. This large and lumpy area is part of a long, low range of morainic hills which extends right across northern Poland, from border to border, breaking only where the Vistula has worn a way through to the sea. The highest point of the Kaszubian area is 329 metres (987 feet), which is high as such hills go, and the various folds of the land have trapped water into innumerable lakes, many of which have campsites and holiday centres on their wooded shores and are a paradise for small-boat sailors, windsurfers and fishermen alike. If there is obviously going to be no time to visit the wilder wetlands of Mazuria, a day here will at least give a flavour of Poland's lakes, so beloved by native city-dwellers and frequently visited by both German and Scandinavian lovers of the outdoors.

The Kaszubians themselves form a separate Slavic ethnic group which has managed to retain its own distinctive language and culture through all the wars and territorial changes that have bedevilled the region. During the long years of partition and in the face of some vigorous Germanization, education in local literature and history was encouraged and the fading language taught, and this Slavic strength weighed in Poland's favour in 1919 when the corridor to the sea was drawn to include most of Kaszubia. There is a great tradition of folk art here and the area's weavers and potters, embroiderers and basket-makers all contribute to the stock of *Cepelia* shops throughout the country. The local capital is **Kartuzy**, just 30 kilometres west of Gdańsk, where a museum on the edge of the little town celebrates native culture with displays on fishing, farming, furniture and ceramics as well as local history. My favourite item in the museum is a wooden bench with a box beneath the seat in which there are two holes covered with perforated sliding doors, the idea being to provide a warm home for a couple of hens in order to keep them laying through the winter.

The name Kartuzy gives a clue to the origins of the settlement, which goes back to 1380 when Carthusian monks were brought to Pomerania from Bohemia. Finding that the Cistercians had the benefits of the coast in hand, they settled here in the hills, building a monastery, church and several hermitages beside the lake. Fragments of the monastery survive, as does the church in its entirety, this latter being a long Gothic building with an unusual baroque roof which rises in three curved layers. The neighbourhood of the lake here is quite lovely, offering plenty of opportunities for long walks through beech and pine woods. A round tour of the Kaszubian region will reveal many small villages remotely situated either in hilly farmland or deep in the thick forests which predominate in the southern area, beyond the village of Kościerzyna. With the sea, the river delta and these hills, Gdańsk is blessed with a fine location.

16

Mazuria

Across the Bay of Gdańsk, due east of the three coastal cities, the new frontier between Poland and Soviet Lithuania slices arbitrarily east-wards for 200 kilometres in an almost straight line. The 100-kilometre band of countryside below this line comprises the Mazurian lake district, a vast tract of thinly peopled, thickly forested post-glacial landscape which makes up one of Europe's great nature reserves. It is known as the land of a thousand lakes, but this is a libellous underestimate. The problem with describing this region is that, with notable exceptions, it is nature's own realm and hardly the country for those mainly interested in the cultural heritage of this insuppressible nation. I have friends, though, who dash off to Mazuria at any opportunity and spend every summer bobbing about on the lakes and without doubt it is a paradise for the inland sailor and perfect for those who want to get away from it all to write or meditate about life. The state tourist organization, *Orbis*, has little wooden cottages available for summer renting – winter here would be positively Siberian – and one fine day I intend to take a family holiday in these idyllic surroundings, but for the purposes of this book I will assume that few non-Polish readers will travel this far just to commune with nature. Suffice it to say that there is an immense wealth of flora and fauna to observe, much of it accompanied in summer by the high-pitched drone of a trillion mosquitoes.

The western margins of the region, which were skirted on the journey down the Vistula, are the most densely populated, but even so the only town of any size is Olsztyn, the old Warmian capital. Within striking distance of the town are several places of interest and beauty as well as one which is gruesome and not a little disturbing. The

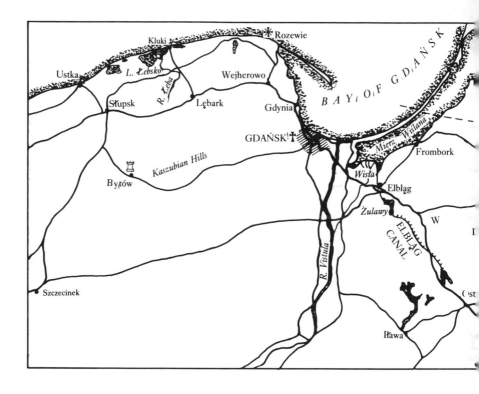

landscape, much like that of Kaszubia, is rolling and wooded with clearings for villages and their farmland and very little industry. The most dramatic way to enter this domain is by way of the Elbląg Canal, an extraordinary 178-kilometre-long waterway which was started in 1845. The problem of changing levels is overcome by hauling the boats up long slopes on trolleys by means of water-powered machines rather than by using conventional locks. This unusual experience is not much use for car-drivers, who arrive deep inland at Iława or Ostróda

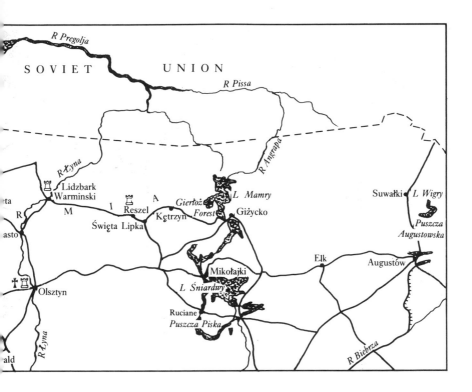

without their vehicles, but it is fun to watch the little white cruisers slowly bumping up through a woodland clearing towards the next stretch of water. The original and ill-fated intention of the canal was to open up the region to development but it has instead turned out to be a perfect tourist attraction.

Both Iława and Ostróda, with plenty of hotels and campsites, are on the only major east-west road through Mazuria and either would make a suitable base for the first port of call. Some 30 kilometres south of

311

Ostróda is a tiny village, still bearing its German name, which is inscribed into European history as deeply as Crécy, Agincourt and Waterloo. **Grunwald** on 15 July 1410 must have been the noisiest and bloodiest place on earth, as the experienced and well equipped army of the Teutonic Knights rode out to meet the more numerous but less professional troops led by King Władysław Jagiełło and Witold, Grand Duke of Lithuania. The engagement began with sorties by groups of Lithuanian cavalry assisted by those fierce warriors the Tartars, who caused confusion among the Knights' mercenary forces and in turn invited the heavy armour of the Knights to charge. And so it went on throughout that awful day. Still it chills the blood to imagine such violence, man to man, horse to horse. The best knights of the order were killed, including the Grand Master, Ulrich von Junginen, and the combined Polish-Lithuanian Army won the battle, pursuing their enemy day after day until the latter had scuttled back to the safety of their fortress at Malbork, 100 kilometres away, which the Poles were unable to penetrate. Grunwald was one of the biggest battles of the Middle Ages, and on the 550th anniversary of an event which proved to be such a watershed for the Teutonic Knights, a large hilltop monument was inaugurated on the battlefield. There is a granite obelisk with the faces of warriors carved into it, a group of 30 steel poles 30 metres high, holding aloft the emblems of the victorious armies, and an amphitheatre with a large-scale map of the battle. Beneath the amphitheatre there is a long, curving gallery where the story of the battle is unfolded and many remains excavated from the site are displayed. It is a remote spot but a must for incorrigible battlefield-visitors.

The Teutonic Order left many castles around the Warmian countryside but the only place to develop into a major town was **Olsztyn**, 42 kilometres east of Ostróda and located amongst pleasant hills and lakes. The first castle here was started in 1334 and the settlement which grew around it gained municipal status only 20 years later. In 1454 its people echoed the actions of Toruń and other northern towns by rising against the Knights and pledging their allegiance to the Polish king. From then on the town flourished, defensive walls were built and many secular buildings erected. From 1516 until 1520, Copernicus acted as the official administrator of the town on behalf of his uncle, the bishop of Warmia, and helped defend it against the Knights in 1520. On a wall in the castle there is still a sundial thought to have been made by the great man during his time here. Following the first partition of 1772, Olsztyn, together with all of Warmia, came under Prussian rule. It was not included in the Polish corridor and remained in the isolated German territory of East Prussia until 1945.

It is not surprising then that much of the development outside the old walled town has a distinctively German look about it; the large town hall in particular, as well as many of the pre-war villas. In fact, when you are travelling in northern or western Poland, one of the surest ways of knowing that you are in old German territory is the style of the railway architecture, particularly of the capped water-towers which loom over so many stations and town approaches and are identical to those found as far west as the Ruhr. In the 1920s, Olsztyn became the headquarters of the Association of Poles in Germany, which was dedicated to keeping Polish culture alive for those within the Reich. Inevitably, such groups were persecuted when Hitler came to power and most members ended their days in the camps. Like so many other towns, Olsztyn paid a high price when the German armies were rolled back and some 40 per cent of the town, including many historic buildings, was destroyed. Today the medieval centre can still be traced and many buildings have been restored, but obviously much of its atmosphere is lost for ever. A handsome old structure such as the fifteenth-century High Gate with its crenellated brick gable now stands alone and a bit forlorn, all its ancient neighbours having disappeared.

But **Olsztyn Castle** still survives, close to the old market square and nicely located above the River Lyna, which flows through a steep little valley that is now a ribbon of parkland. The brick fortress with its round tower was built by the church authorities in the late fifteenth century and extended in both the sixteenth and the eighteenth. In the south-west wing are the old refectory and the living quarters of the chapterhouse administration, where Copernicus lived, and a little chapel survives in the north-east wing. In 1945 the castle was designated a regional museum and it now has several departments devoted to Mazurian and Warmian culture and history with many exhibits which were collected from the formerly German museums of East Prussia, including that at Königsberg, today the Lithuanian coastal city of Kaliningrad. The archaeological section has some 13,000 items in its collection, and those on display include objects recovered from ancient burial sites in the region. Once again the ethnography department is the most glamorous, with its rooms full of old costumes, furniture and folk art, with the Warmian bonnets

313

embroidered with golden threads being especially lovely. Alas, none will be seen on local girls today, who prefer jeans and T-shirts bearing the names of foreign rock groups.

Quite understandably, the history section goes out of its way to emphasize the Polish character of the district which survived 170 years of Germanization. Polish museums are well used by local schools, and in Olsztyn, where the post-war generation consisted mostly of immigrants from the eastern territories that were lost to the Soviet Union, a good museum was an obvious aid in giving these confused people a sense of both place and history in their new home. I have a friend in Olsztyn, an old lady who has lived through two world wars and been moved from pillar to post, never able to strike roots before coming to this almost deserted town in 1945. Her husband had heard that there was work on the railways and ample housing for those who moved quickly. There was little choice of destination in those days.

Perhaps the most pleasantly atmospheric spot in the town is outside the **Cathedral**, which is on the eastern side of the old town centre, a couple of minutes' walk from the square. Beneath mature trees, with old ladies coming from evening service and the sound of the organ still on the air, it is just possible to imagine that no war ever came this way. The church itself is of the Gothic hall type, built in the early fifteenth century, and the solid square tower was added in around 1590. As usual, the interior decoration is mixed, but several late Gothic paintings survive.

The main road eastwards from Olsztyn leads after some 80 kilometres to the largest of the large Mazurian lakes, but a more roundabout route must be taken if the best buildings are to be seen. The road north from the town arrives after 50 kilometres at the tiny but delightful town of **Orneta**, which was founded in 1308 and has survived the centuries better than most places in the region. The market place, in fact, contains the sole surviving Gothic town hall in Warmia, but the real treasure here is the marvellous church which was finished in around 1380. The interior is quite splendid, its warm brick pillars and vault ribbing contrasting with the plain plaster and beautifully setting off the large and richly decorated main altar, the elaborate baroque pulpit and the many side altars and chapels. The basilica construction lends itself to much ornate gabling all around the outside, the eastern façade being particularly fine with its terracotta frieze of grotesque masks. Local people know the attraction of Orneta, of course, but few foreigners venture here.

Eastwards, the road leads through a gently rolling countryside of woods and villages to **Lidzbark Warmiński**, a former capital of the Warmia bishopric. This is the site of one of the best preserved Teutonic castles, a huge block of brick looking like a piece of the Malbork fortress which has drifted east to strand itself on this wooded hill. Being just a single building rather than a great complex like Malbork, it is more typical of the dozens of such structures which the Knights erected as they colonized what was then a very remote region. The Knights first arrived at this spot in 1241, taking over an older fortified settlement and then handing it to the bishops of Warmia, one of whom, Jan of Meissen, moved his headquarters here in 1350. Over the next 50 years the magnificent castle was built and the little town flourished as craftsmen flocked to work on the project. After the Treaty of Toruń the place reverted to Polish rule, and between 1503 and 1510 it was yet another home for Copernicus, who was appointed physician and adviser to his uncle, Bishop Łukasz Watzenrode. Until the 1772 partition Lidzbark was a thriving cultural centre and its bishops included some of the most famous humanists of the time, such as the great historian Marcin Kromer (1512-1589) and, much later, Ignacy Krasicki (1735–1801), who turned to literature when the partition deprived him of his official duties. He was a man much esteemed throughout northern Europe and highly respected by Frederick the Great who, it is reported, once addressed him thus: 'I hope, Archbishop, you will carry me under your episcopal cloak to Paradise.' Whereupon the prelate replied: 'No, sire, your majesty has cut it so short that it will not serve the purpose of concealing contraband goods.' *Touché*. Krasicki was obviously a man of both courage and wit, for as well as producing numerous translations, some popular compilations of fables and one of the first Polish novels, he penned a satire on stupid, uneducated monks addicted to drunkenness and idleness, which, not surprisingly, caused a sensation.

Beyond its formidable and rather plain exterior, **Lidzbark Castle** is one of the most handsome of fortified buildings, with lovely arcaded galleries around its central courtyard. It had been earmarked for demolition in the last century as part of the Germanization programme and would have disappeared had not the local Polish community refused to give their labour for such a cause. So the castle stayed, but all its rich furnishings were shipped back to the German heartland. On the first floor there is an impressive array of rooms, some with mural paintings from the fourteenth and sixteenth centuries, as well as several Renaissance and baroque portals and a chapel with rococo ornamentation. Only three of the wings are part of the original Gothic structure, the east wing having been rebuilt as a bishop's palace in the mid-eighteenth century. The whole building is now managed by the Mazurian Museum at Olsztyn, which each year mounts a large historical exhibition in the monumental and splendidly vaulted Great Refectory.

The castle approach with its sixteenth-century fortifications contrasts with the neighbouring winter garden with its neo-classical orangery, which was laid out by Bishop Krasicki in 1770 and says much about that man's refined taste and preferred lifestyle. The town of Lidzbark did not escape damage in 1945, although the old layout is retained together with some stretches of the walls with their bastions, and the High Gate and parish church still stand. The latter is a mid-fourteenth century Gothic hall church with radial vaults in the nave, a granite font and a 1420 crucifix. There are also many old paintings, tombs and epitaphs, and Renaissance and baroque side altars, but the high altar is a pseudo-Gothic monster installed in 1870. All in all, Lidzbark is a fine place, perched on its hill above the Łyna river, and its castle seems destined to be a landmark for centuries to come.

From here a quiet road continues east for 40 kilometres to **Reszel**, which has a lovely market square, a belfry, a Gothic church and yet another castle. Crossing the River Sujna by a rare Gothic bridge and going on for another six kilometres, you will come to the little village of Święta Lipka which is perched precariously on a narrow strip of land between two lakes and marks the old frontier between Warmia and Mazuria proper. In this spot, of all places, there is a genuine baroque creation of the highest quality; not a remodelling of an earlier building but a real masterpiece of late seventeenth-century frippery, stranded out here in the middle of the forest. The origins of **Święta Lipka Church** go back at least as far as 1400, when there was a shrine here dedicated to the Holy Virgin who is said to have appeared amongst the branches of a nearby lime tree. Pilgrims made their way to the shrine from all over the north-east until it was destroyed by intolerant Protestants from nearby Kętrzyn, but the cult continued and a new chapel was built in 1619 by the secretary to King Zygmunt III Waza. A few years later the Jesuits took it over and started work on the new church complex in 1687.

The architect was a man by the name of Ertly from the Lithuanian capital of Wilno and he put up a small basilica church with an imposing twin-towered façade, built a smart wall around the whole thing and then called in the best local craftsmen to do the decoration and fitting out. The result was a place of worship fit for a king. The front gates, a complex web of wrought-iron foliage surmounted by an explosion of gold, were created by the Schwarz brothers of Reszel and alone are worthy of Versailles or Schönbrunn. They make quite an appropriate overture for the interior of the church, which is a riot of ornate alabaster with fluted columns, bas-relief friezes and golden capitals. The east end is choked by a great three-storey black and gold altar and the west by a quite astonishing organ. Other features include a silver image of Our Lady which is mounted on elaborately carved limewood, a pulpit in French walnut, and many equally exuberant side altars and confessionals. The high altar — three tiers of marbled black columns each framing a large painting and decked out with a dozen gilded figures — dates from 1712, while the main painting of Mary with the boy Christ is the work of a Flemish artist in 1640. The walls surrounding the church are backed by long arcaded walkways which link four corner chapels and, with the adjoining monastery building, complete the extraordinary complex. Faced with such a creation I cannot but agree with Osbert Lancaster's comment on the baroque style: 'A taste for the grandiose,' he wrote, 'like a taste for morphia, is, once it has been fully acquired, difficult to keep within limits.'

Just ten kilometres east is **Kętrzyn**, known until 1945 as Rasten-burg. It is a pleasant enough spot for a small town, dating back to a Teutonic castle which was built in 1329 but the town itself was destroyed in 1945, which is not surprising when you discover what was hidden in the Gierloz Forest just a few kilometres away. The Wolfschanzer or Wolf's Lair was Hitler's main field headquarters throughout the war; a war which for him was directed eastwards against the Soviet Union. The place has a morbid magnetism, but none of the style of the fortresses built centuries before by those earlier Germanic warlords. Eighteen hectares (27 acres) of three- to five-metre thick concrete bunkers take some hiding even in a Mazurian forest; so the clearings were festooned with green leaf-like material suspended on wires and the whole place, with its separate bunkers up to eight storeys deep for all the gang leaders, was permanently mined with a single plunger always ready to fire the charges which would shatter the concrete. As it happened, Europe crumbled more readily than did the German concrete. In the face of the Soviet advance the plunger was depressed, but most of the concrete simply cracked and this is what can be seen today by the curious: huge slabs of concrete which the botanical world is doing its best to cover with trees, plants and lichen.

It must have been a strange place to be incarcerated while the world above tore itself to pieces. At the Nuremberg trials, General Alfred Jodl described the atmosphere at the headquarters as 'a mixture of cloister and concentration camp. Very little news from the outer world penetrated into this holy of holies.' In fact this grim place should by rights have been famous as the tomb of one of the world's greatest madmen, but the assassination attempt here on 20 July 1944, though it killed four people, merely blew Hitler out of a wooden tea-room which was being used for a meeting because the bunker was considered too warm that day. Had the same explosion occurred in the concrete bunker, as was the intention, the solid walls would have contained the force and Hitler would certainly have been killed. And think how much destruction Poland would have been saved if the Germans had sued for peace at that stage in the war.

Just a few kilometres east through the forest is the shore of the second largest of the Mazurian lakes, Lake Mamry, which covers 105 square kilometres, and a 30-kilometre journey by road leads to **Giżycko** on its eastern shore. This is one of the great holiday centres of the lake district, where summer visitors attempt to outnumber the mosquitoes while boats flap their sails like sun-blinded moths and colliding canoes rattle against the landing stages. Boat-building and -servicing must be a good business to be in here, although many people make their own. The great advantage of Mazuria for the sailor, and even more for the canoeist, is that these lakes are not isolated pools but vast and complex expanses of water where long peninsulas of forest and a hundred hidden corners are to be found. Best of all, there are canals and rivers which lead to other lakes, enabling the strong and hearty to paddle or sail for several hundred kilometres.

Giżycko, formerly known as Lec, seems to have been the ancient centre of Teutonic bee-keeping, for a large colony of keepers grew up around the old castle here. Today, for 'bees' read 'tourists'. The foreign visitor to these parts may prefer somewhere quieter, off the beaten track, and plenty such places do exist, but just as caution is urged upon the inexperienced who set out into the mountains, so must the forest be approached with care.

Some 30 kilometres south of Giżycko is another lakeside centre,

Mikołajki; much favoured by Poles, this serves the very largest of the lakes, Śniardwy, which is more regular in shape than Lake Mamry and offers a wider sheet of open water for the testing of sailing skills. For those who prefer a more passive approach to water there are many boat excursions available from Mikołajki, which, not so long ago, was no more than a remote village. The best excursion takes one south through narrow waterways, with the forest closing overhead, to the village of Ruciane, another place where water and lumber occupy the local population. One of the largest stretches of woodland in the country, the Puszcza Piska, stretches south from Ruciane, around and beyond a 50-kilometre long winding waterway which eventually ends up back in Lake Śniardwy.

The village resorts around here are too numerous to list but all give access to wild country and tame water and to many controlled nature reserves where one can observe the birds and study the unusual plant life. There is even the chance that the experienced naturalist or the lost walker will see beavers at work damming their streams.

The alternative centres for lake-lovers lie 90 kilometres to the east at Suwałki and Augustów. Both of these sit at the western extremity of another vast tract of forest, the Puszcza Augustowska, which extends far over the Soviet border to the Niemen river and beyond in one of the continent's great areas of wilderness. It is a region best suited to those with large grants to study forest fungi, bog botany or the most private habits of the short-toed eagle. Without an expert to guide and explain it can be a frightening, almost subterranean world of dense green and gloomy humidity. The forest edges, however, can be fascinating, and both Augustów in the south and Suwałki, 30 kilometres further north, provide an abundance of opportunities to sample this rather alien world. A focus for both the timber industry and the more delicate pastime of folk weaving, **Augustów** was founded by King Zygmunt August in 1561, probably as a base for hunting. In 1824 the construction of a 100-kilometre-long canal was begun through the forest to connect the Vistula tributaries with the River Niemen and thus with the eastern Baltic, the idea being to ease the extraction of timber and generally to open up the region. But just as in the case of the Elbląg Canal, boat rides and canoe trips are now the most popular use of the waterway and they are certainly the safest and most pleasant way to experience the forest. Alternatively, the canal can be followed south though more open and cultivated countryside to the lovely River Biebrza and thence to the Narew, from where it is quite possible, through hard work, to canoe back to Gdańsk via the Vistula.

Suwałki was established only in the eighteenth century and is just a bit bigger than Augustów. The forest thins out in the north but the lakes are bigger; **Lake Wigry** is another of those wandering tentacular waters which twist and turn with the landscape. Descending to 73 metres (219 feet) at its deepest point, it is full of fish and therefore a favourite place for those who pursue the barbarous sport of angling. In Poland, Lake Wigry is considered the most beautiful of all the lakes and its southern shoreline is high enough to provide a magnificent view over water, islands and rolling forest. In the autumn when the birch trees are a shiver of gold, the air sharp and clear, this view is breathtaking. On a low peninsula at the northern end of the lake the typically baroque silhouette of a church rises as if from the water, part of a monastery that was founded in this remotest of spots by King Władysław IV Waza in 1667 for the Carmoldolite Order. The monks, far from contemplating their navels, were very industrious, building saw- and corn-mills powered by streams and distilling almost anything that grew. Destroyed in both world wars, the monastery has now been rebuilt as a holiday hotel and must be one of the most tranquil in the world. By a very sensible policy, motor boats are banned on many of the lakes, including this one, and if there is one overriding memory to be brought away from Mazuria it is of a great stillness once the main centres have been left behind. And these days that is not the easiest thing to find.

17

Pomerania and the Baltic Coast

There are probably just as many lakes to the west of the Vistula, in Pomerania, as there are to the east, but none is as large as Mazuria's Mamry, Śniardwy or Wigry. And although Pomerania is not without its forests, it does not have the same wild atmosphere or the wildlife that is so abundant in the east, which is not to say that there are no lovely spots in Poland's north-west. There are, after all, perhaps 300 kilometres of sandy beaches, counting all the ins and outs of the coastline between the Odra and Vistula rivers. But I doubt that the foreigner will visit Poland for the sea-bathing, and if forests and lakes are the priority then Mazuria is the answer. So what is there in this large region that was for so long a part of various German empires? Szczecin, right against Poland's western border, is certainly no Gdańsk, however busy a port it is now and has been for centuries past. Of the other coastal towns, only Kołobrzeg, Koszalin and Słupsk are of any size, and they were all so battered in 1945 that, apart from the odd church or gateway, little has survived from what was an interesting medieval period. But for centuries Pomerania has been both an important prize and a political pawn in the Baltic arena, and consequently on the larger European stage.

All European coastal regions have had settlers for many millennia and Pomerania was always more culturally and economically advanced than Mazuria, where it has been estimated that the Stone Age lasted some 500 years longer. 2,000 years ago the region was populated by a Slavic people known to the Romans as the Veneti, but how pure this group remained during the following centuries when the Scandinavian Goths and other northern tribes moved into the area it is impossible to say. By the ninth century the region of the two largest river-mouths, the Vistula and Odra, was densely populated by what can most conveniently be called Pomeranian Slavs, along with several spots along the open coast of which Kołobrzeg was the most important. Once again trade can be seen as a measure of a region's prosperity: a tenth-century site on Wolin Island, which lies in the estuary of the Odra, has produced Persian coins and Egyptian beads, and it is known that there was then a population of between 5,000 and 10,000, which is larger than today's.

So Pomerania has a long and interesting history, following the typical Polish pattern. It was indisputably a part of the early Piast kingdom, for Mieszko I settled his son Światopełk in the province and Bolesław the Brave founded a bishopric in Kołobrzeg in AD 1000, but after Bolesław's death most of the region broke away from the kingdom and became an independent dukedom. Eastern Pomerania did remain within the Polish orbit but the western region looked more and more to the German and western Scandinavian world for a living. Self-governing towns developed, basing their structure on Lübeck or Magdeburg Law, by which the real control was in the hands of merchants who encouraged German craftsmen and settlers. The inland and rural areas retained their Slavic majority despite efforts at German colonization made by various monastic orders, and ties with Poland did remain until 1521 when, under pressure from the eastward expansion of Brandenburg, Pomerania formally acknowledged its allegiance to the German emperor. The next player in the Pomerania game was Sweden, which seized the coastal region — though not Gdańsk — in 1621 and was forced to withdraw only after four years of war. Even then Swedes maintained control of many ports, and later in that Thirty Years War they occupied all of western Pomerania. The 1648 Treaty of Westphalia divided the region between Sweden and Brandenburg and it was from this foothold that the 'Swedish Deluge' of 1655 was launched against Poland. Five more years of fighting did force them to withdraw to their own shores but, along with much of Poland, the towns and villages of Pomerania were left in ruins. When the kingdom of Prussia was founded in 1701, Pomerania's fate was sealed until the twentieth century when the eastern end of the region was incorporated into the Polish Corridor in 1919 and the rest of the territory was awarded to Poland in 1945.

It is unfortunate that the English-speaking world seems to know so little about the events of the Eastern Front in either world war, because even the slightest acquaintance with the facts would add greatly to an understanding not only of Poland but of events in the continent as a whole. The bodily shifting of Poland westward in 1945 was an astonishing event, politically, physically and spiritually, but it had been preceded by a massive exodus of Germany's eastern population in the face of the advancing Soviet armies. First it was the East Prussians from what is now Warmia and Mazuria who fled west to the relative safety of the German heartland and they were followed there by the Germans of Silesia and Pomerania. Events were dramatic, and had

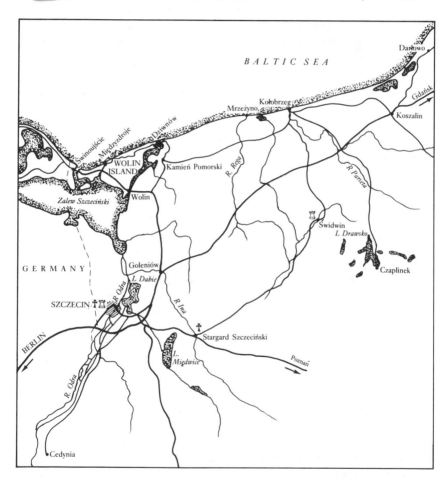

television news coverage existed then as it does now our screens would daily have displayed pictures of country roads here jammed to the horizon with trails of people pushing their belongings in carts and prams or carrying them on their backs, along with some lucky ones, perhaps, who still had horses. Central and eastern Europe in 1944 and 1945 were awash with refugees, uncertain of their status, having no money, food or housing, and not knowing what further terrors fate had in store for them.

Once the new frontiers had become an accepted reality the remaining German population of Pomerania was repatriated and by 1950 there was scarcely a German left in the land which had been theirs for almost 250 years. But the territory now bequeathed to Poland was a shambles. More than half of all urban buildings, residential houses and factories had been destroyed. Much of the fierce last-ditch fighting by the German armies took place on Pomeranian soil. Consequently almost everything along the Odra river and the Baltic coast was a target and suffered accordingly. In many ways, therefore, Pomerania is a young region, whose first generation after the war was made up of strangers, pioneers in a landscape from which a new life had to be built almost from scratch. Railways, ports, schools and factories, all had been destroyed and all were replaced in remarkably quick time. Gdańsk was reassembled brick by brick, but Szczecin, Kołobrzeg, Koszalin and Słupsk, which for centuries had had no Polish connections, were not; they were built as new towns.

The purpose of all this history is not to suggest that Pomerania is a place to avoid but to make it clear why such treasures as do exist are so thin on the ground. I have a great affection for the area, as Szczecin was my first-ever point of arrival in Poland and western Pomerania was the first leg of my Baltic to Byzantium walk. It is from long-standing personal experience, therefore, that I recommend the hospitality of the country folk hereabouts and the tranquil beauty of the lakes around Czaplinek and Szczecinek. I was once taken to an island here by holidaying students and had to remain for four days, singing, eating, drinking and teaching English, before my hosts reluctantly rowed me back to the shore. Popular as these lakes are, Pomerania to most Poles means the sea and, although the idea of a north-facing Baltic beach may not be immediately appealing to those with easy access to the Mediterranean, this shore does have its features of interest, even the occasional heat wave.

The eastern end of the Pomeranian coast is also the northernmost tip of Poland, and the Rozewie Lighthouse, 50 kilometres north of Gdańsk, marks the actual spot. However the essence of this coast can perhaps best be captured 50 kilometres west, around the old fishing village of Łeba, where by 1570 the high shifting dunes had buried the original settlement, complete with its Teutonic castle, forcing a new site to be developed across on the east bank of the little river which enters the sea here. Today the ruins of the old Gothic church can once again be seen, emerging from the sand which is the great attraction here, as it provides some of the country's best bathing beaches. The ornithologist will be drawn by the two great lakes, once sea lagoons, which stretch for 30 kilometres westward along the coast and provide an important resting place for about 250 species of migrating birds; they now form the Słowiński National Park. The largest lake is Łebsko, a typically shallow lagoon fed by the River Łeba and now separated from the sea by dunes which are anything up to 38 metres (114 feet) high. The wind moves these steadily eastward, engulfing the trees in its path and then years later revealing their skeletons. At the village of Kluki on the western shore of Lake Łebsko there is an outdoor museum where a collection of regional cottages and farm buildings has been assembled into the familiar Polish ethnographic park.

The next little fishing ports you come to as you move westwards along the coast, Ustka and Darłowo, both have charms which suggest that prior to 1945 they were picturesque places. In fact, **Ustka** was a member of the Hanseatic League and an important town in the fourteenth century, but since the nineteenth it has been better known as a holiday resort, with fishing as a secondary livelihood. **Darłowo** is equally old, having had municipal status since 1271, and has experienced all the political changes of Pomerania at first hand. But with the larger ships of the nineteenth century, the move to new industrial areas and constant problems with shifting sandbanks, port activity here declined; as at Ustka, fishing and leisure boats are all that will be seen here today, along with the modern hotels and campsites which line the shore. Luckier than many, Darłowo has managed to retain or restore some of its oldest buildings and can still boast a market square with a baroque town hall, a fifteenth-century town gate, and a Gothic castle built by the Pomeranian princes in the fourteenth century which now houses an important regional museum. Perhaps the most interesting building is the late Gothic St Gertrude's Chapel, which sits with its unusual twelve-sided ambulatory beyond the old town walls.

The region behind this eastern Pomeranian coast has few places of great historic interest. The towns of Wejherowo, Lębark and Słupsk have little to recommend them as pleasure grounds with only churches and a few old houses remaining from a long and interesting past. But further inland the morainic ridges that run on into the Kaszubian Hills do have their charms and Bytów, a Slav stronghold back in the ninth century, still has a solid Teutonic castle in good condition; built around 1400, it is a fine if basic example of the genre. From Bytów there is a cross-country road which cuts through the woods, past farms large and small and lakes by the score, ending up after 60 kilometres at the village of Biały Bór, a former fortress which sits on a long and lovely finger lake. A further 30 kilometres to the south is Szczecinek, a lakeside town which is the service centre for many widely scattered villages as well as an army of summer visitors who sail and canoe on the local waters. But if there is one place above all others amongst the Pomeranian lakes which makes a fine centre it is Czaplinek, 40 kilometres west along a winding, wooded road. A small town at the southern end of the many-islanded Lake Drawsko, this was another early Slavic forest stronghold and managed to stay within the Polish realm from 1368 until 1657 before succumbing to Brandenburg rule. How such a remote place came to be an important cloth-producer in the eighteenth century I do not know, but wooden houses from the period survive to give the place some charm and storks still nest on many of the chimneypots — which must lead to a few cold rooms below, for it remains unlucky to disturb these lovable great birds. Being right on the German Army's Pomeranian Wall defensive line in 1945, it was luckier than many other places in not being completely flattened as the Red Army pushed through towards Berlin.

Lake Drawsko is a lovely place. Lying in a hollow where several streams meet, it extends up their valleys to form a vaguely cross-shaped stretch of water some ten kilometres long by two kilometres at its widest point. Like those in Mazuria, this lake connects with others by way of short slow rivers, perfect for the fleets of canoeists who venture out every summer in kayak-club convoys, travelling through the forest from one happy, drunken campsite to the next. Many city-dwellers have built little summer houses here; easy enough if you can get the materials, because local planning regulations seem to be either very liberal or quite unenforceable. The island on which I stayed at the northern end of Lake Drawsko is occupied by just two farmers, who apparently never speak to each other, and about a hundred little cabins, ranging from rotting wooden tents to sturdy brick sheds, all of which are crammed during the season. The pattern seems to be that Grandad gets up early, sneaking out in a boat to catch fish and escape the kids and women, returning hours later to spend the rest of the day with his cronies, wreathed in smoke as they attempt to cook the day's catch without cremating it. Much of my time there was spent trying to avoid the millions of baby frogs which literally smothered the grass around the lake shore, making it impossible to tread without squashing them.

Moving back towards the coast, I feel impelled to mention the obscure little town of Świdwin where the great-grandmothers of my young twins both live and through which I walked in 1980, little suspecting the connection that would ensue from my repeated visits to this fascinating and frustrating land. Both families were washed up here by that great wave of people displaced from the east; which was not entirely inappropriate, for, Świdwin is another ancient Slav site which has changed hands more times than can be recalled. Wends, Brandenburgs, Mecklenburgs, Prussians and Swedes have all raised their banner over the little castle which stands to this day. From Świdwin there is a road due north which hits the sea at **Kołobrzeg**. Unlike Koszalin and other Baltic towns, this has not been silted up but remains on the open coast at the mouth of the little Parsęta river.

Kołobrzeg's origins date back to saltworks which are known to have been trading from here in the seventh century and around which a fortified village developed. Later, it became an important coastal port for the Piast kings, where Bolesław the Brave founded the first bishopric in the year 1000. In the following centuries the town grew, trading its salt as far afield as Byzantium and the Middle East, until the thirteenth century when an adjoining German colony joined the Hanseatic League and rather took the old town over. The Thirty Years War and the Swedish wars saw the familiar decline, which was reversed only at the end of the last century, when tourism became big business and Kołobrzeg found itself host to new hotels and spas as the fashion for sea-bathing and sunshine caught on. The horrors of the last war left most of the town in ruins but also contributed a famous gesture to the rich annals of Polish history. On 18 March 1945, following days of bloody fighting, the town was captured by troops of the 1st Polish Army who had fought westwards alongside the Soviet Army. A group of these fighting people, finally on a Baltic coast which they considered rightfully to be theirs, swore an oath that the famous

327

old city of the Piasts would remain forever Polish and, in a ceremony known as Poland's Marriage with the Sea, a woman officer flung her wedding ring into the sea in a symbolic act of union. A large monument now stands on this spot, not far from the lighthouse and almost as tall.

The long, sandy and tideless beaches here are popular not only with Poles but also with thousands of Swedes who travel each summer to languish on what to them is a southern shore. The town itself now has many tree-filled spaces where ancient houses once stood, but the huge **Collegiate Church of St Mary** has been rebuilt, and a large red-brick lump it is. Originally built in 1321, it was enlarged into a five-nave hall church later in the same century, and so solid was the construction that 1945 photographs show the slab-like west tower as one of the few structures to have survived the bombardment and fires. It was only during the early 1980s that restoration was carried out, but fortunately many of the most precious fitments had been preserved. In order to stretch its season, Kołobrzeg has introduced October cello recitals in a special festival devoted to that sonorous instrument, but I will wager that there are few bathers around at that time. Baltic summers are not Europe's longest.

The 90 kilometres from Kołobrzeg to the German frontier at Świnoujście take one through a succession of unremarkable resorts. Mrzeżyno at least is a tiny river-mouth fishing village, although behind the dunes lurk the usual unglamorous holiday homes, often three-storey blocks owned by a factory or state farm where employees can enjoy a subsidized holiday.

The coast changes for the better at the mouth of the Odra River. The road crosses here to the large lump of **Wolin Island**, around which the river flows on its way to the sea. This is one of those ancient sites which is steeped as much in mythology as in fact but, according to Scandinavian chronicles, it was inhabited by Slavs by the end of the eighth century. It is rightly considered to be the most beautiful stretch of the Baltic coast, as well as the warmest, and has thick beech and pine forests ending in high sandy cliffs which are constantly being eroded by the sea.

The 50-kilometre-long Baltic beach of Wolin Island terminates at its western extremity by the main mouth of the Odra river, beyond which is the little port town of **Świnoujście**. Here ferries ply to and from Ystad in Sweden, providing that country with one of its busiest routes to the European mainland. In summer a procession of overloaded Volvos can be seen between the port and Szczecin where the road meets up with the *autobahn* system of the German Democratic Republic, which in its turn gives easy access to the more southerly regions of Europe. As well as the ferry terminal, Świnoujście has a modern fishing port and several spas, but the main beach resort on the Wolin coast is **Międzyzdroje**, a dozen kilometres east, which has all the trappings of a holiday town: hotels, bars, discos and bandstands, landing stages for boat trips around the bay, and even the statue of a sailor in a town centre which can boast several art-nouveau-style buildings in its main shopping street. The town also has a natural history museum with several thousand exhibits portraying the geology, flora and wildlife of Wolin, much of which is a National Park. Since 1976, the island has been home to a small family of bison, reintroduced into the forest to ensure that straying picnickers have something to talk about when they get home.

The vast Szczecin Lagoon, which stretches for some 40 kilometres from east to west and is up to 20 kilometres wide, was once an even larger sea-bay, but continual silting from the Odra which feeds it has reduced it to its present extent and also to its five- to seven-metre depth. Half of the lagoon is in the GDR, including one of its links with the Baltic, but for the inhabitants of Szczecin too it is a handy way of reaching the coast, with ferries and a hydrofoil providing a regular service. Having such an enclosed and secure haven for shipping, it is hardly surprising that the area was developed long ago; as with the Vistula, the population spread up the river exploiting the converging trade routes and cultivating the fertile valley soils to the south. This rich area, adjacent to the natural frontier of the river, has been fought over throughout recorded history. One of the most famous spots for a patriotic Pole is close to the village of **Cedynia**, some 70 kilometres upstream from Szczecin. Here, on 24 June 972, a great battle was fought in which Mieszko I and his brother Czcibor, having recently occupied the Odra estuary, defended their prize by defeating a large German force led by the Emperor Otto II. As fate would have it, the final thrust on Berlin was triggered from this very same spot on 16 April 1945. A giant concrete pillar topped with an eagle now stands on the hilltop from which the distant haze of the German city, a mere 60 kilometres away, can be seen.

By far the most attractive town in the area is **Stargard Szczeciński**, which lies 26 kilometres east of the Odra and is the only place here which has attempted to rebuild its ancient centre. Its history is barely different from that of its neighbours; the first mention of it in the records is an 1124 reference to a stronghold then known as Stary Gród or Old Township. On a trade route to the coast and surrounded by fertile soil, the town prospered, enjoying many privileges, and under Brandenburg rule it was the seat of government for western Pomerania until 1720 when Szczecin was taken. The market square has some fine old houses and a gorgeous late Gothic town hall from 1569 with a high Renaissance gable decorated with swirling terracotta tracery which was added in 1638. Next door is an arcaded former guard-house which is now home to a small local museum.

The Old Town is still almost entirely surrounded by its medieval walls, complete with most of their bastions and gates and the most interesting of these is the fifteenth-century Miller's Gate (Brama Młyńska) which spans not a road but the River Ina and once guarded the town's old docks. The town's star architectural attraction, though, is the large **St Mary's Church**, built at the end of the thirteenth century by Heinrich Brunsberg, one of the more renowned church designers of the late Gothic period. It has an ambulatory and an octagonal chapel dedicated to Our Lady and, most unusually, the outside walls are covered with ceramic decorations.

Szczecin is now just 26 kilometres away on the high west bank of the Odra and is reached by a long causeway across the Dąbie Lake, a remnant of the larger lagoon to the north. The initial impression is not promising, with factories and docks on the approaches and, thanks to the last war, few ancient or striking buildings now stand above the far side of the river. But there are some interesting remnants to be found in this city of 400,000 souls, mostly close to the river in the area known as Podzamcze, meaning 'below the castle', which lies immediately beyond the older of the bridges. This area is the medieval Old Town, once rich with narrow streets and ancient buildings but totally destroyed in the war, since which only a few buildings have been restored.

Close to the river, in Ulica Wielka, stands the high roof of the **Cathedral Church of St James**, now risen from the heap of rubble that it so recently was. Just the portals, one out of a total of 30 chapels, and the great bell survived intact, and even now the tower rises only to half of its pre-war height. It is a three-nave Gothic hall church with an ambulatory and a ring of chapels which are slotted in between the large buttresses. The presbytery was started in 1375 and the main body of the building, once covered in ceramic decorations, was added a few years later, the whole thing rising from the foundations of a Romanesque church which had been built 200 years previously. With all the original fitments and decorations gone the interior has a rather hollow and empty atmosphere, but that one surviving chapel still has its lovely vaulted ceiling. Although not so large as St Mary's in Gdańsk, the building can still hold 10,000 people and so is quite a substantial edifice. The bell tower is still incomplete, so the old bell, cast in 1681 and weighing 5.7 tonnes, rests today on a special cradle outside the church, just next door to a fourteenth- and fifteenth-century vicarage which has also been restored.

From the north side of the cathedral the narrow cobbled Ulica Grodzka leads up to the **Castle of the Pomeranian Princes**, which sits on a platform above the river, commanding the approaches to the city from the east. The building seen today is the cumulative result of four major construction programmes which started in 1346 on the site of an earlier wooden stronghold. It was enlarged in the sixteenth century into a Renaissance residence and then remodelled once more in the 1720s. Finally, thanks to a 1944 air raid, the whole thing had to be reassembled in the years since the war and it now contains a museum as well as a large café with views over the river. In Prussian times the castle suffered the usual indignities, with its most precious furnishings removed to Berlin and the building used as both an arsenal and a brewery. During the last war the Nazis mounted anti-aircraft guns here, inviting attacks which duly came.

The castle consists of four wings built around the Bastion Courtyard and a fifth museum wing on the west side which overlooks the smaller Mint Yard. In the north-west corner there is a square **Bell Tower** which, from the top of its 200 steps, provides a panorama of the city and the large port. Regrettably, the bugle call which sounds from the tower at noon and 6 p.m. is now a tape-recording. Beneath the tower is a post-war statue of Duke Bolesław X of Pomerania and his wife the Princess Anna, daughter of the Polish monarch Kazimierz the Jagiellon. The separate **West Wing** was erected in 1619 as a 'seat of art and learning' and must have been one of the first purpose-built museums in Europe. Its three floors originally featured an exhibition of weapons, a library and an art gallery, in ascending order, and now display collections of paintings, coins and books.

The square Bastion Courtyard was for several years the scene of intensive archaeological digging but has now been resurfaced with those huge, ankle-twisting cobblestones which the Poles call cat's-

331

Poland

heads. The foundations of a wooden settlement were discovered here with huts and narrow streets much like those at Biskupin and thought to date back to the same Lusatian culture some 2,500 years ago. The main gate to the castle dates from the 1736 building programme and is decorated with the expected eagle and its mixed-up cousin, the griffin.

Many of the castle interiors are still being restored and may not yet be open, but each year should see another section completed and even more galleries open to visitors. The busiest part of the building today is the eastern **Odra Wing** which dates from the fourteenth century and has been rebuilt with all its arcades, crenellations and spiral motifs. The cellars here contain funeral vaults and the sarcophagi of several Pomeranian dukes, mostly from the early seventeenth century, while upstairs a theatre and other facilities for the city's House of Culture have been installed. But without doubt one of the most popular of local meeting-places is the large and elegant café in the north-east corner, hung with interesting pictures of the old town which give some idea of what the war destroyed. The **North Wing** is the oldest part of the castle, started in 1346 and rebuilt in Renaissance style in the 1570s. It has been restored and contains a model of the whole castle complex as well as a chapel which is now a concert hall. This chamber with its barrel-vaulted ceiling and two tiers of balconies is a splendid auditorium for the daily concerts given on the newly installed organ and many other musical events. The upper floors contain exhibition rooms named after various historical figures and displaying modern Polish paintings among other *objets d'art*. From the promenade on the river side of the castle much activity can be seen across the water at the smaller of the docks, but dominating even the ancient Seven Cats Tower is the newly constructed and less than beautiful concrete road bridge, curling away on to the east bank where it links up with the main Stargard road.

Immediately to the south of the castle and standing naked amongst modern buildings in what used to be the old market place is the prettiest thing in the whole city. The red-brick **Town Hall** is a gem, originally erected in the fourteenth century and modernized in the fifteenth before being thoroughly rebuilt in 1677 in the baroque style by the Swedes. The destruction of this building in 1945 provided Polish historians and architects with one of their favourite tasks, the recreation of a long-lost building, and after much study of the ruins it was decided that the town hall should be rebuilt as it had been in the early fifteenth century. Today this brand-new Gothic building in all its

332

glory is a monument to their perseverance. The basic structure is a simple, well-proportioned box with a steep roof, and it is the two splendid but completely different gables which so raise the spirits. The western end is arcaded at ground level and topped by a typical northern European plastered gable, whereas the eastern façade is crowned with a mad assemblage of five slender, missile-like pillars, decorated with geometric patterns and linked with the finest of terracotta open meshes. A branch of the National Museum devoted to the history of the city is housed within.

The main branch of the museum is a few minutes' walk north along the embankment where several large buildings glare down upon the water from the avenue called Wały Chrobrego. The largest, at the far end, is a so-called neo-Renaissance pile built in 1906 as the county administration headquarters. Before that, opposite a massive statue of Hercules battling with a centaur which is an example of mock-heroics typical of its period, is the **National Museum** building. Built in 1908 as a gift to the then-German city by its prosperous merchants, it has been undergoing extensive modernization in recent years which should by now be complete, with all the invaluable artistic treasures back on display. The collection includes sculptures, paintings and crafted objects, mainly from the thirteenth to the fifteenth century, modern paintings, and several historical exhibitions which tell the story of Poland's long relationship with the Baltic. These include models of sailing vessels active from the thirteenth to the nineteenth century and examples of the ancient folk culture of western Pomerania.

The exhibition of Gothic Art stresses the similarities between local sculpture and that of other cultures around the Baltic. Particularly memorable are the thirteenth-century madonna from the local village of Gardno, the group of delicately carved columns from the Cistercian monastery at Kołbacz, and the fourteenth-century crucifix from Kamień Pomorski. Other delights range from a 1563 triptych to a fine set of door knockers cast many centuries ago in a Kołobrzeg workshop, and there is also a great deal of princely gold and jewellery. Maybe it is not so odd for a port with an ocean-going fleet that the museum should also have an exhibition called the Culture of West Africa, which displays many everyday items from the region including a large collection of musical instruments. Closer to home and equally fascinating is a display illustrating the history of 'Artistic Blacksmithery' in western Pomerania, which includes decorative ironwork and products of those highly skilled men, the locksmith and the armourer.

Poland

Moving back towards the castle and then turning away from the river, you will come to Ulica Wyszaka and past the lovely Gothic **Church of SS Peter and Paul**, a brick basilica built in 1370. The doorway has a rose window above it and the façade is topped by another of those delicate pointed gables, very similar to the one on the old town hall. Between the windows there are medallions showing craftsmen, porters, fishermen and merchants of the late fifteenth-century city, while built into the north doorway are Romanesque pillars which were brought here from an old monastery at the village of Grabów.

One block further on, this road crosses the main shopping street of the modern city, the long and busy Aleja Niepodległósci, Independence Avenue, where most of the shops, cafés and restaurants will be found. This avenue, with the area beyond, was laid out at the beginning of the century to a plan inspired by Haussmann's Paris, a fact of which the local guide-books boast. Unfortunately it was the Old Town and not this one which was destroyed in the war; not that it is so very unattractive with its long tree-filled avenues and numerous squares and circuses, but neither is it Paris. The most useful square for visitors to seek out is easily identified by the **Port Gate (Brama Portowa)**, standing in the middle of a road junction just past the large neo-Gothic post office, which is on the west side of Aleja Niepodległósci. At one time this was the main western gate to the old city and the baroque splendour of its 1725 decorations can just be discerned under the grime, although I understand that it is shortly to be cleaned. A right turn here leads to Plac Zywcięstwa, Victory Square, with its two large churches, its cafés and the *Orbis* travel and exchange office. On the south side there are several small *Cepelia* shops selling hand-crafted wooden items for the kitchen, such as spoons and spice boxes, and a good variety of ceramic pots and textiles.

Inevitably, Szczecin makes great play of the large amount of water in its neighbourhood, and there are two points in the city at which boats can be boarded either to go right up to the coast, which is 70 minutes away by hydrofoil, or to potter around the local shipyard, home of the major industry in this area. When this was a German town, the shipyards were an important producer of ocean-going vessels and, although the yards were destroyed in the war, it did not take the Poles, good shipbuilders themselves, very long to get them working again. Today Szczecin exports most of the ships it produces, selling them all around the world.

APPENDICES

An essential Polish vocabulary
Polish is one of the Slavonic languages and is considered quite difficult to learn, with its very precise grammar and clusters of consonants which are hard for Westerners to pronounce. Dictionaries from pocket- to library-sized editions are published in Poland, but the visitor would be well advised to purchase a good phrase-book before leaving home. The Berlitz pocket-book *Polish for Travellers* is very good, well laid out and cheap. The following are a few useful expressions which can be easily learned, especially if you listen to the everyday expressions heard in the street or hotel to check on pronunciation and stress, which is usually on the penultimate syllable.

English	Polish	Pronounced
Hello/How do you do?	*Dzień dobry*	dzhen dobri
Good morning/good afternoon/good evening	*Dobry wieczór*	dobri vyehchoor
Good night	*Dobranoc*	dobrahnots
Goodbye	*Do widzenia*	do veedzehnyah
See you later	*Do zobaczenia*	do zobahchenyah
Yes	*Tak*	tahk
No	*Nie*	nyeh
Please	*Proszę*	prosheh
Thank you	*Dziękuję*	dzehnkooyeh
Thank you very much	*Dziękuję bardzo*	dzehnkooyeh bahrdzo
That's all right	*Proszę bardzo*	prosheh bahrdzo
Excuse me	*Przepraszam*	psheprasham
Do you speak English?	*Czy pan (pani* to a woman*) mówi po nagielsku?*	chi pahn/pahnee moovec po ahngyehlskoo?

335

| I do not understand | *Nie rozumiem* | nyeh rozoomyehm |
| I understand | *Rozumiem* | rozoomyehm |

Where?	*Gdzie?*	gdzheh?
Where is...?	*Gdzie jest...?*	gdzheh yehst?
When?	*Kiedy?*	kyehdi?
What?	*Co?*	tso?
How?	*Jak?*	yahk?
Who?	*Kto?*	kto?
Why?	*Dlaczego?*	dlahchehgo?
Which?	*Który?*	ktoori?

How much does it cost?	*Ile to kosztuje?*	eeleh koshtooyeh?
How much?/how many?	*Ile?*	eeleh?
May I have ...?	*Czy mogę dostać?*	chi mogeh dostahtsh?

Toilet	*Toaleta*	toaleta
— for men	*Panowie*	pahnovyeh
— for women	*Panie*	pahneeyeh
Toilet charge	*Platna*	pwatna
Vacant	*Wolny*	volnee
Occupied	*Zajęty*	zayenti
Hot	*Gorąca*	gorontsa
Cold	*Zimna*	zheemna

Arrival	*Przylot*	pshilot
Departure	*Odlot*	odlot
Entrance	*Wejście*	veyshche
Exit	*Wyjście*	viyshche
Closed (for stocktaking)	*Remanent*	remahnont
Closed (for renovation)	*Remont*	remont
Right	*Prawy*	prahvi
Left	*Lewy*	lehvi
Diversion	*Objazd*	obyazd

| Post Office | *Poczta* | pochtah |
| Stamps | *Znaczki* | znahchkee |

Polish kings

963–92	Mieszko I
992–1026	Bolesław the Brave
1026–37	Mieszko II
1038–58	Kazimierz I the Restorer
1058–79	Bolesław II the Generous
1079–1102	Władysław I Herman
1102–38	Bolesław III the Wrymouth
1138–46	Władysław II the Exile
1146–77	Bolesław IV the Curly
1177–94	Kazimierz II the Just
1194–1202	Mieszko III
1202–27	Leszek the White
1228–31	Władysław III Spindleshanks
1231–38	Henryk I the Bearded
1238–41	Henryk II the Pious
1241–43	Konrad I
1243–79	Bolesław V the Chaste
1279–88	Leszek the Black
1288–90	Henryk IV the Righteous
1290–1300	Przemysł I
1300–05	Wacław II, King of Bohemia and Poland
1305–06	Wacław III, King of Bohemia and Poland
1306–33	Władysław I the Short
1333–70	Kazimierz III the Great
1370–82	Louis of Anjou, also King of Hungary 1342–1382
1384–6	Queen Jadwiga, married Jagiełło, Grand Duke of Lithuania, 1386
1386–1444	Władysław Jagiełło
1444–92	Kazimierz IV the Jagiellon
1492–1501	Jan Olbracht
1501–06	Aleksander
1506–48	Zygmunt I the Old
1548–72	Zygmunt August

Elected kings

1573–74	Henri Valois, King of France 1574–1589
1576–86	Stefan Batory, Prince of Transylvania

1587–1632	Zygmunt III Waza, King of Sweden 1593–1604
1632–48	Władysław IV Waza
1648–68	Jan II Kazimierz Waza
1669–73	Michał Korybut Wiśniowiecki
1674–96	Jan III Sobieski
1697–1704	August II Wettin, Elector of Saxony
1704–10	Stanisław Leszczyński
1710–33	August II Wettin (for the second time)
1733	Stanisław Leszczyński (briefly, for the second time)
1733–63	August III Wettin, Elector of Saxony
1764–95	Stanisław-August Poniatowski

Historical chronology

Mid-ninth century	Foundation of small Slavonic states in the Odra and Vistula basins
963–992	Reign of Mieszko I.
966	Polish Court adopts Christianity.
1000	German Emperor Otto III recognizes Poland's independence. Foundation of the first archbishopric in Gniezno.
1025	Bolesław I crowned king of Poland.
1038	Bohemian invasion of Poland.
1138	Death of King Bolesław III the Wrymouth. Poland divided into duchies.
1226	Prince Konrad of Mazovia invites Teutonic Knights to Poland.
1241	First Tartar invasion. Battle of Legnica. Kraków burned.
1308	Teutonic Knights take Gdańsk and eastern Pomerania.
1325	Polish-Lithuanian alliance against Knights.
1333–70	Reign of Kazimierz the Great (Kazimierz Wielki).
1364	Foundation of Kraków University.
1410	Battle of Grunwald. Defeat of Teutonic Knights.
1466	Treaty of Toruń. Peace with Teutonic Knights.
1525	Teutonic leader pays homage to Polish king.
1543	Copernicus publishes his revolutionary book on planetary motion.
1569	The Union of Lublin. Poland and Lithuania unite.
1573	The principle of the free election of kings is adopted.
1600	First war with Sweden.
1618–48	Thirty Years War.
1655–60	The Swedish Deluge. War with invading Swedes.
1683	King Jan III Sobieski relieves Vienna from Turkish siege.
1702	Swedes invade again.
1772	First partition of Poland.

1793	Second partition of Poland.
1794	Kościuszko's Insurrection.
1795	Third and final partition. Poland no longer a state.
1830	The November Insurrection.
Mid-nineteenth century	Many uprisings and underground movements active in Poland, especially in the Revolutionary Year of 1848, directed at Russian, German and Austrian rule.
1892	Foundation of the Polish Socialist Party.
1901	Strike of schoolchildren against Germanization of schools.
1905	Revolution in Russian Poland.
1915	Russian Poland occupied by German and Austrian forces.
1918	Independent Polish state formed, led by Józef Piłsudski.
1919–20	Polish-Soviet War. Pilsudski invades Soviet Union.
1932	Non-aggression pact with Soviet Union.
1934	Non-aggression pact with Germany.
1939	Germany invades Poland. Soviet forces occupy eastern Poland.
1943	Uprising in Warsaw ghetto.
1944	Warsaw uprising against Nazis (63 days). December: Provisional Communist government formed in Lublin.
1945	January: Warsaw liberated by Red Army. July: Potsdam Agreement. Poland's frontiers redrawn.
1948	Polish Workers' Party and Polish Socialist Party merge to form the ruling Polish United Workers' Party (PZPR).
1952	July: Inauguration of the new constitution of the Polish People's Republic.

SELECT BIBLIOGRAPHY

Ascherson, Neal *The Struggles for Poland* (Michael Joseph, 1987)

Ciechanowski, Jan *The Warsaw Rising of 1944* (Cambridge University Press, 1974)

Davies, Norman *Heart of Europe: A Short History of Poland* (Oxford University Press pbk., 1986)

Halecki, Oscar *A History of Poland* (Routledge & Kegan Paul, 1978)

Lengyel, Olga *Five Chimneys* (Granada pbk., 1972)

Leslie, R. F. *The History of Poland Since 1863* (Cambridge University Press, 1980)

Miłosz, Czesław *The Seizure of Power* (Abacus Press, 1985)

Zamoyski, Adam *The Polish Way* (John Murray, 1987)

INDEX

Index

343

Index

345

Index

Index